The Johnson Circle

Samuel Johnson, after James Barry, c. 1778.
Source: Author's personal collection.

The Johnson Circle

A Group Portrait

Lyle Larsen

FAIRLEIGH DICKINSON UNIVERSITY PRESS
Madison • Teaneck

Published by Fairleigh Dickinson University Press
Copublished by The Rowman & Littlefield Publishing Group, Inc.
4501 Forbes Boulevard, Suite 200, Lanham, Maryland 20706
www.rowman.com

Unit A, Whitacre Mews, 26-34 Stannary Street, London SE11 4AB

British Library Cataloguing in Publication Information Available

Library of Congress Cataloging-in-Publication Data

ISBN 978-1-68393-115-7 (cloth : alk. paper)
ISBN 978-1-68393-116-4 (electronic)

∞™ The paper used in this publication meets the minimum requirements of
American National Standard for Information Sciences—Permanence of Paper
for Printed Library Materials, ANSI/NISO Z39.48-1992.

Printed in the United States of America

Contents

List of Illustrations   vii

Preface   ix

Principal Figures of the Johnson Circle   xiii

1   His Trade was Wisdom   1

2   The Great Field of Genius and Exertion   25

3   Deadman's Place   57

4   Blunders, Ridicule, and a Fine Malignity   73

5   Incident in the Haymarket   97

6   Between Comedy and Tragedy   109

7   Retaliation   125

8   Domestic Issues   145

9   A Variety of Private Cases   163

10   Like Embroidery upon Gauze   189

11   The Flight of Time   211

12   A Wicked, False, Ungrateful Little Vixen   229

13   Torn Friendships   251

14   A Pattern of Resignation   285

Appendix: Bennet Langton's Children   311

Selected Bibliography   315

Index   325

About the Author   333

List of Illustrations

Samuel Johnson, after James Barry, c. 1778.   ii
David Garrick by Thomas Gainsborough, 1770. ©National
    Portrait Gallery, London.   9
Joseph Baretti, after James Barry, c. 1773.   15
Sir Joshua Reynolds by Angelica Kauffmann, 1767. The National
    Trust.   28
Bennet Langton by Sir Joshua Reynolds, 1777. Gunby Hall, The
    Montgomery-Massingberd Collection (The National Trust).   31
Topham Beauclerk by George Perfect Harding. ©Trustees of the
    British Museum.   35
Oliver Goldsmith by William Henry Bunbury, c. 1765. ©Trustees
    of the British Museum.   43
Hester Lynch Thrale, after Robert Edge Pine, 1781.   65
Lady Diana Beauclerk. Anna Stowe / Alamy Stock Photo.   89
Garrick between Comedy and Tragedy, after Sir Joshua Reynolds,
    1760-61. ©Trustees of the British Museum.   112
Oliver Goldsmith by Sir Joshua Reynolds, 1769. ©National
    Portrait Gallery, London.   141
Charles Burney by George Dance, 1794. ©National Portrait
    Gallery, London.   158
Henry Thrale, after Sir Joshua Reynolds, 1777. ©Trustees of the
    British Museum.   179
Joseph Baretti, after Sir Joshua Reynolds, 1773. ©Trustees of the
    British Museum.   195
James Boswell, after George Langton. ©Trustees of the British
    Museum.   205

Gabriel Piozzi by George Dance, 1793. ©National Portrait
  Gallery, London.   233
Frances Burney by Edward Francesco Burney, 1785. ©National
  Portrait Gallery, London.   255
James Boswell by George Dance, 1793. ©National Portrait
  Gallery, London.   263
Hester Lynch Piozzi by George Dance, 1793. ©National Portrait
  Gallery, London.   277
Bennet Langton by George Dance, 1798. ©Trustees of the British
  Museum.   288

Preface

"The number of my friends was never great," wrote Samuel Johnson in his last *Rambler* essay. The periodical had reached the end of its two-year run, but Johnson did not expect the paper's demise to cause much regret, "for I have never been much a favourite of the publick." He had often sat down to work, he said, with a mind harassed with anxieties and a body weakened by disease, yet he knew that he had no grounds to complain for, as he stated, "I have seldom descended to the arts by which favour is obtained."

Johnson had likewise, for much of his life, rarely stooped to those arts by which friendship is obtained. From early boyhood, he lived with the knowledge that his homely face, large and ungainly body, loud voice, and odd mannerisms put people off. He later confessed that he had never made an effort to please until past thirty, "considering the matter as hopeless."[1] At times he adopted a cynical attitude, disparaging the impulses that produced friendship and feigning indifference to it. As if to show how little his inability to please others troubled him, he sometimes went out of his way to *dis*please them. His occasional rudeness became notorious. To cite but two examples: as he came out of Lichfield Cathedral one morning following service, a stranger accosted him too familiarly by saying, "Dr. Johnson, we have had a most excellent Discourse to day," to which Johnson responded, "That may be, Sir, but it is impossible for you to know it."[2] On another occasion, the baronet of Combermere Abbey in Wales asked him what he thought of Lord Kilmorey, a neighbor, and Johnson replied, "A dull, commonplace sort of man, just like you and your brother."[3] He sometimes made similar cutting remarks to those closest to him. When he once verbally abused Sir Joshua Reynolds, the mildest of men, Reynolds observed that it was "a humbling thing that Johnson might say such things without people taking notice of them."[4] Actually, people did take notice of them, and these sudden outbursts occasionally

ix

strained relations. Fortunately, they were thought to be so much a part of Johnson's character, and were spread so widely among his acquaintance, that they usually caused no lasting resentment.

Johnson set forth his philosophy of friendship in a number of sermons and letters and also in various *Idler* and *Rambler* essays. The essence of his thought was that, while grand and virtuous in the ideal, it is in reality fragile and painfully transitory. "Life has no pleasure higher or nobler than that of friendship," he wrote. Yet people possess such dissimilar temperaments and variations of disposition that true friendship is rare. "So many qualities are indeed requisite to the possibility of friendship, and so many accidents must concur to its rise and its continuance, that the greatest part of mankind content themselves without it." Friendship, once found, is likewise frail. Long separation cripples or sometimes kills it. So does a gradual shift in interests, an alteration in one's daily affairs, a change in social status, wealth, or fame, or numerous other conditions. "It is painful to consider, that this sublime enjoyment may be impaired or destroyed by innumerable causes, and that there is no human possession of which the duration is less certain."[5]

He refused to accept the notion that friendship ordinarily arises from generous or virtuous motives. "How many friendships have you known formed upon principles of virtue?" he asked James Boswell. "Most friendships are formed by caprice or by chance, mere confederacies in vice or leagues in folly."[6] He held that friendship, like most other human endeavors, springs from what he termed "the vacuity of life." Once the necessities of living have been met, people must somehow fill up their time, and this accounted for most human activities and attachments, including friendship.

Yet despite his skepticism and his misgivings about his own abilities to please, he managed to gather about him as friends, especially during the last quarter of his life, some of the most fascinating and accomplished people of the day. These friendships were not always smooth and some did not endure, but Johnson valued the individuals nonetheless. Most would have left a mark on some aspect of history had they never been associated with the principal literary figure of the age. Actor, painter, playwright, novelist, Greek scholar, miscellaneous writer, biographer, leading bluestocking, wealthy man-of-fashion: they represented a wide range of talents and personalities. Johnson brought them together as a group, and all testified that in knowing him they became far better persons than they otherwise would have been. "Those very people whom he has brought to think rightly," exclaimed Reynolds, "will occasionally criticise the opinions of their master when he nods. But we should always recollect that it is he himself who taught us and enabled us to do it."[7]

This book focuses on ten key figures, aside from Johnson himself, of the so-called Johnson circle. It explores their characters, their contributions to society, their relationships with one another, and their indebtedness to Samuel Johnson.

NOTES

1. Hester Lynch Thrale Piozzi, *Anecdotes of the Late Samuel Johnson, LL.D., during the Last Twenty Years of His Life* with William Shaw's *Memoirs of the Life and Writings of the Late Dr. Samuel Johnson*, ed. Arthur Sherbo (London: Oxford University Press, 1974), 145.

2. Joseph Cradock, *Literary and Miscellaneous Memoirs*, second edition, 4 vols. (London, 1826), 1:74.

3. Abraham Hayward, ed., *Autobiography, Letters and Literary Remains of Mrs. Piozzi (Thrale)*, second edition, 2 vols. (London, 1861), 1:88.

4. The incident happened while Reynolds and Johnson were visiting in Devonshire. "The company, and Sir Joshua among the rest, had been out a-hunting," writes Boswell, who recounted the story as told him by Reynolds; "so at dinner Dr. Johnson was left out of the conversation. Sir Joshua with a polite desire to bring him into it said, just by way of saying what occurred first, 'Well, Sir, I have been galloping over fields and jumping hedges and ditches today, and that is one thing I can do better than you.' Johnson angrily answered, 'Sir, when I have as mean a mind as you, I shall be vain of such things'" (James Boswell, *Boswell: The Ominous Years, 1774–1776*, ed. Charles Ryskamp and Frederick A. Pottle [New York: McGraw-Hill, 1963], 335).

5. *Idler* #23, Sermon #1, *Rambler* #64.

6. James Boswell, *The Life of Samuel Johnson, LL.D. Together with Boswell's Journal of a Tour to the Hebrides*, ed. G. B. Hill, rev. L. F. Powell, 6 vols. (Oxford: Clarendon Press, 1934–1964), 4:280.

7. Charles Robert Leslie and Tom Taylor, *Life and Times of Sir Joshua Reynolds*, 2 vols. (London, 1865), 2:461.

Principal Figures of the Johnson Circle (in order of birth)

Samuel Johnson	1709–1784
David Garrick	1717–1779
Joseph Baretti	1719–1789
Sir Joshua Reynolds	1723–1792
Oliver Goldsmith	1728/30?–1774
Henry Thrale	1728/29?–1781
Bennet Langton	1737–1801
Topham Beauclerk	1739–1780
James Boswell	1740–1795
Hester Lynch Thrale	1741–1821
Frances Burney	1752–1840

Chapter One

His Trade Was Wisdom

When Samuel Johnson and David Garrick arrived in London together in the spring of 1737, they came seeking opportunities not available to them in their hometown in the West Midlands. Johnson, twenty-seven years old, carried with him the manuscript of a tragedy he hoped to get produced and that he expected would launch him on a successful literary career. Garrick, age twenty, sought to further his education. His family could not afford to send him to a university, so he planned to take private instruction in mathematics and philosophy, intending eventually to enter the Temple and study law. Years later the two recalled how, with only one horse between them, they "rode and tied" the 120 or so miles to London, Johnson quipping that he arrived with only two-pence half-penny in his pocket and David but three half-pence in his.[1]

Both men had been raised in Lichfield, a cathedral and garrison town of three thousand, about twelve miles north of Birmingham. They had known each other from boyhood, their homes situated only a short walking distance apart, but the two became even closer in 1735 when Johnson opened an academy for young scholars in the nearby village of Edial, where eighteen-year-old David and his twelve-year-old brother George made up nearly half the class. The school closed after only six months, however, for lack of pupils. Johnson was not an especially good teacher anyway, for he could not bring his lofty ideas down to a level where young, unformed minds could easily grasp them, and David was not a particularly good student, for success in local amateur productions had already excited his theatrical ambitions. Instead of doing his school assignments, he often spent his time composing scenes for comedies.

Soon after arriving in the metropolis, Garrick decided that practicing law required too much drudgery for one of his sprightly temperament. Looking for other ways to earn a livelihood, he turned to commerce. Having learned something of the wine business from a prosperous uncle in the trade, he joined his older brother Peter and formed Garrick & Co., dealers in wines and spirits. It was a small operation in which David purchased and stored merchandise in London that Peter later sold in Lichfield. But David quickly discovered that commerce did not suit his temperament any better than law. His real interest lay in the theater. He had already begun to cultivate the acquaintance of actors and managers in and around Covent Garden and had also cautiously begun to act.

He performed his first significant roles in 1741 at the theater in Ipswich, nearly seventy miles northeast of London. There he acted anonymously or under a stage name in a series of summer plays. In one of them, an old piece by Thomas Southerne titled *Oroonoko*, he played the part of Aboan, companion and friend of the title character, an African prince. It was a part he performed in blackface. No one in the audience would have recognized him, which was fine with David, for if he made a complete fool of himself, he did not want his London friends to learn of it. He later said that had he failed as an actor, he was prepared to give up so dangerous a profession and content himself with a life in business. But his debut at Ipswich proved a success, and he immediately began taking on more challenging roles at Goodman's Fields Theatre in east London. On October 19, billed as "A GENTLEMAN, (who never appeared on any Stage)," he played the title role in Shakespeare's *Richard III*, wherein his natural delivery and energetic stage presence, contrasted with the histrionic delivery and measured gestures of the other players, caused a sensation. People began crowding into the theater every night to see this extraordinary new actor play the villainous and humpbacked Richard in a manner they had never witnessed before.

What now concerned David most was how to tell Peter that he wanted to quit the wine business and devote himself entirely to acting and writing for the stage. His brother knew that David loved to perform for people and had done so from childhood, but he probably did not think him rash enough to consider following acting as a profession. In a letter to Peter, David casually remarked that "Last Night I play'd Richard ye Third to ye Surprize of Every Body & as I shall make very near £300 p Annum by It & as it is really what I doat upon I am resolv'd to pursue it." Peter became outraged, apparently fearing that his younger brother would be embarking on a life of intemperance, degradation, and failure while at the same time bringing disgrace and humiliation to the family. Everyone knew how dissolute actors were. But David assured him that he had the gifts of an actor with none of the vices and that he had every expectation of succeeding financially. "My Genius that Way (by ye best Judges) is thought Wonderfull," he wrote to Peter. "My Friends who at first were Surpriz'd at my intent, by seeing me on yᵉ Stage, are now well convinc'd twas impossible for Me to keep of [*sic*]."²

When Peter remained adamantly opposed to his plan, David responded, "I am very Sorry You still Seem so utterly Averse to What I am so greatly Inclin'd & to What yᵉ best Judges think I have yᵉ Greatest Genius for—The Great nay incredible Success & approbation I have met with from yᵉ Greatest Persons in England have almost made Me resolve (tho Im sorry to Say it against Yʳ Entreaties) to pursue it as I certainly shall make a fortune by it, if Health continues." He went on to boast that William Pitt, "who is reckon'd yᵉ Greatest Orator in the house of Commons, said I was yᵉ best Actor yᵉ English Stage had produc'd."³

On October 28, following his successful run as Richard III, he performed his first comedic role as Clodio in Colley Cibber's *Love Makes a Man, or, The Fop's Fortune.* On November 6 he played another comic role, that of Chamont in Thomas Otway's *The Orphan*, and three days later he appeared as Jack Smatter in an adaptation of Samuel Richardson's novel *Pamela.* Then on November 30 he produced his own two-act comedy *The Lying Valet*, in which he played the male lead, and on December 2 he took on the dramatic role of Lothario in Nicholas Rowe's *The Fair Penitent.* One week after that he appeared as the ghost in *Hamlet*. This hectic pace continued into the new year. By the close of the theatrical season in April, he had played about 140 times, appearing in eighteen different characters. It had been a spectacular debut season, and the theater public could not get enough of this sprightly and innovative young actor. David wrote to his brother in Lichfield, "I may now venture to tell You I am very near quite resolv'd to be a player; as I have yᵉ Judgment of yᵉ best Judges (Who to a Man are of Opinion) that I shall turn out (nay they Say I am) not only yᵉ Best Trajedian but Comedian in England."⁴ As David's fame and fortune increased, Peter eventually grew reconciled to his brother's choice of acting as a career.

Yet despite David Garrick's growing popularity, not everyone wished to abandon the histrionic style of acting they had grown accustomed to and that was seen to greatest advantage in the performances of Thomas Betterton, Barton Booth, and James Quin. Horace Walpole, art historian, prolific letter writer, and author of the gothic novel *The Castle of Otranto*, wrote to a friend that "all the run is now after Garrick, a wine merchant who is turned player at Goodman's Fields." Walpole granted that Garrick could play a variety of roles and that he was a very good mimic, but he hesitated to go beyond that. "His acting I have seen, and may say to you, who will not tell it again here, I see nothing wonderful in it; but it is heresy to say so."⁵ At about the same time, poet Thomas Gray wrote to one of his own friends, "Did I tell you about

Mr. Garrick, that the town are horn-mad after: there are a dozen Dukes of a night at Goodmansfields sometimes, and yet I am stiff in the opposition."[6]

Many, in fact, remained stiff in opposition to Garrick's dynamic kind of acting. They held fast to the old way of doing things and resisted any innovations. Theatergoers then began lining up on both sides of the issue, making a head-to-head competition inevitable. The public demanded a competition whereby the leading representatives of the rival styles would face one another on the same stage, in the same play, on the same night. A crucial showdown occurred on the evening of November 14, 1746, when James Quin, a veteran of more than thirty seasons, appeared as Horatio on the stage of Covent Garden Theatre in Rowe's *The Fair Penitent.* Dressed in a green velvet coat, a huge full bottomed periwig, rolled stockings, and high-heeled square-toed shoes, he moved slowly about the stage with an air of solemn dignity and imposing stateliness. Delivering his lines in a deep, sonorous, well-modulated voice, but with little variation in cadence, he accompanied his declamation with a kind of sawing motion of his body. Opposite him in the role of Calista, Susannah Maria Cibber, in a high-pitched but sweet voice, "sung or rather recitatived Rowe's harmonious strain, something in the manner of the Improvisatories," recalled Richard Cumberland, who sat in the front row. Cumberland, fourteen years old at the time, who later became an essayist, novelist, and popular playwright of sentimental comedies, thought Susannah Cibber's voice lacked contrast, and "though it did not wound the ear, it wearied it; when she had once recited two or three speeches, I could anticipate the manner of every succeeding one; it was like a long old legendary ballad of innumerable stanzas, every one of which is sung to the same tune, eternally chiming in the ear without variation or relief."[7]

Quin and Susannah Cibber typified the established acting style of the day, one that emphasized the poetic beauty of the lines and was characterized by a resonant tone and cadenced delivery. The performance of a play like *The Fair Penitent* was essentially an exchange of recitations accompanied by gestures, something like an operatic performance, but with the lines spoken instead of sung. Later in the play, with Quin beautifully rounding his *O*s, one foot thrust forward and a hand in the breast of his coat, twenty-nine-year-old David Garrick as Lothario came bounding onto the stage. He was "light and alive in every muscle and in every feature," remarked Cumberland; "heavens, what a transition!—it seemed as if a whole century had been stept over in the transition of a single scene; old things were done away, and a new order at once brought forward, bright and luminous."[8]

What surprised most people was that Garrick's acting hardly seemed like acting at all. His speech and movements appeared so natural. Other players looked wooden in comparison. Quin later remarked that if the young man was right, he "and the rest of the players, had been all wrong."[9] When the actress Anne Bracegirdle declared the young upstart to be an actor of merit, Colley Cibber, an old warhorse of the stage and Susannah Cibber's father-in-law, reluctantly agreed: "Why, faith, Bracey, I believe you are right—The young fellow is clever."[10] Mrs. Porter, another stage veteran, exclaimed, "Good God, what will he be in time?"[11] Alexander Pope commented, "That young man never had his *equal* as an actor, and he will never have a rival."[12] And Lord Chesterfield remarked that Garrick was not only the best tragedian in the world at the time, but the best that ever *was* in the world.[13] As a consequence of such widespread acclaim, Garrick rose rapidly to the top of his profession, becoming the most celebrated and innovative actor of his time. He eventually grew to be one of the richest men in London and, aside from the king, the best-known man in England.

As David Garrick rose rapidly in his profession, his former tutor and fellow townsman Samuel Johnson struggled. Fully aware of his superior intellect, learning, and conversational powers, Johnson initially fantasized about the respect and recognition his talents would bring him. Years afterward he revealed that the eastern tale comprising his *Idler* essay number 75 was meant to represent this period, his early entry into London life. Like the character in his tale, he imagined that his superior abilities would set him apart from the common run of men and win him distinctions:

> I shall see the eyes of those who predicted my greatness sparkling with exultation, and the faces of those that once despised me, clouded with envy, or counterfeiting kindness by artificial smiles. I will shew my wisdom by my discourse, and my moderation by my silence; I will instruct the modest with easy gentleness, and repress the ostentatious by seasonable superciliousness. My apartments will be crouded by the inquisitive and the vain, by those that honour and those that rival me.

With such hopes running through his mind, he submitted his play to the manager of Drury Lane Theatre only to have it rejected. After meticulous revision, he later attempted to get the play printed, but that also failed. He eventually realized that "the poor have no leisure to be pleased with eloquence," nor should he expect to find his apartments crowded with admirers and rivals, for "who will be pleased or instructed in the mansions of poverty?" Even his brilliant conversation was met with silence by the sophisticated, who went away to censure his arrogance and pedantry, while "the dull listened quietly for a while, and then wondered why any man should take pains to obtain so much knowledge which would never do him good."[14]

After three frustrating months in London, he returned briefly to Lichfield to fetch his wife. Elizabeth, or "Tetty" as Johnson affectionately called her, was twenty years older than her husband. As a young woman living in Birmingham, she had been fairly attractive with dark blue eyes, high forehead, and wheat-colored hair. She married a woolen-draper of Birmingham, Henry Porter, in 1714 and bore him a daughter and two sons. Porter died in 1734, and a year later, against the wishes of her sons, she married Sam Johnson. Over the years she put on weight, began rouging her puffy cheeks, and would have dyed her hair black had Johnson not absolutely forbidden it. Descended from an ancient and distinguished family that now had little to show for it, she liked to buy herself fine things—a little lace here, a pair of gloves there—and she occasionally ran up small debts that Johnson could not pay. Although she possessed a good understanding, people detected a slight affectation of gentility in her speech and carriage, and although Johnson loved her, Garrick saw in her no more than a little painted puppet.

About a year after bringing Tetty to London, Johnson finally made some headway by contributing a variety of articles to *The Gentleman's Magazine*. In 1738 he published his first major work, the poem "London," and in 1744 *An Account of the Life of Richard Savage* appeared. These works brought him critical notice but little money. Then in 1747, about the time Garrick had fully established himself as England's foremost actor, Johnson announced "The Plan of a Dictionary of the English Language," a project that would take him nearly nine years to complete, carried on under the pressures of chronic illness and continuing poverty. In his "Plan" he proposed compiling "a dictionary by which the pronunciation of our language may be fixed, and its attainment facilitated; by which its purity may be preserved, its use ascertained, and its duration lengthened."[15] This proposal was similar to the stated goals of national academies that had sprung up in countries throughout Europe, particularly in Spain, Portugal, Germany, and France. The main purpose of these state-sponsored academies was to standardize and regulate their respective languages, primarily through the compilation of grammars and dictionaries. The greatest of these institutions was the French Academy, which produced a dictionary of the French language in 1694.

Some talked of establishing an English academy, but Johnson strongly opposed the idea. He thought frequency of translation a much greater menace to the language than mere ignorance of its rules. "No book was ever turned from one language into another," he stated, "without imparting something of its native idiom; this is the most mischievous and comprehensive innovation." He found the number of works translated from French into English especially alarming. If an English academy *were* to be established, he said, "let them, instead of compiling grammars and dictionaries, endeavour, with all their influence, to stop the licence of translatours, whose idleness and ignorance, if it be suffered to proceed, will reduce us to babble a dialect of *France*."[16] Toiling every day as a private individual at his own dictionary, he had pretty much lost hope of ever seeing his tragedy performed, but David Garrick's spectacular rise in the theater world would soon change that.

In addition to his triumphs as an actor, Garrick wrote a number of successful comedies, prologues, and farces. With money pouring in, he soon had enough to buy half ownership of Drury Lane Theatre, one of the premier houses in London. As co-manager, he supervised theatrical productions, while his partner, James Lacy, attended primarily to the theater building and its contents. In the summer of 1749 Garrick married a beautiful Viennese dancer, twenty-five-year-old Eva Maria Veigel, and they settled into a fashionable house at 27 Southampton Street, Covent Garden, a short walk from Drury Lane Theatre.

Hailed as the English Roscius (after the legendary actor of ancient Rome), Garrick now dined like a prince at the tables of the great and wealthy, where he was acknowledged to be a young man of unsurpassed wit and vivacity as well as the greatest actor of his day. Within a remarkably short time, he had risen to the top of the social and theatrical world. Detractors, however, would plague him throughout his career. Some found fault with his innovative acting technique, accusing him of taking the poetry out of spoken lines and merely replacing the usual "ti-tum-ti" manner of speaking with a "hobble-ti-trot" manner.[17] But all agreed that Garrick was born to be noticed. Whether dressed for the role of private man at the dinner table or costumed as a character on stage, he captured attention by the utter vitality of his person.

People often remarked that on stage and off, he possessed remarkable energy and agility. Throughout life he jumped, skipped, danced, and ran like a youth of sixteen, and although he put on weight as he grew older, he never lost his grace, dexterity, and exuberance. In addition to his lively spirits, he possessed a number of physical attributes that served him well as a performer. His face was plain rather than handsome, yet the individual features were strongly marked, and he had the ability to mold them into whatever he wished. Many expressed amazement that he could alter his expression so as to look like an entirely different person than what he appeared only moments before. A foreign visitor remarked that in changing from one stage character to another, "he becomes so different from his own self that his face and body change, and we can scarce believe it is the same man. One can contort one's face of course; but with Garrick there is no face-pulling or exaggeration; all the changes in his features come from the way in which he makes himself feel inwardly."[18] For the entertainment of company after dinner, he would occasionally act his "rounds" as he called it. Getting behind a chair and leaning on the back of it, he ran through every conceivable emotion by a series of nearly imperceptible changes in expression. "At one moment the company laughed," said miscellaneous writer William Cooke, who witnessed some of these bravura performances; "at another, cried; now melted into pity; now terrified; and presently they conceived in *themselves* something horrible, he seemed so much terrified at what he saw. . . . In short, his face was what he obliged you to fancy it—age—youth—joy—grief—every thing he assumed."[19]

Always given to boyish pranks, he sometimes used his pliable face to create mischief. Once, for example, he sat for his portrait to Thomas Gainsborough, and after the painter had worked for some time getting his facial features just right, Garrick seized the opportunity, as the artist looked away, to change his appearance. The artist, noticing that his picture somehow seemed faulty, patiently altered it so as to look like the face he now saw. But again, when he turned his head aside, Garrick changed his appearance a third time, "which, when the poor tantalized artist perceived, he, in a great rage, threw down his pallet and pencils on the floor, saying, he believed he was painting from the devil, and would do no more to the picture."[20] Garrick is said to have played the same trick at Le Raincy in 1765 on the French artist Carmontelle. While he was being drawn, "as his liveliness prevents him from remaining quiet for one moment, he practised passing, by imperceptible shades, from extreme joy to extreme sadness, and even to despair and horror."[21] Garrick once frightened the painter William Hogarth by assuming the look of Hogarth's dead friend Henry Fielding, the novelist, and pretending to be his ghost. Hogarth never spoke of the incident afterward without visible agitation.[22]

The most striking feature of Garrick's otherwise ordinary face was his eyes. They were exceptionally large and dark beneath high arching brows. Hester Lynch Thrale later described them as black, Garrick and a female friend of hers being the only two people she knew with truly black eyes.[23] Such eyes proved a great asset in a candlelit theater, and Garrick used them to great effect. Critics continually referred to "his matchless eyes," the "sprightliness of eyes," "the finest eye ever seen on a stage," "black, piercing, and full of fire," "they looked into the very soul."[24] A minor actor named Marr got the nickname "Dagger" Marr after bragging that he could play the dagger scene in *Macbeth* better than Garrick if Garrick would only lend him his eyes.[25]

Another feature contributing to Garrick's success on stage was his voice. Described as versatile, clear, and harmonious, it lacked the drawling monot-

David Garrick by Thomas Gainsborough, 1770.
Source: National Portrait Gallery, London.

ony and affectation that characterized other actors of the day. He had to work, however, at eliminating the provincial dialect of his native Lichfield, where people said *theer* for *there*, *heerd* for *heard*, and *woonce* for *once*. The reader of James Boswell's *Life of Samuel Johnson* recalls how Garrick mimicked the same dialect in Johnson "by squeezing a lemon into a punchbowl, with uncouth gesticulations, looking round the company, and calling out, 'Who's for *poonsh*?'" But apparently Garrick never got the better of such words as *supreme* and *superior*, which he pronounced in the Lichfield manner of *shupreme* and *shuperior*, and Johnson claimed to have cured him of saying *feyther* for *father*.[26]

In private conversation Garrick also had a way of halting, hesitating, and repeating words when he spoke. "Hey, now! Now—what—all," he said to the actor Tate Wilkinson, who had auditioned for a part in a play. "How—really this—this—is—Why—well—well—Do call on me again on Monday."[27] Wilkinson thought this peculiar mannerism arose from affectation and not wanting to make definite commitments. Garrick said to Wilkinson on another occasion, "By—nay—why—now if you will not—why I cannot say but I may settle that matter, and as I shall see you on Tuesday, why then—Hey! you know that—But Mrs. Garrick is waiting—and you now—I say now—hey—now Tuesday. You will remember Tuesday?"[28] Boswell records talking to the comic actor and playwright Samuel Foote, an excellent mimic and harsh critic of Garrick, who "took off his *aw–aw–aw* hesitating way of speaking, which is indeed strange, and added, 'Sir, a man born never to finish a sentence.'"[29]

But on stage he was as much the master of his voice as he was his facial expressions. One critic early in Garrick's career described his utterance as neither "whining, bellowing, or grumbling, but . . . perfectly easy in its Transitions, natural in its Cadence, and beautiful in its Elocution."[30] Another critic said that his voice pierced the heart like the sound of a trumpet.[31] Among the many things Garrick could do with his voice is produce a remarkable stage whisper. It carried distinctly to all parts of the theater while the declamation of other actors sometimes proved unintelligible. "The reason," Garrick explained, "is, that many of the actors have no idea of *distinctness in their pronunciation*, and forget the lesson of acquiring 'a temperance that may give it smoothness.'"[32] As for taking the poetry out of spoken lines, Garrick said that from the very start of his career he had tried to escape the shackles of mere poetic cadence, but instead gave special attention "to the Passion, and the Meaning of the Author."[33]

Spectators sometimes mentioned as a refreshing innovation that Garrick, unlike other players, always remained in character, even when he had no lines to deliver. A common practice at the time was for players to be in character only when speaking. Between speeches they pretty much stood around, gazed out into the audience, or did whatever they chose until it came time for them to speak again. During a trip to Paris in 1775, Mrs. Thrale expressed amazement at how good the French players were, but she was equally offended to see an actress "turn aside after a Rant to spit & hawk in a Corner. . . . [W]iping the Sweat off their Faces too in Tragedy is quite a common Trick with them."[34] These practices were likewise common in London theaters until Garrick helped put a stop to them. As actor and manager, he brought greater discipline to the stage. He set an example by always knowing his lines and always staying in character. "When three or four are on the Stage with him," wrote one reviewer approvingly, "he is attentive to whatever is spoke, and never drops his Character when he has finish'd a Speech, by either looking contemptibly on an inferior Performer, unnecessary spitting, or suffering his Eyes to wander thro' the whole Circle of Spectators."[35]

Those who preferred the old oratorical style, the style exemplified by James Quin, were not as appreciative of Garrick's use of "stage business" and staying in character between speeches. Believing that a play was essentially a dramatic recitation of poetic lines, they thought Garrick's constant byplay excessive. It upstaged the other players. It particularly drew attention away from the character speaking at the moment. Fellow actor Charles Macklin claimed that Garrick's art consisted in incessantly "pawing and hawling the Characters about, with whom he was concerned in the scene—and when he did not paw or hawl the Character, he stalked between them and the Audience; and that generally when they were speaking the most important and interesting passage in the Scene." When Garrick himself spoke, "he pulled about the Character he spoke to, and squeezed his hat, hung forward, and stood almost upon one foot, with no part of the other to the ground but the toe of it." Macklin grumbled that in the role of Lear, Garrick, at one point in the play, while not saying a word, slowly becomes drowsy, eventually falls asleep, and is finally carried from the stage to end the scene. Such an action, and others like it, Macklin considered "an excrescence of the worst sort," a paltry stage trick, which, instead of being applauded, should be greeted with indignation and contempt. "Why did he fall asleep in *Lear*?" Macklin fumed. "Is the act necessary in the Play? What is the intent? It is not conducive to forward the Fable. It does not produce any incident, speech, sentiment, passion, or reflection.—It does not mark or develop any part of the Character."[36]

Actor and playwright Theophilus Cibber, son of Colley Cibber and husband of Susannah Cibber, also found fault with Garrick's "studied Tricks, his Over-fondness for extravagant Attitudes, frequent affected Starts, convulsive Twitchings, Jerkings of the Body . . . slapping the Breast and Pockets . . . his pantomimical Manner of acting, every Word in a Sentence;—his unnatural Pauses in the Middle of a Sentence," and his neglect of harmony in delivering a sentiment that "demands a graceful Cadence in the Delivery."[37] Cibber maintained that Garrick's gestures and byplay were entirely overdone: "His favourite Gestures were a hasty Shrugging of the Shoulder-bone, a sudden Dart of his Right-hand to his Left-breast, as if there bit by a Flea, or a Slap therewith on his Thigh, as if seized with a Cramp; sometimes a distorted throwing back of his Left-arm, as if contracted."[38] One of his favorite props was a hat, which, according to Cibber, "was twitched from Hand to Hand, frequently drawn cross the Eyes of the (thereby) startled Person he spoke to;—then, with both Hands, was moulded on his Stomach, and with ungraceful Vehemence slapped upon the Thigh." Like Macklin, Cibber disapproved of such tricks, preferring instead the stately presence of older, more traditional actors who focused on the dramatic recitation of the spoken word and "whose Manner was expressive of a spirited Delicacy, and genteel Deportment."[39] But general audiences loved Garrick's animated byplay, for he was always fascinating to watch, always acting, always doing something, whether he had lines to speak or not. Garrick was, in fact, perhaps the first actor of the modern fully enclosed theater who completely understood the importance of stage business. As a first-rate mimic and pantomimist, he knew how much more pertained to acting than simply reciting words gracefully and dramatically, as Cibber and other advocates of the declamatory school would have it.

One of the staunchest advocates of the old school and the least appreciative of Garrick's stage tricks, at least in the beginning, was Samuel Johnson. He maintained that a play was merely "a book recited with concomitants that encrease or diminish its effect." He insisted that spectators came to the theater "to hear a certain number of lines recited with just gesture and elegant modulation."[40] Johnson felt that drama was first and foremost literature and that its value as a performing art was, by comparison, of little consequence. Actors themselves were of little consequence. When Boswell once accused him of being heretical in never allowing merit to a player, Johnson replied, "What, Sir, a fellow who claps a hump on his back and a lump on his leg, and cries 'I am Richard the Third?'" Johnson claimed that a ballad singer was superior to a mere player, for the ballad singer supplied both recitation *and* music. "The player only recites."

Boswell objected, saying, "*Who* can repeat Hamlet's soliloquy, 'To be or not to be,' as Garrick does it?"

"Anybody may," replied Johnson. "Jemmy, there (Mr. Fieldhouse's son, a boy about eight years old) will do it as well in a week."[41]

Despite Johnson's increasingly outmoded views on how a play should be acted, and despite his low opinion of actors and acting in general, Garrick nevertheless, once he became manager of Drury Lane Theater, decided to stage his friend's tragedy under the title *Mahomet and Irene*. He did this mostly out of respect for his long friendship with Johnson, for he realized that the play in its current form would not be popular, and he even encouraged Johnson to alter it to make it more acceptable. The playwright Arthur Murphy recalled that the plot of *Mahomet and Irene*, later printed as simply *Irene*, proceeded "without an incident to alarm the passions, in a calm philosophic stile."[42] The scenes possessed drama of a poetic nature, but they were not likely to arouse any emotions in a theater audience. As Garrick once observed in a letter, "Speeches & mere poetry will no more make a Play, than planks & timbers in y[e] dock-Yard can be call'd a Ship—It is Fable, passion & Action which constitute a Tragedy, & without them, we might as well exhibit one of Tillotsons Sermons."[43] To help enliven the play, Garrick urged Johnson to write a mad scene for the last act, promising to put forth his best efforts to end the tragedy successfully. Johnson refused and a heated dispute followed, Johnson later complaining to a friend, "Sir, (said he) the fellow wants me to make Mahomet run mad, that he may have an opportunity of tossing his hands and kicking his heels."[44] Garrick complained in turn, "When Johnson writes *tragedy, declamation roars, and passion sleeps.*"[45]

Garrick at last prevailed, however, and the revised play ran for nine performances during the month of February 1749, a respectable run at the time, though not spectacular. Garrick had employed some of the best actors available—Spranger Barry, Susannah Cibber, Hannah Pritchard, and himself in the role of Mahomet—but it was the quality of the acting and the spectacle of costume and scenery that proved a greater draw than the play itself, which was generally regarded as cumbersome and tedious, and no one sought to revive it. When someone later asked Johnson how he felt about the cool reception his tragedy had received, he replied, "Like the Monument." In other words, he remained as steady and unshaken as that memorial to the Great Fire.

Of greater significance for Johnson than *Mahomet and Irene* was a twice-weekly series of essays he began publishing on March 20, 1750. Titled *The Rambler*, the essays appeared every Tuesday and Saturday, priced two pence per copy. Johnson's aim was to inculcate virtue and to guide readers in the proper regulation of their lives and thoughts. Written for the most part in balanced tones and measured sentences, the essays conveyed a sense of gravity, stability, and wisdom. After the first few numbers, Tetty Johnson told her husband that while she thought well of his abilities before, she never thought him capable of anything so good. Johnson himself later said that his other works were wine and water, but his *Rambler* was pure wine.[46] The paper ran for two years, ending with the issue of Saturday, March 14, 1752, three days before Tetty Johnson died at the age of sixty-three.

Johnson now entered one of the darkest periods of his life. Still working at his dictionary, but now burdened with personal grief compounded by poverty and feelings of public neglect, he sometimes spent nights aimlessly walking the streets. Years later he confessed that the pain and gloomy irritability he experienced following his wife's death had never left him. On the seventeenth anniversary of her passing, he wrote in his diary that "when I recollect the time in which we lived together, my grief for her departure is not abated, and I have less pleasure in any good that befals me, because she does not partake it."[47]

The *Rambler* increased Johnson's literary reputation, but not his financial condition. Perhaps the most valuable thing the essays brought him at this time was a brief visit from an exceptionally tall, thin youth who introduced himself as Bennet Langton from Langton-near-Spilsby in Lincolnshire. The sixteen year old had been so impressed by the learning and wisdom displayed in the essays that he had traveled the 150 miles to London principally to meet the author. When he rapped on Johnson's door, he expected to find a decent, well-dressed philosopher. Instead he encountered a massive, ungainly figure with his clothes hanging loosely about him and wearing a little black wig too small for his head. The young man stood for a moment dumbfounded, but as Johnson began to speak, his conversation proved so forceful, so replete with knowledge and wisdom, that Langton formed a lasting veneration for the large, uncouth person before him, and he remained one of Johnson's most devoted admirers for the rest of his life.

Another new acquaintance for Johnson in 1752 was thirty-four-year-old Joseph Baretti, a native of Italy. He would prove to be the most difficult and temperamental of the Johnson circle. Even as a child growing up in Turin, Giuseppe MarcAntonio Baretti, the eldest of four sons, showed the head-strong, fiery disposition that marked his character throughout life. At age sixteen, when his mother died and his father, a month later, married a girl of eighteen, Giuseppe grew so angry that he drew his sword on his father.[48] He then left home and went to live with an uncle at Guastalla, in the Po Valley, where he associated with literary men, began to study diligently, and started to write verses.

A man of medium height and sturdy build, he "wore his hair" as the phrase was, rather than a wig, and due to poor eyesight, he usually read with spectacles, or sometimes a monocle, which he carried on a broad black ribbon around his neck, prompting his Italian friends to dub him *Cavaliere del Ordine del Laccio*, or Knight of the Order of the String. Literature became his vocation, and diligence soon marked his character as much as choler and rashness. As he moved from Guastalla to Venice, then to Milan, and later back to Turin, he learned how difficult gaining a literary reputation could be and how nearly impossible it was to earn a livelihood with a pen in Italy. Perhaps half a dozen writers received small incomes translating works from French and English, but otherwise prospects were dismal. Italian writers often

Joseph Baretti, after James Barry, c. 1773.
Source: Author's personal collection.

stared in disbelief when told there were authors in England who made a living by their writings alone. Part of the problem in Italy was the small reading public. Each province spoke a dialect nearly unintelligible to people in neighboring provinces. Another problem was the severe censorship imposed on authors and publishers. Everything printed in Italy had to be licensed by two or more reviewers appointed by civil and ecclesiastical authorities. Yet in spite of these difficulties, Baretti persevered.

Underscoring his passionate temper was his emphatic speech. He slipped easily into hyperbole, often claiming to be ruined, devastated, or nearly slain by the hardships of life. An example of this occurred when his father died in 1744 and Baretti told a friend that it "has spoilt my life. In addition to this I have suffered a cruel blow, which affected me so seriously that it nearly killed me, in the death of a girl whom I loved above everything else on earth. It has pierced my very soul."[49] Despite such overcharged emotions, he continued to work hard and earned a pittance translating Italian works into French. From Venice in 1747 he wrote to a friend that he usually spent the entire day at his desk translating and revising proofs, his only recreation being a few hours spent in the evening in the company of some poets. "This is my mode of life, entirely in accordance with my wishes, though the weariness of it all is killing me."[50] To the same friend, whom he had not seen in some time, he described his present character as that of

> a fiery fellow who turns savage in a moment and whose hand flies to his sword; who speaks several Italian dialects tolerably well, who sings Italian songs and little musical airs in the French style; who could make a stone laugh at times; agreeable and most obliging with the ladies, but without compliment or ceremony towards a man; with no great literary attainments, though he knows a mere babbler when he sees him and hates a dullard or a disagreeable boor, no matter what his position, and is as bitter, sarcastic, and rough with them as he is sincere, cordial, frank, and as generous as his means allow with all who are neither dullards nor disagreeable boors. Put all this together, and you will have some idea of Baretti, who is loved in Venice, in Mantua, in Milan, in Turin, and wherever he has been by all who love the lovers of virtue—and there's an end to my panegyric.[51]

After moving back to Turin in 1750, he showed how bitter and sarcastic he could be when he published an article titled "Primo Cicalamento" [Splendid Chattering], in which he attacked the prevailing craze in Italy for archeology and the proliferation of antiquarians. He ridiculed Giuseppe Bartoli in particular, a professor of literature at Turin University, for his long-winded speculations, spun out in several volumes, on a single artifact. Men like Bartoli, wrote Baretti, should be sent to an asylum rather than be taken seriously. The nobility might undertake such trivial occupations as archeology, it being a better use of their time than gambling, but a professor should encourage students to study languages, rhetoric, and philosophy—subjects that prepare young men to earn a living and that benefit society.

He meant for the article to create a stir, and it did. Various persons, offended by his scathing comments, convinced authorities that an attack on a professor was an attack on the king who appointed him. Summoned before the president of the Senate and the chancellor of Turin University, Baretti received a strong reprimand and was prohibited from publishing any more "Cicalamenti." Under the circumstances, he got off lightly and later said of the whole affair,

> If I were not something of a savage and a fearless wild beast, and had I not answered the President of the Senate proudly and boldly, things would have gone badly for me, for the King had bidden this same President threaten to shut me up in the fortress for the rest of my days on account of the Cicalamento, which was regarded as a libel upon His Majesty before I was sent for; but I was desperate and I spoke desperately, and managed to undeceive the world and come out in safety: it is a bad business, however.[52]

Realizing that his literary career was over before it really got started, he decided to emigrate to England. He loved travel. Few things delighted him more than encountering new cultures and learning new customs. He had wanted to see England for at least two years, when, in the course of studying English, he happened on a *Spectator* essay and thought that if the lighter productions were so good, how wonderful the weightier ones must be. He arrived in London in March 1751.

The English at this period, lower-class Londoners in particular, did not in general look favorably on foreigners. In the midst of heightened nationalism, Londoners often regarded foreigners as irritants at best, dangerous parasites at worst. Americans, owing to their increasingly quarrelsome disposition toward the mother country, were widely castigated, especially by the Tory segment of the population. The Scots were often reviled as a poor, rapacious, half-civilized race who, following the unification of Britain, were eager to live off their more prosperous neighbors to the south. The French were the most detested of all. Years of intermittent wars with France and constant economic competition sometimes made it dangerous for a Frenchman to appear on the streets. Italians fared better than most. Due to its climate, its status as birthplace of the Renaissance, and its wealth of art and historical monuments, Italy was a favored destination of English travelers. Italian burlettas were then fashionable entertainment in London, and the Italian tongue was the foreign language most in vogue among people of quality.

Baretti's chief concerns after arriving in London were to master the language and to find employment. Although he knew relatively little English, he exaggerated his ignorance when later recalling this period:

> For the first two months I could not understand a single syllable; but when I had succeeded in fixing in my head a few hundred words by continually working at

nouns, verbs, and other parts of speech, I made every one I came across read me out these words not once only, but ten times and more, and tried all the while to pronounce the most difficult; and thus, by gradually accustoming my ears to the sound, I made what was considered extraordinary progress in that strange and most irregular tongue. It is true that nature has given me some facility in learning languages, and that my frequent changes from place to place in early life have increased this facility, for I have always tried to speak the dialect of every place where I have ever made a short stay.[53]

Even though he soon found work with the Italian Opera House in London and began teaching Italian, his early months in London proved difficult and lonely, but by frequenting coffeehouses, speaking with those who appeared to be gentlemen, and studying the customs and language of the people, he made progress. English weather also seemed to do him good. He wrote humorously to a friend in Italy, "This temperate climate was all that was needed to cool my fiery blood, and though my character has not changed, the cider and the beer have calmed me to such a degree that I hope that in a year or two I shall never laugh, except when I am absolutely forced to do so." He likewise found English women much to his taste, claiming they were, "as a rule, angels incarnate, behaving with more reserve and circumspection than those of Italy."[54]

One evening the husband of Charlotte Lennox, author of the novel *The Female Quixote*, entered the Prince of Orange Coffee House in the Haymarket, a gathering place for foreigners, and enquired if anyone there would be able to teach his wife Italian in exchange for lessons in English. Mrs. Lennox, much respected by Samuel Johnson, wished to learn enough Italian to investigate the sources for some of Shakespeare's plays. Baretti accepted the offer, and it was through Mrs. Lennox that he met Johnson.

Early in 1755, Oxford University conferred on Johnson the honorary degree of Master of Arts. He received the award, said the university chancellor, for "a series of essays, excellently calculated to form the manners of the people, and in which the cause of religion and morality is every where maintained by the strongest powers of argument and language." Of additional consideration was the *Dictionary of the English Language*, "executed with the greatest labour and judgement,"[55] published in two large volumes in April and containing 42,773 entries and nearly 114,000 quotations to illustrate precisely how the words are used.[56] In his original "Plan," Johnson had said, "All change is of itself an evil," and he made clear that "one great end of this undertaking is to fix the English language."[57] By "fix" he meant give the language final form so that it would be immutable, not subject to change. But as he progressed in his labors, he realized that he had "indulged expectation which neither reason nor experience can justify." Too many factors contributed to the slow, inexorable mutation of language over time. Following nine years of digging through words and their meanings, he had come to the conclusion that change in language is irresistible, and all we can do is "acquiesce with silence." Because language cannot ultimately be fixed, "it remains that we retard what we cannot repel, that we palliate what we cannot cure."[58] *The Dictionary of the English Language* may not have fixed the language, but it remained a standard reference work for nearly a century and assured Johnson's place in the pantheon of literature.

In the following year, hoping to earn more money, he issued proposals for a new edition of Shakespeare's plays with commentaries. He hoped to complete the work and see it published before Christmas of 1757, about eighteen months hence. In the meantime, he wrote a number of short pieces for various magazines and also assisted Baretti in small ways with books he was writing. Unlike Johnson, who occasionally lapsed into long periods of idleness, Baretti steadily persevered. He studied hard, wrote diligently, and soon mastered English. But all was not toil. Conversing with beautiful women and attempting to charm them were among his greatest pastimes and pleasures. Still, "I have not fallen really in love once," he wrote to an Italian friend, "though, without boasting, I may say that I have been on intimate terms with several ladies worthy of the love of any man, not to mention an old fool like myself."[59]

In 1753 he published two comical pamphlets in French concerning difficulties between the actors and the lessee of the Italian Opera House, and he also published in English a *Dissertation on the Italian Poets*. His *Introduction to the Italian Language* and *The Italian Library* appeared in English in 1757. These were followed in 1760 by his most important work to date, a *Dictionary of the English and Italian Languages*. This was long the standard work of its kind and contained a dedication to the Marquis of Abreu, the Envoy-Extraordinary from Spain, written for Baretti by Johnson.

Encouraged by his moderate literary success in England, he decided to try his fortunes once again in Italy. Perhaps now he possessed enough experience and strong enough credentials to succeed in his own language and country. Departing London on August 14, 1760, he made a leisurely excursion through Portugal, Spain, and France, arriving in Genoa in mid-November. Johnson, fitfully at work on his edition of Shakespeare, had urged him before he left to keep a travel journal, advice that Baretti followed and made good use of later. But conditions in Italy, as events soon proved, still did not accord with Baretti's temperament. After visiting his brothers in Turin, he settled in Milan, where he published the first volume of *Lettere familiari a suoi tre fratelli Filippo, Giovanni e Amadeo* [Familiar Letters to His Three Brothers Filippo,

Giovanni and Amadeo] in 1762. "I am frank of speech and tell the truth quite bluntly," he said of himself. "In literature a certain noble arrogance is not out of place. . . . I like modesty, and consider myself modest in my actions; but once I take a pen in hand, I write without fear—that is, without modesty."[60] But his noble arrogance and frankness embroiled him in another controversy, for some critical remarks on Lisbon in his *Lettere familiari* offended the Portuguese minister, who used his influence to get the work suppressed.

Baretti felt devastated. Writing to Johnson on July 21, 1762, he described his situation. "When I left England," he said, "I firmly proposed, my Johnson, to write to you pretty often, and you yourself in all probability expected I would do so, being sure as you must be, that I love and honour you above all other men." But having met with so many reversals since coming to Italy, he had no heart to write anyone about anything. As an instance, he complained of a patron, Count Firmian, the Austrian Plenipotentiary in Milan, who had strung him along for more than a year with displays of friendship and promises of favor and financial support. Yet he proved to be "a goodfornothing Man" at last. "And so, my Johnson, here am I, brimfull of discontent, with my health disorder'd by this long agitation between hope and fear." He had recently spent some time at a friend's villa on Lake Como and felt somewhat better. "But though I have recover'd part of my bodily health, grief and anger still pray upon my heart, and I think my mental faculties are impaired by the prevalence of those incessant thoughts, that the Plenipotentiary's strange behaviour has given a rise to in my disturbed brains."

For some months, he told Johnson, he had sought consolation in philosophical and religious books, "and your Ramblers among others are often in my hands; but my affliction is unconquerable, and my sadness is made deeper and deeper by another unhappy passion that has taken too strong a possession of my heart. What this passion be, I am ashamed to tell, considering that I am on the wrong side of forty." This unhappy passion was a love for Rosina Fuentes, the young daughter of a close friend. "Towards the latter end of past May I made a violent effort, and went for three weeks into Monferrat; but Grief destroyed me visibly; and my hopeless and unruly passion [for Rosina] brought me here [to Milan] again. I wish I had never left England! I had never left Johnson! but what signifies wishing?" He assured Johnson that he had not forgotten his friend and that he always inquired after him:

> I am informed that you continue to live on in idleness, and that you have not finished your Shakespeare. This, my Johnson, is blameable, very blameable. Yet I dare not now fall too hard upon you. I cannot conquer my stubborn Love as you cannot conquer your Idleness and I have lost my right of scolding my Friend for his not overcoming his Passion since I cannot overcome mine. Indeed, Johnson, we are two miserable Mortals in spight of our superiour talents! God direct us,

and give us strength to mend our ways, for our ways are not good. Nay to be in love and to be idle are very bad ways!

He concluded, "Be well, my Johnson, cure yourself of your Idleness, and do never forget your affectionate Baretti."[61]

In his reply of December 21, Johnson advised Baretti not to let such evils overwhelm him, "as thousands have suffered and thousands have surmounted. . . . Your patron's weakness or insensibility will finally do you little hurt, if he is not assisted by your own passions." As for his love of Rosina Fuentes, "There is indeed nothing that so much seduces reason from her vigilance, as the thought of passing life with an amiable woman; and if all would happen that a lover fancies, I know not what other terrestrial happiness would deserve pursuit." But life, love, and lovers are ever changeable. "A woman we are sure will not be always fair; we are not sure she will always be virtuous; and man cannot retain through life that respect and assiduity by which he pleases for a day or for a month. I do not however pretend to have discovered that life has any thing more to be desired than a prudent and virtuous marriage; therefore know not what counsel to give you."[62] Baretti treasured this and other letters from his friend, for as he later remarked of Johnson, "His trade was wisdom."[63]

Still much dejected, Baretti moved to Venice, where in 1763 he published the second volume of *Lettere familiari* with all critical references to the Portuguese government expunged. Yet he continued to stir up controversy and resentment in other quarters. He began publishing *La Frusta Letteraria* [The Literary Scourge], a periodical denouncing what he saw as the worthless books and bad Italian authors of the day. In so doing, he adopted much the same bitter and sarcastic tone he had used earlier, for as he told a friend, "the world prefers scathing criticism, biting satire, good ridicule of a definite person to a thousand encomiums on a thousand persons. This is human nature."[64] Yet it was not long before some of those he ridiculed in *La Frusta* got the paper suppressed after twenty-five issues. Reportedly the shock and disappointment affected Baretti so severely that he took to his bed for almost two months.

NOTES

1. Boswell, *Life*, 1:101n1.
2. David Garrick, *The Letters of David Garrick*, ed. David M. Little and George M. Kahrl, 3 vols. (London: Oxford University Press, 1963), 28 and 30.
3. Ibid., 31.
4. Ibid., 32.

5. Horace Walpole, *Horace Walpole's Correspondence*, ed. W. S. Lewis, 48 vols. (New Haven: Yale University Press, 1948–1983), 17:435.

6. Thomas Gray, *The Letters of Thomas Gray*, ed. Duncan C. Tovey, 3 vols. (London, 1909), 1:106.

7. Richard Cumberland, *Memoirs of Richard Cumberland*, 2 vols. (London, 1807), 1:80–81. Cumberland's opinion of Mrs. Cibber's acting is contradicted by others. Garrick prized her ability and often played opposite her. The two were close enough in height and overall features to pass for siblings. Thomas Davies wrote of Mrs. Cibber, "In love, grief and tenderness, she greatly excelled all competitors; and was also unrivalled in the more ardent emotions of jealous love and frantic rage, which she expressed with a degree of sensibility in voice, look, and action, that she never failed to draw tears from the most unfeeling" (Thomas Davies, *The Life of David Garrick*, 2 vols. [London, 1780], 1:80).

8. Cumberland, *Memoirs*, 1:81.

9. Davies, *Life of Garrick*, 1:44.

10. Ibid., 1:46.

11. Mrs. Clement Parsons, *Garrick and His Circle* (London: Methuen, 1906), 58; see also Percy Fitzgerald, *The Life of David Garrick*, 2 vols. (London, 1868), 1:99.

12. Maynard Mack, *Alexander Pope: A Life* (New York: W. W. Norton, 1985), 760.

13. Carola Oman, *David Garrick* (Great Britain: Hodder and Stoughton, 1958), 94.

14. Samuel Johnson, *The Yale Edition of the Works of Samuel Johnson*, 23 vols. (New Haven and London: Yale University Press, 1958–2016), 2:57.

15. Ibid., 18:57.

16. Ibid., 18:108–9.

17. Bertram Joseph, *The Tragic Actor* (London: Routledge and Kegan Paul, 1959), 91.

18. Friedrich Melchior, Baron von Grimm, quoted in Jean Benedetti, *David Garrick and the Birth of Modern Theatre* (London: Methuen, 2001), 192–93.

19. William Cooke, *Memoirs of Charles Macklin, Comedian, with the Dramatic Characters, Manners, Anecdotes, &c. of the Age in Which He Lived* (London, 1804), 112.

20. James Northcote, *The Life of Sir Joshua Reynolds*, 2 vols. (London, 1818), 1:106; William Cotton, *Sir Joshua Reynolds, and His Works. Gleanings from His Diary, Unpublished Manuscripts, and from Other Sources* (London, 1856), 95; Richard Wendorf, *Sir Joshua Reynolds: The Painter in Society* (Cambridge, MA: Harvard University Press, 1996), 125. Cotton states unequivocally that the painter was Gainsborough while Wendorf thinks it may instead have been Hogarth.

21. Frank A. Hedgcock, *A Cosmopolitan Actor: David Garrick and His French Friends* (London: Stanley Paul and Co., 1912?), 51.

22. Cooke, *Macklin*, 112.

23. Hester Lynch Thrale Piozzi, *Thraliana: The Diary of Mrs. Hester Lynch Thrale (Later Mrs. Piozzi), 1776–1809*, ed. Katharine G. Balderston, 2 vols. (Oxford: Clarendon Press, 1951), 271n1.

24. Joseph, *The Tragic Actor*, 109–23; *The Theatrical Review; or, Annals of the Drama,* (London, 1763), 76; Tate Wilkinson, *The Wandering Patentee: or, A History of the Yorkshire Theatres*, 4 vols. (York, 1795), 2:50; Old Comedian, *The Life and Death of David Garrick, Esq. The Celebrated English Roscius. In Which His Powers Both in Tragedy and Comedy Are Considered* (London, 1779), 11.

25. William Cooke, *Memoirs of Samuel Foote, Esq. with a Collection of His Genuine Bon-Mots, Anecdotes, Opinions, &c. Mostly Original*, 3 vols. (London, 1805), 3:25.

26. Boswell, *Life*, 2:463–64; Boswell, *The Life of Samuel Johnson, LL.D. by James Boswell With Marginal Comments and Markings from Two Copies Annotated by Hester Lynch Thrale Piozzi*, ed. Edward G. Fletcher, 3 vols. (New York: Heritage Press, 1963), 2:250; John Wilson Croker, *Johnsoniana; or, Supplement to Boswell* (Philadelphia, 1842), 422.

27. Tate Wilkinson, *Memoirs of His Own Life*, 4 vols. (York, 1790), 1:126.

28. Ibid., 1:236.

29. James Boswell, *Boswell for the Defence, 1769–1774*, ed. William K. Wimsatt Jr. and Frederick A. Pottle (New York: McGraw-Hill, 1959), 80.

30. "The Character of Mr. Garrick," *Gentleman's Magazine* 12 (October 12, 1742): 527.

31. John Hill, *The Actor: or, A Treatise on the Art of Playing* (London, 1755), 207.

32. Cooke, *Memoirs of Foote*, 3:98.

33. Garrick, *Letters*, 92.

34. Moses Tyson and Henry Guppy, eds., *The French Journals of Mrs. Thrale and Doctor Johnson* (Manchester: Manchester University Press, 1932), 140.

35. "The Character of Mr. Garrick," 527.

36. James Thomas Kirkman, *Memoirs of the Life of Charles Macklin, Esq. Principally Compiled from His Own Papers and Memorandums*, 2 vols. (London, 1799), 2:265 and 259.

37. Theophilus Cibber, *Theophilus Cibber, to David Garrick, Esq; with Dissertations on Theatrical Subjects* (London, 1759), 56.

38. Theophilus Cibber, *Dissertations on Theatrical Subjects, As They Have Several Times Been Delivered to the Public, (With General Approbation)* (London, 1756), 22.

39. Ibid., 21 and 25.

40. Johnson, *Works*, 7:79 and 77.

41. James Boswell, *Boswell in Extremes, 1776–1778*, ed. Charles McC. Weis and Frederick A. Pottle (New York: McGraw-Hill, 1970), 175–76.

42. Arthur Murphy, *The Life of David Garrick, Esq.*, 2 vols. (London, 1801), 1:159–60.

43. Garrick, *Letters*, 788. John Tillotson (1630–1694) was a highly respected curate and rector and the Archbishop of Canterbury from 1691 until his death. Various editions of his sermons, discourses, and letters appeared during the eighteenth century.

44. Boswell, *Life*, 1:196. See also Joseph Cradock, *Literary and Miscellaneous Memoirs*, 1:240–41.

45. Garrick's reference is to a couplet in the prologue Johnson wrote for the actor to recite at the opening of Drury Lane Theater, in September 1747, under the new management of Garrick and Lacy:

From Bard, to Bard the frigid Caution crept,
Till Declamation roar'd, while Passion slept.

Samuel Johnson, *Samuel Johnson's Prologue Spoken at the Opening of the Theatre in Drury-Lane in 1747 with Garrick's Epilogue: A Facsimile of the Hitherto Undiscovered First Edition*, preface by Austin Dobson, introduction and notes by A. S. W. Rosenbach (New York, 1902), 5.

46. Boswell, *Life*, 1:210 and n1.

47. Johnson, *Works*, 1:127.

48. Piozzi, *Thraliana*, 154.

49. Lacy Collison-Morley, *Giuseppe Baretti and His Friends* (London, 1909), 46–47.

50. Ibid., 46.

51. Ibid., 47–48.

52. Ibid., 55.

53. Ibid., 62–63.

54. Ibid., 91 and 117.

55. Boswell, *Life*, 1:280.

56. Samuel Johnson, *Samuel Johnson's Dictionary: Selections from the 1755 Work that Defined the English Language*, ed. Jack Lynch (Delray Beach, FL: Levenger Press, 2004), 8 and 12.

57. Johnson, *Works*, 18:36 and 38.

58. Ibid., 18:109.

59. Collison-Morley, *Giuseppe Baretti*, 116–17.

60. Ibid., 41 and 156.

61. Alan T. McKenzie, "Two Letters from Giuseppe Baretti to Samuel Johnson," *PMLA* 86, no. 2 (March 1971): 218–24.

62. Samuel Johnson, *The Letters of Samuel Johnson*, ed. Bruce Redford, 5 vols. (Princeton, NJ: Princeton University Press, 1992, 1994), 1:213–14.

63. Samuel Johnson, *Letters of Samuel Johnson, LL.D.*, ed. George Birkbeck Hill, 2 vols. (New York: 1892), 2:215n1.

64. Collison-Morley, *Giuseppe Baretti*, 160.

Chapter Two

The Great Field
of Genius and Exertion

Within a relatively short period—from the late 1750s through the early 1760s—Samuel Johnson made several more friendships that would last throughout his life. In addition to Garrick, Baretti, and Langton, he added four new acquaintances, all young men in their twenties or thirties with most of their lives and achievements before them. The first of these was the artist Joshua Reynolds, a man with a temperament almost the exact opposite of Joseph Baretti. While Baretti was the most passionate of the Johnson circle, Reynolds was the most placid.

The initial meeting occurred about four years prior to Baretti leaving for Italy and took place at the home of two ladies who, at one point during the evening, expressed sorrow over the recent death of a friend to whom they owed many obligations. "You have, however," said Reynolds, "the comfort of being relieved from the burthen of gratitude." The apparent callousness of the remark shocked the ladies, but Johnson defended Reynolds, saying that the comment showed a profound understanding of life and was similar to the reflections of Rochefoucault.[1] Indeed, it sounded like something Johnson himself might have said, and from that time forward Johnson held Reynolds in high esteem, saying, "Sir I know no man who has passed through life with more observation than Reynolds."[2]

At age thirty-seven, he had already achieved considerable success in his profession and was well on his way to establishing himself as England's pre-eminent portrait painter. For more than half a century prior to this, the finest portrait painters in England had come from abroad: Hans Holbein and Peter Paul Rubens from Germany, Anthony van Dyck from Antwerp, Peter Lely from Holland, and Godfrey Kneller from the city-state of Lübeck. English-born portraitists in the half-century prior to Reynolds—William Dobson, Jonathan Richardson, and Thomas Hudson—never achieved the stature of their foreign-born counterparts. William Hogarth, while he painted portraits, was known chiefly for his satirical pictures of London life. George Romney and particularly Thomas Gainsborough would later become strong rivals, yet throughout his career, Reynolds continued to maintain his dominant position as England's foremost portrait painter. This was due not only to the quality of his work, but also to his sociable personality. As someone who knew him commented, "His exemplary moral conduct, his amiable and well-regulated temper, the polished suavity of his manners, a deportment always easy and unaffected, made his society agreeable to everyone. At [this] period . . . his house in Leicester-fields was resorted to by the most distinguished characters in the country."[3]

In 1760, several years after first meeting Johnson, Reynolds obtained a forty-seven-year lease at a cost of £1,650 on a narrow but elegant house on the west side of what would later be called Leicester Square and was then still known as Leicester Fields. For an additional £1,500 he added a gallery; work rooms for copyists, drapery men, and students; and an octagonal paint-ing room for himself. The painting room measured about twenty feet long by sixteen feet wide and stood fifteen feet from floor to ceiling. A small, square window, nine feet four inches from the floor, illuminated the interior, and by its light Reynolds worked. Paintings not yet sold, or those not yet claimed, hung on the walls. Besides the easel and the fireplace for cold winter morn-ings, the room was furnished with sofas for the comfort of visitors. The sitter occupied a mahogany armchair covered in leather and mounted on castors for easy positioning. The chair rested on a dais eighteen inches high, bringing the sitter to eye level with the painter, for Reynolds always worked standing up. He liked to paint for a while and then walk back some distance to view the subject and portrait side by side. To gain additional distance or to observe the sitter from an unusual angle, he often viewed the subject reflected in a mirror. For nearly thirty-two years Reynolds spent the better part of his day in his modest painting room, from about nine o'clock in the morning until late in the afternoon, turning out the finest portraits of the eighteenth century.

Everything ran methodically in the Leicester Fields house, for Reynolds embodied the neoclassic ideals of restraint, discipline, and regulation. His daily routine changed little from one week to the next, from one year to another. He rose early and, after breakfast, entered his studio to arrange his implements and either touch up work from the previous day or put down an idea in a rough sketch. From nine o'clock, when the first sitter arrived, straight through until three or four he painted. Occasionally he devoted the entire period to one sitter, but usually three or four—sometimes six or seven—appeared during the course of a day, Reynolds switching from one canvas to another in turn. At any given time he might have half a dozen or more works in progress. He devoted his evenings to social relaxation, accepting dinner invitations two or three times a week, and once or twice a week hosting a dinner party of his own or having a few friends in for whist. Being naturally shy and retiring, he drank moderate amounts of wine to stimulate good fellowship and conversation, and he also took snuff, his favorite mixture being Hardham's 37, obtained at Hardham's snuff shop in Fleet Street.[4]

Possessing a florid complexion, round features, and a slightly cleft chin, he stood half an inch under five foot six and, having been born and raised in Plympton, spoke with a Devonshire accent.[5] During his youth he wore his thick brown hair full and down to his shoulders, but as his reputation and social obligations increased, he kept his hair closely trimmed to accommodate wigs. His overall appearance, if not remarkable, was thought pleasing. A portrait of him done by Angelica Kauffmann in 1767 captures the genial person most people knew. In Kauffmann's picture, the spirit of Michelangelo looks down on the placid English painter. Dressed informally, he sits in a relaxed posture looking out of the portrait with soft but intelligent eyes and a kindly expression. The picture makes an interesting contrast to Reynolds's portraits of himself as the working painter with eyes fixed on his subject and mouth slightly open in concentration.

In his twenties, while studying pictures in Italy, he grew hard of hearing. He claimed this to be the result of having caught cold as he stood painting near a hot stove in the damp Vatican, but his deafness may have had more to do with heredity, for he had a young niece who was also hard of hearing.[6] He never went totally deaf and could hear well enough to carry on a conversation with one other person in the room, but in a group, among many voices, he required the aid of a hearing trumpet. It was also on his trip to the Continent, while passing through Minorca, that he severely lacerated his face when his horse plunged down a precipice, an accident that delayed his journey two months while he recovered. He wrote to a young lady friend back home, explaining that "my lips are spoiled now for kissing for my upper lip was so bruisd that a great part was cut off and the rest so disfigured that I have but a [sorry face?] to look at."[7] The injury to his lip left a permanent scar that can barely be seen in his later self-portraits, but the bowed shape of the lip is a Reynolds family trait and is not a result of the fall.

While Reynolds's conversation lacked brilliance, it revealed a strong understanding and sound judgment. In once comparing the insights into human manners furnished by the stories of the clever actor Samuel Foote and those of Reynolds, Johnson said, "When Foote has told me something, I dismiss it from my mind like a passing shadow: when Reynolds tells me something, I consider myself as possessed of an idea the more."[8] Nevertheless, Johnson denied that Reynolds possessed wit or the sort of good humor that advances

Sir Joshua Reynolds by Angelica Kauffmann, 1767.
Source: The National Trust.

conversation.[9] One of his greatest defects, according to Johnson, was how easily superior intellects influenced his thinking. Johnson once remarked, "Sir Joshua is too much under [Charles James] Fox and [Edmund] Burke at present. He's under the Fox Star and the Irish Constellation at present. He's always under *some* planet."[10] In painting, however, Reynolds relied entirely on his own judgment. The advice and opinions of others carried no weight whatsoever. If anyone offered suggestions as to color, dress, position of the sitter, and so on, Reynolds listened politely and then proceeded to do what he thought best. When he entered his octagonal painting room in the morning, he entered a world over which he had total command. He went to work confident in knowing that he had no living superior.

Bennet Langton, following his first visit in 1752, continued to call on Johnson from time to time, even after he began studies at Trinity College, Oxford, in May 1757. Johnson found Langton an easy, pleasant companion, intelligent and learned for his years, even if somewhat prolix and meandering in his talk. Sir John Hawkins recalled Johnson once attempting to give a specimen of Langton's eloquent though elaborate style of conversing, "and assuming his manner, he [Johnson], in a connected speech on a familiar subject, uttered a succession of sentences, in language resembling the style of metaphysics, but, though fluent, so obscured by parentheses and other involutions, that I was unable to collect from it a single idea." Said Johnson after the demonstration, "This is the manner in which * * * * [Langton] entertains me whenever he comes here."[11]

Langton nevertheless soon became a favorite in the Hawkins household, Sir John's daughter, Lætitia-Matilda, later recalling his long visits with pleasure. Langton possessed a pleasant smile as he sat in his chair, one leg twisted around the other and hands clasped over a knee. When conversation began, he would produce an oblong gold-mounted snuffbox from his waistcoat pocket and hold it between his long fingers or place it on a nearby table, resorting to its contents when deep in thought. Miss Hawkins said that whenever Langton paid her father a call, "we females of the family might get through much occupation of the after-breakfast description, drive out for two or three hours, return and dress, and my mother might turn in her mind the postponement of dinner, all within the compass of a morning-visit from Bennet Langton." Yet despite his prolonged visits, her father never grew tired of his conversation, and no one complained of him as a visitor. "Unwilling as he always manifested himself to shift his place, the smallest perception of intrusion would have wounded him to the quick."[12] And although his conversation tended toward the intricate and convoluted, it displayed humor as well as learning. "His manner of exciting mirth was the most gentlemanly," said Miss Hawkins, "every line of his face smiled, but he was never tickled by his own excitation."[13] Every topic he introduced seemed to have been carefully considered beforehand.

A friend recalled a typical visit from Bennet Langton in the Minster Yard at Lincoln: "In the course of conversation he took out a small pocket album, containing bon-mots or heads and notices of bon-mots, which he filled out and commented upon in a most amusing manner." In explaining, for instance, how rude and violent Edmund Burke could be in dispute, Langton said, "If any one asserted that the United States were in the wrong in their quarrel with the mother country, or that England had a right to tax America, Burke, instead of answering his arguments, would, if seated next to him, turn away in such a manner as to throw the end of his own tail into the face of the arguer."[14]

Langton possessed a pleasant voice and a gift for recitation. Being an excellent Greek scholar, he would sometimes begin reciting from a favorite work, suddenly "breaking off," Miss Hawkins said, "for fear of wearying, by saying, 'and so it goes on,' accompanying his words with a gentle wave of his hand."[15] Although he did not surpass David Garrick in general acting ability, a friend told of him reading Shakespeare "with such animation, such just intonation and inflexion of the voice, that they who heard him declared themselves more delighted with his recitation than with an exhibition of the same dramatic piece on the stage."[16] He clearly surpassed Garrick in one area, however, for what the great actor lacked in height, Bennet Langton more than made up for. In contrast to Garrick's sprightly five-foot-four-inch height, the slow and attenuated Langton stood about six foot six.[17] An acquaintance appropriately described him as resembling a stork standing on one leg near the shore in one of Raphael's drawings.

His exceptional height and thinness inspired other witty comments, all of which Langton bore good naturedly. He once had occasion to speak before a public gathering and was interrupted when someone in the crowd called out, "Don't mind what that fellow says, . . . you see he only wants a place in the Victualling Office."[18]

One evening at a party, Garrick fretted impatiently because Langton's tardiness delayed dinner, and when Langton finally arrived and approached Garrick to say something, the actor jumped up on a chair as if to hear him better. But as Garrick got back down, Langton reversed the joke by dropping down on one knee to shake Garrick's hand.[19] An incident he told of himself occurred one severe winter when all the blank walls in London were plastered with advertisements of rival tailors offering greatcoats for men of all sizes. Langton went to a shop where another customer was a short fat man. The tailor could not fit either of them from his garments in stock, and when they reminded him of his advertisements, he said, "Gentlemen, I do indeed undertake to furnish great coats for persons of all sizes; but I do not make them for hop *sacks* or for hop *poles*."[20]

In a portrait of Langton in his early thirties, Reynolds captures three of Langton's most distinguishing traits—his physical indolence, his devotion to learning, and his remarkable height. Apart from the intelligent eyes and the

Bennet Langton by Sir Joshua Reynolds, 1777.
Source: Gunby Hall, The Montgomery-Massingberd Collection (The National Trust).

characteristic pointed nose and chin, the picture shows Langton slouching in a chair, leaning casually on a volume of Clarendon's *History of the Rebellion and Civil Wars in England.* The book's compact mass forms a contrast with the sprawling, angular figure. The extraordinarily long row of coat buttons, snaking diagonally across the picture, points to Langton's height, although he is sitting. For a man of normal stature, this might have been a full-length seated portrait, but here it seems impossible to get enough of the sitter's legs in. Reynolds positions the figure, with its length of torso and limbs, in a languid sinuosity that is emphasized not only by the long row of buttons, but also by the long, unpowdered hair, brushed back from the forehead and curling over the right shoulder.

At the time Reynolds painted this picture, Langton had recently become head of his family. It was an ancient Lincolnshire family that could trace its male line back to the same spot of Langton-near-Spilsby more than six hundred years. The direct male line ended with the death of John Langton in 1989, but it remains one of the few families in England that still maintains close ties with the village from which its name derives. George Langton, Bennet's eldest son, once showed to a friend, Henry Digby Beste, a pedigree that traced the family from the twelfth century down to the time of Queen Elizabeth. It was written on a sheet of parchment about ten inches wide and twelve or fifteen feet long. When Beste asked why he did not bring it down to the present day, George Langton answered, "That can be done at any time. I should be proud of your Digbys, but I am not proud of the antiquity of my own family: it has not produced any famous men."[21]

In Johnson's day, the family bordered on the eccentric. Its oddities were often a topic of conversation among others of the Johnson circle. Bennet Langton senior, for instance, or "Old Mr. Langton," as he was called to distinguish him from his son, had a peculiar cast of mind. Johnson respected him as a thoroughgoing gentleman, knowledgeable in literature and divinity, and living an exemplary life; "and Sir," added Johnson, who detested sentimental display, "he has no grimace, no gesticulation, no bursts of admiration on trivial occasions; he never embraces you with an overacted cordiality."[22] But he had one flaw: "He never clarified his notions, by filtrating them through other minds."[23] As a landed Lincolnshire gentleman of independent means and ancient descent, he acted entirely on his own judgment, which sometimes appeared singular. He once dug a channel where the bank in one place was too low to hold in the water. A neighbor suggested he simply build the bank higher, but Mr. Langton insisted that digging the channel deeper at that spot would answer better, and that is what he did.[24] Another time he received half of a £1,000 legacy, the other portion going to a man to whom he owed £100. He agreed to have the debt subtracted from his part of the legacy, but he later protested on learning that the other man ended up with £200 more than what he got. When shown the mathematics involved, he admitted that it might be true on paper but could not be so in practice.[25]

Old Langton was not successful in exercising much control over his family, especially his daughters, who disregarded his authority and did pretty much as they pleased. They would come down to dinner in the middle of the second course or leave the house dressed in a manner of which their father disapproved. One of the daughters, Elizabeth, once stated that she would be a whore except for three things—first, it would endanger her salvation, second, it would endanger her health, "& the other I have forgot," said Hester Thrale, who recorded the story in her diary, "but it was not that She should disgrace her Family; for says Johnson who told it me—No hang her She was *above that*."[26] Elizabeth demonstrated a trait her brother Bennet possessed, that of being easily offended. She once wrote Johnson to complain of his frigidity in last writing to her "and to tell me," said Johnson, "that she neither hopes nor desires to excite greater warmth. That my first salutation *Madam* surprised her as if an old friend newly meeting her, had thrown a glass of cold water in her face, and that she does not design to renew our conversations when I *condescend* to visit them." Johnson had never meant to insult her, for he customarily addressed letters to women with the salutation *Madam*. Now he felt puzzled what to do next: "I dare neither write with *frigidity* nor with fire."[27] But the misunderstanding eventually got smoothed over and the two remained friends.

Diana Langton, the mother, always pestered her husband to go to London, for she doted on the actors. Johnson said that for more than twenty years she failed to regulate her family, neglected her household duties, and postponed necessary repairs to the house and furniture because she always planned to go to London the following year to see the players, "who made all the subject of her Conversation, settling the Merits of Mrs Cibber & Mrs Pritchard in the midst of a Family ruined by Mismanagement, and running to speedy Decay; and in a Neighborhood of Country Gentlewomen who had never seen nor were likely to see them." Johnson, while once visiting her son in Lincolnshire, tried curing her of always talking of the players, but given the isolated location of the family estate, he could find no other subject close at hand to interest her: "I felt myself in the Situation of a Physician who should prescribe light Food and light Wines to a dying Sailor in the South Seas, where nothing but salt Provisions were to be got."[28]

The entire family possessed a knack for squandering money, not so much by spending it on opulent living, but by letting it dribble away on trivialities, they knew not where or how. Johnson told of Diana Langton taking one of her daughters to Knightsbridge in London and paying five guineas a week "for a lodging and a warm bath; that is, mere warm water. *That*, you know, could not be had in *Lincolnshire!* She said, it was made either too hot or too cold there."[29] When someone asked Old Mr. Langton how his brother Peregrine lived on £200 a year better than he did on £2,000, he replied that it was easy to be an economist with little.[30] The younger Bennet Langton inherited many of these family quirks, yet he possessed such genteel manners and pleasant disposition that people easily excused his little foibles. Being a thoughtfully religious man, he carried about him an aura of virtue and piety without the narrowness that sometimes accompanies those qualities. To censure him for being indolent, careless of money, and sometimes a little dull, would be like chastising him for being too tall. Johnson was heard to say that Langton approached the nearest to his idea of an angel as any man he ever knew.[31] "I know not who will go to heaven if Langton does not," he declared. "Sir, I could almost say, 'Sit anima mea cum Langtono [May my soul be with Langton].'"[32]

While visiting Bennet Langton at Oxford in 1759, Johnson met Langton's brilliant but dissolute friend Topham Beauclerk. Two years older than Langton, Beauclerk traced his descent from Nell Gwyn and Charles II. Nell Gwyn, reportedly born in a brothel to an apple woman, had risen by her fresh good looks, intelligence, sharp tongue, and saucy manner to become a fine comic actress and mistress of the king. She eventually bore the king a bastard son, Charles Beauclerk, First Duke of St. Albans, who in turn fathered a son, Sidney Beauclerk, reputed to be, in many ways, the male counterpart of "pretty witty Nell," as diarist Samuel Pepys called her.[33]

"The Man in England that gives the greatest pleasure and the greatest pain," wrote Lady Mary Wortley Montagu of Lord Sidney Beauclerk in 1727, "is a Youth of Royal blood, with all his Grandmother's beauty, Wit, and good Qualitys; in short, he is Nell Guin in person with the Sex alter'd, and occasions such fracas amongst the Ladys of Galantry that it passes belief."[34] A notorious rake and fortune hunter, Lord Beauclerk eventually earned the names "Worthless Sidney" and "Sid the Beggar." His son, Topham, named for Lord Beauclerk's friend Richard Topham, is said to have resembled Charles II in some ways, while his good looks, cleverness, and sarcastic wit suggested his kinship to pretty witty Nell.

Lord Beauclerk, upon the death of Richard Topham, received a sizeable bequest of land and money that passed on to his son when Lord Beauclerk died in 1744. Later, at his mother's death in 1766, Topham Beauclerk inherited additional land and nearly £3,000 a year.[35] If all this did not amount to a spectacular fortune, it still allowed Topham to live comfortably, sometimes beyond his means, for the rest of his life. On the surface, given his rank, wealth, and reputation for loose living, young Beauclerk appeared ill-suited as a boon companion for Samuel Johnson. He normally circulated within the genteel corridors of fashion and among persons of rank and wealth. His world

Topham Beauclerk by George Perfect Harding.
Source: Trustees of the British Museum.

was that of "forms, fashions, frolicks, of routs, drums, hurricanes, balls, assemblies, ridottos, masquerades, auctions, plays, operas, puppet-shows, and bear-gardens," a social world that Samuel Johnson ridiculed in *Rambler* 100. "Little oaths, polite dissimulation, tea-table scandal, delightful indolence, the glitter of finery, the triumph of precedence, the enchantment of flattery" comprised his social milieu. Yet he also possessed learning, curiosity, and a keen intellect, without which he would have been just another frivolous pop-injay in satin coat and lace ruffles. With his more solid mental attributes, he cultivated a taste for books, science, and the company of such learned men as Bennet Langton and Samuel Johnson.

He met Langton when both entered Trinity College in 1757. Though it would be difficult to find two men more dissimilar in character—the one lively, dissipated, and profane; the other lethargic, scholarly, and devout—Beauclerk had such a love of literature and such a strong intellect that he and Langton soon became friends. Johnson at first thought it strange, wrote James Boswell later, "that Langton should associate so much with one who had the character of being loose, both in his principles and practice; but, by degrees, he himself was fascinated." Besides the appeal of his quick mind, sarcastic wit, and fluent talk, Beauclerk's resemblance to Charles II helped "to throw a lustre upon his other qualities; and, in a short time, the moral, pious Johnson, and the gay, dissipated Beauclerk, were companions."[36]

David Garrick, on learning of this new relationship, exclaimed, "What a coalition! I shall have my old friend to bail out of the Round-House."[37] But Garrick in due course fell under Beauclerk's spell himself. Both were avid book collectors, and they later purchased books together in Italy, Garrick while on leave from the rigors of the theater, and Beauclerk while attempting to recover his health after leaving Oxford without taking a degree. Langton accompanied his friend on this trip as far as Paris and then returned to England. Beauclerk, after a brief affair with a Parisian actress, continued on to Italy. In Venice he met Garrick, and the two made the rounds of the booksellers together. He also met Joseph Baretti, to whom Johnson had written a letter of introduction, saying, "I beg that you will show Mr. Beauclerk all the civilities which you have in your power; for he has always been kind to me."[38] Throughout the trip, Beauclerk apparently lived in high style, mingling with the rich and fashionable, money being no object to him. Garrick wrote to a friend in England that his young companion had lost £10,000 in one night of gaming.[39]

About the time Beauclerk was squandering his money on the Continent, a new and entirely different personality entered the Johnson circle back in London. Oliver Goldsmith's origins and upbringing were as provincial as Beauclerk's were patrician. While Beauclerk had been shaped by fashion-able London society, Goldsmith had been formed by the rural people in and around County Westmeath, Ireland. By the time Goldsmith arrived in London at age twenty-six, no amount of fashionable society could refine his rustic ways. "The Doctor came late into the great world," explained Joshua Reynolds, the one in London who came to know him best. "He had lived a great part of his life with mean people. All his old habits were against him. It was too late to learn new ones, or at least for the new to sit easy on him."[40] But even so, he was odd. In fact, the entire Goldsmith family seemed odd. One familiar with the three branches of the family said that they seldom acted like other people; "their hearts were always in the right place, but their heads seemed to be doing anything but what they ought."[41] Yet it was a close-knit, supportive family, the Reverend Charles Goldsmith, the father, instilling in his seven children the Christian virtues of charity to those less fortunate and goodwill toward everyone.

Mrs. Elizabeth Delap remembered Noll Goldsmith as a child. As village schoolmistress at Lissoy, fifty miles or so west of Dublin, she had taught him to read. She recalled that he was "impenetrably stupid," one of the dullest boys ever placed under her care.[42] The Reverend Doctor Strean, who succeeded to the local curacy in 1768 on the death of the Reverend Henry Goldsmith, Oliver's older brother, found that others in the village held similar recollections. Said Strean, who never met Oliver himself, "He was considered by his contemporaries and school-fellows, with whom I have often conversed on the subject, as a stupid, heavy blockhead, little better than a fool, whom every one made fun of."[43]

Catherine Goldsmith Hodson remembered her brother being serious and reserved as a child yet remarkably humorous on occasion. Unfortunately, young Oliver was short, homely, and awkward, which accounted for much of his shyness. His apparent dullness arose more out of self-consciousness than stupidity. A case of smallpox at age nine had left his cheeks deeply scarred, and this further undermined his looks and self-confidence and subjected him to more ridicule. "He realy cut an ugly figure," recalled his sister.[44] Yet despite his reserve, he showed a quick temper when slighted. "Why, Noll, you are become a fright," said a relative to him following his bout with smallpox; "when do you mean to get handsome again?" The relative was something of a reprobate. "I mean to get better, Sir, when you do," the boy answered smartly.[45]

Ann Goldsmith, for one, recognized that her son was not a blockhead and not a fool, but rather a shy, sensitive boy who possessed talent. As young as seven years of age, he showed a flair for making clever rhymes that amused his father and his father's friends. He would sometimes sit and write little poems and then throw them into the fire. Some of them were once retrieved and handed to Ann, who thought they showed promise. A kindly uncle, Thomas Contarine, a man of modest independence who married one of Goldsmith's sisters, also discerned more in Noll than just a blockhead. He liked the clever youngster and agreed with his mother that the boy deserved proper schooling. As the immediate family was poor, Contarine put up money to prepare

Oliver for a university education. The boy spent two years at a school in Athlone, seven or eight miles away, and he spent more than three years at Edgeworthstown, seventeen miles northeast of Lissoy, where he studied the classics. He liked Horace and Ovid, loved Tacitus and Livy, but hated Cicero. At first backward and diffident, he started to emerge from his defensive shell while at Edgeworthstown, and soon he began to take a leading role in sports and typical boyhood activities. He taught himself the flute and learned to sing many Irish songs with verve and expression. People at Edgeworthstown later remembered him as extremely sensitive and quick to anger but also as ready to forgive.

He progressed well enough in school that at seventeen he passed the examination to enter Trinity College, Dublin. He entered not as a pensioner, however, able to pay his own way, but as a sizar, a poor scholar who acts as servant to other students, for which he receives an allowance toward college expenses. Dressed in a sizar's customary coarse black gown and red cap, Oliver was expected to do such menial chores as carry dishes into the dining hall, sweep and scrub floors, and perform other odd jobs as they arose. He found the situation demeaning and thought it a contradiction "for men to be at once learning the *liberal* arts, and at the same time treated as *slaves*, at once studying freedom, and practising servitude."[46] But in spite of his degraded position and slow academic progress, he developed a keen interest in college social life. His natural cheerfulness, together with the humiliating experiences of childhood, made him eager to be liked, so he increasingly neglected his studies and became more gregarious. One of his classmates later recalled him "perpetually lounging about the college gate," and he was known to have injured his health and finances by "too often mixing in scenes of dissipation."[47] His short, stocky build, awkward movements, and homely features still made him the butt of sarcastic remarks, but when chafed to anger, he often picked up his flute and played it "with a kind of mechanical vehemence till his equanimity of temper returned."[48]

At some point in his teens or early twenties he discovered that if he could not conceal his defects, he could at least lessen the pain they caused him. By accentuating his peculiarities and pointing out his own shortcomings, he developed a talent for buffoonery. As a social clown he could laugh with those who laughed at him and thereby gain attention and a measure of acceptance. Later, as this penchant for buffoonery became more deeply ingrained in his personality and as his literary talents matured, people were often baffled by the contradictions in his character. They hardly knew what to make of the brisk little Irishman, who appeared to be at times little more than a zany, yet who, at other times, displayed flashes of brilliance.

On February 27, 1750, he took the degree of Bachelor of Arts, bringing to a close his undistinguished and generally unhappy college career. During his absence his father had died and his mother had moved to a cottage in Ballymahon. At twenty-three years of age, with a college degree and no prospects of employment, he joined his mother and entered into a period of idleness. A villager remembered often seeing him sitting in the window of his mother's house playing his flute. He also spent much time across the road at George Conway's inn, where he met with the lads to swap stories, play cards, and sing songs. He often took solitary walks up the Inny, hunted otters along the Shannon, and one summer won a prize for throwing the sledgehammer at the Ballymahon fair. His father, his brother Henry, and his Uncle Contarine having all been clergymen, friends and family now thought that Oliver, too, should enter the profession. But Oliver disliked the idea. He thought himself temperamentally unsuited to the calling, yet he nevertheless applied for orders to the Bishop of Elphin, who, after meeting with the young man, turned him down. Catherine Hodson believed the bishop rejected her brother due to his youth; a priest had to be at least twenty-four years old. But the Reverend Strean later heard rumors that the bishop had been annoyed with Oliver for showing up to his interview dressed in scarlet breeches.

His friends and relations, having failed to make Oliver a clergyman, next thought he might do well in the medical profession, so Uncle Contarine sent him off with a little money in the fall of 1752 to attend medical classes at Edinburgh University. But the new surroundings, combined with his low self-esteem and lack of friends, only made him lonely. He wrote to his uncle that he was unknown to everybody except for a few students who attended the professors as he did. Writing to his brother-in-law, Daniel Hodson, he lamented, "During the day I am obligd to attend the Publick Lectures. At night I am in my Lodging. I have hardly any other society but a Folio book[,] a skeleton[,] my cat and my meagre landlady." Even so, he acknowledged Uncle Contarine's assistance in enabling him to come to Scotland rather than rusticate in Ireland, where "I was despised by most, and hateful to myself. Poverty, hopeless poverty, was my lot, and Melancholy was beginning to make me her own."[49]

His naturally gregarious nature, however, eventually led him to become more socially active and to make new acquaintances. For a couple of weeks he dined every other day with the Duke and Duchess of Hamilton, where he showed his comic talent and earned the name "the facetious Irish man." But that soon wore thin and he stopped going, for "it seems they like me more as a *jester* than as a companion; so I disdained so servile an employment."[50] The Scots, in general, were a new experience for him. The somber young people he saw at the popular assembly balls in Edinburgh were far different from the boisterous youths he had known in Irish alehouses. "When a stranger enters the danceing-hall," he wrote home, "he sees one end of the room taken up by the Lady's, who sit dismally in a Groupe by themselves. On the other end stand their pensive partners, that are to be, but no more intercourse between the sexes than there is between two Countrys at war." Couples walked through the minuet, he said, quietly and with a formality approaching despondency. "I told a scotch Gentleman that such a profound silence resembled the ancient procession of the Roman Matrons in honour of Ceres and the scotch Gentleman told me, (and I beleive he was right) that I was a very great pedant." Still, Oliver claimed to love Scotland, particularly the lasses, whom he thought ten thousand times finer and better looking than Irish women. The Scottish ladies had such fine skin and eyes, and the broad Scots dialect complemented their pretty mouths. Unfortunately, he had to admire the lovely misses from afar. "There are 'tis certain handsome women here," he repined, "and tis as certain they have handsome men to keep them company. An ugly and a poor man is society only for himself and such society the world lets me enjoy in great abundance." Edinburgh with all its pretty women left him leisure to "sit down and laugh at the world, and at myself—the most ridiculous object in it."[51]

He finally left Edinburgh in 1754 to complete his medical training at Leyden, in Holland, but gambling debts soon forced him to leave without taking a degree. From Leyden he set out with no money in February 1755 to travel parts of Europe on foot. In a year's time he passed through Flanders, Belgium, France, Germany, Switzerland, and Italy before heading toward England. He survived by sleeping in barns, accepting the hospitality of friars in convents, and earning a meager living playing his flute.[52] He may have picked up the degree of medical bachelor in Padua, Italy, or in Louvain, east of Brussels, which authorized him to practice medicine and to assume the title *doctor*, though no record of his having earned a medical degree or certificate has turned up at any European institution.

Arriving at Dover around the beginning of February 1756, he made his way to London two weeks later with a few half-pence in his pocket. After much difficulty, he found work for a time as a tutor, or usher, in a boys' academy, a position he found demeaning and one that he detested. That having failed, he hoped his medical training might gain him employment, but due to his Irish accent and his shabby appearance, he found nothing but rejection from the apothecaries to whom he applied. "You may Easily imagine what difficulties I had to encounter," he wrote to his brother-in-law, "left as I was without Friends, recommendations, money, or impudence; and that in a Country where my being born an Irishman was sufficient to keep me unemploy'd." Many others in similar circumstances, he said, might have turned to the friar's cord or the suicide's rope. "But with all my follies I had principle to resist the one, and resolution to combat the other." Poor and lonely, he often thought about his friends in Ballymahon and displayed the ambivalent feelings of many immigrant Irish toward their native land: "Unaccountable fondness for country, this maladie du Pays, as the french call it. Unaccountable, that he should still have an affection for a place, who never received when in it above civil contempt, who never brought out of it, except his brogue and his blunders." He found work as a physician among the poor along Bankside, Southwark, but he got no fees. His patients could not afford to pay him. Desperately needing money, and always having possessed an easy facility with the pen, he turned to writing occasional essays and critiques for the *Monthly Review.* These occasional pieces were marked by a congenial manner, good sense, and a graceful prose style. "By a very little practice as a Physician and a very little reputation as an author I make a shift to live," he told his brother-in-law. "Nothing more apt to introduce us to the gates of the muses than Poverty."[53]

Eventually the publication of *An Enquiry into the Present State of Learning in Europe* in 1759, along with increasing success at periodical work, especially his "Chinese Letters" in the *Public Ledger*, brought him a widening group of friends. An early acquaintance was Thomas Percy, whom Goldsmith met through a mutual friend in early 1759 at the Temple Exchange Coffee House. The two had similar interests. Percy was engaged in compiling his *Reliques of Ancient English Poetry*, published in 1765, the most significant work of the eighteenth century in reviving interest in old English ballads. Goldsmith for his part was knowledgeable in Irish folklore and ballads, so the two had much to discuss. Percy was also a friend of Samuel Johnson, and one evening he brought the great lexicographer to a dinner Goldsmith hosted at his chambers in Wine Office Court on the last day of May 1761. The meeting proved successful, and soon Goldsmith found himself on easy terms with Johnson and those close to him. All thought Goldsmith unusual, but Johnson and Reynolds felt him talented and amiable enough to include in the original eight members of the Club, which they established in 1764. The original members included Reynolds, who first proposed the Club; Johnson; Edmund Burke; Christopher Nugent, a physician and Burke's father-in-law; Goldsmith; Topham Beauclerk; Bennet Langton; Anthony Chamier, Under-Secretary of State; and Sir John Hawkins. They met for supper and conversation every Monday evening about seven at the Turk's Head, Gerrard Street, Soho.

Although gifted, lively, and fundamentally good natured, Goldsmith was the most unconventional member of the Club and the most eccentric character of the Johnson circle. Much of his unconventional behavior arose from a conflict between his deep feelings of insecurity and a just understanding of his talents. Had he been good looking, or even so much as plain, the diverse elements of his character would have been better integrated, but his ugliness placed a heavy burden on him. It forced him into behavior that people could not reconcile with his literary talents. His homely features had been the great affliction of his childhood, and, although he could joke about it now, it still preyed on his mind as an adult. "I have sent my cousin Jenny a miniature picture of myself," he wrote to his brother Maurice. "The face you well know is ugly enough but it is finely painted."[54]

In full manhood he stood about five foot five or six inches tall with a compact, muscular build. He had brown hair and fair complexion with a receding chin, large mouth, and protruding brow and upper lip. As homely as he was, he felt that his struggles since leaving Ireland had made him look worse. He wrote to his older brother Henry, "Tho' I never had a day's sickness since I saw you yet I am not that strong active man you once knew me. You scarce can conceive how much eight years of disappointment anguish and study have worn me down." He asked Henry to imagine "a pale melancholly visage with two great wrinkles between the eye brows, with an eye disgustingly severe and big wig, and you may have a perfect picture of my present appearance." Since leaving Ireland, he said, he had picked up a disagreeable, hesitating manner of speaking "and a visage that looks illnature itself."[55]

To help detract from his ugliness, he developed a taste for flamboyant clothing early in life. On arriving in London in 1756 to set up as a physician, he had little money to indulge this inclination, but as he later wrote of Beau Nash, he "dressed to the very edge of his finances."[56] An acquaintance from Ireland, who met him on the street at the time, described him as dressed in an old faded suit of green and gold, with a shirt and neck cloth that looked like they had been worn at least a fortnight.[57] Later he managed to get hold of a secondhand velvet coat more in a style favored by physicians. It had evidently once belonged to an aristocrat, the star on the left breast having been cut off and the coat mended. Yet the spot where the patch had once been showed so clearly that Goldsmith had to carry his hat over his left breast to conceal it.

The author Percival Stockdale first encountered Goldsmith in Tom Davies's bookshop in Russell Street, Covent Garden. This is the place where James Boswell would first meet Samuel Johnson a short time later. Stockdale claimed that he had never seen a man look more like a tailor than Goldsmith.[58] Such was the impression his uncouth appearance initially made on people. Joshua Reynold's sister, Frances, said of him, "Dr. Goldsmith was indeed very ugly, he had a vulgar mean aspect, more the look of a journeyman taylor from head to foot than any man I ever saw." She mentioned that his general aspect impressed everyone at first that he was either a journeyman tailor or a common laborer. She told of him one day entering a gathering of ladies and gentlemen at her brother's residence and complaining of being insulted by a stranger at a coffeehouse: "'The fellow,' he said, 'took me for a tailor!' on which all the Party either laugh'd aloud or shew'd they suppress'd a laugh."[59]

Oliver Goldsmith by William Henry Bunbury, c. 1765.
Source: Trustees of the British Museum.

James Boswell's encounter with Johnson in Tom Davies's bookshop on Monday, May 16, 1763, proved to be the most significant meeting of the young Scotsman's life, an event he later described in the now well-known passage in his *Life of Johnson*. On Davies introducing the two, Boswell, recalling reports that Johnson had a prejudice against the Scots, told Davies facetiously not to tell where he came from. "From Scotland," Davies blurted out.

Boswell admitted that he did indeed come from Scotland but said that he couldn't help it. "That, Sir, I find," replied Johnson, "is what a great many of your countrymen cannot help." After the three sat down, Johnson said to Davies, "What do you think of Garrick?" The actor had refused him a complimentary theater order, or pass, for Anna Williams, a blind poetess and former friend of Tetty Johnson, who was among a growing number of destitute people Johnson cared for in his house. Garrick had refused the pass, complained Johnson, "because he knows the house will be full, and that an order would be worth three shillings."

"O, Sir," interjected Boswell, "I cannot think Mr. Garrick would grudge such a trifle to you."

"Sir," Johnson shot back, "I have known David Garrick longer than you have done: and I know no right you have to talk to me on the subject."

Mortified by this rough check and lapsing into silence, Boswell thought that his long-held ambition of gaining Johnson's acquaintance had been dashed. Johnson, however, treated him more courteously as the evening progressed, convincing Boswell "that though there was a roughness in his manner, there was no ill nature in his disposition." When Boswell later had to leave the bookshop to keep another engagement, he complained to Davies, who accompanied him to the door, of the "hard blows" Johnson had given him, but Davies reassured him, saying, "Don't be uneasy. I can see he likes you very well."

Boswell acknowledged to himself that contradicting Johnson's criticism of his old friend and pupil had been presumptuous, yet attempting to make himself conspicuous, especially to celebrated persons, was one of his most prominent traits. Upon arriving in London the previous year, he had proclaimed, "Surely I am a man of genius. I deserve to be taken notice of."[60] But the statement, though full of bravado, expressed more hope than conviction, for Boswell, at age twenty-two, actually saw himself, when stripped of all pretensions, as a timorous and poorly educated individual. Yet he also wanted to believe himself unique, possessed of certain attributes that, when coupled with boundless energy, helped compensate for what his upbringing had failed to provide. Thus driven by a strong ambition to be noticed, and blessed with abundance of charm, he determined not to let his shortcomings prevent him from cultivating the acquaintance of superior men like Johnson.

He saw his native Scotland, however, as too confining. To remain there, he said, would be to yoke a Newmarket courser to a dung cart.[61] Edinburgh in particular seemed vulgar and provincial compared to the variety and excitement that London had to offer. So he quit Scotland and came to London, "the great field of genius and exertion" as he called it, "where talents of every kind have the fullest scope, and the highest encouragement."[62] Here he hoped to perfect his character and demonstrate to the world his unmatched spirit and unique personality. With much enthusiasm and some trepidation, he remarked, "My great object is to attain a proper conduct in life. How sad will it be, if I turn out no better than I am."[63]

Before leaving Edinburgh, he began keeping a journal, not merely to record the events of his life, but to trace the development of his personality.

"What a singular Being do I find myself!" he noted several years later. "Let this my Journal shew what variety my mind is capable of."[64] The journal became a ledger of sorts into which he might look at any time to see what progress he had made in shaping his character. Yet coming to a final determination of what kind of person he was proved elusive, a goal he ultimately never achieved. Despite attending to his feelings and actions and meticulously setting them down in his journal, he remained to the end of his life a man in search of himself. Friends sometimes accused him of being vain and self-centered, a charge he readily acknowledged. He admitted that he magnified all events in his own favor, inflating them all out of proportion due to vanity. To an acquaintance he wrote, "Have you ever seen a man so vain as I am? I am sure you never have. I cannot divest myself of vanity for a single instant."[65] Yet he justified his egotism by stating, "It is not enough merely to be proud or vain; it is necessary at the same time that other people should think we have a right to be so."[66] As with many people of like disposition, his vanity sprang from self-doubt rather than overconfidence. His pride rested on a shaky foundation of deep insecurities while his vanity propped up an unstable ego. Nonetheless, a strong determination to fashion himself into a man of substance had already carried him a long way from Jamie Boswell, the cringing, hypochondriacal, fastidious boy who only a few years earlier slunk through the streets of Edinburgh, fearful of everything.

Throughout childhood he had been tugged in different directions by a strict father, indulgent mother, and a stern Presbyterian upbringing. "My mother was extremely kind," he recalled in a sketch of his early life, written for the philosopher Jean–Jacques Rousseau, "but she was too anxious when I had some small ailment. If I did not feel well, I was treated with excessive attention." She did not make him go to school when he felt sick but gave him candy and various trinkets to amuse him. Because he hated school, Jamie might have lied about being ill but for his father impressing upon him the importance of always speaking the truth. "Accordingly I never lied, but I hung my head down towards the floor until I got a headache, and then I complained that I was ill." Although he often skipped school, he had to attend church every Sunday "when I was made to remember the terrible Being whom those about me called God. The Scots Presbyterians are excessively rigid with regard to the observance of the Sabbath. I was taken to church, where I was obliged to hear three sermons in the same day, with a great many impromptu prayers and a great many sung psalms, all rendered in a stern and doleful manner." Taught not to do his own work, speak his own words, or think his own thoughts on holy days, "I tried in sincerity of heart to conform to that command; especially not to think my own thoughts."[67]

His religious training made such a deep impression that he afterward always associated Presbyterianism with fear and gloom. A Presbyterian kirk made him tremble, while card playing depressed his spirits, just like he felt when listening to a Presbyterian sermon.[68] As much as he tried to suppress his gloomy thoughts in later life, he never completely succeeded: "The meanest and most frightfull presbyterian notions, at times recurr upon me," he wrote to a friend. "My ideas of Virtue & Vice are not fixed. Shall I ever be a sollid uniform & happy man?"[69] In addition to the gloomy feelings that often overwhelmed him, the servants when he was a boy used to frighten him with stories of robbers, murderers, witches, and ghosts. All these influences conspired to crush his spirit, leaving him in youth "no noble hope. Terribly afraid of ghosts. Up to eighteen could not be alone at night. . . . Afraid of the cold and everything else. A complete poltroon in the streets of Edinburgh. . . . Black ideas even at that age. Ignorant—terrified by everything I did not understand."[70] Matters grew so desperate that at seventeen he suffered an emotional breakdown.

Feeling that he had become the most timid and despicable of beings, he grew determined to reshape himself into what he wished to be—a steady, dignified, and respectable gentleman. Keeping a journal, he told himself, would help him discover his intrinsic character and allow him to fashion a new and stronger Boswell. He remarked that "as a lady adjusts her dress before a mirror, a man adjusts his character by looking at his journal."[71] He believed that to some degree people can be whatever they choose, but in trying to find a suitable image for himself, he became all the more confused about who he really was. While his journal later served, among other things, as a repository of Johnsoniana, it remained the place where he endeavored to sort out and comprehend his own perplexing nature. His journal served as a register of faults he wished to correct and a catalog of virtues he hoped to attain. His wife, Margaret Montgomerie, whom he married in 1769, once told him that in keeping a journal he left himself emboweled to posterity, but he cared less about posterity at the time than in methodically anatomizing his personality in order to make himself worthy of the notice of men like Samuel Johnson.[72]

Johnson's curt rebuke in Davies's bookshop might have discouraged anyone of less determination, but Johnson was too big a prize for Boswell to let get away. Consequently, he called on Johnson several days later and was courteously received. Johnson became another exemplar in a growing collection of great men, both living and dead, whose lives Boswell studied and whose conduct he wished to emulate. By the time he reached twenty-five, he had attached himself to a number of distinguished individuals who served as models for his own behavior. These included Thomas Sheridan ("My Mentor! My Socrates!"), Samuel Johnson ("my great friend and instructor"), and General Pasquale Paoli, leader of the patriots in Corsica.[73] Early journal entries record his search among these and other individuals for an appropriate persona to model himself after. He tried on identities as another man might try on coats to see which fit him best: "Study [to be] like Lord Chesterfield, manly"—"Be Johnson"—"You resemble Johnson; imitate him"—"Let us imitate the amiable Pitfour"—"Be [Thomas] Gray"—"Be content to be known as [Dr.] Armstrong"—"I felt a strong disposition to be Mr. [Joseph] Addison"—"Be like Sir Richard Steele."[74] Often, when he had executed his part well in company, he congratulated himself on his sterling performance: "I was in fine cheerful spirits tonight, spoke a good deal, fancied myself like Burke"—"I was quite happy, quite [West] Digges"—"Was powerful like Johnson."[75]

He thus acquired the habit of acting parts as in a play. It became a custom he found useful at the time, but one that further confused his notions of who he really was. Eventually affectation became a permanent part of his character, but a feature that made him uneasy. Among his many reasons for admiring Lord Marischal, the seventy-year-old Scotsman who had been a leader of the Rebellion of 1715, was his lordship's lack of affectation, something Boswell could not quite understand, as he was much plagued by it.[76] He wondered how a man as illustrious as Lord Marischal could have no affectation. In Germany, while on his Grand Tour, he encountered a celebrated bluestocking who spoke in an affected manner as if she enjoyed hearing herself talk. He admitted to sometimes putting on a similar display by talking too much, and he acknowledged this to be a great fault, yet excusable. "All affected people have it," he said, "and as I was ill educated, I am obliged to affect more genteel manners and so have learnt the habit of playing a part."[77]

Although he never lost the habit of role-playing, he realized the futility of trying to be someone else. "I saw my error in suffering so much from the contemplation of others. I can never be them; therefore let me not vainly attempt it, in imagination. . . . I must be Mr. Boswell of Auchinleck and no other. Let me make him as perfect as possible." But just who was Mr. Boswell of Auchinleck? What was he supposed to be, and how was he to act? These perplexing questions he never fully resolved as he occasionally wrote in his journal such queries and notations as "*What* am I?" and "Mem.: know who you are and what you are."[78]

In attempting to compensate for the timidity and priggishness of his childhood, he swung to the other extreme and developed into a boisterous, outgoing, and morally lax adult. By violently throwing off his earlier constraints, he lost the faculty of self-restraint, becoming compulsively self-centered, self-indulgent, contradictory, and vacillating. Looking back to this transitional period in his life, he commented that

> like a man who takes to drinking to banish care, I threw myself loose as a heedless, dissipated, rattling fellow who might say or do every ridiculous thing. This

made me sought after by everybody for the present hour, but I found myself a
very inferior being; and I found many people presuming to treat me as such,
which notwithstanding of my appearance of undiscerning gaiety, gave me much
pain. I was, in short, a character very different from what GOD intended me
and I myself chose.[79]

The perplexing question remained, however, that if the dissipated, rattling
fellow was not the genuine Boswell, what was? And if the inferior being
many people saw was only a mask, why could he not rid himself of it?

In thus struggling to define himself, Boswell isolated certain key traits in
his nature. For one thing, he saw that he was a man of sentiment and passion
rather than reason. Having been discouraged as a child from thinking his own
thoughts, he had developed the habit of indulging his feelings. He became
the kind of man to snatch a present gratification rather than cultivate a lasting
comfort. He remarked that he was a being that consisted mostly of feelings.
"I have some fixed principles. But my existence is chiefly conducted by the
powers of fancy and sensation."[80] He often regretted not being more sensible,
but happiness in life, he maintained, was not found along one path alone. In
this so-called Age of Reason, he was a confirmed romantic: "Reason is not
the sole guide. Inclination must chiefly direct us."[81]

Another of his traits was an often debilitating melancholy, made worse,
certainly, by his Presbyterian upbringing, but a disorder he attributed ultimately to heredity. His mother, grandfather, and an uncle suffered from it.
Although in society he projected an image of perpetual gaiety, he acknowledged privately that he had an essentially melancholy nature, "which dissipation relieves by making me thoughtless, and therefore, an easier, tho' a more
contemptible, animal."[82] Often without warning, and for no apparent reason,
he sank into a deep depression that might last days or months. At such times
he resembled, he said, a room in which someone has accidentally snuffed
out the candles.[83] While the distemper lasted, he dreaded getting out of bed,
saw no hope or purpose in life, and often sought diversion in low jocularity,
obsessive drinking, and compulsive whoring. He maintained that dissipation,
after all, was better than melancholy. But then, just as quickly as it had come,
the depression suddenly lifted, and he felt gloriously alive and happy.

The one fault that required special attention was that of talking too much,
especially about himself. He cautioned himself time and again in his journal,
"Be *retenu* [reserved]"—"Pray, pray be *retenu*. O man, thou hast a sad inclination to talk; now is thy time to cure it!"—"Learn by all means *retenue* and
being easy without talking of yourself."[84] Although he recognized the problem, he seemed powerless to control it. "I am too open and have a desire to let
all my affairs be known," he said. "This I must endeavour to correct."[85] But
once he got started, nothing seemed too private for him to divulge: "Yester-

day you was still too jocular and talked of yourself, particularly of your whoring, which was shameful."[86] Even his closest friends sometimes lost patience
with him. During a walk one day in St. James's Park with several others, he
went on so long about himself and his affairs that his close friend William
Johnson Temple said to him, "We have heard of many kinds of hobby-horses,
but, Boswell, you ride upon yourself."[87]

Yet in spite of his egotism, he possessed a charming manner that most
people found irresistible. Johnson took a liking to the young man the more
he saw of him. Unfortunately, less than two months after the meeting in Davies's bookshop, Boswell had to leave for Holland to pursue his law studies,
and Johnson accompanied him to Harwich to see him aboard ship. Boswell
spent a dull and mostly unpleasant year in Holland before embarking on a
two-year Grand Tour of the Continent. In keeping with his desire to associate
with great men, he pressed himself on the sickly Jean-Jacques Rousseau at
his retreat in Môtiers, Switzerland, presenting himself as "a man of singular
merit" who deserved Rousseau's attention.[88] He enjoyed five interviews with
the reclusive philosopher, who was at first irritable and disinclined to be both-
ered, but who, like Johnson, soon warmed to the young man. Rousseau felt
alarmed, however, by certain things Boswell disclosed about himself. In a letter of introduction he wrote for Boswell, Rousseau disclosed to a friend, "In
his youth he got his head confused with a smattering of harsh Calvinistic the-
ology, and he still retains, because of it, a troubled soul and gloomy notions.
. . . He is a convalescent whom the least relapse will infallibly destroy."[89]

From Switzerland, Boswell moved on to Ferney, France, near Geneva,
where he pressed himself on the ailing Voltaire. Though not as easily charmed
as Rousseau, Voltaire impressed Boswell as a thoroughly brilliant talker, constantly throwing off flashes of wit. In comparing the two great men, Boswell
thought Voltaire a poet who flew very high and Rousseau a philosopher who
went very deep. Continuing his tour, Bowell visited Joseph Baretti in Venice. He had not met Baretti before, but he wished to pay a courtesy call on
"Johnson's translator," Baretti having recently made a French translation of
Rasselas that was never published. Four days later Baretti returned the visit,
and Boswell recorded in his journal, "Yesterday morning came Baretti, Johnson's friend; curious Italian."[90] The following day, after showing Boswell the
letters Johnson had written him, Baretti erupted into violent expressions of
misery and bitterness. He spoke contemptuously of immortality and said the
devil had created man. He exclaimed, "As man dies like a dog, let him lie
like a dog. I hate mankind, for I think myself one of the best of them, and I
know how bad I am." When Boswell reported this conversation to Johnson at
the Mitre Tavern in Fleet Street seven months later on his return to England,
Johnson grew annoyed. Having little patience for such querulous discontent,

he replied, "*If* he dies like a dog, *let* him lie like a dog." As for Baretti's comparing himself with others, Johnson said, "Sir, he must be very singular in his opinion, if he thinks himself one of the best of men; for none of his friends think him so."[91]

Still miserable and bitter, Baretti finally returned to England for good in the fall of 1766, having despaired of ever earning a decent living as an author in Italy. He now contented himself with becoming "a kind of demi-Englishman," as he phrased it.[92] He went to work with the same diligence as formerly and soon published *An Account of the Manners and Customs of Italy.* The work brought him a welcome income and much attention. He wrote to his brother Filippo that "there is no one of literary note in this city who is not anxious to make my acquaintance. The other evening a beautiful lady, famous for her wit, her charm, her modesty, and many other good qualities, kissed me without ceremony in a very large assembly, saying she did so as a return for the pleasure which my second volume especially had given her."[93]

Johnson also spoke highly of the work and of Baretti in general, telling Boswell, "His *Account of Italy* is a very entertaining book; and, Sir, I know no man who carries his head higher in conversation than Baretti. There are strong powers in his mind. He has not indeed so many hooks as he might have had; but so far as his hooks reach, he lays hold of objects very forcibly."[94] The king thought well enough of Baretti's book that he appointed him Secretary of Foreign Correspondence to the newly instituted Royal Academy of Painting, Sculpture, and Architecture upon recommendation of its president, Sir Joshua Reynolds. On Reynolds being elected the first president of the Academy by a unanimous vote of its members, George III had knighted him to give the institution greater distinction. In addition to Baretti's appointment, the king further named Samuel Johnson Professor of Ancient Literature and Oliver Goldsmith Professor of Ancient History. These were entirely honorary positions. They carried no salaries and no responsibilities and were intended to augment the institution's prestige. The titles allowed the three authors to attend Academy meetings if they wished and ensured them seats at the Academy's annual dinner. Goldsmith wrote to his brother Maurice in Ireland that he accepted the position "rather as a compliment to the institution than any benefit to myself. Honours to one in my situation are something like ruffles to a man that wants a shirt." By contrast, Baretti felt elated. He found the honor especially remarkable considering that English laws did not favor outsiders and those of a different religion. He rejoiced to think of the respect accorded him in England, where even a foreigner might succeed according to his merit, compared to the scorn he had received in Italy. He remarked, "In Venice, instead of heaping honours and favours on me for having written such a book, they would almost have thrown me into the Canal Orfano. What a difference between the Venetians and the English!"[95]

NOTES

1. Leslie and Taylor, *Life and Times*, 1:118–19.

2. *The Correspondence and Other Papers of James Boswell Relating to the Making of the* Life of Johnson, second edition, corrected and enlarged, ed. Marshall Waingrow (Edinburgh: Edinburgh University Press and New Haven: Yale University Press, 2001), 277.

3. Joseph Farington, *Memoirs of the Life of Sir Joshua Reynolds; with Some Observations on His Talents and Character* (London, 1819), 64.

4. Derek Hudson, *Sir Joshua Reynolds: A Personal Study* (London: Geoffrey Bles, 1957), 73–74; Wendorf, *Sir Joshua Reynolds*, 112–14; John Timbs, *Anecdote Biography; or, Scenes and Events in the Lives of Distinguished Persons* (London, 1860), 144.

5. Sir Joshua's sister Mary Palmer captured a comical rustic version of this dialect in *A Devonshire Dialogue, in Four Parts*, edited by Mrs. Gwatkin and published in London in 1839, of which the following is a sample, taken from pages 19 and 20:

ROBIN. I was a'gest thee widn't a' come, as et began to misslee.[z]

BETTY. I can't zay I like to walk in zich vady,[a] hazy weather: I zem es shall ha' a slotteringb walk o'te.

RAB. This dribbl'ingc rain will break up bam by.[d] Look'e, d'ye zee, there's blue enew in the sky to make thee a rocket.

BET. Po, your eyes mistree.[e]

RAB. I can zee, tho', thee hast a cruel pritty gownd on.

BET. I've a' waddl'd[f] en up vor vear of a scud,[g] vor if it's wet 'twill cockle.[h]

RAB. 'Tis an over modest colour, spick and span new,[i] is'n it? You must pay beverage,[k] Bet.

BET. I zay zo, too: why, I bot[l] en last Ridmas[m] come twelvemonth, of a runabout. Dame zaith, I was catch'd by the vinger. There's many scovy[n] places in en, it wan't wear well; I shall ha' more wit next. I'm very chary[o] over en; it never zees zin, but upon choice times. Come! pray dont'e clum[p] en zo.

[z]To rain in small drops, like a mist.

[a]Damp.

[b]Dirty, wet.	[i]Quite new, first worn.
[c]Small rain	[k]A treat upon wearing a suit of new clothes
[d]By and by.	[l]Bought.
[e]Dim-sighted.	[m]Roodmas. [14 September]
[f]Folded.	[n]Thin, uneven.
[g]Shower.	[o]Careful.
[h]Wrinkle	[p]Paw or handle.

6. Frances Burney, *Diary & Letters of Madame d'Arblay (1778–1840)*, ed. Charlotte Barrett, preface and notes Austin Dobson, 6 vols. (London, 1904–1905), 4:23.

7. Sir Joshua Reynolds, *The Letters of Sir Joshua Reynolds*, ed. John Ingamells and John Edgcumbe (New Haven: Yale University Press, 2000), 7.

8. Piozzi, *Anecdotes*, 98.

9. See Boswell, *Boswell: The Ominous Years*, 149n6, and *Boswell in Extremes*, 315.

10. *Boswell in Extremes*, 261. Joseph Farington writes that Reynolds "thought Dr. Johnson possessed a wonderful strength of mind, but that Mr. Burke had a more comprehensive capacity, a more exact judgment, and also that his knowledge was more extensive; with the most profound respect for the talents of both, he therefore decided that Mr. Burke was the superior character. Sir Joshua and Mr. Burke were for a great length of time warmly attached to each other" (*Memoirs*, 82–83).

11. Sir John Hawkins, *The Life of Samuel Johnson, LL.D.* (London, 1787), 387–88.

12. Lætitia-Matilda Hawkins, *Memoirs, Anecdotes, Facts and Opinions Collected and Preserved by Lætitia-Matilda Hawkins* (London, 1824), 1:234–35.

13. Hawkins, *Memoirs*, 1:289.

14. Henry Digby Beste, *Personal and Literary Memorials* (London, 1829), 63.

15. Hawkins, *Memoirs*, 1:279 and 288.

16. Beste, *Personal and Literary Memorials*, 62.

17. Miss Hawkins says that Langton was six foot six (*Memoirs*, 1:148), and Peregrine Langton states that his father, "thinner than any man I almost ever saw," stood six foot four (James Boswell, *The Correspondence of James Boswell with Certain Members of the Club*, ed. Charles N. Fifer [New York: McGraw-Hill, 1976], lxixn60).

18. Hawkins, *Memoirs*, 1:285.

19. Lætitia-Matilda Hawkins, *Anecdotes, Biographical Sketches and Memoirs; Collected by Lætitia-Matilda Hawkins* (London, 1822), 319–20.

20. Hawkins, *Memoirs*, 1:285.

21. Beste, *Personal and Literary Memorials*, 66–67. The Lincolnshire historian Terence R. Leach says of the Langtons, "Their tenacity and ability to produce male heirs over so many generations is their main, but not their only, claim to fame. The members of the family who have owned Langton, and some of the family who have not, have been interesting rather than distinguished" (*Lincolnshire Country Houses & Their Families: Part One* [Lincoln: Laece Books, 1990], 26). If the Langton family has not produced any famous men, it has at least produced a succession of tall, angular ones. Bennet Langton's sons, for instance, were tall men. Lætitia-Matilda Hawkins writes that when in France, they "amused the good people of Paris, by raising their arms to let them pass [under]" (Hawkins, *Memoirs*, 1:285). This writer was told by a present-day member of the family that while at school, the late John Langton and one or two of his brothers, due to their height and slenderness, were called the Kipper Langtons.

22. Boswell, *Life*, 4:27.

23. Ibid., 3:47 and n1.

24. Ibid., 3:47. See also Piozzi, *Thraliana*, 104–5.

25. George Birkbeck Hill, *Dr. Johnson: His Friends and His Critics* (London, 1878), 253.

26. Piozzi, *Thraliana*, 105.

27. SJ to Mrs. Thrale, July 20, 1771, Johnson, *Letters*, Redford, 1:373–74. See also SJ to Elizabeth Langton, April 17, 1771, 1:358–59.

28. Piozzi, *Thraliana*, 105 and 170.

29. Boswell, *Life*, 5:286.

30. Piozzi, *Thraliana*, 105.

31. Samuel Johnson (Reynolds's nephew of that name) to Miss Elizabeth Johnson, February 6, 1775; Susan M. Radcliffe, *Sir Joshua's Nephew* (London: Murray, 1930), 39.

32. James Boswell, *Boswell: The Applause of the Jury, 1782–1785*, ed. Irma S. Lustig and Frederick A. Pottle (New York: McGraw-Hill, 1981), 215. See also Boswell, *Life*, 4:280.

33. Samuel Pepys, *The Diary of Samuel Pepys*, ed. Robert Latham and William Matthews, 11 vols. (Berkeley: University of California Press, 1970–1983), April 3, 1665, 6:73.

34. Lady Mary Wortley Montagu, *The Complete Letters of Lady Mary Wortley Montagu*, ed. Robert Halsband, 3 vols. (Oxford: Clarendon Press, 1966), 2:74.

35. Lady Mary Coke, *The Letters and Journals of Lady Mary Coke*, ed. J. A. Holmes, 4 vols. (Bath: Kingsmead Reprints, 1970), 2:127.

36. Boswell, *Life*, 1:248–49.

37. Ibid., 1:249.

38. Johnson, *Letters*, Redford, 1:207.

39. Garrick, *Letters*, 425–26. See also John Heneage Jesse, *George Selwyn and His Contemporaries*, 4 vols. (London: 1843–1844), 2:121, in which Gilly Williams in London writes to Selwyn on December 26, 1766, "Topham Beauclerk is arrived. I hear he lost £10,000 to a thief at Venice."

40. Sir Joshua Reynolds, *Portraits by Sir Joshua Reynolds*, ed. Frederick W. Hilles (New York: McGraw-Hill, 1952), 47.

41. James Prior, *The Life of Oliver Goldsmith*, 2 vols. (London, 1837), 1:101.

42. Ibid., 1:22–23.

43. Ibid., 1:23.

44. Oliver Goldsmith, *The Collected Letters of Oliver Goldsmith*, ed. Katharine C. Balderston (Cambridge: Cambridge University Press, 1928), 162–63 and 165.

45. Prior, *Goldsmith*, 1:29–30.

46. Oliver Goldsmith, *An Inquiry into the Present State of Polite Learning in Europe* in *The Collected Works of Oliver Goldsmith*, ed. Arthur Friedman, 5 vols. (Oxford: Clarendon Press, 1966), 1:336.

47. Thomas Percy, *The Life of Dr. Oliver Goldsmith*, ed. Richard L. Harp (Salzburg: Institut für Englische Sprache und Literatur, 1976), 15 and 21.

48. Prior, *Goldsmith*, 1:73.

49. Goldsmith, *Letters*, 3 and 16.

50. James, Sixth Duke of Hamilton (1724–1758), was a Scottish peer who, in 1752, married Elizabeth Gunning (1733–1790). James died at age thirty-three from a

cold contracted while out hunting. Elizabeth later served from 1761 to 1784 as Lady of the Bedchamber to Queen Charlotte. It is not known how Goldsmith made the couple's acquaintance. See Goldsmith, *Letters*, 18n3, and Ralph M. Wardle, *Oliver Goldsmith* (Lawrence: University of Kansas Press, 1957), 54–55.

51. Goldsmith, *Letters*, 18, 17, 10–11, and 13.

52. William Cooke, "Table Talk; or, Characters, Anecdotes, &c. of Illustrious and Celebrated British Characters, During the Last Fifty Years," *European Magazine* 24 (August 1793): 91–92.

53. Goldsmith, *Letters*, 27–28.

54. Ibid., 85–86.

55. Ibid., 57–58.

56. *The Life of Richard Nash* in Goldsmith, *Collected Works*, 3:293.

57. Prior, *Goldsmith*, 1:214–15.

58. Ibid., 2:238–39.

59. Frances Reynolds, *Recollections of Dr. Johnson*, in *Johnsonian Miscellanies*, ed. George Birckbeck Hill, 2 vols. (New York, 1897), 2:269.

60. James Boswell, *Boswell's London Journal, 1762–1763*, ed. Frederick A. Pottle (New York: McGraw-Hill, 1950), 181.

61. *The Correspondence of James Boswell and William Johnson Temple 1756–1795*, vol. 1, ed. Thomas Crawford (Edinburgh: Edinburgh University Press and New Haven: Yale University Press, 1997), 33.

62. Boswell, *Life*, 1:101.

63. JB to Sir David Dalrymple, June 25, 1763; James Boswell, *Letters of James Boswell*, ed. Chauncey Brewster Tinker, 2 vols. (Oxford: Clarendon Press, 1924), 12.

64. James Boswell, *James Boswell: The Journal of His German and Swiss Travels, 1764*, ed. Marlies K. Danziger (Edinburgh: Edinburgh University Press and New Haven: Yale University Press, 2008), 327.

65. James Boswell, *Boswell on the Grand Tour: Germany and Switzerland, 1764*, ed. Frederick A. Pottle (New York: McGraw-Hill, 1953), 55.

66. James Boswell, *Boswell in Holland, 1763–1764*, ed. Frederick A. Pottle (New York: McGraw-Hill, 1952), 127.

67. Frederick A. Pottle, *James Boswell: The Earlier Years, 1740–1769* (New York: McGraw-Hill, 1966), 1–3.

68. James Boswell, *Boswell on the Grand Tour: Italy, Corsica, and France, 1765–1766*, ed. Frank Brady and Frederick A. Pottle (New York: McGraw-Hill, 1955), 57; Boswell, *Grand Tour: Germany*, 185.

69. Boswell, *Correspondence of Boswell and Temple*, 98.

70. Pottle, *Boswell: Earlier Years*, 16.

71. Boswell, *Life*, 3:228.

72. Boswell, *Ominous Years*, 174–75.

73. Boswell, *London Journal*, 9; *Boswell in Extremes*, 214.

74. Boswell, *Boswell in Holland*, 4 and 231; *Grand Tour: Italy*, 50; *Boswell in Holland*, 212 and 249; *Grand Tour: Italy*, 65; *London Journal*, 62 and 113. Dr. John Armstrong was a Scottish physician.

75. Boswell, *Ominous Years*, 60; *Journal of German and Swiss Travels*, 33; and *Boswell in Search of a Wife, 1766–1769*, ed. Frank Brady and Frederick A. Pottle (New York: McGraw-Hill, 1956), 25. West Digges was an actor whom Boswell admired for his elegance and affability.

76. Boswell, *Journal of German and Swiss Travels*, 117.

77. Ibid., 169.

78. Ibid., 65; Boswell, *Boswell in Holland*, 231; *Applause of the Jury*, 114.

79. Boswell, *London Journal*, 62.

80. Boswell, *Ominous Years*, 97–98.

81. Boswell, *London Journal*, 123.

82. Boswell, *Letters*, 12.

83. Boswell, *Correspondence of Boswell and Temple*, 34.

84. Boswell, *Boswell in Holland*, 249, 76, and 40.

85. Boswell, *London Journal*, 110.

86. Boswell, *Boswell in Holland*, 51.

87. James Boswell, *Boswelliana: The Commonplace Book of James Boswell*, ed. Charles Rogers (London, 1874), 208.

88. Boswell, *Grand Tour: Germany*, 218.

89. Ibid., 275.

90. Boswell, *Grand Tour: Italy*, 94 and 98.

91. Boswell, *Life*, 2:8.

92. Collison-Morley, *Giuseppe Baretti*, 359.

93. Ibid., 188.

94. Boswell, *Boswell in Search of a Wife*, 156. See also Boswell, *Life*, 2:57.

95. Goldsmith, *Letters*, 84; Collison-Morley, *Giuseppe Baretti*, 199–200.

Chapter Three

Deadman's Place

During the years that Baretti tried unsuccessfully to reestablish himself in Italy, and as Garrick and Reynolds increased their fortunes and reputations in their respective arts, Samuel Johnson continued to scratch out a meager living with his pen. Although he did not earn much, he gradually advanced his status as writer, scholar, thinker, and moral philosopher. In April 1758 he had begun publishing a new series of periodical essays titled *The Idler*, the articles appearing every Saturday for a two-year period in *The Universal Chronicle, or Weekly Gazette*. Produced largely out of financial necessity, they were sometimes written at the last possible moment, Johnson occasionally sending them off to the printer the night before they were needed without first reading them over. Also out of financial necessity he wrote *Rasselas, Prince of Abyssinia*, a philosophical fable in the form of an Oriental tale, published in 1759. He wrote the work during the evenings of one week in order to pay his mother's funeral expenses and to discharge some of her small debts.

While these works demonstrated Johnson's ability to compose rapidly when the need arose, the long-delayed edition of Shakespeare's plays exhibited an equally strong propensity to idle away his time. In his *Miscellaneous Observations on the Tragedy Macbeth*, published in 1745, he had revealed his intent to bring out the complete plays with notes, but the announcement attracted such little interest that it may have dampened his enthusiasm. The project therefore languished for eleven years, but then in 1756 he again announced "Proposals" for a new edition of the plays, which, he stated, would be out before Christmas of 1757. The day before Christmas, however, he wrote to music historian Charles Burney that the work would be delayed until March. In March he wrote Burney again apologizing for another delay: "It will, however, be published before summer." Yet summer came and went and still no Shakespeare. Three years later, in 1760, he wrote to Baretti in Milan, "I intend that you shall soon receive Shakspeare," but five more summers passed. After delays totaling eighteen years, *The Plays of William Shakspeare, in Eight Volumes, with Notes* finally came out in October 1765. The edition received mixed reviews and was largely superseded twenty-five years later by Edmond Malone's edition, but Johnson's "Preface" to the plays is now recognized as the best piece of Shakespeare criticism to appear in the eighteenth century.[1]

The same year the *Plays of Shakspeare* was published, Johnson met a wealthy couple who would become part of the growing circle of diverse characters closely associated with him. The wife in particular would become perhaps the most significant person in his later life. Raised in a physically and intellectually vigorous family, Hester Lynch Salusbury loved the outdoors, especially the rugged countryside of her native Caernarvonshire, Wales, where she learned to ride and to hunt at an early age. She loved rural pleasures, later prompting Johnson to sometimes chide her for tending her chickens when she should be cultivating her mind. At home she received an excellent education from her mother and an aunt and envisioned becoming a writer. Due to financial troubles, the family later moved to the Hertfordshire estate of Sir Thomas Salusbury, her father's brother, and there, at age seventeen, she began serious academic studies under Arthur Collier, doctor of divinity, Oxford graduate, and classical scholar. Thirty-four years older than Hester, he instructed her primarily in rhetoric, logic, Latin, and Greek, and became the greatest influence on her early intellectual growth. As friend, tutor, and advisor, he filled the position Johnson would eventually occupy. A close friend of the novelist Henry Fielding and his family, he had also tutored Fielding's sister Sarah, who went on to become a novelist herself. Hester later described Collier as a man of great erudition and polished manners, totally free of rancor and malice. Yet he loved to debate metaphysical and philosophical issues to the point at which others sometimes grew resentful that he pressed his arguments with too much tenacity, "but nobody ever did feel more fond & true Affection for another, than I did for my dear Dr Collier, & he for his *sweetest Angel* as he call'd me."[2] Under Collier's guidance, Hester made good progress, eventually becoming fluent in Latin, Greek, Italian, and Spanish. In addition, she wrote verses to amuse her father and uncle, knew the Bible intimately, conversed fluently, and possessed natural charm and grace.

Despite her intelligence and high spirits, she strove to be an obedient daughter. Both father and mother wanted the best for her, yet they often worked at cross purposes, leaving Hester caught in the middle and struggling to please both. The result was that throughout life, although possessing a strong will of her own, she frequently found herself torn between competing loyalties and uncertain which way to turn. She felt ambivalent anyway about her father, John Salusbury. An effusive man with a robust sense of humor, he could be extremely generous and obliging, though, according to Hester, he often made family life miserable with his "red-hot temper."[3] The mother, on the other hand, Hester idolized. She regarded Hester Maria Salusbury as the most accomplished female she ever beheld, her "Shape so accurate, her Carriage so graceful, her Eyes so brilliant, her Knowledge so extensive, & her Manners so pleasing." In Hester's eyes she was the essence of female intelligence and virtue. Her mother's every wish became her own desire, her mother's rectitude a model for her own behavior. Hester said that until the day she married, she had never been away from her mother more than twelve hours at a time.[4]

Hester particularly admired her mother's patience and determination in the face of adversity. In the early days of her marriage, Mrs. Salusbury some-times opposed her husband's will, an action Hester thought so perilous, given her father's temper, that she wondered how her mother had escaped with her life, which, she heard, had sometimes actually been in danger.[5] The contrast between her mother's perseverance and her father's temper showed itself clearly when Henry Thrale began courting their daughter. John Salusbury at first knew nothing of Thrale's intentions. The family still lived with Salus-bury's brother, Sir Thomas, at Offley Park in Hertfordshire, just north of Lon-don. One day when Salusbury was away on business, Sir Thomas entered and announced to Hester and her mother that he had met an excellent young man named Thrale. According to Sir Thomas, Thrale was a most incomparable in-dividual, a model of perfection, and a real sportsman. Hester felt like laughing at her uncle's extravagant praise, but Sir Thomas looked at her gravely and said he expected Mrs. Salusbury and Hester to like the gentleman.[6]

Henry Thrale arrived the next day, tall and handsome, Oxford educated, articulate, and well bred. His father, Ralph Thrale, had worked his way up from small business owner to amass a fortune in the brewing business. He gave his son the best education and a large stipend, both of which allowed Henry to develop a taste for genial company and epicurean pleasures. After leaving Oxford without taking a degree, young Thrale settled in London on a thousand-pound-a-year allowance and became a beau, often associating with the brilliant and somewhat profligate Irish playwright Arthur Murphy. With Thrale's money and Murphy's knowledge of London's various amusements, they enjoyed themselves immensely.

Upon the death of his father in 1758, Henry Thrale inherited the house and brewery in Southwark along with a handsome country villa at Streatham Park, six miles from town. Contrary to the expectations of his merry London friends, young Thrale applied himself to the brewing trade and demonstrated an entrepreneurial talent to rival his father's. Several years later, with business prospering, Henry decided to take a wife and start raising a family. He principally wanted a male heir to whom he could eventually pass on his name, business, and fortune. He sought the hand of several young women, but none would agree to live in the depressing and rundown area of Southwark Borough where the brewery stood. A chance meeting with Sir Thomas Salusbury of Offley Park led him to Hester Lynch Salusbury, who was not so particular.

Sir Thomas and Thrale got along well from the start. Both were avid sportsmen, and in the course of conversation at the home of a mutual friend, Sir Thomas learned that Thrale's father had been born at Offley Park. Sir Thomas immediately invited Thrale to visit the place, which Thrale eagerly agreed to do, and during his visit he met Hester. He found her cheerful, attractive, and intelligent. Being the quick and decisive businessman that he was, this brief encounter convinced him that Hester would do for a wife, so he immediately laid siege to her mother as the surest way to win Hester's hand. Thrale "applied himself so diligently to gain my mother's attention—aye, and her heart, too," recalled Hester years later, "—that there was little doubt of her approving the pretensions of so very showy a suitor—if suitor he was to *me*, who certainly had not a common share in the compliments he paid to my mother's wit, beauty, and elegance."[7] Mrs. Salusbury was so much impressed by Thrale's conduct and appearance, she told her daughter that this was the man for her to marry.[8]

Everything so far had been kept secret from Hester's father, for everyone knew what his reaction would be. The family had been through a similar situation before. Several years earlier, when Hester was nineteen, Dr. James Marriott of Twinstead Hall in Essex had made his addresses, which sent Salusbury into a fit of rage. He wrote to Marriott

Sir,
   My daughter shewed me an extraordinary letter from you. She resents the ill-treatment as conscious that she never gave any pretence to take such liberties with Her. I think it hard that insolence and Impudence should be suffered to interrupt the tranquil state of youth and innocence.
   I therefore insist on no altercations—no more trash on the subject. But should you continue to insult my poor child I do assume the Father, I shall take the Insult to myself; be then most certainly assured that I will be avenged on you, much to the detriment of your person. So help me God.

John Salusbury[9]

The dismissed suitor went on to a distinguished career as a judge in the High Court of Admiralty, was later knighted, and in the 1780s served as Member of Parliament for Sudbury.

Henry Thrale was now charting the same perilous course that had brought Salusbury's wrath down on Marriott. Meanwhile, another suitor, a local parson, vexed at being cut out by this London dandy, informed Salusbury of the intrigues going on behind his back. Salusbury predictably erupted into a violent passion. Finding Hester "already half disposed," as he called it, without his consent, he swore that his daughter would "not be exchanged for a barrel of porter."[10] He knew all about Thrale's reputation as a man-about-town, "protested his scorn of Mr. Thrale's low birth and flashy dress, his fashionable manners too, wearing [his mistress] Miss Hart's portrait outside his snuff-box, and boasting of gallantries my father knew too much of to approve in a son-in-law."[11] He warned his daughter that Thrale was nothing but "a Beau Brewer, would soon be a Bankrupt &c. told me what Mistresses he kept, & what Enormities he committed, and charged me never to have him."[12] Salusbury badgered his wife and brother so much with complaints about what he thought a family conspiracy against him that finally Sir Thomas asked him to leave the estate. Salusbury then moved his wife and daughter to a London house in Dean Street, Soho, where they all got on one another's nerves and where Henry Thrale continued to visit on the sly, only adding to Hester's anxieties.[13]

Thrale made his calls when he knew John Salusbury would be away, for his visits were designed primarily to stay on good terms with the mother and to keep his prospects with Hester alive. Dreading the consequences if her father learned of these secret appointments, she found the situation terrifying. One day Salusbury grew suspicious of a letter she received. That evening he accused her of carrying on a secret correspondence with Thrale, a charge she denied. The two argued for hours until Hester, emotionally exhausted, fainted, whereupon her father seized the letter he thought from Thrale, found it was not, and had to apologize—"and in this fond misery," said Hester, "spent we the hours till four o'clock in the morning."[14]

They arose about five hours later and prepared to go about their separate business for the day. Both felt ill, so they thought it prudent to invite their family doctor to dinner that evening, "but by the time he came, my father died, and was brought us home a corpse, before the dining hour."[15] Hester maintained that her father's violent exhibition the night before had brought on the apoplectic stroke that killed him. He had always been violent in his affections and hatreds. She conceded that he loved his wife, doted on his brother, and often showed her exceptional tenderness and affection, "yet I think we all three felt as if relieved by his Death."[16]

Mrs. Salusbury saw that only one minor obstacle now stood in the way of her daughter marrying the wealthy Southwark brewer, thus providing a secure future for Hester and perhaps a comfortable retirement for herself. That obstacle was Dr. Collier. Mrs. Salusbury knew that he sided with her husband in opposing Hester's marriage to Thrale. She furthermore did not like some of Collier's doctrines and was jealous of the influence he exercised over Hester's mind. Consequently, she instigated a quarrel between the two over some trivial matter and then used the quarrel as an excuse to dismiss Collier. With no further impediments remaining, she arranged for Hester to marry Henry Thrale at St. Anne's Church, Dean Street, not far from her current residence. Hester was then twenty-two years old, Thrale thirty-four.

Hester had no objections to the marriage even though Thrale had been her mother's choice for her and not her own, "however we never differed either on that or any other Occasion—her Pleasure was my Delight, her Will my Law."[17] Hester, in fact, viewed the marriage stoically, as an act of providence, and as their union was "not founded on Passion but on Reason," she expected to derive some happiness from it.[18] If she did not fully understand the business side of the arrangement at first, "I soon saw that I was married from prudential Motives, as a passive, tho' well born & educated Girl." Henry Thrale, it is true, devoted more attention to brewing ale and enjoying London's many diversions than to pleasing his new bride, but nevertheless "we lived on Terms of great Civility & Politeness, if not of strong Alliance and Connection."[19]

Hester first saw her new house in Southwark the day she moved into it as Thrale's wife. The dingy, four-story stone building adjacent to the sprawling nine-acre brewery complex stood just off Dirty Lane in Deadman's Place. Here corpses had been flung into pits during the Great Plague of 1665, hence its name. Although she thought her surroundings depressing, Hester actually found her husband "much kinder than I counted on, to a *plain girl*, who had not one attraction in his eyes."[20] Despite the fact that no passionate feelings existed on either side, Thrale performed his conjugal responsibilities in a businesslike and efficient manner: "I believe he might visit my Chamber two or Three Times a Week in a sort of formal Way, which my Mother said was *quite right*,—& therefore I appeared to think so too."[21]

Thrale had specific notions concerning a wife's duties. These duties involved little more than looking attractive and bearing children. The husband, of course, made all the important family decisions. Thrale himself, reserved and even-tempered by nature, not at all high-handed or imperious, still possessed a dignified, imposing manner that gained compliance to his wishes, however quietly expressed. Being a sportsman, he kept a hunting lodge with superb fox hounds near Croydon, and even though Hester was an accomplished equestrian, Thrale told her that it was masculine for ladies to ride, so she quit riding. He also objected to her minding the kitchen, so she usually had no idea what was for dinner until it was served. Galloping over fields and fussing with housework simply were not proper occupations for a wife, "whose place he said was either in the drawing-room or the bed-chamber."[22] While Thrale spent his days at the brewery and his evenings entertaining cronies at the opera or other places of amusement, Hester stayed home to entertain her mother. She read to her in the mornings, played backgammon with her in the afternoons, and worked carpets with her in the evenings. She did her best to keep her mother happy, for Mrs. Salusbury was about the only person she saw, and if her mother was not happy, her own life would have been wretched.

Hester, however, did manage to find time to write poetry to her husband. This was an attempt to win Thrale's affections as she had once charmed her father and uncle. "I was now a married Woman: young enough to be proud of being such,—& silly enough to expect that my husband's heart was to be won by the same empty Tricks that had pleased my Father & my Uncle. so I wrote Verses in *his* Praise instead of *theirs*." But Thrale was a different sort of man altogether from her father and her uncle. Possessing no trace of romantic sentiment, he appeared completely unmoved by her poems. "It seemed odd when I observed them repress'd as Impertinent, or rejected as superfluous: but it was Natural to try, & try again: so Instead of Dressing showily, or behaving usefully—I sate at home & wrote Verses."[23] She eventually behaved usefully, however, by becoming pregnant, and Thrale was delighted when she gave birth to a healthy girl whom they named Hester Maria (Mrs. Salusbury's name), the child later acquiring the nickname Queeney. A boy followed a few years after and then came a child almost annually for the next eleven years, a total of twelve children altogether, only four of whom survived to adulthood, all girls.

Mrs. Salusbury and Thrale, working in concert, made sure that nothing distracted Hester from being a good wife and attentive mother. Having friends was discouraged. "Married Women should have no *Friends* my Mother said but their Husbands."[24] They prohibited her from attending the theater, saying that young wives should seek their pleasures in domestic activities. Hester remarked that her domestic activities consisted mainly of throwing up in a basin for six months out of the year due to pregnancy. She spent another three months at Thrale's country villa at Streatham Park, one month at Brighthelmstone on holiday, and the rest at Deadman's Place in Southwark, where she lay awake nights listening for Thrale's carriage to return at two, three, or four o'clock in the morning. Bearing children and being a patient wife did not, of course, relieve her of obligations to her mother. Following Hester's

convalescence after the first child, Mrs. Salusbury returned to Dean Street "&
I to my Occupation of daddling after her,"[25] that is, traveling almost every
day from Deadman's Place in Southwark to her mother's house in Soho and
back again.

Thrale's friend Arthur Murphy was also a friend of Samuel Johnson, and
about this time Murphy grew eager to introduce the two. Thrale, anxious to
raise the general quality of his companions and intrigued by Murphy's account of Johnson, enthusiastically endorsed the plan. It then became a matter
of how and when to invite Johnson. They finally decided to invite him to dinner under the pretext of meeting the "shoemaker poet," James Woodhouse,
whose verse was then in vogue, and so it was that Henry and Hester Thrale
first met Johnson on January 10, 1765. Woodhouse left no deep impression
on anyone, but Johnson and the Thrales took to one another immediately, and
the relationship flourished. Hester Thrale was delighted in having someone
to talk to other than her mother and occasionally Murphy, someone to really
exchange ideas with, while Johnson loved the attention of this articulate and
intelligent young woman. Johnson particularly enjoyed Hester's spirited nature, later recalling that when he first entered the Thrale residence, "there was
the gay Mistress of the House, who I expected to see a fine Lady; but soon
found she was a funny little Thing."[26]

Johnson respected Henry Thrale's wealth, position, intelligence, and business acumen, but he quickly developed a special rapport with Hester. They
fed off each other's strengths and were able to exchange confidences that
established strong personal ties. Johnson said to her one day, "I do certainly
love you better than any human Being I ever saw—better I think than even
poor dear Bathurst, and esteem you more, though that would be unjust too,
for I have never seen you in distress, & till I have I cannot rank you with a
Man who acted in such trying situations with such uniformity of Virtue."[27]
Richard Bathurst, who had only recently died, had been one of Johnson's
closest early London friends. Johnson described him to Hester as "a man to
my very heart's content: he hated a fool, and he hated a rogue, and he hated
a *whig*; he was a very good *hater*."[28]

Johnson felt close enough to Hester Thrale that he occasionally told her
"such Secrets" as he would not have entrusted to anyone else. These secrets
had to do primarily with his fears of insanity. Hester, for her part, told Johnson about her domestic difficulties, and one evening she happened to mention her husband's cold indifference to her. She did so with no bitterness or
resentment, for she felt no animosity, but Johnson's blunt response startled
her. He said,

Why how for Heaven's Sake Dearest Madam should any Man delight in a Wife
that is to him neither Use nor Ornament? He cannot talk to you about his Busi-

Hester Lynch Thrale, after Robert Edge Pine, 1781.
Source: Author's personal collection.

ness, which you do not understand; nor about his Pleasures which you do not partake; if you have Wit or Beauty you shew them nowhere, so he has none of the Reputation; if you have Economy or Understanding you employ neither in Attention to his Property. You divide your Time between your Mamma & your Babies, & wonder you do not by that means become agreable to your Husband.[29]

Hester said it was this admonition, along with similar remarks from time to time, that first opened her eyes to the odd kind of life she led.

Johnson advised her to make better use of her intellectual gifts. He encouraged her to be more assertive and independent. In once criticizing her circumscribed life, he told her in front of her mother "that I lived like my husband's kept mistress,—shut from the world, its pleasures, or its cares."[30] Her mother did not appreciate the comment, and later, when Hester expressed an interest in learning the brewing trade, Mrs. Salusbury told her flatly that nursing and teaching her children was "better Employment than turning into *My Lady Mashtub.*" So with her new intentions quashed, "I went on in the old Way, brought a Baby once a Year, lost some of them & grew so anxious about the rest, that I now fairly cared for nothing else." Johnson remained her true friend, "though I could not break thro' my Chains to take his Advice."[31] She was now close to thirty with little more independence than one of her own children.

In 1766 Johnson fell into a state of deep depression. Henry Thrale grew concerned for his health and had him move to Streatham Park for three months to see if a change in company and scenery would not improve his spirits. From then on, Johnson spent much of his time at Streatham, having a bedroom reserved especially for him. He returned home on weekends only long enough to make sure that his odd collection of inmates were well and that they had enough to eat. Some who lived in his house and benefited from his assistance made relatively brief stays and drifted on, while others became more or less permanent fixtures. Among the long-term dependents he helped support was Anna Williams, a blind poetess and former friend of his wife, Tetty. Another was Francis Barber, a young former Jamaican slave whom Richard Bathurst had given to Johnson as a domestic servant soon after Tetty's death. In addition was Robert Levett, an unlicensed practitioner of physic who earned a paltry income among the poorest classes of the city and who was destitute himself. Some of those who survived on Johnson's charity, especially Anna Williams and Frank Barber, did not get along well, so, besides ensuring they were satisfactorily provided for, Johnson sometimes had to mediate disputes that had arisen during his absence.[32]

Hester assumed primary care of Johnson when he was at Streatham, injuring her own health, she said, by staying up late to keep him company and sometimes brewing endless cups of tea for him until four o'clock in the morning.[33] Thrale, meanwhile, focused most of his attention on brewing beer and enjoying his evenings in town, though in 1765 he stood for and in December was elected a Member of Parliament, representing Southwark, a position he held for nearly fifteen years. His wife, in addition to looking after Johnson, divided her time, as usual, between entertaining her mother and tending her children. Her life seemed as dreary as Southwark itself. Thrale had torn down a wall to make an opening before the windows of the house, and Hester could now look across an alley toward the river over the drab, gloomy borough and see the crumbled ruins of Shakespeare's Globe Theatre close by. She noted, "there were really curious remains of the old Globe Playhouse, which, though hexagonal in form without, was round within." She developed something of a morbid fascination for the old theater, seeing it as a symbol for her own dreary situation: "For a long time, then,—or I thought it such,—my fate was bound up with the old Globe Theatre, upon the Bankside, Southwark."[34]

Besides Johnson and occasionally Murphy, the Thrales entertained few guests. "Our Society at the Borough House was exceedingly circumscribed," said Hester. Few people wanted to visit such a drab location as Deadman's Place in Southwark. Her husband kept two carriages, one of which she used to visit her mother in Soho, and she could have used it for other social calls if her mother had approved. "My mother however thought the closer I kept home the better."[35]

Johnson eventually managed to overcome his depression and to exert himself for a charitable cause by helping to get published *Miscellanies in Prose and Verse* by Anna Williams. Mrs. Williams needed the little money such a work might produce, but her poems alone were not enough to make a satisfactory volume, so Johnson asked Hester Thrale if she had any verses to contribute that had not been seen before. She showed him a verse tale called "The Three Warnings" that he decided would do nicely. He then told Hester, "Come Mistress, now *I'll* write a Tale and your Character shall be in it,"[36] and he quickly composed "The Fountains: A Fairy Tale," which would also appear in the *Miscellanies.* Of minor importance in the entire body of Johnson's work, the tale is notable chiefly for what it says about Hester Thrale's character as Johnson perceived it after little more than a year's acquaintance.

In the tale, set in Hester's native Wales, the sensitive Floretta rescues a goldfinch that has become entangled in a lime twig and is being threatened by a hawk. Floretta's domineering mother wants to put the bird in a cage to hang outside the window, thinking how pleasant to hear it sing every morning, but Floretta cannot endure imprisoning the bird and sets it free. The bird turns out to be a fairy that the queen of fairies had transformed into a goldfinch as punishment for some minor transgression "till some human being shall show thee kindness without any prospect of interest." For five years the goldfinch had experienced many perilous adventures, encountering numerous people motivated by self-interest like Floretta's mother. To reward Floretta for her kindness, the queen of fairies authorizes her to enter a nearby cavern and to drink at the Spring of Joy, by which she may have any wish she desires. She also enjoys the unprecedented liberty of retracting any wishes she later regrets by drinking at the Spring of Sorrow. Floretta's "first desire was the increase of her beauty. She had some disproportion of features." Floretta drinks from the Spring of Joy, wishing only for agreeable looks, but she finds the water so pleasantly sweet that she refills her cup and wishes "for a rosy bloom upon her cheeks," then for a sparkling eye, and then for perfect beauty. Her perfect beauty prompts her mother to push her into a life of social activities that Floretta quickly finds intolerable, so she returns to the cave, drinks away her perfect beauty in the bitter waters of sorrow, leaving herself only attractive.

A short time later, "being on some occasion thwarted by her mother's authority," Floretta drinks at the Spring of Joy "for a spirit to do her own way." Returning home, "every thought was contempt, and every action was rebellion: She had drunk into herself a spirit to resist, but could not give her mother a disposition to yield; the old lady asserted her right to govern." The house becomes a perpetual chaos as the daughter's impetuosity meets the mother's intransigence. Finally convinced that her spirit to resist has transformed her into a shrew, she drinks again from the Spring of Sorrow, after which she "replaced herself under her mother's care, and quitted her spirit, and her own way."

Following similar experiences of alternating surfeit and repentance, Floretta grows weary of the fountains altogether and contents herself with simple amusements as they occur, but one day "there arose in her imagination a strong desire to become a wit." Eager to enjoy the pleasures this new character promises her, she returns to the cave and drinks from the fountain of joy. As she does so, "she felt new successions of imagery rise in her mind." She sees objects in new ways and notes relationships between things that before seemed to have no connection. As accompaniment to her wit, she also acquires the powers of discernment, ease of expression, impatience, and an element of harshness in her criticism. "To laugh was something, but it was much more to make others laugh. As every deformity of character made a strong impression upon her, she could not always forbear to transmit it to others." She now laughs at affectation, censures imperfections, and ridicules defects. The result is that strangers come to fear her and friends to desert her. "With all this Floretta made sport at first, but in time grew weary of general hostility." She finally returns to the Spring of Sorrow, dips her cup into the bitter water, and is about to drink, but suddenly she dashes the cup to the ground and resolves "to keep her wit with all its consequences."

"The Fountains" is a cautionary tale, addressed to the public at large but to Hester in particular, illustrating the dangers of excess and the virtues of moderation. In giving Hester Thrale's character under the guise of Floretta, Johnson portrays a generous and sensitive individual with a spirit of independence and a disposition to rebel, yet a woman susceptible to the power of authority. She is an impulsive young woman with the talent and ambition to be a wit; a woman restive in her actions, critical in her views, and harsh in her judgments.

In actual life for the present, Hester Thrale carried on with her daily routine, chafing under the restrictions imposed on her by her mother, husband, child, and friend. Her natural spirit was always that of a young filly longing to run free—one who never feels content in harness, no matter how light the hand on the reins. Yet she knew she had little to complain about. Her husband, while not affectionate, was rich and easy to live with; she had bright, handsome children; and she claimed as a friend perhaps the greatest literary figure of the day. Her life, if circumscribed and dull, was at least tolerable.

But matters took a sudden turn in 1772. As a businessman, Thrale had become overconfident and ambitious. Growing more determined to overtake his rivals Whitbread and Calvert, he adopted speculative and reckless business practices, and he became obsessed with increasing the size of his brewery and its beer production. In his rashness, he adopted a hair-brained scheme suggested by an inventor, Humphrey Jackson, to brew beer without malt and hops. Thrale devoted an entire year's production to this method, which failed miserably. As a result, he lost many customers. Jackson also talked him into buying land in East Smithfield, where Thrale planned to build twenty enormous copper vats in which to mix a substance for use on the bottoms of ships to keep out worms. The metal alone cost £2,000. That scheme also failed. And to make matters worse, financial panic shook London in June with a large bank failure that plunged many businesses into bankruptcy and threatened universal collapse.

The year's events proved so devastating to Thrale's self-confidence that he withdrew into himself, beginning a slow decline into depression and poor health. His wife wrote years afterward, "Mr. Thrale was a very merry talking man in 1760; but the distress of 1772, which affected his health, his hopes, and his whole soul, affected his temper too. Perkins [the brewery superintendent] called it being planet struck, and I am not sure he was ever completely the same man again."[37] Expecting her eighth child in almost as many years, and with her husband emotionally debilitated, Hester felt the burden to do something fall upon her, "whose Spirits always rise on an Exigence whereas his sink."[38] When harassed by misfortune, Thrale tended to withdraw into himself, while "Vomiting and fainting is my regular Practice when any thing goes wrong."[39] With Johnson furnishing useful advice and encouragement, Hester began rushing about borrowing money and pacifying disgruntled brewery workers. Eventually she managed to fend off disaster at the cost of going more than £130,000 into debt and losing her expected child. In September she gave birth to Penelope, who "liv'd but 10 hours, looked black & could not breathe freely—poor little Maid! one cannot grieve after her much, and I have just now other things to think of."[40]

One of the things weighing on her mind was her mother's deteriorating health. Mrs. Salusbury grew worse into the new year and finally died in July at age sixty-six. At first devastated by the loss and exhausted by her other problems, Hester nevertheless soon emerged from these ordeals as the woman most people now recognize as the eccentric, flighty, and irrepressible Mrs. Thrale—for as Henry Thrale's health and spirits steadily waned, her own confidence rose. With her mother's death, Hester, in her thirty-second year, realized that a great burden had been lifted from her life, and she could now take wing and begin to soar.

NOTES

1. See Boswell, *Life*, 1:175, 318–19, and 496n3. Bertrand H. Bronson forcefully argues that indolence had little to do with the long delay of Johnson's *Shakspeare*. "Whatever the causes of Johnson's delay, however," writes Bronson, "his conduct in this whole business, with its initial impressive drive and sudden neglect, does not deserve the name of 'indolence'" (*Works of Johnson*, 7:xxv). Boswell, Baretti, Reynolds, and others close to Johnson nevertheless thought that indolence played a significant role.

2. Piozzi, *Thraliana*, 297n1.

3. Hayward, *Autobiography*, 2:19.

4. Piozzi, *Thraliana*, 6 and 54–55.

5. Ibid., 281.

6. Hayward, *Autobiography*, 2:19.

7. Hayward, *Autobiography*, 2:19–20.

8. Piozzi, *Thraliana*, 300.

9. A. M. Broadley, *Doctor Johnson and Mrs Thrale* (London, 1910), 105.

10. Hayward, *Autobiography*, 2:20.

11. John Tearle, *Mrs. Piozzi's Tall Young Beau: William Augustus Conway* (Rutherford, NJ: Fairleigh Dickinson University Press, 1991), 39.

12. Piozzi, *Thraliana*, 302.

13. Ibid., 303.

14. Hayward, *Autobiography*, 2:21.

15. Ibid., 2:22.

16. Piozzi, *Thraliana*, 127.

17. Ibid., 55.

18. James L. Clifford, *Hester Lynch Piozzi* (Oxford: Clarendon Press, 1968), 45.

19. Piozzi, *Thraliana*, 307.

20. Hayward, *Autobiography*, 2:22.

21. Piozzi, *Thraliana*, 308.

22. Hayward, *Autobiography*, 2:24.

23. Clifford, *Hester Lynch Piozzi*, 50.

24. Piozzi, *Thraliana*, 305n4.

25. Ibid., 308.

26. Tearle, *Mrs. Piozzi's Tall Young Beau*, 93. In a 1779 letter, Johnson wrote to Mrs. Thrale, "keep yourself airy [sprightly] and be a *funny little thing*" (Johnson, *Letters*, Redford, 3:176). "It was a Hack-Joke to call me a funny little thing," she explained in an annotated presentation copy, given to Sir James Fellows, of her *Letters to and from the Late Samuel Johnson, LL.D.* (London, 1788), 2:56.

27. Clifford, *Hester Lynch Piozzi*, 88.

28. Piozzi, *Anecdotes*, 88. Richard Bathurst was a young physician in London. "In the course of his studies," wrote Sir John Hawkins, "he became acquainted with Johnson, and was greatly beloved by him for the pregnancy of his parts and the elegance of his manners" (Hawkins, *Life*, 234). Besides hating fools, rogues, and whigs, Bathurst also hated slavery, and it was he who sent the former Jamaican slave Francis Barber to live with Johnson following Tetty Johnson's death in 1752. Bathurst, after ten years of fruitless struggle to establish a practice in London, sailed for the West Indies, but died in 1762 of fever aboard ship off Havana.

29. Piozzi, *Thraliana*, 309.

30. Hayward, *Autobiography*, 2:25.

31. Piozzi, *Thraliana*, 309–10.

32. For the history of Johnson's dependents, see Lyle Larsen, *Dr. Johnson's Household* (Hamden, CT: Archon Books, 1985), and for a full account of Barber, see Michael Bundock, *The Fortunes of Francis Barber: The True Story of the Jamaican Slave Who Became Samuel Johnson's Heir* (New Haven and London: Yale University Press, 2015).

33. Piozzi, *Anecdotes*, 101.

34. Hayward, *Autobiography*, 2:33.

35. Clifford, *Hester Lynch Piozzi*, 52.

36. Ibid., 61.

37. Hayward, *Autobiography*, 1:49.

38. Mary Hyde, *The Thrales of Streatham Park* (Cambridge, MA: Harvard University Press, 1977), 201.

39. Hester Lynch Thrale Piozzi, *The Piozzi Letters: Correspondence of Hester Lynch Piozzi, 1784–1821 (formerly Mrs. Thrale)*, ed. Edward A. Bloom and Lillian D. Bloom, 6 vols. (Newark: University of Delaware Press, 1989–2002), 2:140.

40. Clifford, *Hester Lynch Piozzi*, 94.

Chapter Four

Blunders, Ridicule,
and a Fine Malignity

The brewery eventually recovered, though it returned to the brink of ruin several more times over the years. Thrale grew increasingly reserved and more self-indulgent, and he developed a near-obsession to build. Just before Mrs. Salusbury's death, he started work on renovating the villa at Streatham. He added a library wing, gave Johnson money to help stock it with excellent books, and began commissioning Sir Joshua Reynolds to decorate it with portraits of Streatham's most distinguished guests. Thrale then added another wing and more rooms, built a small lake with an island, reconstructed a two-mile walk around the grounds, put in rolling lawns, fruit trees, and vegetable gardens, and succeeded in converting what once had been a handsome country villa into a fine country mansion and estate. Eventually Streatham boasted twelve bedrooms, not counting separate quarters for eighteen to twenty servants, and was now a comfortable place to live and entertain. Among the prominent guests besides Johnson to frequent Thrale's splendid estate and dine at his sumptuous table were lawyer Robert Chambers, Charles Burney, Arthur Murphy, and Edmund Burke.

The Thrales, over time, got to know Johnson's intimate circle of friends. Hester Thrale found some of them amusing, especially Oliver Goldsmith, whom she referred to in her diary as "our odd little Doctor."[1] His fortunes by now had somewhat improved. He dressed more smartly, for he hoped that fine clothing might command the respect and attention that his homely features could not. "Dress has a mechanical influence upon the mind," he wrote in *The Life of Nash*, "and we naturally are awed into respect and esteem at the elegance of those whom even our reason would teach us to contemn."[2] To aid him in his efforts to look more elegant, he engaged the services of William Filby, a fashionable tailor near the Strand. He first bought from Filby a pair of purple silk knee breeches, a scarlet roquelaure, a large wig, a sword, and a gold-headed cane. Physicians traditionally wore large, bushy wigs and carried gold-headed canes as marks of their profession. Later he spent over eight pounds for a suit in crimson and light blue silk. A bill dated October 16, 1769, shows that Filby brought him a half-dress suit of wool lined with satin, a pair of silk stocking breeches, and a pair of bloom-colored breeches, all of which cost about sixteen pounds. The bill does not mention a bloom-colored coat that Goldsmith wore to a dinner party that evening hosted by Boswell. The coat must have been delivered earlier. But about the time dinner was to be served, and while Boswell's company waited for another guest to arrive, Goldsmith comically strutted up and down showing off his coat and bragging about how fine he looked. Garrick said, "Come, come, talk no more of that. You are, perhaps, the worst—eh, eh!" Goldsmith began to protest, but Garrick laughingly replied, "Nay, you will always *look* like a gentleman, but I am talking of being well or ill *dressed.*"

"Well, let me tell you," replied Goldsmith, "when my tailor brought home my bloom-coloured coat, he said, 'Sir, I have a favour to beg of you. When anybody asks you who made your clothes, say John [*sic*] Filby at the Harrow in Water Lane.'"

"Why, Sir," said Johnson, "that was because he knew the strange colour would attract crowds to gaze at it, and thus they might hear of him and see how well he might make a coat even of so absurd a colour."[3]

Goldsmith's fine clothing certainly gained him attention, though not the respect he so much desired, for the flashy attire on his short, stocky build only made him look more ridiculous. Once as he walked down the Strand with his sword at his hip, he encountered two fops. One pointed at him and said loudly to his friend, "Look at that fly with a long pin stuck through it." Goldsmith heard the remark and called out to passersby to watch out for that pair of disguised pickpockets. He then moved off to a side street, half drew his sword, and beckoned the men to follow him, but they slunk off down the Strand to the jeers of the crowd.[4] In a passage Boswell struck from his *Life of Johnson,* he wrote that Goldsmith's "dress was unsuitably gawdy and without taste."[5] In addition to his gaudy attire was his inclination to act the buffoon. Many who knew him were at a loss what to make of his eccentric dress and odd behavior. They could not decide whether he was a low comic, a genuine fool, or a combination of both. Dr. James Beattie, Scottish poet and philosopher, after spending an evening with him, wrote in his diary, "Goldsmith's common conversation was a strange mixture of absurdity and silliness; of silliness so great, as to make me sometimes think that he affected it."[6]

Indeed, it was often difficult to tell if Goldsmith was serious in what he said or if he was jesting. Once when he and Johnson were visiting Reynolds, the conversation turned to a popular tragedy of the day, Thomas Otway's

Venice Preserved. Goldsmith contended that of all modern tragedies, this play was the nearest to Shakespeare in excellence. Johnson scoffed at the notion, claiming there were not forty good lines in the entire play. "Pooh!" he snorted, "what stuff are these lines:—'What feminine tales hast thou been listening to, of unaired shirts, catarrhs, and tooth-ach got by thin soled shoes?'"

"True," responded Goldsmith, "to be sure that is very like Shakspeare."[7] Was the comment serious or was he only jesting? People were left to ponder.

Boswell had first encountered Goldsmith in Tom Davies's bookshop in December 1762 and thought him "a curious, odd, pedantic fellow with some genius." Those present—Boswell, Goldsmith, Davies, and publisher Robert Dodsley—began taking about poetry and the relative merits of various poets. Goldsmith seemed to disparage every poet mentioned. He even sneered at Shakespeare. "Here I said nothing," wrote Boswell later in his journal, "but thought him a most impudent puppy."[8]

Horace Walpole heard him talk occasionally and referred to him in various letters as "the silly Dr Goldsmith," "piddling Goldsmith," and "an idiot, with once or twice a fit of parts." Other factors also contributed to the image of an idiot who happened to possess some genius. One was his natural clumsiness. He seemed always to be barking his shins on furniture, falling down, or tumbling into water. One evening at Streatham among a large assembly of women, a servant presented him with a cup of tea, but as he reached out to take it, he upset the tea things. The astonished women looked at one another and began to laugh. Johnson turned to Mrs. Thrale and said, "Madam, can you tell how a man who shocks so much in company, can give so many charms to his writings?"[9] Yet some of his blunders were certainly intentional pratfalls made to gain attention, as when he once accompanied a group viewing the ornamental fountains and other attractions at Versailles. A friendly dispute arose as to whether a nearby water channel was narrow enough to leap over. Goldsmith said that it was and made the attempt, but he fell short and landed in the water to the great amusement of all who watched.[10] Another time, in the company of William Stanhope, Second Earl of Harrington, a question came up over the depth of a pond. Goldsmith said that it was not so deep but that he could pick up anything of value thrown into it. Lord Harrington tossed in a guinea, and Goldsmith, in trying to retrieve it, slipped and fell in, but he finally came to the surface with the money in hand and kept it.[11]

He loved to indulge in these outlandish pranks, yet his low humor puzzled the more reserved English and made them think Goldsmith a greater dunce than he actually was. Moreover, his child-like impetuosity often caused him to speak and to act without forethought, thus adding to the image of a fool with once or twice a fit of parts.

People often failed to understand that Goldsmith was simple-hearted rather than simpleminded. Much of what passed for idiocy in his talk and behavior originated in a sense of playfulness, a lack of restraint, and a need for attention. Sir Joshua Reynolds, who admired Goldsmith's lack of pretentiousness, saw "what indeed is self-apparent, that such a genius could not be a fool":

> His more intimate acquaintances easily perceived his absurdities proceeded from other causes than from a feebleness of intellect, and that his follies were not those of a fool.
>
> A great part of Dr. Goldsmith's folly and absurdity proceeded from principle, and partly from a want of early acquaintance with that life to which his reputation afterwards introduced him. . . .
>
> He was of a sociable disposition. He had a very strong desire, which I believe nobody will think very peculiar or culpable, to be liked, to have his company sought after by his friends. To this end, for it was a system, he abandoned his respectable character as a writer or a man of observation to that of a character which nobody was afraid of being humiliated in his presence.[12]

His playfulness showed itself most clearly in his relations with children. He might be said never to have outgrown the innocence of childhood himself. He would sing songs, perform odd dances, turn his wig around on his head, and do any number of things to excite a child's laughter. He would play simple card games and pretend to cheat, play forfeits and blind man's bluff, or just romp around on the floor. Sir John Hawkins's daughter, Lætitia-Matilda, remembered Goldsmith sitting on the floor until dinner was announced, teaching her to play "Jack and Jill" with two pieces of paper stuck to his fingers.[13] The younger George Colman recalled that at five years old he was always glad when Goldsmith visited his father, for "a game of romps constantly ensued." One day Goldsmith placed three hats on the carpet with a shilling under each. "The shillings, he told me, were England, France, and Spain. 'Hey, presto, cockolorum!' cried the Doctor,—and lo!" all three countries were found united under one hat.[14] David Garrick also liked children. He allowed young Colman to run about his gardens, taught him how to play trap ball, and "practised, too, a thousand monkey tricks upon me. . . . All this was very kind and condescending,—but it wanted the *bonhomie* of Goldsmith, who play'd to please the boy; whereas Garrick always seem'd playing to please himself."[15]

Turning his wig around on his head and playing parlor tricks delighted the children, and they loved him for it. When he performed similar antics among adults, they too laughed, but they thought such behavior denoted a fool. Some even spread stories of his absurdities, knowing them to be false. "What Goldsmith intended for humour," said Reynolds, "was purposely repeated as serious."[16] Yet his writings displayed no foolishness; hence he gained the reputation of being a man with two distinct souls—an inspired idiot—one who was foolish when he had not a pen in his hand and wise when he had.[17] Boswell recorded many Goldsmith anecdotes in his *Life of Johnson.* He is one who occasionally took seriously some of the things Goldsmith intended for fun. Among several instances, Boswell refers to the time Goldsmith accompanied the lovely Horneck sisters and their mother through Holland and France. Near Paris, as they looked out a hotel window at a military troop in the square, the beautiful women drew the attention of the soldiers below. Goldsmith, with mock sternness, a common feature of his humor, turned from the window saying that elsewhere he, too, had admirers. Boswell actually believed that Goldsmith was "seriously angry that more attention was paid to them than to him."[18] But years later, one of the sisters told an early Goldsmith biographer, "This was said in mere playfulness, and I was shocked many years afterwards to see it adduced in print as a proof of his envious disposition."[19]

Mrs. Thrale made similar errors. She mentions in her diary, for example, that "The Doctor was a Man eminently ugly, but wonderfully fond of his Person." To illustrate her point, she describes an incident at Streatham when Goldsmith was told that a play by his rival Hugh Kelly had been applauded. This happened at a time when his own play *The Good-Natured Man* had been hissed on opening night. But Goldsmith pretended not to mind. Looking into a nearby mirror, he simply exclaimed, "A handsomer Fellow than Kelly however."[20] Mrs. Thrale took the remark seriously.

Goldsmith complained to a friend about the number of people who tried to make him into something ridiculous. They maliciously ascribed all his comments and actions, he said, to absurdity or folly. "Sir," he remarked, "I am as a lion baited with curs."[21] These people acted either from malice or from a total misunderstanding of his character and intentions. The English in general had never taken much trouble to understand the cultural idiosyncrasies of their Irish neighbors. Goldsmith, on the other hand, was always fascinated by national differences, something reflected in a number of his works. "There is a cast of humour, as well as of manners, peculiar to each country," he noted in one of his essays. He was particularly alive to the differences between the people of Ireland and those of England. "To begin with Ireland," he wrote in another essay,

> the natives are particularly remarkable for the gaiety and levity of their dispositions: the English, transplanted there, in time lose their melancholy serious air,

and become gay and thoughtless, more fond of pleasure, and less addicted to reasoning. . . . [The Irish] have no important national concerns to make them anxious, or cloud their tempers with the solemnity of pride. In such circumstances they are contented with indolence and pleasure, take every happiness as it presents, are easily excited to resent, and as easily induced to submission.[22]

Londoners were not accustomed to Irish humor, and they could not easily tell when Goldsmith was simply indulging in buffoonery. One evening he and a number of others went to the popular Italian puppet show in Panton Street. Supposedly Johnson and Reynolds praised the dexterity of the puppets, particularly one that tossed a spontoon, or pike. "Pooh! pooh! there's nothing in it," Goldsmith reportedly said with some warmth. "Give me a spontoon, and I'll do it as well myself."[23] Boswell, who was not present, tells a version of this story in his *Life of Johnson* as an instance of Goldsmith's excessive envy. He adds that after the show, Goldsmith went with a group to Edmund Burke's house, where he barked his shin trying to demonstrate that he could leap over a stick better than the puppets.[24] Apparently Boswell did not consider that Goldsmith might have been clowning or that the story may not have been true at all. Joseph Cradock, one of the party that night, later recalled nothing unusual happening except that "we were all greatly entertained, and many idle remarks might possibly be made by all of us during the evening." Cradock suspected that the anecdote about Goldsmith barking his shin was a fabrication: "It was always thought fair by some persons to make what stories they pleased of Dr. Goldsmith."[25]

What made these stories all the more plausible is that Goldsmith was, in fact, genuinely envious of highly successful people, all of whom he regarded as rivals for the attention he craved for himself. It is what Reynolds described as a "fighting, absurdity, and ridiculous kind of envy," not "that black malignant kind which excites hatred and disgust."[26] Goldsmith harbored a childish impulse, rooted in his deep insecurity, that whatever approval other authors gained by their works, they stole from him. He could not stand to hear other writers praised without feeling something akin to physical pain. Once when someone went on too long praising Johnson, Goldsmith interrupted by saying, "No more, I desire you; you harrow up my soul!"[27]

Johnson, soon after his celebrated meeting with George III in the library at Buckingham House, related the event to a group at Sir Joshua's. Goldsmith sat apart on a sofa, pretending to be uninterested. Those present suspected that he was being petulant out of envy for the honor Johnson had received. But soon he jumped up from the sofa, approached Johnson, and congratulated him on the composure he had shown during the interview, for had it been him, he said, "I should have bowed and stammered through the whole of it."[28] This was typical of Goldsmith. His envy, absurd as it was, never lasted for long. It flared up, like a child's, only to fade as quickly. "Whatever appeared of this kind was a mere momentary sensation," observed Thomas Percy, "which he knew not how like other men to conceal. It was never the result of principle, or the suggestion of reflection; it never imbittered his heart, nor influenced his conduct."[29]

Goldsmith freely admitted to being envious, and he knew it was a childish way to act. Most people found his candor refreshing, and they laughed at his foibles along with him. Boswell told Johnson that they ought not be angry with him as he was so frank in confessing his envy. "Nay, Sir," replied Johnson, "we must be angry that a man has such a superabundance of an odious quality, that he cannot keep it within his own breast, but it boils over."

"In my opinion, however," wrote Boswell privately, "Goldsmith had not more of it than other people have, but only talked of it freely." Boswell further maintained that Goldsmith was what the French termed *un étourdi*, one who acts without thought.[30]

Yet envy and acting without thought were not Goldsmith's worst traits. At times his words and actions revealed a trace of deceitfulness. Bennet Langton recounted the story of Goldsmith once stopping by a roadside inn and noticing in the parlor a portrait he thought might be the work of an old master. He found the landlady ignorant of its value, so he told her that the picture reminded him of his Aunt Salisbury, and he arranged to buy the portrait for a nominal sum. He made a handsome profit when he resold the painting, for it turned out to be a Van Dyke. A similar story of deceit was told by Thomas Cadell, the publisher, to Lætitia-Matilda Hawkins. Goldsmith had signed a contract with Cadell and other publishers to compile a history of England for which he would receive five hundred guineas twelve months after publication. But Goldsmith soon came to Cadell saying he desperately needed the money to pay off creditors, for he was about to be arrested for debt. Cadell called a meeting of the other publishers and convinced them to advance most of the five hundred guineas immediately. As Goldsmith left with the money, Cadell somehow grew suspicious, "and after following him to Hyde-Park Corner," wrote Miss Hawkins, "saw him get into a post-chaise, in which a woman of the town was waiting for him, and with whom, it afterwards appeared, he went to Bath to dissipate what he had thus fraudulently obtained."[31]

He also sometimes told the most transparent lies. Boswell thought he did so to appear more consequential. For instance, he once bragged to a church dignitary that his brother was the Dean of Durham, a lie so easily detected that Boswell was surprised he would venture it.[32] He admitted to telling such lies but claimed they were only white lies, light as feathers, which he blew into the air, and on whomever they fell, no one was injured. Johnson told him, "I wish you would take the trouble of moulting your feathers."[33]

Another flaw was that in speaking of others, he now and then appeared spiteful. When Johnson lived at Streatham during one of his recurring bouts of depression, Goldsmith, according to Mrs. Thrale, seemed to rejoice in his illness. He whispered to Henry Thrale that Johnson would never again be the man he was, and he said it in such a malicious way that Thrale never respected him afterward. Another time somebody remarked that Goldsmith must like the Thrales very much, for he never abused *them*. No, Johnson replied, "but he would be glad to hear they were parted tomorrow Morning, never to meet more."[34]

Fortunately, these were not Goldsmith's most predominant traits. They dwindled in comparison to his other qualities like his frequent blunders, his generosity, and his compassion for others. Those who came to social events expressly to laugh at his follies often went away disappointed. With people he did not like or in situations in which he felt uncomfortable, he remained silent. Some thought his silence indicated ill-nature, but he explained, "People are greatly mistaken in me: a notion goes about, that when I am silent I mean to be impudent; but I assure you, gentlemen, my silence arises from bashfulness."[35] Thomas Percy said that although his conversation was never totally free of buffoonery, in polite society he always behaved with the utmost decorum.[36]

In less formal settings, he made himself easier. Few were better at breaking down the initial stiff reserve and uneasy tension at social gatherings. People nearly always found him entertaining. "When Goldsmith entered a room, Sir," said James Northcote, Reynolds's apprentice, "people who did not know him became for a moment silent from awe of his literary reputation; when he came out again, they were riding upon his back."[37] Although he easily chattered away on any topic under discussion, whether he knew anything about it or not, he liked nothing better than to be asked to sing. He often sang comic songs like the one about the old woman tossed in a blanket seventeen times as high as the moon. But "Johnny Armstrong's Last Good Night," "Barbara Allen," and "Death and the Lady" were his favorites. "In singing the last," said Reynolds, "he endeavoured to humour the dialogue by looking very fierce and speaking in a very rough voice for Death, which he suddenly changed when he came to the lady's part, putting on what he fancied to be a lady-like sweetness of countenance with a thin, shrill voice."[38] He also sang his own compositions like Tony Lumpkin's song from *She Stoops to Conquer*, the words of which he set to an Irish air. Boswell, a passable singer himself, thought Goldsmith acquitted himself well in these situations, though Reynolds found Goldsmith's vocal skills only passable, "but whilst he was thus employed he was a conspicuous figure at least and was relieved from that horror which he entertained of being overlooked by the company."[39]

As easy as he made himself in general society, in the company of a few intimate friends he felt particularly free. He observed that the wisest of men have friends with whom they feel comfortable enough to play the fool,[40] and playing the fool to him meant being completely natural and unaffected. "Come now and let us play the fool a little," he sometimes said as an invitation to good fellowship.[41] Being a fool was simply the act of being spontaneous. In one of his poems he speaks of himself as "magnanimous Goldsmith, a gooseberry fool,"[42] and his writings in general demonstrate his aversion to all stiffness and formality. On the contrary, his works show a love for natural, simple people. "Were I to be angry at men for being fools," he wrote, "I could here have found ample room for declamation; but, alas! I have been a fool myself, and why should I be angry with them for being something so natural to every child of humanity."[43]

"The misfortune of Goldsmith in conversation is this," Johnson told Boswell, "he goes on without knowing how he is to get off. His genius is great, but his knowledge is small." Johnson believed that Goldsmith often talked "to keep you in mind of him, for fear you should forget he is there."

"Yes," said Boswell, "he stands forward."

"True, Sir, but if a man is to stand forward, he would choose to do it not in an awkward posture, not in rags."

"I like very well to hear honest Goldsmith talk away carelessly," replied Boswell.

"Why, yes, Sir; but he should not like to hear himself."[44]

And it was in his talk, not just his actions, that Goldsmith made some of his most notable blunders. He often rattled away little knowing or caring what he said and heedless of where his words took him. At one of Reynolds's dinner parties, a dish of peas was brought in that had turned yellow in cooking. Someone suggested they be sent to Hammersmith, for that was the way to Turnham Green. (Hammersmith and Turnham Green were villages on the outskirts of London.) Goldsmith thought this an excellent joke and asked permission to spring it on Edmund Burke, who loved a pun. The next time he dined at Burke's and the vegetables were brought in, Goldsmith hastily announced that they ought to be sent to Hammersmith: "That is the way to *make* 'em green." No one laughed. "I mean that is the *road* to turn 'em green." Still, no one got the point, and Goldsmith, flustered and embarrassed, got up and left the table.[45]

Sometimes he would enter into debate with Johnson or someone else and usually get bested, for his impetuosity hurried him into contradictions or ridiculous statements. Then when he got caught in an absurdity it made him all the more flustered, and soon he would be, in Johnson's phrase, "as irascible as a hornet."[46] Johnson said to Reynolds, "It is amazing how little Goldsmith knows. He seldom comes where he is not more ignorant than any one else."

"Yet there is no man whose company is more liked."

"To be sure, Sir. When people find a man of the most distinguished abilities as a writer, their inferiour while he is with them, it must be highly gratifying to them. What Goldsmith comically says of himself is very true,—he always gets the better when he argues alone; meaning, that he is master of a subject in his study, and can write well upon it; but when he comes into company, grows confused, and unable to talk." Johnson attributed most of his absurdities in conversation to a desire to shine as a man of literary parts. He thought this unwise, for Goldsmith had little to gain and much to lose. It was like a man laying a wager at odds of a hundred to one—he can win only a guinea but stands to lose a hundred. "Goldsmith is in this state. When he contends, if he gets the better, it is a very little addition to a man of his literary reputation: if he does not get the better, he is miserably vexed."[47]

Reynolds disagreed that Goldsmith tried to set himself forward as a literary figure. "He talked without knowledge," Reynolds contended, "not so much for the sake of shining as from an impatience of neglect by being left out of the conversation. He would therefore, to draw the attention of the company upon himself, sing, stand upon his head, or dance about the room."[48]

Yet despite his numerous faults and frailties, he still carried with him the lessons he had learned in youth about charity to the less fortunate. His country upbringing and his own chronic poverty had made him sensitive to human suffering. Having been raised in a charitable home in which no appeal for alms went unanswered, he could not stand to witness distress without trying to alleviate it. "Why, why was I born a man, and yet see the sufferings of wretches I cannot relieve!" he wrote in *The Citizen of the World.* "Why was this heart of mine formed with so much sensibility! or why was not my fortune adapted to its impulse! Tenderness, without a capacity of relieving, only makes the man that feels it more wretched than the object which sues for assistance."[49] One reason he had so little money and possessions during much of his life is that he usually gave them away to those with greater need. A former Trinity classmate remembered calling for him at his rooms one cold winter morning and hearing Goldsmith shout from inside that he was a prisoner in his bed and could not get out. After forcing open the door, the friend discovered Goldsmith held fast in the ticking of his mattress where he had wriggled for protection from the cold. The friend learned that the night before he had carried his blankets to the college gate and given them to a poor woman and her five little children who needed them more.[50] He was particularly susceptible to the distresses of his own countrymen, who, like himself, found it hard to earn a living in the English capital. He assisted poor writers and helped support several widows in the neighborhood, and if he had no money to give them, he sent them away with shirts, old clothes, or occasionally food from his table, saying once, "Now let me only suppose I have eat a much heartier breakfast than usual, and I'm nothing out of pocket."[51]

Reynolds observed that Goldsmith often had to ask a friend for the loan of ten pounds or so to relieve his own needs, "yet, if by accident a distressed petitioner told him a piteous tale—nay, if a subscription for any folly was proposed to him—he without any thought of his own poverty would with an air of generosity freely bestow on the person who solicited for it the very loan he had himself but just before obtained."[52] In this way he was easy prey to sharpers who played upon his innocence and generosity. Thomas Percy stated that "there never were a heart and purse so open to the calls of pity, and the applications of distress, whether real or pretended, as Dr. Goldsmith's." Almost every request made to him he granted. "Emigrants from his own country, and especially the poor scribblers from it constantly lived upon him; but indeed adventurers from all countries found access to him, and emptied his pockets."[53]

One day at the home of Sir William Chambers, while playing cards with Sir William, his wife, and Joseph Baretti, Goldsmith suddenly put down his cards, jumped up, and ran outside. He returned a short time later and sat down again. Sir William asked why he had rushed outside; he hoped it had not been because of the heat in the room. "Not at all," answered Goldsmith, "but in truth I could not bear to hear that unfortunate woman in the street half singing, half sobbing, for such tones could only arise from the extremity of distress." The sound had been so painful to him that he had gone out to give her something and send her on her way.[54]

These qualities of kindliness and compassion appear throughout his literary works. Ironically, the personal characteristics that so often made him look foolish in society also helped give his writings their distinctive allure. His simplicity, child-like exuberance, benevolence, and lack of studied formality determined his material, formed his sentiments, and shaped his style.

As odd and amusing as others of the Johnson circle found Oliver Goldsmith, they found the pious and virtuous Bennet Langton almost as comical. Johnson exclaimed with great enthusiasm on one occasion, "The earth does not bear a worthier man than Bennet Langton,"[55] and eventually the term *worthy*

attached to the name like a Homeric epithet as people spoke affectionately of "the worthy Langton." In the *Life of Johnson*, when Boswell refers anonymously to "a worthy friend of ours," "one of our friends, a very worthy man," or the like, it is clear from the adjective whom he means.

Yet Langton's worthiness, piety, virtue, and gentle manners, when mixed with his usually grave demeanor, sober conversation, sluggish habits, and absurd height, combined to produce a most striking seriocomic character. Unlike Goldsmith, he was not absurd in what he said or how he behaved. It is true he affected more gaiety at times than he naturally possessed, the result perhaps of his close connection with Topham Beauclerk, yet Langton's manners were highly polished, and his conversation always proper and sensible. Still, everyone agreed to there being something slightly ludicrous in his overall composition. When Boswell once made the commonplace remark that Bennet Langton was a worthy man, Johnson replied, "Sir, the earth has not a better man. But ridicule is inherent in him. There is no separating them."[56]

Mrs. Thrale thought the same. She wrote in her diary that he stood in an odd light among the rest of them: "he is acknowledged Learned, Pious, and elegant of Manners—yet he is always a Person unrespected and commonly ridiculous; When he made his Will we were all bursting with Laughter—Langton's Will was the Mot de Guerre and every body was tittering."[57] The topic became a theme of merriment for some time, turning up in conversation for years afterward. One had only to mention Langton's will to start Johnson off on a string of humorous suppositions and roars of laughter. There was little remarkable in the incident itself, nothing at all absurd on the face of it, yet something in the idea of Bennet Langton solemnly making his will excited Johnson's mirth. Boswell described the initial episode in his journal but left out several particulars when he transferred the tale to the pages of his *Life.*

The affair began with Langton telling Boswell one morning at breakfast that he was on his way to the lawyer Robert Chambers to make his will, and barring male offspring of his own, he meant to leave his estate to his three sisters rather than to a remote male heir. Boswell held strong views in favor of male succession, and when later that day he met Johnson by prearrangement at Chambers's home, he told Johnson what Langton had done. Johnson agreed with Boswell in maintaining the tradition of male succession, and he labeled Langton's sisters "three *dowdies.*" He then began laughing at the idea of Langton making his will, calling him "Langton the *testator*" and speculating on what a mighty thing Langton must think he had done. "He won't stay till he gets home to produce this wonderful deed," said Johnson, shaking with laughter. "He'll call up the landlord of the first inn on the road, and after a suitable preface upon mortality and the uncertainty of life will tell him that he should not delay making his will. 'And here, Sir,' will he say, 'is my will, which I have just made with the assistance of one of the ablest lawyers in the kingdom.' And he will read it to him." Continuing to laugh, he said to Chambers, "He believes he has made this will, but he did not make it. You made it for him. I hope you had more conscience than to make him say, 'being of sound understanding.' Ha, ha, ha! I hope he has left me a legacy. He should leave hatbands and gloves to all the Club. I'd have his will turned into verse like a ballad."

Chambers seemed perturbed and was pleased when his visitors finally left, but Johnson continued his uproarious commentary all the way back to Temple Gate, Boswell keeping it alive by calling out, "Langton the testator, Langton Longshanks."

"I wonder to whom he'll leave his legs?" shouted Johnson in near convulsions, holding on to a post for support and bellowing so loudly, said Boswell, "that in the dark silence of the night his voice resounded from Temple Bar to Fleet Ditch."[58]

Langton at this time was already indignant with Johnson over another matter that had occurred a few evenings earlier. The incident affected Langton so strongly that it nearly ended his friendship with the man he reverenced above all others. The incident occurred at the home of Edward Dilly, the bookseller, among a gathering that included Johnson, Boswell, Goldsmith, and several more. Boswell somehow started the subject of toleration, and there followed a heated exchange between Johnson and one of two dissenting clergyman present. Goldsmith tried to interject himself into the debate but was ignored, so he angrily snatched up his hat and prepared to leave. Just then the second clergyman began to talk and Johnson made a sound as if he was about to interrupt. Goldsmith called out to Johnson, "Sir, the gentleman has heard you patiently for an hour. Pray allow him to speak."

Johnson shot back, "Sir, I was not interrupting the gentleman. I was only giving him a signal of my attention. Sir, you are impertinent to me." Goldsmith made no further reply but began to sulk. Langton, meanwhile, quietly looked on. Although he reverenced Johnson almost to idolatry, he always spoke with great discretion in Johnson's presence for fear of exciting the great man's wrath. Through his caution and natural timidity, he had so far escaped the Johnsonian lash that so many others had felt. But then, no one seemed so little actuated by vanity or less bent upon victory in conversation than Bennet Langton, so Johnson found little cause to attack him. Furthermore, Johnson may have shown him more tolerance than was customary, knowing how sensitive he was to criticism. Nevertheless, shortly after Johnson had rebuked Goldsmith, Langton made the mistake of asking, "Is there not a difference between opinions that lead to action and opinions merely speculative—for instance, the doctrine of the Trinity?"

Still agitated by his short exchange with Goldsmith and shocked that anyone would pose such a question before dissenting ministers, Johnson said to Langton, "Sir, I'm surprised that a man of your piety can introduce this subject here."

Langton turned pale and meekly replied, "I only hinted at the question from a desire to hear your opinion upon it." But Johnson scolded him for introducing such a topic in a company in which people held differing religious views.

Later that evening at a meeting of the Club, seeing that Goldsmith continued sullen, Johnson called out to him, "Dr. Goldsmith, something passed today where you and I dined. I ask your pardon."

Goldsmith brightened and replied, "It must be much from you that I take ill." He then fell to chattering away the rest of the evening in his usual carefree manner.

When Johnson later left the room for a short time, Boswell told Goldsmith and Langton that he would have given five guineas rather than miss the evening's spectacle. After being tossed by Johnson so often himself, and Langton laughing about it, it gave him pleasure, he said, finally "to see his long legs in the air!"[59]

Several days afterward, Boswell set out for Scotland, and later in the year, on the eve of Johnson's arrival in Edinburgh to begin their now-famous tour of the Hebrides, he wrote to Langton in Lincolnshire. "What an intellectual feast is before me!" he exclaimed:

> I shall never murmur though he should at times treat me with more roughness than ever. His roughness is an indication of the vigour of his genius.—You know you and I differ a little upon this head. But I am keen for my own opinion. That however is too ample a subject for a letter. I must only say that I cannot help having a kind of joy in recollecting that you with all your timid caution got a drubbing at Dilly's. The truth is, it was observed when you was here [on a visit to Edinburgh and Auchinleck] that you assumed a kind of superiority over me, as if you was never touched by that awful rod, which has been so often applied to my back. It is natural then for me to feel some satisfaction in thinking that you had your share.[60]

But Langton had taken the rebuke more to heart than his friends realized, his sense of humiliation and resentment made more acute, perhaps, because Johnson had apologized to Goldsmith and not to him. Johnson wrote to Boswell not long after the incident that Langton had left London in deep dudgeon without calling and taking leave. "Is not this very childish?" Johnson wrote. "Where is now my legacy?"[61] After Johnson and Boswell had set off from Edinburgh on their jaunt through the Highlands, they spoke of Langton's continuing resentment. Johnson lamented, "What is to come of society if a friendship of twenty years is to be broken off for such a cause?"[62]

Having received no reply to his first letter, and anxious to repair differences, Boswell wrote to Langton again:

> You are a letter in my debt, but I write this because I understand that Mr. Johnson imagines that the reproof which he gave you at Dilly's has made you angry out of all proportion. It seems you left London without calling for him. . . . You know I allways [*sic*] was of opinion that you deserved the reproof which you got. But suppose you did not deserve it, are you for so slight a cause to break with one for whom you cannot but have the highest veneration and to whose counsels you have been much obliged? I am uneasy at the thought.[63]

Langton finally responded, writing to Boswell that he had actually called on Johnson before leaving London, but "very probably I might not have a Card with me, with my Name, to leave, and *so*, he might not have been told of it." Other than clearing up this misunderstanding, "I do not like to say much on the subject of what I confess has given me pain—" but he went on in his typical style to defend himself anyway:

> You say I deserved the Reproof; to which, as You only say it in general, I cannot attempt speaking particularly, except only, that if the introducing one or two Particulars, in what I said at that time, of too serious a Kind was not well advised, as I am afraid it was not, in the manner at least that I did it; I had no Intention of being any way troublesome to Mr. Johnson, and I hope I did not express myself with any want of Complaisance to Him; I could not therefore but think the manner of his checking me unkind. . . . I will not detain You any further on this head than to repeat my Thanks for this Your kind Endeavour to remove any Misunderstanding there might have been on that occasion we are speaking of.[64]

He followed this up with a conciliatory letter to Johnson, a gesture that greatly pleased Boswell, who wrote back to Langton, "It gave me sincere joy to find that there was no reason for the apprehension that he entertained of your having broke with him. The way in which he expressed that apprehension was a proof of his sincere love for you."[65]

With Langton's injured feelings somewhat mollified, Johnson, after returning to London, informed Boswell that "Langton is here; we are all that ever we were. He is a worthy fellow, without malice, though not without resentment."[66] The reason Johnson had rebuked Langton, and the reason Boswell thought he deserved it, was simple: Langton had a habit of introducing religious subjects into conversations and among different types of people without considering what the result might be. "Why, Sir," Johnson once complained to Boswell, "he will introduce religious discourse without seeing whether it will end in instruction and improvement or produce some profane jest."[67]

He had a habit of introducing a subject into company in which he knew two people disagreed.

"But," objected Boswell, "he told me he did it for instruction."

"Sir, whatever the motive be, the man who does so is very pernicious. He has no more right to instruct himself at such a risk than he has to make two people fight a duel, that he may learn how to defend himself."[68] Yet despite his faults, Johnson still maintained that he was as good a man as lives.

"But ridiculous," Boswell reminded him.

"It will do him no harm in the next world. But it makes him be laughed at in this."[69]

Although not at all clownish or ridiculous, Bennet Langton's friend Topham Beauclerk carried about him a certain demeanor, a certain waggish arrogance and nonchalance, that some in the Johnson circle found amusing and others irritating. Mrs. Thrale in particular detested him. Perhaps this had something to do with a fundamental antipathy between the nouveau riche and the established rich, or perhaps it was only Beauclerk's haughty disposition and cavalier attitude that she abhorred.

Before leaving England on his Grand Tour through France and Italy, he had become engaged to one Anna Maria Draycott, a wealthy heiress to some lead mines. Elizabeth Montagu, the most prominent of London's intellectual women, wrote of the pair that "by a certain coldness in his manner she fancied her lead mines were rather the objects of his love than herself, and so after the license was taken out she gave him his *congé* [dismissal]." The rejection did not appear to trouble Beauclerk, however, for according to Mrs. Montagu, "Rosamond's pond was never thought of by the forsaken swain."[70] Rosamond's Pond in St. James's Park was a notorious place for despondent lovers to end their lives.

After returning to England, Beauclerk proved a more successful suitor to Lady Diana Bolingbroke, the former Diana Spencer, wife of Frederick St. John, Second Viscount Bolingbroke. Lady Diana, the eldest of five children belonging to the Duke and Duchess of Marlborough, had grown up among the grandeurs of Blenheim and the comforts of Marlborough House. Attractive, intelligent, and sociable, she was an accomplished artist. Horace Walpole, who became a close friend and frequent host at Strawberry Hill, claimed that her floral designs in particular were equal to anything Michelangelo could have done for a pope's villa.[71] At the time she met Beauclerk, she already had two sons by Lord Bolingbroke, a man she had come to despise, he being idle and debauched, a philandering dipsomaniac who became cruel when deep

Lady Diana Beauclerk.
Source: Anna Stowe/Alamy Stock Photo.

in wine. After ten stormy years of quarrels and reconciliations, she finally decided on a separation. "I believe Lord B. is much the same as mad when he is drunk," wrote one of her friends to an acquaintance, "and that is generally. Lady B.'s reason for parting is that she cannot live with him with safety to her health [that is, from venereal infection]."[72]

Estranged from her husband, Lady Diana quickly attracted several admirers. Her leading suitor was "Mr Beauclair, the most self-sufficient coxcomb, in my opinion, I ever saw," sniffed Caroline Fox, Lady Holland. "Lady Bolingbroke is his passion, if he has any passion but for himself, which is doubted."[73] Even Lady Diana did not at first seem to take Beauclerk's attentions seriously. She reportedly remarked, "Who would [have] thought I should ever flirt with a Macaroni?"[74] Yet soon she began receiving Beauclerk's visits regularly, sometimes two or three times a day and at unusual hours. Servants grew suspicious, upper-class tongues began to wag, and finally Lady Diana confirmed all rumors by giving birth on August 20, 1767, to a girl, later named Mary.

Lord Bolingbroke immediately sought a divorce. The length of time he had been separated from his wife made it impossible for the child to be his. A friend cautioned him against so drastic a move as he intended, advising him instead to take no notice of the matter. Obtaining a divorce was a difficult process that must gain the sanction of Parliament. This could be an ugly procedure and would likely fail. Yet Bolingbroke said he must try. He could not stand the thought of a son born to Lady Diana and Beauclerk inheriting his estate and title should his own two sons die. His petition, therefore, charging his wife with "*crim. con.*" (criminal conversation) with Beauclerk, went forward and ultimately succeeded. Having passed both houses of Parliament, the divorce decree became final on March 12, 1768. Two days later Topham Beauclerk married Lady Diana Spencer at St. George's Church, Hanover Square. The entire episode had been one of those deliciously entertaining scandals that aristocracy sometimes puts on for the rest of society. Boswell, who greatly admired Lady Di's attractiveness and charming conversation, attempted to justify her adulterous conduct to Johnson. He argued that Lord Bolingbroke had been cruel to her, that she could not live with him without damaging her reputation, that she was in the prime of life, and why should she spend years of unhappiness with Bolingbroke when she could live happily with Beauclerk. Johnson listened patiently, but the longer Boswell went on, the feebler his argument seemed, even to himself. Finally Johnson said to him, "My dear Sir, never accustom your mind to mingle virtue and vice. The woman's a whore, and there's an end on't."[75]

Conversing with Boswell on a later occasion, Johnson happened to observe that vice would not injure a man's reputation. Boswell disagreed—debauching a man's wife would. "No, Sir," said Johnson. "Who thinks worse of Beauclerk for it?"

"Lord Bolingbroke was not his friend," countered Boswell.

"Sir, that is a circumstance, a slight distinction. He could not get into the house but by Lord Bolingbroke. A man is chosen Knight of the Shire not the less for having debauched ladies."

"What, Sir? If he has debauched ladies of gentlemen in the country, will there not be a general resentment against him?"

"No, Sir. He will lose these particular gentlemen. But the rest will not trouble their heads about it." Johnson then added, "Ask Mr. Thrale," whose philandering was well known.[76]

Following their marriage, the couple seemed to have lived for a short time in Charles Street, Berkeley Square, where they gave lavish dinners. Later they moved to a town house, No. 3, in the luxurious and newly built Adelphi Terrace in the Strand. David Garrick and his wife now had rooms at No. 4. Boswell, on first visiting the Adelphi, very much admired the elegance of Beauclerk's parlor, especially "his large gilded lion, a cast from the antique, supporting his sideboard."[77] The Beauclerks afterward purchased a country villa on an eight-acre estate at Muswell Hill in what was then a quiet rural area near Highgate. The villa was furnished with the utmost splendor and convenience where Beauclerk could indulge his passions for book collecting, astronomy, and conducting chemical experiments. The estate also became a handsome showplace where curious visitors were allowed to tour the premises after obtaining tickets in advance. Boswell arranged to accompany Beauclerk to see his villa and then to dine with him, but Beauclerk had to cancel due to illness, so Boswell went with Johnson instead. Both were suitably impressed. "He has one of the most numerous & splendid private libraries that I ever saw," Boswell exclaimed. "Greenhouses hothouse Observatory Laboratory for chymical experiments in short every thing princely."[78]

Nearly every aspect of Beauclerk's life, in fact, seemed princely. Elegance showed not only in his houses, furnishings, dress, and collection of fine books, but also in his manner. His deportment always appeared extremely refined and well bred. Some, like Mrs. Thrale, thought it simply pompous. John Wilkes described his personality as "shy, sly, and dry."[79] Yet like his great-grandmother, Nell Gwyn, Beauclerk was an excellent conversationalist, ever ready with an entertaining story or anecdote, which he delivered with a captivating nonchalance and ease of expression. Even Sir John Hawkins, that formal man of business and law, found much in him to admire: "To the character of a scholar, and a man of fine parts, he added that of a man of fashion, of which his dress and equipage shewed him to be emulous." Beauclerk, said Hawkins, became the exemplar "of all who wished, without incurring the censure of foppery, to become conspicuous in the gay world." His travels in Italy had polished his manners and increased his learning. "In painting and sculpture, his taste and judgment were accurate, in classic literature, exquisite; and in the knowledge of history, and the study of antiquities, he had few equals. His conversation was of the most excellent kind; learned, witty, polite, and, where the subject required it, serious; and over all his behaviour there beamed such a sunshine of chearfulness and good humour, as communicated itself to all around him."[80]

Boswell, on the other hand, a man of more zest and animal spirits than Hawkins, never felt quite easy around Beauclerk. The first time the two met, Beauclerk received his guest politely but without much warmth. He seemed distant and aloof, though Boswell thought that what he had first interpreted as distant coldness might only have been Beauclerk's customary high-bred demeanor. Boswell was also willing to overlook any small slights and try to appreciate Beauclerk given his veneration for Johnson and Johnson's love for him. Boswell also had to acknowledge Beauclerk to be "a man of wit, literature, and fashion in a distinguished degree" and grant that he was an excellent raconteur, telling stories in company "in a lively elegant manner, and with the air of *the world* which has I know not what impressive effect, as if there were something more than is expressed, or than perhaps we could perfectly understand."[81] One thing that made Boswell especially uneasy, however, was Beauclerk's scoffing attitude when speaking of religion. He did not indulge in profane or licentious talk around Johnson, for he respected Johnson too much for that, but in the company of more informal companions he felt less constraint. Boswell said it was a discussion of religion one day that produced the most perfect contrast between Bennet Langton and Beauclerk: "The one earnestly and seriously arguing for the truth of Christianity. The other with indifference and vivacity parrying every argument, or springing out of its way. Langton quoted passages from books. Beauclerk threw out immediate sparkles from his own mind." At one point, harkening back to their university days, Beauclerk embarrassed Langton by saying, "The belief in Christianity does not influence a man's conduct. I *know*, Langton, it did not keep you from whoring."[82]

One evening Boswell attended a dinner party wearing a crimson suit, embroidered with silver, made for him in Dublin six years earlier. It was now a bit out of fashion, but he thought he looked handsome in it nevertheless. He told those present, "'I feel myself quite different in this suit from what I am in my frock' (meaning that I felt myself better). Said Beauclerk: 'So should I feel myself quite different, but I should not feel agreeably' (meaning that I was ridiculous). He has a fine malignity about him."[83]

NOTES

1. Piozzi, *Thraliana*, 473.
2. Goldsmith, *Collected Works*, 3:294.
3. Boswell, *Boswell in Search of a Wife*, 317–18.
4. Prior, *Goldsmith*, 2:359–60.
5. Chauncey Brewster Tinker, *Young Boswell: Chapters on James Boswell the Biographer Based Largely on New Material* (Boston: Atlantic Monthly Press, 1922), 232.
6. Beattie to Sir William Forbes, July 10, 1788; Sir William Forbes, *An Account of the Life and Writings of James Beattie, LL.D.*, 2 vols. (London, 1824), 2:220; Boswell, *Life*, 3:518.
7. Northcote, *Life*, 1:288.
8. Boswell, *London Journal*, 105 and 106.
9. Walpole, *Correspondence*, 1:310, 28:41, and 28:277; Boswell, *Life*, 1:412n6; Piozzi, *Anecdotes*, 55–56.
10. Prior, *Goldsmith*, 2:296–97.
11. Ibid., 2:379.
12. Reynolds, *Portraits*, 44–47.
13. Hawkins, *Anecdotes*, 1:7.
14. George Colman Jr., *Random Records*, 2 vols. (London, 1830), 1:111.
15. Ibid., 1:117–18.
16. Reynolds, *Portraits*, 54.
17. Boswell, *Life*, 4:29.
18. Ibid., 1:413–14.
19. Prior, *Goldsmith*, 2:291.
20. Piozzi, *Thraliana*, 83.
21. Prior, *Goldsmith*, 2:349.
22. Goldsmith, *Collected Works*, 1:84–85; Oliver Goldsmith, *New Essays of Oliver Goldsmith*, ed. Ronald S. Crane (Chicago: University of Chicago Press, 1927), 50–51.
23. Leslie and Taylor, *Life and Times*, 1:460.
24. Boswell, *Life*, 1:414n4.
25. Cradock, *Literary and Miscellaneous Memoirs*, 1:232.
26. Reynolds, *Portraits*, 49 and 51.
27. Davies, *Life of Garrick*, 2:145.
28. Boswell, *Life*, 2:42.
29. Percy, *Life of Goldsmith*, 117.
30. Boswell, *Life*, 2:260 and 1:413.
31. Hawkins, *Memoirs*, 1:295–96.
32. Boswell, *Life*, 1:414–15.
33. Reynolds, *Portraits*, 86.
34. Piozzi, *Thraliana*, 84.
35. Hawkins, *Life*, 418–19.
36. Percy, *Life of Goldsmith*, 20 and 141.

37. Prior, *Goldsmith*, 1:440–41.

38. Reynolds, *Portraits*, 50.

39. Boswell, *Boswell for the Defence*, 181; ibid., 50.

40. Goldsmith, *Letters*, 65.

41. Prior, *Goldsmith*, 2:378.

42. "Retaliation," first stanza.

43. Goldsmith, "Description of Various Clubs," *Collected Works*, 3:14.

44. Boswell, *Life*, 2:196; *Boswell for the Defence*, 109–10.

45. Prior, *Goldsmith*, 2:483–84.

46. Boswell, *Life*, 5:97n3.

47. Ibid., 2:235–36 and 2:231.

48. Reynolds, *Portraits*, 48.

49. Goldsmith, "A city night-piece," *Collected Works*, 2:454.

50. Prior, *Goldsmith*, 1:95–96.

51. Cooke, "Table Talk," *European Magazine* 24 (October 1793): 261.

52. Reynolds, *Portraits*, 34.

53. Percy, *Life of Goldsmith*, 98-99.

54. Prior, *Goldsmith*, 2:420–21.

55. Boswell, *Life*, 3:161.

56. James Boswell, *Boswell's Journal of a Tour to the Hebrides with Samuel Johnson, LL.D. 1773*, edited from the original manuscript by Frederick A. Pottle and Charles H. Bennett (New York: McGraw-Hill, 1961), 13n19.

57. Piozzi, *Thraliana*, 106.

58. Boswell, *Boswell for the Defence*, 188–89. See also Boswell, *Life*, 2:262.

59. Boswell, *Boswell for the Defence*, 185–87.

60. Boswell, *Correspondence with Members of the Club*, 33–34.

61. Johnson, *Letters*, Redford, 2:42.

62. Boswell, *Tour to the Hebrides*, 64.

63. Boswell, *Correspondence with Members of the Club*, 35.

64. Ibid., 36–37.

65. Ibid., 41.

66. Johnson, *Letters*, Redford, 2:170.

67. Boswell, *Applause of the Jury*, 123.

68. Boswell, *Boswell in Extremes*, 177.

69. Boswell, *Applause of the Jury*, 151.

70. Hill, *Dr. Johnson*, 287. See also Walpole, *Correspondence*, 10:14, in which Walpole writes to George Montagu on February 22, 1762, "Miss Draycott, within two days of matrimony, has dismissed Mr Beauclerc."

71. Walpole, *Correspondence*, 29:272.

72. Lady Steuart Erskine, *Lady Diana Beauclerk: Her Life and Work* (London, 1903), 56.

73. Emily FitzGerald, *Correspondence of Emily, Duchess of Leinster*, ed. Brian Fitzgerald, 3 vols. (Dublin: Stationery Office, 1949), 1:467.

74. Ibid., 1:467.

75. Boswell, *Life*, 2:246–47. Baretti also found Lady Di a captivating woman. "Of Lady Diana Beauclerc he was saying a thousand fine Things," wrote Mrs. Thrale; "I mention'd her bad Character—Oh yes says he I know She is a Strumpet; had She not been so, She would have sate in Heaven next Jesus Christ" (Piozzi, *Thraliana*, 46–47).

76. Boswell, *Boswell in Extremes*, 341.

77. Boswell, *Boswell for the Defence*, 165.

78. Boswell, *Correspondence of Boswell and Temple*, 373–74.

79. Hill, *Dr. Johnson*, 298.

80. Hawkins, *Life*, 421–22.

81. Boswell, *Boswell for the Defence*, 165; Boswell, *Life*, 1:249 and 3:390.

82. Boswell, *Ominous Years*, 92.

83. Ibid., 140.

Chapter Five

Incident in the Haymarket

The Royal Academy met on the night of October 6, 1769. About nine o'clock, Joseph Baretti, being late for the start of the meeting where he was Secretary of Foreign Correspondence, was striding briskly down the Haymarket toward Pall Mall when a woman seated on some steps near the pavement accosted him and an altercation ensued. Three men saw Baretti strike the woman. The men confronted him, he ran, and they pursued him a short way up Panton Street where the chase ended with Baretti stabbing two of his pursuers, one critically.

The more seriously wounded man, Evan Morgan, was carried to Middlesex Hospital for medical attention, while Constable John Lambert arrested Baretti and took him before magistrate Sir John Fielding, half-brother of Henry Fielding. After hearing what Baretti had to say, Sir John placed him in a room below, allowing him to send a man to fetch Sir Joshua Reynolds from the Royal Academy meeting. Fielding dispatched another man to Middlesex Hospital to ascertain Morgan's condition.

Reynolds arrived a short time later with Oliver Goldsmith and several others. A surgeon also appeared from Middlesex Hospital to take his oath that Morgan's life was in danger. As a result, Baretti could not be released on bail, so Fielding committed him to Tothill Fields Prison. It had been a day of heavy rain. The coachman carrying Baretti, Reynolds, Goldsmith, and a constable lost his way in the dark, and the four passengers had to alight from the carriage and find their way to the prison on foot through the mud. Soon after midnight, Evan Morgan died.

Samuel Johnson and Edmund Burke came to Baretti in his cell the following day and told him that things looked bad. They could not give him much hope. They thought he would probably hang. Baretti placed himself between the two and said, "Why what can he fear that holds two such hands as I do[?]"[1]

Friends quickly rallied to Baretti's support. Johnson, Burke, and others conferred on the best strategy for his defense. Goldsmith, although he did not like Baretti, thinking him an insolent and overbearing foreigner, still responded with characteristic generosity by consoling him and offering him money if he needed it.[2] Only Boswell held back. By this time he detested Baretti. Like Goldsmith, he disliked the Italian's assertive bearing. While Baretti prided himself on being frank, independent, and outspoken, Boswell thought him offensively brutish. He found his manners, even when in good humor, "exceedingly rough, which had not disgusted me when I saw him at Venice, because I was so happy to find there a great admirer of Mr. Samuel Johnson."[3] Boswell had called on him while he was writing his *Journey from London to Genoa*, and he observed that Baretti "was so full of himself, and so assuming and really ferocious in his manner, that he disgusted me not a little."[4]

Furthermore, Boswell's ruling passion at this time was the Corsicans and their struggle for independence against Genoese, and later French, domination. He had spent nearly six weeks during his Grand Tour on the island of Corsica, much of it in the company of General Paoli, leader of the freedom fighters. He found the Corsican general well-bred and intelligent, and he thought the Coriscans themselves brave and devoted to the cause of liberty. Baretti, however, took a different view. He often reviled the Corsicans and ridiculed their supporters. He wrote to Boswell in March 1768 congratulating him on his recently published *Account of Corsica*, calling it a delightful book, but he complained that it libeled the Genoese, "especially in favour of the Corsicans, who upon the very face of your book do not appear to be anything better than bloody-minded savages."[5] Boswell simply could not love or even feign respect for a man like this.

On the eve of trial, six days after the incident in the Haymarket, Boswell quizzed Johnson about feeling distress for the misfortunes of others, and Johnson, as usual, dismissed such sentiments as cant, mere affectation. "But now if I were in danger of being hanged?" Boswell persisted.

"I should do what I could to bail you, but when you were once fairly hanged I should not suffer for you."

"Would you eat your dinner that day, Sir?"

"Yes, Sir, and eat it as if you were eating it with me. Why, there's Baretti who is to be tried for his life tomorrow; friends have risen up for him on every side, but if he should be hanged, none of those friends will eat a slice of plum pudding the less."

Boswell then mentioned Samuel Foote, who had shown him a letter from Tom Davies wherein Davies claimed he had been unable to sleep due to

"This sad affair of Baretti," and in the same letter he recommended to Foote a young man who kept a pickle shop. "Ay, Sir," said Johnson, "here you have a specimen of human sympathy; a friend hanged, and a cucumber pickled."[6]

Four days after the Haymarket incident and three days before the trial was scheduled to begin, Baretti wrote to his brothers in Italy explaining to them what had occurred. He said that when he found himself confronted by the three men and surrounded by a growing crowd in the street, he "bellowed like a bull. My voice and my knife opened the crowd on one side." He ran through the opening and up Panton Street. "I could not run as fast as my pursuers, so that they were upon me, continually beating and pushing me. I struck out with my knife as I fled. I wounded one under the arm-pit as he had his hand raised for a blow." This was a man named Thomas Patman. "The most treacherous of all my assailants—and they were all thorough scoundrels, as afterwards appeared—was a man called Morgan, who made several attempts to seize me by the hair, which I wore in a tail. He beat off my hat with his fist. I gave him two blows, as I fled: the rascal, however, did not feel them, but waited for another, which brought him to the ground, groaning." Seeing an open shop, "I ran into it for protection, quite spent with fatigue, and turned upon the mob, brandishing my knife and threatening to strike any one that entered."[7]

Other details emerged once the trial began on October 13 in Justice Hall of the Old Bailey, Justice Bathurst, one of His Majesty's Judges of the Court of Common Pleas, presiding. Baretti entered the dock accused of murdering Evan Morgan by stabbing him twice in the chest and once in the abdomen. Given the time of night and the locality, there was suspicion that Baretti might have been drinking and trying to pick up prostitutes. Baretti for his part hoped to show that it was a common practice in the Haymarket for prostitutes, working with male accomplices, to rob innocent passersby. He waived his right to present his case before a jury made up half of foreigners, for he did not want it to appear that he received special treatment. This may have been part of the strategy worked out at the meeting of Johnson and Burke.

The first witness called was Elizabeth Ward, the woman Baretti had struck. She testified that between nine and ten on the night of the incident she was sitting on a step in front of a doorway with a woman who had asked her for a penny. She professed never to have seen the woman before, but as Baretti walked past, the woman asked him to give her a glass of wine, "and she put her hand towards him." When asked whereabouts she put her hand, Ward answered, "Towards his breeches; towards his private parts." According to her, Baretti walked about a yard further on "and then turned back and struck me a great blow on the side of my face." He struck her, she said, with his clenched fist. Then three men she claimed not to know immediately came up and asked the gentleman how he could strike a woman. They crowded Baretti, shoving him off the pavement and into the muddy street. "Then he drawed his knife out of the case and held it in his hand; but I did not see him stab either of them. They cried murder, he has a knife out." Baretti then ran about eight or nine doors up Panton Street with the men chasing him, and there he turned about to face them. She could not tell what happened after that. Asked if she or the other girl had called him "French dog" or similar names, she answered, "No. I remember he called us bitches." When asked to recollect what other names she heard, she replied, "I remember hearing some say buggerer, or some such name. Some of them called him so."

Baretti would soon write in his *Journey from London to Genoa* that it was the custom of lower-class Londoners to call every foreigner *French dog.* They seemed to think that the world consisted of only two nations, England and France, and anyone who was not English must be French. "Then they know something of a sea-faring people called the Dutch, for whom they have the greatest contempt. But talk to them of other nations; of the Italians for instance: They have heard something of the Italians; but a'n't the 'Talians French?"[8]

Next to testify was the less seriously wounded man, Thomas Patman. In questioning him, the court sought to establish the sequence of events, determine if there was any provocation for Baretti's actions, and probe whether or not the men and Miss Ward were in collusion. Patman began by stating that on the night of the encounter, as he and John Clark came up the Haymarket, they met Morgan. The three entered a tavern and each had a pint of beer. When Patman and Clark asked Morgan to give them a song, Morgan said he would if the other two accompanied him to a tavern in Golden Square. "We were going along the Haymarket all three together, and just at the corner of Panton Street, coming by, there was a gentleman struck a woman. I saw him strike her on the head. She reeled, and was very near ready to fall. I do not know whether it was me that said he was not a gentleman for striking a woman."

"Did you know the woman?"

"I did not. I had never spoken to her in my life."

"What did the woman say?"

"The woman cried out. I never heard her mention a word before. She said, 'You do not behave like a gentleman.'"

"What did he say?"

"I never heard him speak a word. The other two men were behind me, and they immediately pushed me against the gentleman. I received a blow from him directly on my left side: the blood ran down into my shoes." The push, he said, was not at all forceful. It would not have hurt anybody.

"Did you hear the word buggerer mentioned, or something like?"

"I did not."

"Did you not call him names?"

"I did not call him any names at all." Patman testified further that he had not seen Morgan do anything to the gentleman before he began running up Panton Street. "I did not know he had a knife. Morgan ran after him, to take him, and just by the Hole in the Wall [a tavern] Morgan received a wound. I saw the gentleman strike him as he was running up Panton Street: he struck him on the side of the body."

"Did you see any other blows given?"

"I saw none but that. We pursued him, and cried murder. We saw him go into a chandler's shop. I went just by the door. Morgan was lying on the ground, as they told me. I did not see him. I never lifted a hand against the gentleman, neither did I see any of the others offer to strike him."

"Did you hear any such words as buggerer, or French bugger?"

"No, I did not."

"Had you given him no offense at all?"

"No."

John Clark appeared next. He offered confused and conflicting evidence. He could not recall sworn testimony he had given earlier at a coroner's inquest, and he denied statements that others claimed he made.

John Lambert, the man who had arrested Baretti, took the witness box. "I am a tallow-chandler," he stated, "and was then a constable." On the day in question, at about nine o'clock at night, he had just sat down to supper "when I heard the cry of murderer, or stop murderer, which alarmed me a good deal. I got to my door, and observed the prisoner and two or three men pursuing him: he ran into a grocer's shop just opposite to me. Patman was standing at the door when I went over. He was unbuttoned, and there was blood running down; I observed it through his shirt. I asked him what was the matter; he said he was stabbed by that gentleman, who was then in the shop, and had a knife in his hand. The silver case on it was bloody."

The constable, joined by one or two neighbors, with a mob gathering outside, asked Baretti if he would surrender. Baretti asked in return if they were friends. When Lambert assured him they were and that they would protect him, he started to put his knife back into its case. But not knowing who he was dealing with or what the situation might be, Lambert thought it best to secure the assailant, so he sprang at Baretti, grabbed him by the collar, seized the knife, and attempted to drive it into a tea chest, bending the point of the blade. The knife was duly produced as evidence. Asked if Baretti had tried

to conceal the knife, Lambert replied, "No. I showed him my short staff [em-
blem of a constable], but I believe he did not see it. He appeared to be very
near sighted." Lambert said that when he learned another woman besides
Elizabeth Ward might be involved, "I made it my business to take up several
prostitutes in the Haymarket, and examined them, but could not find any such
person as Ward has mentioned."

John Wyatt, surgeon at Middlesex Hospital, next testified that Morgan had
been stabbed three times. "That wound received in his abdomen was the occasion of his death. Wounds in the lungs do sometimes prove mortal, and sometimes not." After tending to Morgan, Wyatt questioned the other two men in
the hall. Clark told him that after drinking some beers they were coming up
the Haymarket, "where they saw a gentleman abusing a lady, who was an acquaintance of the gentleman's up stairs," meaning Morgan. Wyatt asked him
what provocation the woman had given Baretti, and he said he thought she
"damned him for a French bugger, and said he ought to have his head clove
with a patten." Seeing a crowd gathering in the hall, Wyatt took Clark into a
nearby boardroom and said to him, "This woman was an acquaintance of the
gentleman's up stairs: he then said, 'No, not at all.' Then the gentleman with
me said, 'You rascal, you said so, not two minutes ago.' But he then denied
it: after that, I did not ask him any other questions."

Baretti was then called to present his defense. He began by reading a statement in which he claimed to have seen only one woman on the steps before
the doorway, not two. This woman, he said, "was eight or ten yards from
the corner of Panton Street, and she clapped her hands with such violence
about my private parts, that it gave me great pain. This I instantly resented,
by giving her a blow on the hand, with a few angry words. The woman got
up directly, raised her voice, and finding by my pronunciation I was a foreigner, she called me several bad names in a most contumelious strain; among
which, *French bugger, damned Frenchman*, and a *woman-hater*, were the
most audible." He had gone only a few steps further on when a man hit him
from behind with his fist, asking him how he dared strike a woman: "another
pushed him against me, and pushed me off the pavement; then three or four
more joined them." Others quickly gathered and began beating him, "and all
damning me on every side, in a most frightful manner. I was a Frenchman
in their opinion, which made me apprehensive I must expect no favour nor
protection, but all outrage and blows."

The day's heavy rain had left a large puddle at the corner of Panton Street.
"I could plainly perceive my assailants wanted to throw me into the puddle,
where I might be trampled on; so I cried out murder." Seeing a break in the
circle of people surrounding him, he ran through it. "I was in the greatest
horror, lest I should run against some stones, as I have such bad eyes. I could

not run so fast as my pursuers, so that they were upon me, continually beating and pushing me. Some of them attempting to catch me by the hair-tail: if this had happened, I had been certainly a lost man." He did not recall precisely where he first struck out with his knife: "I remember, somewhere in Panton Street, I gave a quick blow to one who beat off my hat with his fist." A short distance further on he stopped and faced his pursuers. "My confusion was great, and seeing a shop open, I ran into it for protection, quite spent with fatigue. I am certainly sorry for the man, but he owed his death to his own daring impetuosity." Baretti told the court that he hoped it would not think a man of his age, character, and habits of life would suddenly put down his pen to engage in street brawls: "I hope it will easily be conceived that a man almost blind could not but be seized with terror, on such a sudden attack as this. I hope it will be seen, that my knife was neither a weapon of offence or defence: I wear it to carve fruit and sweetmeats, and not to kill my fellow-creatures. It is a general custom in France, not to put knives upon the table, so that even ladies wear them in their pockets for general use." He concluded by reminding the court that he had waived his right as a foreigner to plead his case before a jury comprised half of foreigners. He had relinquished that right for his life and his honor. "I chose to be tried by a Jury of this country; for if my honour is not saved, I cannot much wish for the preservation of my life."

Two commissioners of the peace were then called to testify that such criminal assaults as Baretti experienced were common in the Haymarket area. Justice Kelynge spoke from personal knowledge: "I once was coming from a relation of mine down Panton Street when a woman took hold of me, and endeavoured to put her hand into my breeches. I immediately sprung away. I was going to knock her down, when two men came up to me. I called out watch! watch! very loud," and when a gentleman crossed the street to help, the others ran off. "It is a common case there, I am sorry to say it, notwithstanding all the care we take."

A Major Alerton testified that he had fended off a similar attack about a year previously. "I was attacked by women first, and because I pushed them away, I was attacked by men: they began to jostle me, but I had a pretty good stick in my hand, and they did not chuse to closely attack me."

Next followed a quick succession of character witnesses, whom Boswell termed "a constellation of genius," to testify on Baretti's behalf.[9] Topham Beauclerk was first. He verified that forks only were placed on tables in the public houses and inns of France, and that gentlemen and ladies usually carried knives with them. "I have seen those kind of knives in toy-shops," he stated. Toy shops were shops that sold trinkets, knick knacks, and other small miscellaneous goods. As for Baretti, "He is a gentleman of letters, and a studious man."

Sir Joshua Reynolds in his testimony spoke of Baretti as "a man of great humanity, and very active in endeavouring to help his friends, I have known many instances of it. He is a gentleman of good temper; I never knew him quarrelsome in my life; he is of a sober disposition. He never drank any more than three glasses in my company."

Samuel Johnson next took the witness box. Boswell, who attended the trial but did not participate, said that Johnson "gave his evidence in a slow, deliberate, and distinct manner, which was uncommonly impressive."[10]

Said Johnson, "I believe I began to be acquainted with Mr. Baretti about the year 53 or 54. I have been intimate with him. He is a man of literature, a very studious man, a man of great diligence. He gets his living by study. I have no reason to think he was ever disordered with liquor in his life. A man that I never knew to be otherwise than peaceable, and a man that I take to be rather timorous."

"Was he addicted to pick up women in the street?"

"I never knew that he was."

"How is he as to his eye-sight?"

"He does not see me now, nor I do not see him. I do not believe he could be capable of assaulting any body in the street, without great provocation."

Edmund Burke next testified that Baretti was a man of remarkable humanity who was thoroughly good natured. David Garrick followed and told the court, "I never knew a man of a more active benevolence." When shown the knife, Garrick said that he had one similar to it, "but I have lost mine. Mrs. Garrick has one now, with a steel blade, and gold."

"When you travel abroad, do you carry such knives as this?"

"Yes, or we should have no victuals."

Oliver Goldsmith next swore under oath that Baretti was "a most humane, benevolent, peaceable man. I have heard him speak with regard to these poor creatures in the street, and he has got some in the hospital, who have had bad distempers. I have known him three years. He is a man of as great humanity as any in the world."

Others were prepared to testify along similar lines, but the court thought it unnecessary to call them. The case was next submitted to the members of the jury, who shortly returned acquittals on all charges. After a trial lasting nearly five hours, Baretti was released from custody and his knife returned to him.[11]

All of Baretti's friends and acquaintances were delighted with the trial's outcome—all except Boswell. Based on the evidence, Boswell, a lawyer by profession, thought Baretti guilty of murder and said openly in company that he should have been hanged. These comments eventually got back to Baretti. Garrick and Langton took Boswell aside one day and convinced him that he was wrong to make such statements, whereupon he wrote to Baretti, apologizing for his careless remarks. He was sorry, he said, to have been so prejudiced in his attitude, but Baretti's manner in speaking of the Corsicans had provoked him, "and a certain roughness of behaviour which I could not see you had a title to be indulged in, disgusted me." But now that he saw his error, he hoped Baretti would excuse his conduct with "mild Philosophy . . . while I also begin to lose all my prejudices against you and to make every allowance for difference of opinion or mode of address." Boswell later wrote on the draft copy of this note that it was "a weak, absurd letter," and he quickly reverted to his original opinion that Baretti had been guilty of murder.[12] Baretti was not at all pacified by Boswell's grudging apology, and neither man tried afterward to hide his contempt for the other.

As for having killed a man, Baretti felt no remorse given the circumstances. He said one day at the Prince of Orange Coffee House, when the subject came up of thugs assaulting people in the streets, "Why do they not serve such fellows as I served the man just by here?—That's the only way to stop the evil." Some years later, while in casual conversation with a young woman, he cut a peach in half to share with her. After she had eaten her portion, Baretti told her, "I should, I fear, have spoiled your stomach for the peach, if you had known that the knife I cut it with, was that with which I stabbed the man in the Haymarket."[13]

In the days following the trial, Baretti returned to his usual routine, which meant that he got up around eight o'clock and, after being shaved and powdered, had tea. He then sat down to write until mid-afternoon, after which he dined.

> About six o'clock I drink tea again, always at somebody else's house and in the company of clever, beautiful women and girls. Then I play at quadrille the whole evening every day, supping where I have been spending the evening, after which we drink tea and chatter till past eleven. The houses I frequent are numerous, and would be more numerous did I wish it. My familiarity with English ways and my Italian gaiety—which is usually, I might almost say always, greater here than in Italy—makes people readily open their doors to me. Blessed England! Rascals are as plentiful here as they are in any other country; but good people abound here in a proportion about thirty times as great as in other countries.[14]

He sometimes complained of getting fat from want of exercise and said that he had callouses on his thumb from squeezing his pen so much. Why did he work so hard? "A pretty question indeed . . . faith for no other reason, but because I hate work, and I want to be idle."[15] With poverty always following close upon his heels, he regretted that he was forced to write "in a most confounded hurry," and he considered it a miracle that he was able to obtain bread and cheese "and now and then a beef-steak, by my ill-chopt performances."[16]

In July of 1770 he published the book he had long been at work on, *A Journey from London to Genoa, through England, Portugal, Spain, and France.* He dedicated the four-volume work to Sir Joshua Reynolds, president, and members of the Royal Academy. Far from being an ill-chopped performance, it is now thought to be his best work in English. Presented in the form of travel letters addressed to his three brothers in Italy, it comprises a personal account of places, customs, and people, told in a spirited and entertaining style. In the preface, he explained the purpose of his book and acknowledged a particular debt of gratitude:

> In the descriptions that follow, I hope it will appear that I have spared no pains to carry my reader in some measure along with me; to make him see what I saw, hear what I heard, feel what I felt, and even think and fancy whatever I thought and fancied myself. Should this method prove agreeable, and procure the honour of a favourable reception to my work, I shall owe it in a great part to my most revered friend Dr. Samuel Johnson, who suggested it to me, just as I was setting out on my first journey to Spain. It was he that exhorted me to write daily, and with all possible minuteness: it was he that pointed out the topics which would most interest and most delight in a future publication. To his injunctions I have kept as close as I was able.

The book received wide praise. Said Johnson, "I know not whether the world has ever seen such travels before."[17] Baretti, in fact, had reached the summit of his literary career. He had done more than any single writer to instruct the English in Italian customs and acquaint them with Italian literature. Many eminent people now desired his company, and he claimed to know several wealthy families in town and in the country with whom he could spend a month any time he chose. Certainly he made a lively addition to any social gathering, for, as he himself declared and as others acknowledged, he possessed considerable charm when he chose to exert it. When his friends, some of the foremost men in England, swore under oath at his trial that he was a good-natured, peace-loving man, they did not perjure themselves, but spoke of the individual they most often saw. The actor John O'Keefe, who had seen him frequently at the Prince of Orange Coffee House, confirmed that "Baretti was an agreeable, good-natured man, and, I am sure, of a humane disposition—large fine person—concave, smiling Italian face."[18] Another acquaintance remarked that "his eye when he was inclined to please, or be pleased when he was conversing with young people, and especially young women, [was] chearful and engaging."[19] And Johnson also confirmed that Baretti was a pleasant companion, writing in a letter, "I ran a race in the rain this day, and beat Baretti. Baretti is a fine fellow."[20]

NOTES

1. Piozzi, *Thraliana*, 232.

2. Davies, *Life of Garrick*, 2:162–63.

3. Boswell, *Boswell in Search of a Wife*, 159.

4. Ibid., 293.

5. Ibid., 159n6.

6. Ibid., 323; Boswell, *Life*, 2:94.

7. Collison-Morley, *Giuseppe Baretti*, 204–5.

8. Joseph Baretti, *A Journey from London to Genoa, through England, Portugal, Spain and France*, 4 vols. (London, 1770), 1:64.

9. Boswell, *Life*, 2:97.

10. Ibid., 2:98.

11. The preceding account is based on a transcript of the trial posted at *Proceedings of the Old Bailey, 1643–1913* (www.oldbaileyonline.org), October 1769, trial of Joseph Baretti (t17691018-9).

12. James Boswell, *The General Correspondence of James Boswell, 1766–1769*, ed. Richard C. Cole et al., 2 vols. (Edinburgh: Edinburgh University Press, 1993, 1997), 2:257–58.

13. Lætitia-Matilda Hawkins, *The Countess and Gertrude; or, Modes of Discipline*, 4 vols. (London, 1811), 1:305.

14. Collison-Morley, *Giuseppe Baretti*, 231.

15. Francis Hardy, *Memoirs of the Political and Private Life of James Caulfield, Earl of Charlemont*, 2 vols. (London, 1812), 1:309.

16. "Anecdotes of Joseph Baretti," *European Magazine* (May 1789): 350.

17. Johnson, *Letters*, Redford, 1:348.

18. John O'Keefe, *Recollections of the Life of John O'Keefe*, 2 vols. (London, 1826), 2:22–23.

19. "Anecdotes of Joseph Baretti," *European Magazine* (August 1789): 93.

20. Johnson, *Letters*, Redford, 2:273.

Chapter Six

Between Comedy and Tragedy

By the early 1770s, David Garrick had amassed a sizable fortune and lived in a style unprecedented for a player. In addition to his house at 27 Southampton Street, Covent Garden, he had rooms on six floors of the new and luxurious Adelphi Terrace between the Strand and the river, and a fine country villa at Hampton on the banks of the Thames, thirteen miles from Hyde Park Corner. The villa stood on extensive grounds that sloped down to the water. The property contained a grotto, a temple to Shakespeare, an orangery, and a garden in which grew a mulberry tree grown from a slip of the legendary mulberry tree said to have been planted by Shakespeare in his garden at Stratford. All three of Garrick's residences contained art works and other furnishings of the highest quality and elegance.

In a relatively short period of time he had transformed many aspects of the theater, particularly the art of acting, and despite grumblings from proponents of the old declamatory school, theatergoers in general found him vastly entertaining and thought his animated, more natural style appropriate to the characters he portrayed. Unfortunately for those in the profession, acting prior to the twentieth century was among the most perishable of art forms. A painter, sculptor, or writer could dream of future generations admiring his works, but the art of acting, like singing and the dance, was gone and past retrieving in the moment of creation. A great theatrical performance lived only as long as the memories of those who had seen it. Hannah More, educator, philanthropist, and author, touched on this in 1776 when she wrote in a letter, "I have at last had the entire satisfaction to see Garrick in 'Hamlet.' . . . I pity those who have not. Posterity will never be able to form the slightest idea of his pretensions."[1] Garrick, of course, fully understood the transitory nature of his art. He wrote in the prologue to his play *The Clandestine Marriage*,

> he, who *struts and frets his hour upon the stage*,
> Can scarce extend his fame for half an age,
> Nor pen nor pencil, can the Actor save,
> The art, and artist, share one common grave.

As Hannah More said, later generations may deserve pity for not having seen Garrick act, but we can nevertheless form some idea of his brilliance from what eyewitnesses said about his acting and the effect it had on them. From the accounts we possess, we know that, broadly speaking, his greatness lay in the naturalness of his actions and speech and his ability to rouse his audience's emotions. While other actors concerned themselves primarily with the grave, orbicular, and rotund delivery of poetic lines, Garrick conveyed the drama's inherent sentiments, whether comic or tragic, through a remarkable adaptation of voice, gesture, and facial expression. He played upon his audience much like a great concert virtuoso is able to do with his musical instrument, setting into motion a sympathetic vibration of feelings between the spectator and the character portrayed. "If he was angry, so was you," said a fellow actor; "if he was distressed, so was you; if he was terrified, so was you; if he was merry, so was you; if he was mad, so was you. He was an enchanter, and led you where he pleased."[2]

He seemed to adapt himself flawlessly to whatever role he played. With his clear voice, piercing dark eyes, and pliant features, he seemed, in fact, perfectly adapted to his profession in all aspects but one. That was physical stature. Although sturdily built and well proportioned, he stood only five foot three or four inches high, well below middle size even in the eighteenth century. One critic at the time observed that he was perhaps the shortest actor who ever played the part of a hero.[3] Yet Garrick made as if his size posed no disadvantage either personally or professionally. Makeup, costume, and thick-soled shoes could help create the illusion of a larger man on stage. Off stage he sometimes adopted a gruff, aggressive manner to appear more formidable. Otherwise, he usually avoided the subject of his size and on occasion made light of it. In writing to the dramatist George Colman, a diminutive man himself, Garrick said, "We little Men make nothing of swelling ourselves to a *Hercules* or a *Robinson Crusoe!*"[4] When he first played Romeo at Drury Lane Theater in 1750, the rival house, Covent Garden Theatre, countered by staging the same play with Spranger Barry, a tall, handsome actor with a splendid voice, in the lead role. Although irked by the provocation, Garrick also found humor in the situation, writing the following quatrain:

> Fair Juliet at one house exclaims with a sigh,
> No Romeo is clever that's not six feet high;
> Less ambitiously t'other does Romeo adore,
> Though in size he scarse reaches to five feet and four. [5]

Yet regardless of how serious he considered his one limitation, it produced some incidents that must have been galling. Samuel Foote, for instance, a large man, once planned on bringing out a play at the Haymarket Theatre acted entirely by puppets. A lady of fashion asked him if the puppets were to be life sized. "Oh dear, Madam, no," he said, "not much above the size of Garrick."[6]

On stage he often found that the other actors, and sometimes the leading ladies, towered over him. One evening while acting the role of a suitor in a new play, he exclaimed to his mistress,

> Alas!
> I fear I seem *too little* in your eyes,

whereupon a man in the upper gallery called out, "Why, to be sure you do; it would be very odd if you did not." This set the house in an uproar, and Garrick omitted the lines in the next performance.[7]

He played all Shakespeare's great tragic heroes—Hamlet, Lear, Macbeth, Richard III—but Othello proved to be too much. It was the only Shakespearean tragic role in which his talent could not compensate for his size. It seemed ludicrous that the noble Moor, mighty warrior, and general should stand no more than five foot four and be overshadowed by the other characters. After three performances, Garrick dropped Othello from his repertoire and never resumed it. Another thing that may have helped undermine his confidence was James Quin jeering from the audience at the first night performance. It is said that when Garrick made his entrance in the first act, Quin called out, "Here's Pompey! But where's the tea-kettle and lamp?" *Pompey* was the common term for *black servant*, but Quin referred specifically to the little black boy in the second plate of Hogarth's *Harlot's Progress* who is about to serve tea to Moll Hackabout.[8] Arthur Murphy thought the role not appropriate to Garrick's particular talents anyway. "*Othello* could not be a well-chosen part for a man, who performed wonders with that expressive face," wrote Murphy. "The black complexion disguised his features, and the expression of the mind was wholly lost."[9]

His size also proved a disadvantage in the role of Hotspur. As Thomas Davies pointed out, he simply lacked the necessary bulk. Davies further remarked that Garrick's figure did not assist him in representing the king in *Henry IV, Part 1*, "but the forcible expression of his countenance and his energy of utterance made ample amends for defect of person."[10] Yet aside from the difficulties his short stature presented, the multiplicity of feelings he could excite and the variety of parts he could play were remarkable. Most actors of the day played a specific character type. They built reputations and careers playing the noble patriarch, the London dandy, the country rube, and the like. Due to this typecasting, they performed in either dramas or comedies—seldom both. But Garrick played a wide range of roles from Hamlet, Lear, and Richard III to the vainglorious coxcomb Chamont, the bombastic playwright Bayes, and the lowly tobacconist's assistant Abel Drugger—and he played them equally well. He had a repertoire of ninety-six roles that he could perform on short notice without much preparation or rehearsal, and he made each role, each characterization, unique.[11] "The thing that strikes me above all others," the Reverend Thomas Newton told him, "is that variety in your acting, and your being so totally a different man in Lear from what you are in Richard . . . and in the four parts wherein I have seen you—Richard, Chamont, Bayes, and Lear—I never saw four actors more different from

Garrick between Comedy and Tragedy, after Sir Joshua Reynolds, 1760–1761.
Source: Trustees of the British Museum.

one another than you are from yourself."[12] He played comedy with as much brilliance as he did tragedy, though Johnson actually liked him better in comedy.[13] Sir Joshua Reynolds evidently did as well, for in his famous portrait "Garrick Between Comedy and Tragedy," it is Comedy who succeeds in pulling the actor away as he gestures apologetically to Tragedy.

Among Garrick's most popular comedic roles was that of Bayes in Buckingham's *The Rehearsal.* Bayes was originally intended as a caricature of John Dryden and was traditionally played as a solemn coxcomb of a dramatic poet. But Garrick played Bayes as a flamboyant little garreteer bard and used the character to satirize bad acting and to mimic current actors. "O he was great beyond measure!" said Charles Burney's young daughter Frances, who saw Garrick in the role in April 1772. "I was almost in convulsions with excessive laughter—which he kept me in from the moment he entered, to the End of the Play—never in my life did I see any thing so Entertaining, so ridiculous—so humourous,—so absurd—!"[14] Another of his brilliant comedic characterizations was that of Abel Drugger in Ben Jonson's *The Alchemist.* The part was relatively small, but through his "pantomimical manner of acting" and plenty of stage business, he made it one of the most popular comic roles in his repertoire.

Yet straight drama and tragedy is where his brilliance shown to greatest effect and where he made the most significant contributions to his art. He could express the soft strains of melancholy and sadness like no other actor before him: "At night I went to Drury Lane pit," wrote Boswell in his journal, "and saw the Second Part of *King Henry IV,* where Mr. Garrick in the pathetic scene between the old King and his son drew tears from my eyes."[15] He could sound equally well, and perhaps better, the malevolent depths of a character like Richard III, a role Frances Burney saw him in two months after seeing him as Bayes:

> Garrick was sublimely horrible!—Good Heaven—how he made me shudder whenever he appeared! it is inconceivable, how terribly great he is in this Character. I will never see him so disfigured again—he seemed so truly the monster he performed, that I felt myself glow with indignation every time I saw him. The Applause he met with exceeds all belief of the Absent. I thought, at the End, they would have torn the House down: Our seats shook under us.[16]

James Beattie long remembered seeing Garrick in the role of Macbeth, the effect of which "made me almost throw myself over the front seat of the two-shilling gallery. . . . To be serious, if all actors were like this one, I do not think it would be possible for a person of sensibility to outlive the representation of Hamlet, Lear, or Macbeth."[17]

An acquaintance discovered on visiting him at his lodgings in the Adelphi that he could act Macbeth as well before a friend or two on a Sunday morning as before a full house at Drury Lane:

> After some preliminary conversation, Garrick took up the play; and read several passages with a taste, feeling, and discrimination, *new* even to me, who had seen him so often in this character on the stage. But when he came to the dagger scene, I observed his face instantly assume a mixture of horror, perplexity, and guilt, which I thought it impossible for human nature to *affect*: the glare of his eye was conformable to the range of his features, and he went through the passage in a style totally indescribable.[18]

Another observer told how, at a similar social gathering, a foreigner who understood no English and who was not familiar with *Macbeth* nearly collapsed from horror when Garrick seized the imaginary knife "with the satanic look of a man resolved on murder."[19]

In Act III of the play, during the banquet scene, the murderer enters to inform Macbeth that Banquo has been dispatched. Supposedly during a performance at Drury Lane, Garrick, in the title role, looked at the murderer so intently and said with such conviction, "There's blood upon thy face," that the actor replied, "Is there by G——," instead of "'Tis Banquo's then," thinking, as he said later, he had broken a blood vessel.[20]

It was generally acknowledged, however, that Lear was Garrick's finest dramatic role due to the variety of emotions it allowed him to exhibit. He portrayed Lear as a feeble old man on a crutch—terrible in his wrath, pathetic in his suffering, mad, impotent, and distracted—yet noble. The role allowed Garrick to exhibit the full range of his powers, and the audience might be said to have enjoyed the acute tortures of the experience. Frances Burney wrote, "We had yesterday the—I know not whether to say *pain* or *pleasure*,—of seeing Mr Garrick in the part of Lear. He was exquisitely Great—every idea which I had formed of his talents, although I have ever idolized him, was exceeded——."[21] Three years later, at another performance of *Lear*, both Hannah More and Sir Joshua Reynolds sat in the audience. "It is literally true that my spirits have yet not recovered from the shock they sustained," wrote More nearly a week later. "I called today in Leicester Fields, and Sir Joshua declared it was full three days before he got the better of it."[22]

Garrick's success in roles like Lear was the result of more than just native ability and certain physical attributes. He worked hard at the craft and spent countless hours before the mirror perfecting his facial expressions. He studied not only his lines and character, but also human nature, borrowing from life what he needed to represent the human condition more naturally on stage. He often told company how he came to understand Lear's madness. He knew a man who stood one morning at an upper window of his house dandling his two-year-old daughter, when suddenly she slipped from his hands and fell through the window to her death on the pavement below. The man remained at the window shrieking in horror and grief until neighbors came out to see what had happened and soon returned his daughter's lifeless body to him. He never regained his senses but spent the rest of his life going over the calamity in his mind. He would go to the window happily playing with his imaginary daughter, see her slip from his hands, and then begin screaming in anguish. Later he would sit down and look slowly around as if imploring compassion. Garrick witnessed this scene numerous times, and "there it was," he said, "*that I learned to imitate madness*; I copied nature, and to that owed my success in *King Lear*."[23]

Garrick used to employ this scene as one of his short bravura pieces for the entertainment of guests after dinner. "This writer," said Arthur Murphy, "has often seen him rise in company to give a representation of this unfortunate father. He leaned on the back of a chair, seeming with parental fondness to play with a child, and, after expressing the most heart-felt delight, he suddenly dropped the infant, and instantly broke out in a most violent agony of grief, so tender, so affecting, and pathetic, that every eye in company was moistened with a gush of tears."[24] Denis Diderot, the French philosopher, wrote of Garrick performing the same scene for a group of dinner guests during the actor's visit to Paris in 1751. He picked up a cushion, stood before an open a window, and began caressing and kissing the cushion as though it were an infant child, when suddenly it slipped from his hands and fell through the window. His stunned shock of horror, followed by his cries of agony and despair, so affected the viewers, said Diderot, "that most of them could not bear it and had to leave the room."[25]

On stage in the role of Lear, Garrick moved slowly as if age and wretchedness weighed him down. "He moved his head in the most deliberate manner," recalled Murphy;

> his eyes were fixed, or, if they turned to any one near him, he made a pause, and fixed his look on the person after much delay; his features at the same time telling what he was going to say, before he uttered a word. During the whole time he presented a sight of woe and misery, and a total alienation of mind from every idea, but that of his unkind daughters.[26]

At one point in the play he threw away his crutch, got down on one knee, and, in the words of Tom Davies, made Lear's curse "so terribly affecting to the audience, that, during the utterance of it, they seemed to shrink from it as from a blast of lightning."[27] The actor John O'Keeffe commented on the emotional energy of Garrick's Lear and his effective use of stage business:

> His saying, in the bitterness of his anger, "I will do such things—what they are, I know not," and his sudden recollection of his own want of power, were so pitiable as to touch the heart of every spectator. The simplicity of his saying, "Be these tears wet?—yes, faith," putting his finger to the cheek of Cordelia, and then looking at his finger, was exquisite.[28]

Garrick was a perfectionist. Every character he played he had thoroughly studied—every look, gesture, movement, and inflection of voice carefully weighed and considered. He played tragic and comic characters equally well, from King Lear to Abel Drugger, but his most enduring part, one that many thought less convincing than those he exhibited on stage, was his portrayal of David Garrick.

Off stage as well as on, he was a little dynamo, always lively and constantly on the move. All who knew him attested to his vitality, good humor, and gregariousness. He seemed always eager for a bit of fun, always ready for a prank. One day as he walked in the Strand with Messenger Monsey, a physician, he noticed a man striding briskly ahead humming a tune. He said to Monsey, "I'll get a crowd around that man before he reaches Temple Bar." As he passed the man, he turned his piercing gaze on him, and the man's chipper manner suddenly vanished. Hurrying further down the street, Garrick paused at an apple stall, and as the man approached, he gave him another penetrating stare. "The man began to look if there was anything strange about him that attracted the gentleman's notice," said John Taylor, who relates the story, "and, as Garrick repeated the same experiment, turned himself in all directions, and pulled off his wig, to see if anything ridiculous was attached to him." His odd behavior quickly drew attention, and just as Garrick promised, the man had a crowd around him before he reached Temple Bar.[29]

Another time Monsey came to visit Garrick at his rooms in the Adelphi shortly before a performance of *King Lear*. He found the actor in bed with the covers pulled up under his chin and his night cap on, groaning in discomfort and looking ill. Monsey asked if the play was to be changed. Garrick said no—"Dagger" Marr knew the part of Lear perfectly, had studied Garrick's mannerisms, and, as he resembled Garrick in features and was an excellent mimic, would take his place that evening, and the audience wouldn't know the difference. Monsey protested that this was a preposterous and dangerous trifling with the public's trust, but Garrick moaned that he was too sick to argue. He said he must be left alone to sleep but asked Monsey to attend the play and return later with a report of Marr's success. As soon as Monsey left, Garrick jumped up fully dressed and hurried to the theater to complete his costume and makeup. The play soon began, and Monsey was struck by the astonishing resemblance of Marr to Garrick. But as the audience seemed satisfied that it really was Garrick before them, Monsey began to suspect he had been duped. Following the play, he rushed back to the Adelphi only to find Garrick just as he had left him, sick in bed with his night cap on. Garrick's friends who were privy to the joke, and who had witnessed Monsey's perplexity at the theater, thought it an excellent prank, as Monsey did himself when he learned the particulars the following morning.[30]

Frances Burney (whom friends and family members always called Fanny) saw Garrick often at her house during the time that her father worked on his *History of Music* and was well acquainted with his playfulness. Like Mrs. Thrale, she was struck by his brilliant dark eyes. "I never saw in my life," she said, "such brilliant, piercing Eyes as his are—in looking at him, when I have chanced to meet them, I have really not been able to bear their lustre." But it was his effusive spirits that intrigued her most. All the Burney children loved it when Garrick paid one of his morning calls.[31] He would sometimes chase them, screaming and laughing, up the stairs, banging his stick on the steps as if he intended to cane them. One morning he came in when Dr. Burney was out and the four children were at breakfast. "Dick ran to him as the Door was opened—" wrote Fanny in her diary. "'What! my bright Eyed Beauty![']' cried he—& then flinging himself back in a Theatric posture—'& here ye all are—one—two—three—four—Beauties all—' He then came in, & with a great deal of humour, played with Dick—How many pities that he has no Children, for he is extremely, nay passionately fond of them."[32]

And children were fond of him. Richard Cumberland tells how Garrick would create disorder in the ranks of his six small children, normally quiet and well-behaved, by acting turkey cocks and peacocks to their great amusement and their mother's vexation.[33] He also used to entertain children by placing himself before a wall and pretending to be a wooden puppet operated by wires. Lætitia-Matilda Hawkins remembered the many times when she was a girl that Garrick called on her father at Twickenham. "He might be sitting at a table indoors at our house, but if he saw my brothers on the lawn he would dash off like an arrow from a bow on a spirited chase after them round the garden."[34] One day a group of adults missed Garrick from their midst and later found him in the backyard doing his turkey cock imitations for a little black boy who was convulsed with laughter and crying out, "Massa Garrick, [you] do so make me laugh: I shall die with laughing."[35] But Garrick could suit his playfulness to the company he was in, and adults loved his sportive repartee and funloving exuberance as much as the children. In his journals Boswell often refers to him as "pleasant as usual," and Johnson several times praised his conviviality and sprightly conversation. Garrick's continual stream of drollery, in fact, elevated Johnson to such unusually high spirits in company that he often joined in the good-humored banter. In strictly masculine company, Garrick's humor would at times grow pretty salty, and Arthur Murphy said that with his infectious manner, Garrick could lead Johnson into speaking the plainest bawdy.[36]

On one of his morning calls at the Burney home, Garrick asked Charles Burney, hard at work on his history of music, what books he still kept that Garrick had loaned him. Burney said that he had the ten volumes of the French Academy. "And what others?" asked Garrick.

"I don't know. Do you, Fanny?"

"O—what—" said Garrick, in mock agitation, "I suppose you don't chuse to know of any others?—" Then springing from his chair he began bowing and scraping around the room in a low, formal, obsequious manner, saying, "O very well!—pray Sir make free with me!—pray keep them, if you chuse it. . . . But pray, Doctor, when shall we have the History out? Do let me know in Time, that I may prepare to Blow the Trumpet of Fame—." He then put his walking stick to his lips, assumed the voice and stance of a raree showman, and cried, "Here is the only true History—Gentlemen, please to Buy—please to Buy—Gad, Sir, I shall Blow it in the very Ear of yon scurvy magistrate," meaning Sir John Hawkins, who was then writing his own history of music.[37]

And so flowed his irrepressible banter and cheer. Garrick loved life thoroughly and knew how to enjoy it. He wrote of himself, "I was born with quick lively Spirits. . . . I cannot quit *Peck & Booze*—What's Life without Sack & Sugar! my lips were made to be lick'd, & if the Devil appears to me in the Shape of Turbot & Claret . . . I laugh & Eat till my Navel rosebud is as full blown as a Sun flower."[38] There were few things, apart from the theater, that he loved more than good food and pleasant company. Both Johnson and Reynolds agreed that as great as he was on stage, he was equal if not superior at the table.[39] One morning he dropped by to see Boswell, and finding him not yet up, he left word that "Rantum Scantum" had called. He later returned, calling out as he entered the room, "Here's Rantum Scantum."[40] Such was the image he strove to convey—Rantum Scantum, a combination of disorder and nonsense. Yet despite the boyish pranks, the entertaining banter, and the abundance of good humor and cheer, there seemed to lurk in the background something slightly artificial. No one questioned the inherent exuberance of the man, but once he had put off the costume and grease paint, something a trifle stagy, theatrical, and histrionic remained. Those who detected this thought the cause not hard to find.

Garrick needed an audience. To gain attention, he did not resort to the low buffoonery and antics that characterized Goldsmith's actions but relied more on his wit and conviviality seasoned with a little tomfoolery. Yet he sometimes overdid it. This inspired numerous jests such as Samuel Foote's epigram:

> Garrick's the greatest actor of the age;
> For Garrick acts both on and off the stage.[41]

George Colman the younger, whose father worked closely with Garrick for many years, remarked that despite his superior ability to portray human nature on stage, "it is to be lamented that he outraged her in one character,—and that was his own;—he over-acted the part of Garrick."[42]

Sir Joshua Reynolds complained that he spoiled every company he went into by striving to be the center of attention. Reynolds felt that social gatherings should foster relaxed conversation and good fellowship. Garrick, however, always appeared to have prepared himself as if he was to act a principal part at every social event he attended.[43] In addition, he was so calculating that he often contrived to have himself called away early from a dinner that he might leave his audience yearning for more of his wit and raillery. Even his own dinner parties seemed carefully plotted and choreographed. One such gathering at his country villa included Reynolds, Topham Beauclerk, Edmund Burke, statesman Charles James Fox, historian Edward Gibbon, and playwright Richard Brinsley Sheridan. Immediately following dinner, before his guests had time to finish their wine, Garrick took them out to his spacious lawn where, he said, they would find amusement. The amusement consisted of an old man and a young man running back and forth between two baskets filled with stones, the object being to see who could empty his basket first. Garrick expected his guests to bet on the outcome, but "being dragged from table the instant dinner had been finished," said Reynolds, "no interest whatever was expressed. . . . If Garrick had not laid these plots for merriment, but let conversation taken its common course, all would have gone well. Such men . . . could not have passed a dull day."[44]

His closest friends sometimes wondered if they ever saw the real David Garrick or only a succession of carefully rehearsed performances. Many attributed his artificiality to excessive vanity. He would occasionally irritate acquaintances with his fondness for "lolling with a Lord in his chariot" and for a propensity to drop names. "Well now, Hay," he said to a group of his actors at Drury Lane Theatre, "are you all well: but I can't stay now at your rehearsal, for my Lord Edgcomb is waiting in the carriage for me."[45]

Boswell got annoyed one morning when he called on Garrick at his rooms in the Adelphi and "found him like a little minister of state, standing in the middle of a room, hurried and surrounded with several people . . . talking vainly of his being appointed the executor of a clergyman by 'that great man, Lord Camden.'"[46] Boswell grew irritated another morning when he called on Garrick and found him standing with a dish of tea at a little table with breakfast on it. Without so much as a simple greeting, but with "his instantaneous attitudinal position and smartness," Garrick declared, "I have not a minute to stop." He seemed to expect Boswell to make some fawning or courting remarks about how unlucky he was not to have the great man's attention for a few minutes. Instead, "strutting up close to the little man and (I think) putting my hands on his shoulders, and looking with his own tragi-comic, dubious cast, [I said,] 'Don't give yourself airs.'"[47]

Joseph Baretti, in discussing Garrick's vanity with several others, wondered that Garrick was not vainer, considering his fame. Goldsmith asked how he could be *vainer* unless he actually wore cap and bells to call attention to himself. George Colman remarked that it was not a question of him being vainer than others, but only that he must have a sip every quarter of an hour.[48] Johnson appeared to share Baretti's view. One evening Boswell made a comment about "Garrick's assuming the great man," and Johnson disagreed. He said that Garrick bore his good fortune modestly. Other famous men heard their applause from a distance. "But Garrick had it dashed in his face, sounded in his ear, went home every night with the applause of a thousand in his cranium. . . . Sir, if all this had happened to me, I should have had a couple of fellows with poles walking before me to knock everybody down that stood in the way. Consider if all this had happened to Cibber or Quin; they had have jumped over the moon. Yet Garrick speaks to us (smiling)."[49]

In addition to artificiality and vanity, Garrick was sometimes attacked for being greedy and tightfisted. He could spend great sums on a country house or a fine painting, but his early poverty had taught him the price of a candle, and he never lost the habit of holding on to his loose change. Wags like Foote, a notorious spendthrift, seldom missed a chance to ridicule Garrick's avarice. Foote is said to have placed a bust of Garrick on top of his bureau, saying to it, "There you dog take as much Care of my Money as of your own." Arthur Murphy, who was present, expressed mock surprise that Foote would allow Garrick so near his cash. "Why don't you see," said Foote, "that the Rascal has got no hands."[50] But the actors at Drury Lane Theatre knew better than anyone how stingy Garrick could be. He paid his performers as little as possible. Lead players could usually negotiate higher salaries by threatening to move to another company, but lesser performers had to take whatever pittance Garrick allowed them, which was usually not enough to live on. It was not that Garrick lacked the resources—he personally took in thousands of pounds a year—but it was a matter of business, and in matters of business Garrick was always stinting. Some of the greatest dissentions in the company arose over inadequate pay. For those who had the temerity to bring up the matter of salary, Garrick would assume a dignified manner, fix them with his piercing black eyes, and browbeat them into submission.

Tate Wilkinson recounts in his *Memoirs* numerous examples of Garrick's magisterial ways and niggardly treatment of underlings. In one incident, Garrick sent Wilkinson, a devastating mimic, to Ireland hoping that he would foment trouble among some rival actors. When Wilkinson returned, not having created any problems, knowing that to do so would injure his own career, he went to collect his usual weekly salary, a matter of twenty-five shillings or so. The treasurer would not allow it and told Wilkinson he would have to see the manager. Wilkinson then confronted Garrick, who fixed him with his withering gaze and claimed that he had more than paid Wilkinson's salary by letting him visit Ireland. Arthur Murphy, who later wrote a flattering biography of Garrick, shared Wilkinson's resentment of the manager's sometimes miserly and shifty business practices. Like Wilkinson, Murphy disliked the man even as he admired the actor. He said privately many times, "Off the stage he was a little sneaking rascal, but on the stage, oh, my great God!"[51]

Johnson knew nothing of Garrick's business practices but admitted that Garrick was stinting in private life, "not so much from avarice, as from impotence to spend his money. He cannot find in his heart to pour out a bottle of wine; but he would not much care if it should sour."[52] On the other hand, Johnson often said that Garrick gave away more money to charities and to people in distress than any man in England. He explained that Garrick entered society with a great hunger for money. This was due to his being raised in a family that had difficulty making ends meet. "But when he had got money," said Johnson, "he was liberal."[53] Whenever Johnson solicited money of friends for a worthy cause, it was always Garrick who gave most.

Despite all the speculation as to the nature and extent of Garrick's vanity and avarice, it still remained difficult to pin down his real character. Not even those closest to him knew what really lay beneath the surface. His social and professional talents seemed to conceal, rather than reveal, the inner man. Garrick's conversation, for instance, while more delightful and entertaining than most, discovered no profundity of thought or feeling. As Johnson observed,

"Garrick's conversation is gay and grotesque. It is a dish of all sorts, but all good things. There is no solid meat in it. There is want of sentiment."[54] One may search Garrick's letters from beginning to end and find no deeply held religious convictions or philosophy of life. The letters are all pleasantry or business. His dramatic prologues and epilogues show that he possessed uncommon literary ability, yet these were professional productions. He kept no soul-searching diary as did Johnson and Boswell, composed no prayers or sermons or meditations—nothing, in fact, introspective. From his letters one gets the impression that, aside from the agitation of business, he maintained the same good-natured, convivial demeanor in his closet that he exhibited in society, and the suspicion arises that perhaps Garrick was only shoal water after all. As Boswell said, "Garrick was pure gold, only beat out to thin leaf."[55] There seems to have been no bedrock to Garrick, no fixed standards or principles. The inner Garrick was as shifting and pliable as his face. "I never knew a man," said Johnson, "of whom it could be said with less certainty today what he will do tomorrow than Garrick."[56]

Boswell thought that Garrick being an actor had much to do with his lack of a firm center, for "the greater degree a man is accustomed to assume of artificial feeling, the more probability is there that he has no character of his own on which we can depend."[57] It should be remembered, however, that Garrick was a fundamentally contented man, while Johnson and Boswell were not. What at first may look like shallow water from the surface may actually be an absence of agitation beneath. We have so strong a sense of the deep and sometimes troubled waters of Johnson and Boswell due to the monsters that dwelled there. But with greater opportunities for self-fulfillment, Garrick did not have to wrestle with such demons. He was a man who lived fully in the present, and who thoroughly enjoyed life.

Johnson, by contrast, often tormented himself with recriminations about his own idleness, sometimes hovering on the brink of despair and hoping for a better, more productive future. The struggle between hope and despair became one of the leitmotifs of his life. Boswell, too, in struggling with his personal identity, knew the depths of despair. During feverish rounds of activity, punctuated by long periods of depression, he jotted endless notes to himself on how to behave and wrote copiously about his insecurity and fears. Garrick indulged in none of these things. A man of regular and sober habits, he went to bed betimes and awoke with a purpose to his day. He was a man in control of himself and his own destiny—things that Johnson and Boswell frequently were not.

NOTES

1. William Roberts, *Memoirs of the Life and Correspondence of Mrs. Hannah More*, 4 vols. (London, 1834), 1:88.

2. Old Comedian, *Life and Death of Garrick*, 13.

3. Hill, *The Actor*, 150. German scientist Georg Christoph Lichtenberg, on a visit to London in 1775, described Garrick as strong and muscular: "His shapely legs become gradually thinner from the powerful thighs downwards, until they end in the neatest foot you can imagine; in the same way his large arms taper into a little hand. How imposing the effect of this must be you can well imagine. But this strength is not merely illusory. He is really strong and amazingly dexterous and nimble. In the scene in *The Alchemist* where he boxes, he runs about and skips from one neat leg to the other with such admirable lightness that one would dare swear that he was floating in the air" (*Lichtenberg's Visits to England as Described in His Letters and Diaries*, translated and annotated by Margaret L. Mare and W. H. Quarrell [New York: Benjamin Blom, 1969], 7).

4. Garrick, *Letters*, 1031. "Mr. Garrick, on account of his deficiency of stature, used to wear cork soals, which gave him an *inch* in height" (Old Comedian, *Life and Death of Garrick*, 59).

5. John Taylor, *Records of My Life*, 2 vols. (London, 1832), 1:327.

6. Cooke, *Memoirs of Foote*, 2:58.

7. Ibid., 2:180.

8. See Oman, *David Garrick*, 75; Parsons, *Garrick and His Circle*, 76; Fitzgerald, *Life of Garrick*, 1:153; Murphy, *Life of Garrick*, 1:105.

9. Murphy, *Life of Garrick*, 1:106.

10. Thomas Davies, *Dramatic Micellanies [sic]: Consisting of Critical Observations on Several Plays of Shakespeare*, 3 vols. (London, 1784), 1:225 and 320.

11. Benedetti, *David Garrick and the Birth of Modern Theatre*, 146.

12. Hedgcock, *A Cosmopolitan Actor*, 39.

13. Boswell, *Life*, 4:243.

14. Frances Burney, *The Early Journals and Letters of Fanny Burney*, ed. Lars Troide, Stewart J. Cooke, and Betty Rizzo, 5 vols. (Montreal: McGill-Queens University Press, 1988–2012), 1:200.

15. Boswell, *London Journal*, 134.

16. Burney, *Early Journals*, 1:225.

17. Forbes, *An Account of the Life and Writings of James Beattie*, 1:210.

18. Cooke, *Memoirs of Foote*, 2:209.

19. Joseph, *The Tragic Actor*, 128.

20. Taylor, *Records of My Life*, 1:347.

21. Burney, *Early Journals*, 1:242.

22. Roberts, *Memoirs*, 1:90.

23. Murphy, *Life of Garrick*, 1:30.

24. Ibid., 1:28–30.

25. Quoted in Benedetti, *David Garrick and the Birth of Modern Theatre*, 188.

26. Murphy, *Life of Garrick*, 1:27–28.

27. Davies, *Dramatic Micellanies*, 2:280.

28. O'Keefe, *Recollections*, 1:81–82.

29. Taylor, *Records of My Life*, 1:344–45.

30. Ibid., 2:4–5.

31. Burney, *Early Journals*, 1:151 and 2:95.

32. Ibid., 1:183–84.

33. Cumberland, *Memoirs*, 1:332–33.

34. Lætitia-Matilda Hawkins, *Gossip About Dr. Johnson and Others, Being Chapters from the Memoirs of Miss Lætitia-Matilda Hawkins* (London: Eveleigh Nash and Grayson, 1926), 40.

35. Cumberland, *Memoirs*, 1:339.

36. Boswell, *Ominous Years*, 114. Tate Wilkinson gives an example of Garrick's "low stuff and ribaldry." One day, as Garrick rehearsed Wilkinson in a difficult part and Wilkinson did not speak his lines as well as he should, Garrick exclaimed, "Why hey now, Wilkinson! why this is all shittle-come-sh—te, and my a—e in a bandbox.---Here now was I in eager expectation of a t—d as thick as my wrist, and as long as my arm, and d—n it it is all squitter, S::::r." After relating this anecdote, Wilkinson adds, "The delicate reader will skip this leaf" (Wilkinson, *Memoirs*, 2:131).

37. Burney, *Early Journals*, 2:95–96.

38. Garrick, *Letters*, 818 and 739.

39. Boswell, *Life*, 4:243; Reynolds, *Portraits*, 97.

40. Boswell, *Boswell for the Defence*, 133.

41. Ibid., 80.

42. Colman, *Random Records*, 1:120–21.

43. Reynolds, *Portraits*, 97–98.

44. James Prior, *Life of Edmond Malone, Editor of Shakspeare. With Selections from His Manuscript Anecdotes* (London, 1860), 416–17.

45. Wilkinson, *Wandering Patentee*, 2:50–51.

46. Boswell, *Boswell for the Defence*, 81.

47. Boswell, *Boswell in Extremes*, 307.

48. Boswell, *Boswell: In Search of a Wife*, 308; Boswell, *The Correspondence of James Boswell with David Garrick, Edmund Burke, and Edmond Malone*, ed. George M. Kahrl et al. (London: Heinemann, 1986), 11–12.

49. Boswell, *Boswell in Extremes*, 262.

50. Piozzi, *Thraliana*, 152.

51. Taylor, *Records of My Life*, 1:194.

52. Boswell, *Life*, 3:40.

53. James Boswell, *Boswell: Laird of Auchinleck, 1778–1782*, ed. Joseph W. Reed and Frederick A. Pottle (New York: McGraw-Hill, 1977), 98.

54. Boswell, *Ominous Years*, 292.

55. Boswell, *Laird of Auchinleck*, 98.

56. Boswell, *Boswell in Extremes*, 263.

57. Boswell, *Correspondence of Boswell with Garrick, Burke, and Malone*, 15.

Chapter Seven

Retaliation

Sir Joshua Reynolds, like Garrick, was a man of regular habits. Also like Garrick, he possessed a strong determination to excel in his profession and had acquired a sizable fortune doing what he loved to do most. His passionate love for painting, however, was curiously offset by his calm demeanor. The assertiveness with which he wielded his brush in the studio stood in sharp contrast to the ease with which he carried himself in society.

His equanimity became proverbial. It so clearly marked his personality that someone usually mentioned it whenever his name arose in conversation. Johnson said of him, "Sir Joshua Reynolds is the same all year the round."[1] Boswell, when he dedicated his *Life of Johnson* to Reynolds, listed chief among his qualities "Your equal and placid temper, your variety of conversation, your true politeness, by which you are so amiable in private society, and that enlarged hospitality which has long made your house a common centre of union for the great, the accomplished, the learned, and the ingenious." And Goldsmith, when he later skewered some of his acquaintances in a satirical poem comprised of mock epitaphs, spoke only in positive terms of Reynolds:

> Here Reynolds is laid, and to tell you my mind,
> He has not left a better or wiser behind;
> His pencil was striking, resistless, and grand,
> His manners were gentle, complying, and bland;
> Still born to improve us in every part,
> His pencil our faces, his manners our heart:
> To coxcombs averse, yet most civilly steering,
> When they judged without skill he was still hard of hearing:
> When they talk'd of their Ralphaels, Corregios, and stuff,
> He shifted his trumpet, and only took snuff.

Although his even temper and amiable disposition came naturally to him, he understood that natural gifts must still be cultivated, so throughout life he directed his mind toward improving himself as an artist and strengthening his powers of self-command. While still young, he wrote down maxims to guide the development of his personality. Among them were the following:

Humility is not to despise any thing, especially mankind.
The great principle of being happy in this world is not to regard or be affected with small things.
Magnanimity is not to be disturbed at any thing.[2]

Sounding a great deal like the ancient Roman philosopher Marcus Aurelius, he always maintained that the art of life consisted of not getting upset over trifles, and he told James Northcote, his pupil and assistant, "We should look at the bottom of the account, not at each individual item in it, and see how the balance stands at the end of the year. We should be satisfied if the path of life is clear before us, and not fret at the straws or pebbles that lie in our way."[3]

Northcote said that in his approach to life and in his dealings with other people, Reynolds possessed a "native dignity."[4] He appeared natural and easy in whatever company he found himself, whether common or genteel. In the five years that he worked with him, Northcote never heard Reynolds utter the words "your lordship" or "your ladyship,"

nor did he ever say *Sir* in speaking to any one but Dr. Johnson; and when he did not hear distinctly what the latter said (which often happened) he would then say "Sir?" that he might repeat it. He was in this respect like a Quaker, not from any scruples or affectation of independence, but possibly from some awkwardness and confusion in addressing the variety of characters he met with.[5]

Although easy and affable, Reynolds did not radiate much personal warmth. He was created more to be respected than loved, fashioned more to please than to stir warm feelings of attachment. He said of himself, "I never was . . . a great professor of love and affection."[6] He remained a bachelor all his life, too devoted to his art to make a passionate beau or attentive husband. There is no reason to think, however, that he was indifferent to feminine charms or, as some said, that he had become so used to looking on the greatest beauties of the age in his capacity as painter that women in general left him unaffected. Rumors circulated that he had affairs with some of his sitters, and we know that he became infatuated with several women, including his fellow Royal Academician, the attractive Angelica Kauffmann. We also know that he was very much taken with Mrs. Wymondesold, a rich widow with expressive eyes and dimpled cheeks.[7] But Reynolds confided to Boswell that he would never marry, for every woman he had ever liked eventually grew indifferent to him, so that he was glad he had not married her. He saw no reason why it would not be the same with any other woman.[8]

Yet beneath the placid exterior burned the steady, intense flame of the artist. His outwardly complacent manner concealed a deeply passionate and single-minded ambition to be the foremost painter in England. He acknowledged that his accomplishments in art were not so much an exercise of native genius as an exertion of will. He did not believe that inspiration counted for much in painting anyway, or in any other worthwhile endeavor for that matter. He thought that inspiration and spontaneity often led the artist into false paths. True genius lay in dedication, commitment, and a steady application to one's work. He maintained that "all refined knowledge is gradually obtained, and that by study and exertion alone every excellence of whatever kind might be acquired."[9] In his *Discourses*, delivered annually to students of the Royal Academy, he stressed that "Nothing is denied to well-directed labour; nothing is to be obtained without it." He often reiterated, "Excellence is never granted to man, but as the reward of labour."[10]

His own exertion was remarkable. He sometimes received fifteen to twenty sitters in a month. One year his sitters numbered 150. When he put down his brushes for the last time in 1789, he had produced what is thought to be far more than two thousand paintings. He claimed to have covered more canvas than any painter before him. So persevering was he that he seldom ventured from London, for he said that if he went on a three-day journey, it so unsettled his mind that once he returned, he was another three days in recovering his train of thinking.[11] For months on end he did not leave his house between the hours of nine and three or four but confined himself to his octagonal painting room. He advised his fellow painter James Barry, "Whoever is resolved to excel in painting, or indeed any other art, must bring all his mind to bear upon that one object, from the moment he rises till he goes to bed."[12] He admonished Northcote that "the pupil in art, who looks for the Sunday with pleasure as an idle day, will never make a painter."[13]

The ambition that fueled this tremendous activity developed early. When he was only sixteen, his father could not decide whether to make him an apothecary or let him develop his artistic talents. Reynolds said later that if he had become an apothecary, he would have felt the same determination to be the most eminent physician of his age that he now had to be the most eminent painter.[14] He told Northcote that for a man to attain eminence in his profession, whatever that profession might be, he must focus his entire attention on that alone.[15] "Indeed it was ever his decided opinion," said Northcote, "that the superiority attainable in any pursuit whatever does not originate in an innate propensity of the mind to that pursuit in particular, but depends on

the general strength of the intellect, and on the intense and constant application of that strength to a specific purpose."[16] Reynolds declared more than
once that he labored with his brush as hard as any mechanic worked at his
trade for bread.[17] Yet his labor was not actuated by any sense of grim duty or
puritanical work ethic; it brought him the greatest pleasure possible. "While I
am doing this," he declared, "I am the happiest creature alive."[18]

He was nevertheless aware of the professional advantages to be gained in
carefully maintaining an outwardly gentle and amiable disposition. It would
not do to antagonize potential clients as William Hogarth sometimes did with
his outspoken and abrasive personality. "A painter should sew up his mouth,"
Reynolds would say.[19] Once when Goldsmith in his careless fashion said
something indiscreet, Reynolds remarked, "What a fool he is thus to commit
himself, when he has so much more cause to be careful of his reputation than
I have of mine!"[20]

With a gentle and quiet purposefulness, Reynolds built up a vast number
of acquaintances over the years. Most were politicians (both Whig and Tory),
literary figures, and people of quality. They served two distinct functions:
they made a ready pool of prospective clients, and they helped to expand his
knowledge of the world. He deplored the man who was only a painter, yet he
had little time to devote to study, so he combined social pleasure and edifica-
tion by conversing in the evenings with eminent people in various fields. Sig-
nificantly, none of his friends were painters, for painters were associates and
could not be expected to further his professional or educational interests.

Others of the Johnson circle respected his artistic achievements and his con-
geniality. Johnson particularly admired his character, and he demonstrated his
regard in several ways. He often praised Reynolds to others, as when he once
said, just as Reynolds had left the room, "There goes a man not to be spoiled
by prosperity."[21] Johnson also spared him the affectionate but slightly condescending nicknames he had for others of the circle, such as Bozzy, Goldy,
Lanky, Davy, and Beau. It was always "Sir Joshua" or simply "Reynolds."
The obvious nickname "Renny" he gave to Reynolds's sister Frances. And although Johnson occasionally jostled Reynolds in the give and take of debate,
he seldom tossed and gored him as he sometimes did the others.

Boswell also greatly admired Reynolds and counted himself fortunate in
being numbered among his friends. "I am very lucky in my intimacy with
this eminent man," he said. "It is truly enviable."[22] Yet he did not stand in
awe of Reynolds's artistic genius as he did Johnson's intellectual powers or
Garrick's theatrical fame. Reynolds was too open and guileless for that. Boswell found Reynolds easy and comfortable to be around and retained a just
appreciation for his perseverance and stability, qualities that Boswell lacked
himself. "Rose restless," Boswell wrote in his journal. "Breakfasted with Sir
Joshua. Envied his activity and placid disposition."[23]

Yet of the entire Johnson circle, indeed of all the people whom Reynolds knew on every level of society, Oliver Goldsmith became his dearest friend. On the surface the two seemed total opposites: Reynolds calm, deliberate, stable; Goldsmith excitable, impulsive, unpredictable. Nevertheless, Reynolds was the only one to whom Goldsmith consistently began his letters "My Dear Friend." In dedicating his poem "The Deserted Village" to Reynolds, Goldsmith wrote with his characteristically simple elegance,

> I must be indulged at present in following my affections. The only dedication I ever made was to my brother, because I loved him better than most other men. He is since dead. Permit me to inscribe this Poem to you. . . . I am, Dear Sir, Your sincere friend, and ardent admirer, Oliver Goldsmith.

Goldsmith first made himself known as an author in December 1764 with publication of "The Traveller," a poem based on his earlier travels on the Continent. From there his reputation grew with the novel *The Vicar of Wakefield* in 1766, the play *The Good-Natured Man* in 1768, "The Deserted Village" in 1770, and various other works of history, biography, criticism, and popular science.

At a time in England when many prose writers embraced turgidity, sounding phrases, elaborate parallel structure, and the majestic rise and fall of carefully modulated periodic sentences and studied elegance, Goldsmith wrote in a familiar and even colloquial style. His sentences echoed the words and patterns of everyday speech. The elegance of his style derived from its brevity, simplicity, and aptness of expression. The writing seemed natural and spontaneous rather than deliberate and literary. Johnson remarked, "Is there a man, Sir, now who can pen an essay with such ease and elegance as Goldsmith?"[24]

He was not a deep or systematic thinker. He lacked the perspicuity of Johnson, yet conveyed a sense of good humor, kindliness, and sympathy that readers found attractive. He began *The Life of Nash* with the sentence, "History owes its excellence more to the writer's manner than the materials of which it is composed," and this is where Goldsmith excelled—in the *manner* of his relating what he had to say. He took his materials from his immediate experience and from books. Given his unsettled notions and irregular education, he could find little stored in his own mind. As Johnson remarked, Goldsmith "was a man, who, whatever he wrote, did it better than any other man could do. . . . He had, indeed, been at no pains to fill his mind with knowledge. He transplanted it from one place to another; and it did not settle in his mind; so he could not tell what was in his own books."[25]

He followed no specific principles of composition, but relied on what seemed appropriate to him at the time. He proclaimed himself, in fact, an enemy to rules, for they only gave people something to talk about without aiding the writer in his work. Reynolds said that no man wrote less from rules and more from his own feelings than Goldsmith. Yet Reynolds, who spent a good deal of thought formulating rules to govern his own art, did not mean that Goldsmith, especially as a poet, wrote without deliberation and care. "I mean only that he governed himself by an internal feeling of the right rather than by any written rules of art. He judged, for instance, by his ear, whether the verse was musical, without caring or perhaps knowing whether it would bear examination by the rules of the *prosodia.*" Fortunately, said Reynolds, Goldsmith possessed an excellent ear and excellent judgment: "He felt with great exactness, far above what words can teach, the propriety in composition, how one sentiment breeds another in the mind. . . . In short, he felt by a kind of instinct or intuition all those nice discriminations which to grosser minds appear to have no difference. This instinct is real genius if anything can be so called."[26]

When Goldsmith had anything to write that demanded serious application, he often went into the country for two or three months. His favorite place was an attractive cottage belonging to a Farmer Selby six miles or so from town on the Edgeware Road. The cottage had previously been used as a country retreat by a wealthy London shoemaker, so Goldsmith called it the Shoemaker's Paradise. Here he could work undisturbed by city distractions. Having been raised in rural surroundings, he found the country, unlike others of the Johnson circle, congenial to his temperament. While Johnson thought a tavern chair the throne of human felicity, while Boswell felt imprisoned in a rustic setting, and while Reynolds found his landscapes in the human face, Goldsmith loved walking in the country and puttering for hours in a garden. Once during a stay at Lord Clare's in the country, he designed and built for his lordship an icehouse and a hothouse. He offered to build an icehouse for his friend Joseph Cradock, telling him that he had built two others, and that Cradock's should be perfect and a model for the whole county.[27] Beauclerk wrote a letter to the Irish nobleman Lord Charlemont, urging him to return to London, where he spent much of his time, and threatening that if he did not do so, he would send the Club over to Ireland to live with him and that would drive him back: "Johnson shall spoil your books, Goldsmith pull your flowers, and Boswell talk to you."[28]

Goldsmith wrote prose easily. He seldom had to recopy what he first set down, writing on sheets of paper in a fair hand and leaving wide spaces between the lines for minor revisions and interlineations. Poetry required more care. It took time to focus the sentiments and polish the verse. He usually wrote out his ideas in prose as they occurred to him and then carefully worked them into poetry. "The Deserted Village" took him two years to finish. Whether working on a poem, an essay, or a book, he would jot down ideas or lines of verse on anything that was handy. On his walks in the country he carried paper and pencil to take down notes, and would later, at his desk, develop the ideas or refine the language to suit his ear. While working on *She Stoops to Conquer*, he wrote to Bennet Langton, "Since I had the pleasure of seeing you last I have been almost wholly in the country at a farmer's house quite alone trying to write a Comedy. . . . There have I been strolling about the hedges studying jests with a most tragical countenance."[29] He later began work on a book of natural history. Having lost his Shoemaker's Paradise cottage at Farmer Selby's, he took another place in the same area, and he brought with him two post-chaises loaded with books to furnish information.

"Goldsmith, Sir, will give us a very fine book upon the subject," Johnson said when he learned of the project, "but if he can distinguish a cow from a horse, that, I believe, may be the extent of his knowledge of natural history."[30] But despite Goldsmith's ignorance, Johnson thought his plain narrative would make the work "as entertaining as a Persian Tale."[31]

Boswell and another man attempted to visit Goldsmith shortly after he took up his new country residence: "He was not at home; but having a curiosity to see his apartment, we went in and found curious scraps of descriptions of animals, scrawled upon the walls with a black lead pencil."[32] The finished book contained inevitable errors, such as the statement that cows shed their horns, but it combined useful information with personal observations, all of it told in Goldsmith's easy style, so that the *History of the Earth, and Animated Nature* turned out to be a readable and popular survey of natural science.

Along with his growing reputation as an author came increased wealth. Even though his 1768 play *The Good-Natured Man* had not been the great success he hoped, it still brought him £500. With this and another £100 for works he compiled, he left his rented London rooms and bought rooms at No. 2 Brick Court, Inner Temple, for £400. He furnished his new place with bookshelves, Wilton carpets, chairs, blue curtains, mahogany sofas upholstered in blue, chimney glasses, Pembroke tables, and other furniture he thought suitable for a man of genteel independence.[33] Five years later he would take in about £800 for his second play, *She Stoops to Conquer*.

His second comedy opened at Covent Garden Theatre on March 15, 1773, and ran for twelve nights before the theater closed for the season. The play then opened at the Haymarket Theatre during the summer and was revived at

Covent Garden for Christmas. During its opening run, newspapers printed a number of laudatory verses and articles praising the author and the play. *She Stoops to Conquer* became a stock piece throughout the eighteenth century and has been in the active theatrical repertoire ever since. Said Johnson, "I know of no comedy for many years that has so much exhilarated an audience, that has answered so much the great end of comedy—making an audience merry."[34]

Despite the play's success, some rival factions and malicious wits published verses and articles attacking Goldsmith's "laughing" style of comedy as opposed to the "sentimental" style popular at the time, but these newspaper pieces Goldsmith largely ignored. An Irish friend, however, thought he should not ignore a particularly vicious attack that appeared in the March 24 issue of the *London Packet*. The article was an open letter addressed "To Dr. Goldsmith" that began by accusing him of puffing his own works and of being a literary humbug. It continued in part:

> But the gauze is so thin, that the very foolish part of the world see through it, and discover the doctor's monkey face and cloven foot. Your poetic vanity, is as unpardonable as your personal; would man believe it, and will woman bear it, to be told, that for hours the *great* Goldsmith will stand surveying his grotesque Oranhotan's [orangutan's] figure in a pier glass? Was but the lovely H-----k as much enamoured, you would not sigh my gentle swain in vain.[35]

The Irish friend persuaded Goldsmith that he ought to answer this scurrilous attack, if not for his own honor, then for the honor of Mary Horneck, one of the pretty Horneck sisters, whose family Goldsmith had been close to for years. The two men, therefore, called on the *London Packet*'s publisher, Thomas Evans, in Paternoster Row, and Goldsmith stated his complaint. Evans had no direct involvement in the scurrilous article and probably knew nothing about it, but when be bent over to look under the counter for a copy of the newspaper in question, Goldsmith struck him on the back with his cane. The two men then began trading blows, each giving the other a solid drubbing before sounds of the struggle brought a man in from another room to break up the fracas. Goldsmith then returned to his lodgings, where soon after, Garrick and Beauclerk stopped by to carry him to the Turk's Head in Gerrard Street for a meeting of the Club. Thomas Percy recalled that Beauclerk, "who had all the sportive talents of his ancestor Charles II, and loved a little mischief, persuaded the poor Doctor to go all bruised, as he was to the Club; to show the world how little he was affected by his late encounter."

The other club members were astonished when Goldsmith entered "with his face terribly scratched and torn, his body bruised, & one of his hands swelled & nearly dislocated." They expressed concern and offered him their compassion, "but it was impossible for the most serious not to relax from his gravity at the oddity of the spectacle, and the comic circumstances of the Narrative." Later in the evening Goldsmith, "who was suffering great pain in body and mind, desired leave to retire" and "the poor Doctor was no sooner withdrawn when a laugh burst forth which it was impossible to restrain."[36]

Some days afterward, Boswell remarked to Johnson that this must have been the first time Goldsmith was engaged in such an incident. Johnson replied, "Why, Sir, I believe it is the first time he has *beat*; he may have *been beaten* before. This, Sir, is a new plume to him."[37]

Although his parents had taught Oliver to observe the Christian ideals of charity and generosity, his early years of poverty had not taught him prudence. Money evaporated almost as quickly as it came to hand. Not only was he prodigal, and not only were needy individuals a drain on his finances, but a passion for gaming had plagued him from youth. During the time in Ireland when he was looking for a suitable profession to enter, Uncle Thomas Contarine had sent him off to London with £50 to study law. But at Dublin he got into a card game, lost it all, and returned to Ballymahon in disgrace. Contarine quickly forgave him, though his mother apparently remained long indignant.[38] Later he had to break off his medical studies at Leyden because of gambling debts, and when he first arrived in London in 1757 he wrote to his brother-in-law that "at Present there is hardly a Kingdom in Europe in which I am not a debtor."[39]

Thomas Percy later wrote that Goldsmith "was unfortunately so attached to the pernicious practice of gaming: and from his unsettled habits of life, his supplies being precarious and uncertain, he had been so little accustomed to regulate his expences by any system of economy, that his debts far exceeded his resources."[40] His friend Joseph Cradock further stated, "The greatest fault of Dr. Goldsmith was, that if he had thirty pounds in his pocket, he would go into certain companies in the country, and in hopes of doubling the sum, would generally return to town without any part of it."[41]

No matter how much he took in at the height of his career (in one year he is supposed to have netted £1,800),[42] he was always strapped. He found it increasingly necessary to buy on credit and to request loans from his friends, "and his debts rendered him, at times," said miscellaneous writer and acquaintance William Cooke, "so very melancholy and dejected, that I am sure he felt himself, at least the last years of his life, a very unhappy man."[43]

Growing debt was not the only reason for Goldsmith's dejection. His health had become a problem. Years of struggle, anxiety, and unsettled living had undermined his resilience. In 1772 an ascending urinary tract infection, perhaps contracted or complicated by a commerce with prostitutes, developed into a strangury, an affliction characterized by a slow and painful discharge of urine. The disorder grew serious. The *General Evening Post* for August 13 reported that "Dr. Goldsmith has been dangerously ill of an inflammation in the bladder: he was cut on Sunday last by Mr. [Percivall] Pott, when an amazing discharge of purulent matter proceeded from the part; and it is now thought that he is in a fair way of recovery."[44] But the operation only eased the symptoms without curing the disease. The infection invaded the kidneys and produced uremia, a buildup of toxins in the blood. Yet Goldsmith kept the discomfort and seriousness of his illness to himself and carried on as best he could.

One evening a group sitting at ease in the St. James's Coffee House began discussing Goldsmith's unique character—his appearance, blunders, brogue, literary talent, and so on. They speculated on how Goldsmith would go down to posterity, and Garrick contended that no one could possibly draw Goldsmith's character until he was finally dead and buried. "And then," recalled Garrick years later, "one risible folly bringing on another, I voted him to be dead at that time, that I might give his real character in his epitaph."[45] Others also took up the challenge of writing Goldsmith's epitaph, but Garrick's proved the most successful:

> Here lies Poet Goldsmith, for shortness called Noll,
> Who wrote like an angel, but talk'd like poor Poll.[46]

Goldsmith was not present at the gathering, but after learning of what had passed, he quickly decided to beat the coffeehouse wits at their own game. He had shown no leanings toward satire before, but he now set about composing his own series of epitaphs in his poem "Retaliation." The poem circulated only privately in manuscript, and most who appeared in it were not pleased with what they read, for the epitaphs touched deftly, though not maliciously, on their little vanities and weaknesses. Of Garrick, he wrote in part,

> Here lies David Garrick, describe him who can,
> An abridgment of all that was pleasant in man:
> As an actor, confest without rival to shine:
> As a wit, if not first, in the very first line:
> Yet, with talents like these, and an excellent heart,
> The man had his failings, a dupe to his art. . . .
>
> On stage he was natural, simple, affecting;
> 'Twas only that when he was off, he was acting. . . .

Of praise a mere glutton, he swallow'd what came
And the puff of a dunce he mistook it for fame:
Till his relish grown callous, almost to disease,
Who pepper'd the highest, was surest to please.
But let us be candid, and speak out our mind,
If dunces applauded, he paid them in kind.

Goldsmith proved to be a skilled and dangerous satirist as well as a keen observer of other people's foibles. He had been the easy butt of jests before, but "Retaliation" produced in his acquaintances, according to William Cooke, "more civility and seeming affection" than he had received from them before. Goldsmith decided, however, not to publish the poem right away, but to keep it by him, he said, "as a rod in pickle upon any future occasion."[47]

Meanwhile, he grew more depressed and irritable as his debts mounted and his disease worsened. "Goldsmith I found much altered, and at times very low," said Joseph Cradock. "The day before I set out for Leicestershire, I insisted upon his dining with us [Cradock and his wife]. He replied, 'I will; but on one condition—that you will not ask me to eat any thing.'" He arrived at Cradock's apartment and occupied himself for a time looking through newspapers and pamphlets, but Cradock thought he appeared distracted:

> I had ordered from the tavern some fish, a roasted joint of lamb, and a tart; and the Doctor either sat down or walked about just as he liked. After dinner he took some wine with biscuits; . . . and in the course of the evening he endeavoured to talk and remark, as usual, but all was force. He stayed till midnight, and I insisted on seeing him safe home; and we most cordially shook hands at the Temple-gate.
> Goldsmith did not live long after our return into Leicestershire.[48]

Severe blood poisoning developed, accompanied by fever. On the evening of Friday, March 25, he felt so ill that he sent for his apothecary, William Hawes, who quickly arrived to assess the situation and to prescribe what he thought necessary. Goldsmith related his symptoms. "He complained of a violent pain extending all over the fore-part of his head," Hawes recounted later; "his tongue was moist, he had no cold shiverings or pain in any other part, and his pulse beat about ninety strokes in a minute."[49] Goldsmith said he had taken two ounces of ipecac wine as a vomit and intended to take Dr. James's Fever-Powders, a popular medicine of the day, one of its ingredients being arsenic. Hawes advised against the fever powders and suggested less drastic medication.

When Hawes returned the following day, he learned from a servant that, against Hawes's advice, Goldsmith had taken Dr. James's Fever-Powders, which had induced prolonged vomiting and diarrhea. "I afterwards went into

Dr. GOLDSMITH's chamber," said Hawes, "and found him extremely reduced, and his pulse was now become very quick and small." When asked how he did, Goldsmith replied in a soft voice that he wished he had followed Hawes's advice the night before and not taken the fever powders:

> and this was all he said during this visit, for whatever other questions I thought proper to ask him, he appeared so much exhausted as not to be able to make any reply to them; and I clearly perceived he was so very weak and low, from the large and copious evacuation, that he seemed to have neither strength nor spirits to speak.[50]

Dr. John Turton was summoned on Sunday, March 27, followed by Dr. George Fordyce. They attended Goldsmith into the early days of April. While the disease was dangerous, no one, apparently, thought it immediately fatal, but Goldsmith's inner turmoil, occasioned by mounting debts, aggravated his condition. Dr. Turton said to him, "Your pulse is in greater disorder than it should be from the degree of fever which you have. Is your mind at ease?" Goldsmith answered that it was not.[51]

Events then hurried to an end. He rested easily during the night of April 3, but at about four o'clock in the morning on April 4, Hawes came in to find him in severe convulsions, which continued until a little before five o'clock, when he died. He was only forty-five years old at the time.

Burke wept when he learned of Goldsmith's death. Reynolds put down his brushes and did not paint all that day, a remarkable occurrence for him. The blow was the "severest Sir Joshua ever received" according to Northcote.[52] Boswell got word in Edinburgh on April 9 and wrote to Garrick, "I have not been so much affected with any event that has happened of a long time."[53] Boswell also wrote to other friends in London requesting particulars of Goldsmith's death. Johnson replied,

> Of poor Dr. Goldsmith there is little to be told, more than the papers have made publick. He died of a fever, made, I am afraid, more violent by uneasiness of mind. His debts began to be heavy, and all his resources were exhausted. Sir Joshua is of opinion that he owed not less than two thousand pounds. Was ever poet so trusted before?[54]

Johnson expressed no personal grief at Goldsmith's passing. Perhaps he experienced none. He ranked Goldsmith's talent very high, though he never felt for him the close attachment that he had for men like Henry Thrale and

Reynolds. "He was not an agreeable companion, for he talked always for fame," said Johnson. "A man who does so never can be pleasing."[55] Goldsmith's lack of education, his impulsive nature, his propensity to show off, and his incidental malice were not qualities apt to win Johnson's affections. "Goldsmith referred everything to vanity" said Johnson; "his virtues and his vices too were from that motive. He was not a social man. He never exchanged mind with you."[56]

Goldsmith's feelings for Johnson had been, as might be expected, inconsistent over the years. At times Goldsmith was admiring and respectful, and at others envious and quarrelsome. Johnson had been of great assistance to Goldsmith's career, not only in helping to get *The Vicar of Wakefield* published when Goldsmith fell behind in his rent and was threatened with arrest, but also in being the center of an intellectual group in which he might be accepted and his literary abilities given greater exposure. The mere fact that Johnson acknowledged his merit as a writer gave him encouragement to excel. Johnson exerted influence in other ways, not so much on his literary style as on his behavior. Johnson became the model in Goldsmith's mind for the well-respected and highly esteemed literary man. Goldsmith tried to capture some of that respect and esteem by occasionally assuming in company Johnson's language and imperious manner. Joseph Warton, one of Johnson's friends, noted this characteristic when he first met Goldsmith in 1766: "Of all solemn coxcombs, Goldsmith is the first; yet sensible—but affects to use Johnson's hard words in conversation."[57] Boswell mentioned this trait to John Wilkie, the publisher, Wilkie saying that Goldsmith was then Johnson in duodecimo.[58] Yet imitating Johnson's talk may have been done mostly in jest. Sir John Hawkins said that Goldsmith "affected Johnson's style and manner of conversation, and, when he had uttered, as he often would, a laboured sentence, so tumid as to be scarce intelligible, would ask, if that was not truly Johnsonian."[59]

Most of the time Johnson received Goldsmith's temperamental outbursts with uncharacteristic restraint. He tolerated gibes from Goldsmith he would not endure from anyone else, Topham Beauclerk excepted. He perhaps realized that Goldsmith was incorrigible and that censure might only provoke him further. Once when Goldsmith spoke of having a theater in London that produced only new plays, and Johnson treated the idea lightly, Goldsmith said, "Ay, ay, this may be nothing to you, who can now shelter yourself behind the corner of a pension." Surprisingly, Johnson good humoredly let the comment pass.[60]

"You are all of you," said Goldsmith to a group of friends, "absolutely afraid of Johnson,—now I attack him boldly, and without the least reserve." They admitted it was true. "If it were not for me, he would be insufferable."[61]

One evening as Goldsmith questioned a young American about the customs and manners of the "North American Savages," Johnson interrupted by saying, "I'm surprized, Goldsmith[,] that you can ask the young man so many frivolous questions. I am sure none but a *Savage* could think of plaguing him so."

Goldsmith answered, "I'm sure[,] Doctor, that none but a *Savage* could interrupt a man so abruptly in his conversation."[62]

Despite these occasional flare-ups, Goldsmith dedicated *She Stoops to Conquer*, his greatest literary success, to Johnson. It stood as an acknowledgment for all that Johnson had done to assist him. He wrote,

> By inscribing this slight performance to you, I do not mean so much to compliment you as myself. It may do me some honour to inform the publick, that I have lived many years in intimacy with you. It may serve the interests of mankind also to inform them, that the greatest wit may be found in a character, without impairing the most unaffected piety.

The words express more admiration, however, than intimate friendship. They stand in contrast to Goldsmith's more affectionate dedication of "The Deserted Village" to Reynolds.

Boswell never much altered his first impression of Goldsmith. His initial feeling mellowed over the years, but he always saw Goldsmith as essentially the "curious, odd, pedantic fellow with some genius." In the first years of their relationship, Boswell looked upon Goldsmith somewhat condescendingly, much as he would a gifted but unpredictable child. Only gradually did he learn to appreciate Goldsmith's candor and good spirits. For a time Boswell may have seen Goldsmith as a potential rival. He was already an accomplished biographer and he seemed the likely candidate to write Johnson's life. Johnson once asked Mrs. Thrale, "I wonder who will be my Biographer?"

She replied, "Goldsmith to be sure if you should go first—and he would do it better than any body."

"The dog would write it best to be sure," said Johnson, "but his particular malice towards me, and general disregard for truth, would make the book useless to all, and injurious to my character."[63]

But rivalry from any quarter never deterred Boswell from gathering Johnsoniana with the intention of writing Johnson's life himself. Little given to envy, he saw Goldsmith's death not as the passing of a rival biographer, but as a loss to good fellowship. Goldsmith's death truly affected him. A year after the event, following an evening at the home of philanthropist and social reformer General James Oglethorpe, where he and Goldsmith used to dine, Boswell wrote in his journal, "We had a good dinner and Sicilian wine as usual. But I missed poor Goldsmith."[64]

When Boswell came to publish the *Life of Johnson*, Goldsmith occupied more space in the work than anyone except Johnson himself. In the narrative portions, Boswell spoke in balanced terms of both Goldsmith's talents and his foolishness. But when he brought his picture to life through anecdote, the foolish aspects of Goldsmith's character predominated. Boswell seems never to have understood Goldsmith's peculiar Irish sense of humor, and he disputed Reynolds's assessment of what motivated Goldsmith's odd behavior:

> Sir Joshua Reynolds mentioned to me that he frequently heard Goldsmith talk warmly of the pleasure of being liked. . . . Sir Joshua was convinced that he was intentionally more absurd, in order to lessen himself in social intercourse, trusting that his character would be sufficiently supported by his works. If it indeed was his intention to appear absurd in company, he was often very successful. But with due deference to Sir Joshua's ingenuity, I think the conjecture too refined.[65]

When the *Life* first appeared, it generated controversy for a number of reasons. Perhaps the strongest objections arose over its depiction of Goldsmith. Once in speaking with a woman who disapproved of the way Boswell presented Goldsmith, Edmund Burke said, "What rational opinion, my dear madam, could you expect a lawyer to give of a poet?" John Wilkes made much the same point when he observed, "A Scotch lawyer and an Irish poet I hold to be about as opposite as the antipodes: if they agreed in any thing, I should marvel much, and least of all in forming a favourable opinion of each other." The acerbic Shakespearian commentator George Stevens added, "Why, Sir, it is not unusual for a man who has much genius to be censured by one who has none."[66]

Edmond Malone, who worked closely with Boswell during the writing of the *Life*, added his voice to those who thought the portrait of Goldsmith a caricature. In a letter to Thomas Percy in 1807 he wrote, "I always made battle against Boswell's representation of him also in the Life of Johnson, and often expressed to him my opinion that he rated Goldsmith much too low."[67]

Goldsmith's view of Boswell, as one might expect, was inconsistent. He seemed to enjoy Boswell's company and always treated him well, but he told several friends that Johnson conferred too much attention on him. Boswell, he said, could not justify such notice either by his conversational powers or his literary abilities.[68] Someone remarked that Boswell was a "Scotch cur," whereupon Goldsmith objected, "No, no, you are too severe; he is merely a Scotch *bur*. Tom Davies threw him at Johnson in sport, and he has the faculty of *sticking*."[69] Whether this expressed Goldsmith's true sentiments or was merely the sally of a moment, it is difficult to say. Goldsmith said spiteful things at one time or another about nearly everyone except Sir Joshua

Reynolds. For Reynolds he had the warmest affection, which Reynolds returned in full measure. Because they were of different professions, theirs was a friendship free from jealousy and petty competition. And despite the great dissimilarity in their temperaments, they were both men who loved simplicity in others and who scorned social ceremony. Goldsmith spent more time at Reynolds's table playing draughts or whist or in just talking than anyone else; and Reynolds, for his part, found in Goldsmith the companion who was easiest on his mind. When Goldsmith warmly dedicated "The Deserted Village" to Reynolds, Sir Joshua hurriedly painted the picture "Resignation," had it engraved, and inscribed on it, "This attempt to express a character in the *Deserted Village* is dedicated to Doctor Goldsmith, by his sincere friend and admirer, Joshua Reynolds." The picture shows a bearded old man seated in an armchair before a column, his right arm resting on a table with books on it.

Sir Joshua painted his celebrated portrait of Goldsmith in early 1769. He preserved in this portrait not the public Goldsmith so many people knew—the strutting, absurd little Irishman in bushy wig and gaudy clothes. Instead he captured the informal and intelligent individual he knew and loved. Goldsmith, book in hand, bare-headed with open collar, looks out upon the world with penetrating gaze. It is not a handsome face, but it wears a noble expression. In 1772 Reynolds painted a copy of this portrait to hang in the Thrale library among the other Streatham worthies.

Mrs. Thrale liked to write verse characters in her diary, modeled on Goldsmith's "Retaliation," as companion pieces to the Reynolds portraits. She admitted she had little intimacy with Goldsmith and that it was difficult to draw his character, "yet I will say these Lines are not bad":

> From our Goldsmith's anomalous Character, who,
> Can withhold his Contempt—and his Reverence too?
> From a Poet so polish'd, so paltry a Fellow,
> From Critick, Historian, or vile Punchinello?
> From a Heart in which Meanness had fix'd her Abode,
> From a Foot that each Path of Vulgarity trod;
> From a Head to invent, and a hand to adorn,
> Unskilled in the Schools—a Philosopher born. . . .
> All Deformity seeming in some points of View,
> In others quite regular, uniform, true:
> Till the Student no more sees the figure that shock'd her,
> But all in his Likeness—our odd little Doctor.[70]

Mrs. Thrale summed up Goldsmith as "A man made up of Contradictions— Knowledge & Ignorance, Artlessness and Design, Delicacy & Grossness. Poor dear little Dr Adieu."

Oliver Goldsmith by Sir Joshua Reynolds, 1769.
Source: National Portrait Gallery, London.

In the days following Goldsmith's death, Reynolds acted as executor. He raised several subscriptions toward a magnificent public funeral scheduled to take place the coming Monday. He proposed that Goldsmith be buried in Westminster Abbey. The pallbearers would be himself, Lord Sherburn, Lord Louth, Edmund Burke, David Garrick, and Topham Beauclerk. But after the list of official mourners was announced, *"excuses came from all*;

light and frivolous enough," according to William Cooke. Garrick is supposed to have sent word "that it was cursed unlucky the funeral should be of a Monday, when they ought to know [Mr. Garrick] never came to town on that day."[71] The burial was then rescheduled for Saturday afternoon, April 9, in the Temple. Present at the services were Sir Joshua's nephew, the Reverend Joseph Palmer; Goldsmith's dramatic rival, Hugh Kelly; longtime Irish friends John and Robert Day; Goldsmith's apothecary, William Hawes; and a Mr. Etherington.

None of the Johnson circle attended.

"His numerous friends neglected him shamefully at last," said Horace Walpole, "as if they had no business with him when it was too serious to laugh." Walpole thought the neglect might be attributable to Goldsmith's satiric poem "Retaliation" and its mock epitaphs, "some of which hurt, and perhaps made them not sorry that his own was the first necessary."[72] Another factor had to do with the prevailing attitude toward Goldsmith personally. Most admired his work and prized his good nature and benevolence, but they had no deep reverence for the man himself—certainly not enough to lay him among Britain's immortal authors. People had spent too much time laughing at his zany antics to enshrine him within the ancient, solemn, and consecrated walls of the old abbey.

The subscription money raised for the public funeral went to pay for a memorial portrait and tablet executed in marble by Joseph Nollekens and containing an inscription in Latin by Johnson. Sir Joshua went to Westminster Abbey and personally chose the spot for the cenotaph commemorating his friend. There it still hangs above the door leading into St. Faith's Chapel, while on the lawn, near the northeast side of Temple Church, reposes a white, weather-worn stone, shaped like a coffin lid, and bearing the simple inscription "Here lies Oliver Goldsmith."

NOTES

1. Boswell, *Life*, 3:5.

2. James Northcote, *Memoirs of Sir Joshua Reynolds* (Philadelphia, 1817), 196–97.

3. William Hazlitt, *Conversations of James Northcote, R.A.*, ed. Edmund Gosse (London, 1894), 152.

4. William T. Whitley, *Artists and Their Friends in England 1770–1799* (London, 1928), 1:255.

5. Hazlitt, *Conversations of James Northcote*, 237–38.

6. Reynolds, *Letters*, 69.

7. Boswell, *Boswell in Extremes*, 256n5.

8. James Boswell, *Boswell: The English Experiment, 1785–1789*, ed. Irma S. Lustig and Frederick A. Pottle (New York: McGraw-Hill, 1986), 205.

9. Farington, *Memoirs of the Life of Sir Joshua Reynolds*, 28.

10. Second Discourse.

11. Farington, *Memoirs*, 85.

12. Reynolds, *Letters*, 29.

13. Northcote, *Life*, 1:119.

14. Ibid., 1:10.

15. Northcote, *Memoirs*, 196.

16. Northcote, *Life*, 10–11.

17. Sir Joshua Reynolds, *The Works of Sir Joshua Reynolds, Knight; Late President of the Royal Academy*, ed. Edmond Malone, 3 vols. (London, 1809), xcix.

18. Cotton, *Sir Joshua Reynolds*, 51–52.

19. Hazlitt, *Conversations of James Northcote*, 56.

20. Northcote, *Life*, 1:251.

21. Piozzi, *Anecdotes*, 129.

22. Boswell, *Applause of the Jury*, 339.

23. Boswell, *English Experiment*, 147.

24. Percy, *Life of Goldsmith*, 110.

25. Boswell, *Life*, 3:253.

26. Reynolds, *Portraits*, 57.

27. Prior, *Goldsmith*, 2:368.

28. Hardy, *Memoirs*, 1:347.

29. Goldsmith, *Letters*, 102–5.

30. Boswell, *Life*, 3:84n2.

31. Ibid., 2:237.

32. Ibid., 2:181–82.

33. John Forster, *The Life and Times of Oliver Goldsmith* (London, 1890), 299.

34. Boswell, *Life*, 2:233.

35. Percy, *Life of Goldsmith*, 103–4.

36. Ibid., 192–93.

37. Boswell, *Life*, 2:210.

38. Forster, *Life and Times of Oliver Goldsmith*, 30.

39. Goldsmith, *Letters*, 32.

40. Percy, *Life of Goldsmith*, 111.

41. Cradock, *Literary and Miscellaneous Memoirs*, 1:232.

42. Hawkins, *Life*, 421.

43. Cooke, "Table Talk," *European Magazine* 24 (September 1793): 173.

44. Boswell, *Life*, 3:500–501.

45. Frances Burney, *Memoirs of Doctor Burney, Arranged from His Own Manuscripts, from Family Papers, and from Personal Recollections by His Daughter, Madame d'Arblay* [Frances Burney], 3 vols. (London, 1832), 1:359.

46. Prior, *Goldsmith*, 2:492.

47. Cooke, "Table Talk," *European Magazine* 24 (September 1793): 174.

48. Cradock, *Literary and Miscellaneous Memoirs*, 1:234–36.

49. William Hawes, *An Account of the Late Dr. Goldsmith's Illness, So Far as Relates to the Exhibition of Dr. James's Powders* (London, 1774), 1.

50. Ibid., 6–7.

51. Boswell, *Boswell in Extremes*, 163.

52. Forster, *Life and Times of Oliver Goldsmith*, 462.

53. Boswell, *Correspondence of Boswell with Garrick, Burke, and Malone*, 60.

54. Johnson, *Letters*, Redford, 2:146.

55. Boswell, *Life*, 3:247.

56. Boswell, *Ominous Years*, 330.

57. John Wooll, *Biographical Memoirs of the Late Revd. Joseph Warton, D.D.* (London, 1806), 312.

58. Boswell, *Boswell in Extremes*, 299.

59. Hawkins, *Life*, 416.

60. Boswell, *Life*, 4:113.

61. Cradock, *Literary and Miscellaneous Memoirs*, 1:231.

62. Boswell, *Correspondence Relating to the Life*, 411.

63. Piozzi, *Thraliana*, 173; Piozzi, *Anecdotes*, 70.

64. Boswell, *Ominous Years*, 137–38.

65. Boswell, *Life*, 1:412–13n6.

66. Prior, *Goldsmith*, 1:444–45.

67. Thomas Percy, *The Percy Letters: The Correspondence of Thomas Percy & Edmond Malone*, ed. Arthur Tillotson (Clinton, MA: Louisiana State University Press, 1944), 234.

68. Prior, *Goldsmith*, 1:430.

69. Ibid., 1:435–36.

70. Piozzi, *Thraliana*, 472–73.

71. Cooke, "Table Talk," *European Magazine* 24 (October 1793): 258.

72. Walpole, *Correspondence*, 28:144.

Chapter Eight

Domestic Issues

Three months after Goldsmith's burial, Johnson wrote to Bennet Langton in Lincolnshire, bringing him up to date on recent happenings in London. He explained that Goldsmith's fever had increased toward the end, aggravated by the fear of distress, and that Goldsmith had squandered much money through folly. "But let not his frailties be remembred," Johnson wrote. "He was a very great Man."[1]

Langton had, for some time, been out of touch with events in London as a result of increasing domestic obligations. In May 1770, at age thirty-three, he married the widow of a Scottish peer, John Leslie, Tenth Earl of Rothes. The match, according to Mrs. Thrale, surprised and disappointed many. She wrote in her diary, "To the Grief and Astonishment of all his true Friends they now behold him tied to a Thing without Beauty, Birth, Money or Talents," a judgment probably too harsh though substantially true.[2] Johnson told Boswell, "He has done a very foolish thing, Sir; he has married a widow, when he might have had a maid."[3] What apparently disappointed his friends most was that following his marriage, he settled into a life of quiet domesticity, never fulfilling his earlier potential.

Johnson had spoken of him in 1759 as "towering in the confidence of twenty one,"[4] and as a youth in his teens, he had demonstrated uncommon diligence. His curiosity extended in many directions, though he took particular interest in historical scholarship, ancient Greek literature, and the practice of painting. In his early twenties he entered Trinity College, Oxford, where he excelled in Greek but also became an excellent Latinist. In addition, he acquired fluency in French, Hebrew, Italian, Spanish, and Portuguese. He had already become acquainted with several of the nation's most prominent literary men, one of whom was Edward Young the poet, author of *Night Thoughts*. Another was Joseph Spence, the friend of Pope and author of *Observations, Anecdotes, and Characters of Books and Men.* But most important was Samuel Johnson. All three recognized young Langton's abilities and encouraged his ambitions. Edward Young wrote to him in 1755, "Proceed, Dear Sr, in yr litterary Pursuits; Heaven bless you in them. And if your Progress is equall to yr setting out, I will venture to prophecy that ye Name of a Langton will be frequent in the mouth of late Posterity."[5]

Joseph Spence also acknowledged the young man's potential, yet he noticed what would eventually become Langton's greatest shortcomings—a lack of focus and a general dispersion of his talents. Spence wrote his young friend a kindly letter of advice saying he had discovered at their last meeting "two or three symptoms of his being a Crow-Pelter, in a certain Gentleman that I love, and esteem, very much," a "crow-pelter" presumably being one who chases after crows while neglecting his crops. Spence said that when he mentioned the British Museum at their first meeting, Langton wanted to return to London and study the curiosities there for two or three weeks. Then when Spence praised a certain mathematics book, Langton immediately wanted to take a course in mathematics. "Now as I wish as well to the said Gentleman, as I do to any man in the world; I can't help wishing, and that most earnestly, That he wou'd fix some settled Aim (or Aims) for so much industry, and such an extream Desire to excell; and add a regular Method of pursuing those Aims, to the uncommon Abilities that Heaven has blest him with." Spence advised him to focus his energies on only two goals, for instance, "the excelling in the knowledge of History, and in the Practice of Painting; one for Business, and the other for Diversion."[6]

As for Langton excelling at painting, it is now difficult to estimate his ability, for none of his paintings are known to exist. Based on a number of pen and pencil sketches scattered throughout his extant memorandum books for the years 1758 to 1764, his talent appears to have been respectable though not exceptional. Several sketches depict heads of men and women. One man wears a Roman helmet. Another wears a crown and is labeled "Robert Bruce." A landscape in pencil shows a river flowing beneath a cliff, while another depicts Langton Hall. The end paper of one memorandum book carries an ink drawing of a state carriage, and the end paper of another book displays a pencil sketch of a horse and rider. None of these drawings demonstrate talents above a moderately gifted amateur.

Peregrine Langton, however, Bennet's second son, claimed that his father's brushwork was good enough to fool Sir Joshua Reynolds. He states that Sir Joshua once loaned his father an excellent old battle piece to copy. When Langton later returned his copy as the original, Sir Joshua said he hadn't remembered it being so good, and upon being told of the switch, he expressed surprise that with so little experience, Langton was able to deceive him. Assuming this story to be true, it is difficult to believe that Reynolds could be so easily tricked and that he was not simply stooping to flattery.[7] Spence's suggestion that Langton excel in history proved more in keeping with the young man's character, for Langton naturally possessed the tastes and temperament of a scholar and continued to read ancient history and literature throughout his life. At home he surrounded himself with books and papers, and though the public never gained the benefit of his extensive learning, much of his conversation consisted of quotations, recitations, and reflections on what he had read. Johnson once complained to Boswell that some of their friends talked too much from books, particularly Langton. "Garrick," he said, "would talk from Books if he talked seriously. *I* do not talk from Books. You do not talk from Books."[88] Boswell's friend William Temple criticized Langton for the same thing: "Mr. L. talks too much & quotes too much & too minutely," he wrote in his diary. "I trust [he is] too apprehensive about the times we live in: yet full of science & information."[9]

Besides a tendency to inertia, his inability to regulate expenses further kept him from making better use of his time and talents. His memorandum book for 1764 shows expenditures for May, June, and July totaling more than £380, including £127.10 "to Mr. Fleedder in discharge of his bond" and £68.0.6 "to Mr. Long Coachmaker." His accounts for the same three months the following year total more than £650, including such miscellaneous items now beyond our means to understand as £180.10 "to Mr. Couth for Mr. Fane," and £175 "to George Langton in full for my Fathers and Uncle Sam's contributions to his Brother." By contrast, Boswell and his wife in Edinburgh spent the same amount of £650 for the entire year of 1775 and thought that extravagant.[10]

With the death of his father in 1769 and his marriage in 1770, Langton acquired the responsibilities of overseeing the family estate and raising children of his own. But these new obligations, rather than inciting him to greater exertion, only settled him deeper into lethargy and financial mismanagement. His wife, Lady Rothes, who retained her title after marrying Langton, bore him ten children between 1772 and 1787, all of them living at least into early adulthood.[11] As these children grew, they became nearly the sole focus of Langton's attention. He sometimes brought them into fashionable society where he was invited, and like the overattentive father that he was, got them to recite, parrot-like, little things he had taught them, much to the annoyance of his friends. Johnson told a gathering at Thrale's that the *progenies Langtoniana* "might be very good Children, if they were let alone; but the Father is never easy when he is not making them do some thing which they can *not* do; they must repeat a Fable,—or a speech,—or the Hebrew alphabet;—& they might as well *Count Twenty*, for what they know of the matter: however, the

Father says *half,* for he *prompts* every other Word. But he could not have chosen a man who would have been less entertained by such means."

"I believe not!" exclaimed Mrs. Thrale; "nothing is more ridiculous than people's cramming their Children's nonsence down other people's Throats!" She asked if Langton took better care of his affairs than formerly.

"No, Madam, & never will; he complains of the ill effects of *habit,* & rests contentedly upon a *Confest indolence.* He told his Father himself that he had *no turn to oeconomy;*—but a Thief might as well plead that he *had no turn to Honesty.*"[12]

Boswell and Topham Beauclerk, both fathers themselves by this time, also felt disgust at Langton's plaguing people with his children. He seemed to have no sense of social decorum. They attempted to check what they considered his extravagant attachment to his offspring, but to no avail. Langton seemed totally oblivious to their efforts and advice.[13] Mrs. Thrale recalled a day at Sir Joshua Reynolds's country house on Richmond Hill in which a small group met intending to make a pleasant day of it, but Garrick felt sick and the Langtons created complications by bringing two of their children along, both under six years old. The children made so much noise that the adults had a difficult time conversing. "The Wits wanted to be talking & could not be heard, The Family folks fretted—but Langton & his Wife with a triumphant Insensibility kissed their Children and listened to nothing with Pleasure but what they said." Just before dinner, to nearly everyone's relief, Reynolds and his sister had a maid take the children outside for a walk, the parents fretting all the while lest their little ones become overheated. Garrick, because of his illness, requested a small table by himself near an open window, and when the children returned, Langton's wife, Lady Rothes, gave them some food and told them to go to Mr. Garrick's table and eat. "He was sick before," said Mrs. Thrale, "and I actually saw him change Colour at their approach, however he was civiller to them than anybody there except myself." After the party ended and people began to disperse, "some said how ill bred Lady Rothes & her Husband were, some said how foolish, to be repeating Bons Mots of Babies among people of Wit & Understanding."[14]

Wishing to keep his children about him as much as possible, and because he mistrusted public schools, Langton decided to instruct his offspring at home himself. His daughters, he told Sir John Hawkins, were to have the same education as the boys. He would make the girls perfect Greek scholars so that one might read Homer aloud while the others sewed and embroidered.[15]

Years later, Peregrine Langton wrote that his father had a dread of needlework that nothing could overcome, so that it was in vain that my mother attempted to bring my sisters into any method or regularity in their hours for needle work—They had governesses, but what could governesses achieve, where all order & regularity was set at defiance—The two youngest daughters luckily were sent to school, and there they learnt French, & such other acquirements as girls at school are taught—and, as in the case of French, with this my father was much pleased—from him they never would have learnt any thing; Tho' as I have already repeated it, & shall again refer to, than himself, if he had taken pains, there was not a man in England more capable of teaching than he was.

Peregrine Langton described a typical day of instruction in the Langton household. His father, clad in a white flannel dressing gown that hung down to his heels, would seldom enter the parlor before nine o'clock, and usually much later. Carrying several papers and a book or two, a comb, and a tape with which to tie up his hair, he would start scolding because his girls were so late, "just as if the other 364 days of the year it had not *always* been invariably the same." Once the girls straggled in, tea was made and their father's hair was combed and tied up, "during which operation Thomas a Kempis, or some other book of the kind was read out, and breakfast was begun—this would bring us towards eleven oClock." If Langton did not have to leave the house for an engagement, "then breakfast would continue on and on and on till *one*, or probably two oClock; except that sometimes my Mother used to come down stairs, which from very indifferent health she was frequently prevented from doing, and then occasionally I have known the breakfast cloth remain till near three oClock, and immediately relaid for dinner." Following breakfast, if it ended early enough, the lessons started. "My father . . . would . . . scrape together a few books, and begin with them before him a desultory conversation that treated of all that was ingenious, and improving, and entertaining to the highest degree; but that probably had no reference, after the first five minutes, to the book or books out of which it was intend'd to instruct his children seated around him." Peregrine concluded that while this account of his father "is by no means an exaggerated one" and portrays much that seems ridiculous, "I have drawn the picture of a wise, learned, pious, good man."[16]

Langton's friends agreed to his being wise, learned, pious, and good, but they expressed concern at how he was ruining himself and his family by neglecting his financial affairs. Johnson and others, said Mrs. Thrale, constantly hectored him about his bad management, "whether benefiting him—I know not."[17] Langton claimed to have no idea where his money went, though Johnson said his excuse was that of all spendthrifts. "I am afraid he has always something to hide."[18] His money certainly did not go toward entertaining guests, for his poor suppers became proverbial. "Sir," said Johnson in complaining of Langton's coarse table, "when a man is invited to dinner, he is disappointed if he does not get something good," and a man seldom got anything good at Langton's.[19] Mrs. Thrale, relating only what she had heard secondhand, probably from Johnson, said that Langton and his wife "ask their Friends to dine with them—Lords, Ladies, any body—upon a Piece of boyl'd Beef or a Loyn of Veal *only* without anything else: all this with an Insensibility truly admirable."[20]

Part of Langton's difficulty was that he was too lethargic to prosper in the city, and too gregarious and well educated to enjoy a retired country life. Rather than live quietly and frugally on his Lincolnshire estate and tend to that, he preferred living in London where he found life much more stimulating though far more expensive. Although he claimed an ancient name and property, he possessed no great fortune, yet he maintained a carriage and lived for a time in fashionable Harley Street. As his family grew and his patrimony decreased, he felt an even greater aversion to residing in Lincolnshire. "I believe he cannot bear the thought of living at [Langton] in a state of diminution," said Johnson, "and of appearing among the gentlemen of the neighbourhood *shorn of his beams*. This is natural, but it is cowardly."[21] Hearing that he meant to sell a parcel of land to pay his bills, Johnson told Boswell that if he were Langton, he would move to France and live on £100 a year rather than sell land that his family could never recover.[22] "To pass over the flowery path of extravagance is very well," Johnson observed, but Langton was ruining himself without receiving any pleasure from it.[23] "Wasting a fortune is evaporation by a thousand imperceptible means. If it were a stream, they'd stop it." He urged Boswell to speak to him. "It is really miserable," said Johnson:

> Were he a gamester, it could be said he had hopes of winning. Were he a bankrupt in trade, he might have grown rich. But he has neither spirit to spend nor resolution to spare. He does not spend fast enough to have pleasure from it. He has the crime of prodigality and the misery of parsimony. If a man is killed in a duel, he is killed as many a one has been killed. But it is a sad thing for a man to lie down and die, to bleed to death because he has not resolution to cicatrize [sear] the wound or even to stitch it up.[24]

Boswell mentioned Lady Rothes hesitating to cut into a pickled mango that cost two shillings, yet not pausing to lay out £8 a week in rent. "Sir," replied Johnson, "that is the blundering economy of a narrow understanding. Stopping one chink in a sieve."[25] Boswell retold the mango anecdote in the *Life* but left out Lady Rothes's name. Lætitia-Matilda Hawkins later verified that the mango was a fact, "but the prohibition had no foundation; and the price was a guess." According to Hawkins, when Lady Rothes read the anecdote in the *Life*, she knew that she was meant, and "she asked Boswell how he could so falsify the truth; he replied, 'Why, madam, it is no more than is done by landscape-painters: the landscape is from nature, but the tree in the foreground is an embellishment.'"[26]

While Langton sank deeper into domestic indolence and mismanagement, Mrs. Thrale soared ever higher in her own situation. Her mother's death and her husband's waning health and spirits allowed her to take Johnson's advice and break through her chains. She now began to excel in the drawing room, one of two areas sanctioned by her husband as the proper place for a wife. Like Floretta in "The Fountains," she became a wit, her fashionable guests at Streatham offering her a wider and more select audience than what her father, mother, and uncle had provided.

With Johnson now spending much of his time with the Thrales, Streatham became the meeting place for several of those closest to him. Joseph Baretti occasionally made up part of the company at the Thrales' country estate. He mixed well with the extraordinary people who gathered there, and he appealed to madam's fondness for rough characters. Mrs. Thrale particularly admired Baretti's conversation, finding it "always copious, always nervous [energetic], always full of various allusions." She said that it extended much beyond the ability of nineteen in twenty native speakers. He knew both "the solemn language and the gay, could be sublime with Johnson, or blackguard with the groom; could dispute, could rally, could quibble in our language." Besides possessing a fund of sardonic humor, he also sang pleasantly in a bass voice and could mimic in falsetto nearly any singer he heard. "These accomplishments," she said, "with his extensive power over every modern language, make him a most pleasing companion while he is in good humour."[27]

Mrs. Thrale wanted her eldest daughter, Queeney, then nine years old, to learn Italian. Next to French, Italian was the fashionable language for people to know, just as it became German in the following century. Baretti was the best teacher of Italian available, and he also got on exceptionally well with children. At Mrs. Thrale's urging, Johnson persuaded Baretti to take up residence in the Thrale household and start teaching Queeney Italian. At first things went well. Queeney could be difficult—sometimes sullen and uncooperative, sometimes hyperactive—but Baretti handled her with patience and sensitivity, and she made good progress. Baretti made good progress himself. Having entered the household as teacher and guest, he soon occupied a significant place in the Thrale ménage, joining the family at mealtimes and in various activities. He became so highly regarded that Henry Thrale commissioned Sir Joshua Reynolds to paint his portrait, which afterward hung in the library along with portraits of the other "Streatham worthies."

Dr. Thomas Campbell, an Irish clergyman, on a visit to London for the purpose of meeting Johnson, dined one evening at Streatham, where he observed some of those who assembled there. He wrote in his diary, "Baretti is a plain sensible man, who seems to know the world well." He noted that Baretti could "keep his ground" in conversation: "Talking as we all were at Tea of the magnitude of the Beer vessels [in Thrale's brewery]—he said there was one thing in Mr Thrale's house still more extraordinary—meaning his wife. She gulped the pill very prettily."[28] Campbell had been told earlier that Baretti and Boswell hated each other. Mrs. Thrale and Arthur Murphy explained to him how Boswell had expressed the opinion that Baretti should have been hanged for the Haymarket incident. "Upon this hint I went & without any sagacity it was easily discernable for upon Barretti [*sic*] entering Boswell did not rise, & upon Barretti's descry of Boswell, he grinned a perterbed glance."[29]

The unfriendly relations between the Scotsman and the Italian may account in some measure for Boswell never becoming a truly intimate member of the Thrale household. He never felt completely at ease there, especially with Baretti around. In his journal he mentions spending an evening at the Thrales' home in Southwark and records his relief when "Baretti, happily for me, went to bed pretty early, having fallen asleep at the fireside."[30] Another time, anxious to see Johnson, Boswell hurried to Southwark and knocked at Thrale's door: "Just as the servant opened it, Baretti appeared. I coldly asked him how he did. Methought there was a shade of murderous blood upon his pale face. I soon made a transition from this disagreeable object to the parlour, where Mrs. Thrale and Dr. Johnson were at breakfast."[31]

Baretti for his part thought Boswell boorish and ill-bred, and further speculated that he "is not quite right-headed in my humble opinion."[32]

In 1775 the Thrales made a two-month journey into France. The party included Henry and Hester Thrale, Queeney, Dr. Johnson, various servants, and Baretti as guide and general factotum. Baretti got the company up in the mornings and on their way. He arranged lodgings and sight-seeing excursions, and did everything, in fact, to ensure a relatively smooth and rewarding trip. Said Mrs. Thrale, "France displayed all Mr. Baretti's powers—he bustled for us, he catered for us, he took care of the child [Queeney], he secured an apartment for the maid, he provided for our safety, our amusement, our repose; without him the pleasure of that journey would never have balanced the pain."[33] Years later, Baretti referred to himself on this trip as "the chief mover of too large a caravan, most members of which had a good proportion of wants and whims."[34]

Baretti got along well with the easy-going Henry Thrale, and he might have remained in the household indefinitely but for Hester Thrale's knack for bringing out the worst traits in some of her friends and family. Queeney, for instance, who inherited her father's reserve, came to regard her mother with quiet scorn and frigid hostility. Mrs. Thrale could frequently chafe Johnson into petty displays of petulance, and she soon rubbed Baretti's volatile temper into a scalding malignity. Besides teaching Italian, he often looked after Queeney and her two younger sisters while their mother occupied herself elsewhere. He did so with pleasure, for as he remarked, "every body that knows me, knows that I am and always was fond of children."[35] But his notions of tending the youngsters differed greatly from their mother's. Mrs. Thrale demanded strict adherence to her authority. She expected her children to come running when she called or when she blew the ivory whistle she always carried in her pocket for the purpose of summoning them. Often too busy with her own affairs to pay them much attention, she stifled them at other times with unwanted attendance and inflexible rules. She accepted the old adage about sparing the rod and spoiling the child, for she freely cuffed and scolded them when they misbehaved. Her inconsistent behavior made her unsuccessful as a mother, for three of her four daughters grew up to despise her.

Baretti, on the other hand, held to a loose system of management. He believed that when not assigned specific tasks, children should be allowed to play and enjoy themselves. Years later he recalled that the Thrale girls "were never so happy as when their mother was away, who did nothing but scold or beat them for the most trivial faults or omissions. As to me, when I had done teaching Queeny, I made them run merrily about, and no body check'd their mirth but their beastly mother."[36]

The first serious clash occurred when Baretti took the girls across a drawbridge at Streatham and into a nearby field. There he encouraged them to tumble in the grass and have a good time. He did not know that Mrs. Thrale had forbidden the girls to play in the field because it contained a pond, and she was afraid the youngsters might fall into it and drown. When she came out of the house and saw her daughters in the forbidden field, it "kindled her rage at once," said Baretti. She blew her ivory whistle and "the frighted girls ran instantly to her with no small trepidation and hurry." Storming at them for disobeying her injunction, she then turned her rage on Baretti for endangering their lives by taking them near the pond. "Had they gone near it while you were poring on your book," she said, "could they not have drowned themselves? What do children know of the difference between land and water? They might very well have run themselves into the pond, taking it to be as solid as the field, and miserably perished in it!"

Baretti stood astonished. "This foolish speech made me presently aware that the woman was so grossly ignorant, as to think that children knew nothing of the difference between solids and fluids."[37] Another point of friction arose when Baretti began chiding Mrs. Thrale in the style Johnson often used. "Johnson could scarcely sit an hour with her," he said, "without abusing her for her failing in talking nonsense, or telling lies, which she did every day of her life."[38] As if it were part of his assigned duties, Baretti started abusing her as well, telling his brothers in a letter, "I live with him [Henry Thrale] like a brother, and scold his wife before his face when I think it necessary, for I regard her more in the light of a daughter."[39] But Mrs. Thrale thought Baretti not entitled to the same freedom Johnson enjoyed. Nor did she appreciate the inferior status to which Baretti's conduct reduced her.

She wrote to Johnson, then in Lichfield, complaining of Baretti's rudeness. Johnson wrote back, "Poor Baretti! do not quarrel with him, to neglect him a little will be sufficient. He means only to be frank, and manly, and independent, and perhaps, as you say, a little wise. To be frank he thinks is to be cynical, and to be independent, is to be rude." He asked her to forgive Baretti, "because of his misbehaviour, I am afraid, he learned part of me. I hope to set him hereafter a better example."[40] Yet Baretti did not much regard what Mrs. Thrale thought. Boswell heard Johnson remark one day that Baretti lived at the Thrales' as at an inn: "I suppose he meant, gave value for what he got, and did not mind whether the landlady liked him or no."[41]

The greatest point of contention arose from Mrs. Thrale's fondness for dabbling in physic. When the children got sick, their mother tended them herself, dosing them with a variety of questionable concoctions, a practice Baretti strongly opposed. Ralph Thrale, the youngest son, died when he was little more than a year and a half old, and Baretti insinuated long after that his mother hastened the boy's death. Baretti said that Ralph "died within the year of the inoculated small pox, during which the mother used to wash him in cold water in consequence of her great skill in physick."[42] The older son, Harry, on whom Henry Thrale placed so much hope as heir to his name and business fortune, also died young, at age nine. Baretti later claimed that one of Mrs. Thrale's medicines had killed him. He wondered if she ever disclosed to Johnson

> that she herself poisoned little Harry, or did she not? I think she suppressed that particularity, and attributed his death to convulsions, or some other complaint of that kind, as Johnson seemed the remainder of his life ignorant of the accident that caused the Boy's death, and I would not tell him, lest his attachment to her should make him discredit my words, and of course cause a serious quarrel between us.[43]

Immediately following young Harry's death, Baretti accompanied Mrs. Thrale and Queeney to Bath—Mrs. Thrale to recover from her grief at having lost her son and Queeney to find relief from a persistent case of intestinal worms. There Mrs. Thrale and Baretti had their greatest falling out. Mrs. Thrale showed Baretti a letter she had just received from Dr. Richard Jebb, one of the most eminent physicians of the day. Jebb had learned, probably from a family nurse, that Mrs. Thrale was giving her ten-year-old daughter tin pills. Mrs. Thrale had already tried giving Queeney two popular purgatives, Anderson's Scot's Pills and Glauber's Salt, but when they did not produce the desired result, she ventured on something stronger. Dr. Jebb warned her that the tin pills would probably kill the worms but might also cause her daughter serious injury. Handing Baretti the letter to read, she said, according to him, "See, see what fools these physicians are! They presume to know better how to manage children than their mothers themselves." She obviously expected a sympathetic response, for Baretti also mistrusted physicians, often calling them vultures and speaking derisively of their profession. But his fondness for Queeney, coupled with what he knew of Mrs. Thrale's medical skills and the news that she was giving Queeney tin pills, greatly alarmed him—"my bile suddenly rose to such a degree," he said,

> that I am sure I uttered my indignation in the most severe terms, and swore that she would soon send the daughter to keep company with the son, if she gave her any more of her damn'd pills: and not satisfied with this, I informed the daughter of the horrid quality of the physic that her good mamma administered her against the positive order of Dr. Jebb, of whose letter I told her the contents, exhorting her to resist the taking of any tin pills, and assuring her that they would soon destroy her.

Mrs. Thrale then erupted in fury and there followed "a pretty long exchange of very strong words."[44]

Mrs. Thrale complained to Johnson in a letter, "Baretti alone tried to irritate a wound so very deeply inflicted, and he will find few to approve his cruelty." Next to this passage in his copy of Mrs. Thrale's *Letters to and from the Late Samuel Johnson, LL.D.*, published twelve years later, Baretti wrote in the margin,

> The Bitch alludes to the quarrel I had with her to prevent her giving tin-pills to Queeny. But she was the cause of it by showing me a letter of Doctor Jebb, that intreated her to forebear those pills; and as I visibly saw that the Girl grew worse and worse by them, sided with the Doctor, and was obliged to be very violent to keep her from sending Hetty where she had just sent Harry. And take notice, that she suppresses Johnson's answer to this charge of cruelty, which, had it been true, would have immediately parted us for ever.[45]

But the final break came at Streatham over a continuing dispute about servants and guests. Baretti by that time had grown so disgusted with his situation that one morning in the summer of 1776, in the middle of breakfast, he put down his tea, retired to his room long enough to pack his belongings, picked up his hat and stick, and without so much as taking leave, walked off to London. He wrote in the margin of *Letters to and from the Late Samuel Johnson, LL.D.*, next to Johnson's letter of June 4,

> On this day I quitted Streatham without taking leave, perfectly tired with the impertinance of the Lady, who took every opportunity to disgust me, unable to pardon the violent efforts I had made at Bath to hinder her from giving tin-pills to Queeney. I had by that time been in a manner one of the family during six years and a half, teaching Queeny Spanish and Italian from morn to night, at her earnest desire originally, and Johnson, who had made me hope, that Thrale would at last give me an annuity for my pains: but, never receiving a shilling from him or from her, I grew tired at last, and on some provocation from her, left them abruptly.[46]

Not long after his departure, Baretti began telling others malicious tales and "abusing me for a Vixen," complained Mrs. Thrale; "it is really very unjust, & below a fellow of his Parts and Knowledge to be traducing one so." She thought him a scoundrel for living among people, setting them at defiance, and then telling stories about them to strangers; "besides that I was always willing to love Baretti—it was Baretti that hated *me*. He made [James] Barry the Painter believe such strange Things of my *Shrewship*, that when I met the Man casually t'other Night at a Visit, he told the people of the House that my mildness had amazed him—Good heavens what did he expect?"[47]

One day when Baretti still lived at Streatham, Johnson asked Mrs. Thrale to save him from the biographers who one day would scramble to write his life. He urged *her* to do it. He said that his old companions Dr. John Taylor, Dr. William Adams, and Edmund Hector could furnish her with early anecdotes, and she could ask Baretti about later events, for, he said, "I think Baretti is a Lyar only when he speaks of himself."

"Oh!" replied Mrs. Thrale, eager to undeceive him. "Baretti told me Yesterday that you got by Heart six Pages of Machiavel's History once, & repeated 'em thirty Years afterwards Word for Word."

"O why this indeed is a *gross* Lye," replied Johnson. "I never read the Book at all."

"Baretti too told me of *you* that you once kept 16 Cats in your Chamber, & y^t they scratch'd your Legs to such a degree, you were forced to use Mercurial Plaisters for some Time after."

"Why this is an unprovoked Lye indeed: I thought the Fellow would not have broken thro' divine & Human Laws thus, to make Puss his Heroine— but I see I was mistaken."[48] The extent of Baretti's lying may have surprised Johnson at the time, but it was a lie that eventually ended their friendship of over thirty years.

Like Mrs. Thrale, Fanny Burney was much impressed with Baretti the first time she met him in April 1772. She admitted to having a great enthusiasm for authors and therefore felt honored to see Joseph Baretti, whom she thought "a very good looking man."[49] She did not get to speak with him much at their first meeting, however, nor was she able to gage his character until nearly a year later, when she wrote in her diary,

> Mr. Baretti appears to be very *facetious*; he amused himself very much with Charlotte [Fanny's twelve-year-old sister], whom he calls *Churlotte*, & kissed whether she will or no, always calmly saying, 'Kiss a me, *Chur*lotte!' He asked if she had Read Robinson Crusoe? Charlotte coloured, & *tittered*, & answered, Yes Sir '& pray, how many years *vas* he on *de* Uninhabited Island?' 'O Sir, I can't tell that—! its so long since I read it—*Vat*! don't you remember *vat* you Read? *den*, my pretty Churlotte, you might spare your Eye sight!'
> 'But, can you remember *vat vas de* name of Robinson Crusoe's Island?—'
> 'O Sir, no, that I can't indeed!'
> 'And could you Read all *dat* Book, & not find out, *dat* it has no Name at all?'[50]

Later, when the public learned that Charles Burney's shy young daughter Fanny had written the best-selling novel *Evelina*, published anonymously in 1778, Baretti said to her next time they met, "I see what it is you can do, you little witch—it is, that you can hang us all up for laughing-stocks; but hear me this one thing—don't you meddle with me. I see what they are, your powers; but, remember, when you provoke an Italian you run a dagger into your own breast!" Fanny realized this was only Baretti's gruff manner of teasing, but still, "I half shuddered at the fearful caution from him, because the dagger was a word of unfortunate recollection."[51]

Baretti's sudden departure from the Thrale household cleared the way for a new favorite, Charles Burney, Baretti's "perfect Opposite," as Mrs. Thrale called him.[52] Dr. Burney was always pleasing, friendly, and well-mannered, whereas Baretti, said Mrs. Thrale, had been invariably "Haughty & Insolent and breathing defiance against all Mankind."[53] Burney, due to his active social life, had long been acquainted with Johnson, Garrick, Reynolds, Baretti, and many other notable people. It was through a mutual friend, William

Charles Burney by George Dance, 1794.
Source: National Portrait Gallery, London.

Seward, that Burney was introduced to the Thrales not long before Baretti left Streatham, and it was perhaps through Johnson that he began instructing Queeney in the harpsichord as Baretti had instructed her in Italian. Burney was engaged to come out to Streatham once a week for that purpose, "but such was the fertility of his Mind," said Mrs. Thrale, "and the extent of his Knowledge; such the Goodness of his Heart and Suavity of his Manners that we began in good earnest to sollicit his Company, and gain his Friendship."[54]

Burney occasionally brought one or more of his children with him to Streatham, and so it was that some of the younger Burneys came to meet the spirited hostess and the great Samuel Johnson. Charlotte Burney was tremendously impressed with Mrs. Thrale. Charlotte claimed to have known "many Genius's, & Famous & charming people" through their association with her father, but "I have never met with any one with manners & conversation so captivating, her wit so sweet temper'd, her humour so spontaneous & comic, her observations so original, her repartee so ready & brilliant, her quotations & allusions so impressively applied."[55]

Fanny also found Mrs. Thrale irresistible, once exclaiming, "Mrs. Thrale!—She, she is the Goddess of my Idolatry!"[56] Fanny also remarked, "She is extremely lively and chatty; . . . she is full of sport, remarkably gay, and excessively agreeable."[57] Her conversation overall was "so entertaining, so gay, so enlivening, when she is in spirits, and so intelligent and instructive when she is otherwise, that I almost as much wish to record all she says, as all Dr. Johnson says."[58] If she had any flaw, it was that her entrance into a room "was rather florid and flourishing, as who should say, 'It's I!—No less a person than Mrs. Thrale!'"[59]

Johnson assured Fanny on one of her early visits that the Thrales were as fine a people as she could be with—they were good-natured and nothing made them angry.[60] Fanny soon agreed that Mrs. Thrale was "a sweet Creature, & *never* angry; she has a Temper the most delightful of *any* woman I ever knew."[61] Mrs. Thrale initially felt indifferent about the precocious Fanny, but she was so delighted with her father that she could not help wishing well "to every thing that bears the name of *Burney.*"[62]

NOTES

1. Johnson, *Letters*, Redford, 2:147.
2. Piozzi, *Thraliana*, 106.
3. Boswell, *Life*, 2:77.
4. Johnson, *Letters*, Redford, 1:171.
5. Edward Young, *The Correspondence of Edward Young, 1683–1765*, ed. Henry Pettit (Oxford: Clarendon Press, 1971), 423.
6. Boswell, *Correspondence with Members of the Club*, 422–23.
7. Ibid., 32–33 and n4.
8. Ibid., 359.
9. William Johns[t]on Temple, *Diaries of William Johnston Temple, 1780–1796*, ed. Lewis Bettany (Oxford: Clarendon Press, 1929), 147.

10. Boswell, *Ominous Years*, 210.

11. On the back flyleaf of one of his letter books, Peregrine Langton wrote, "Bennet Langton by his marriage with the Dowr Countess of Rothes had ten children—viz

George
Mary
Diana
Jane
Elizabeth
Peregrine
Algernon
Isabella
Charles
Margaret"

12. Burney, *Early Journals*, 3:85–87.

13. See Boswell, *Ominous Years*, 330.

14. Piozzi, *Thraliana*, 108–9 and n3.

15. Hawkins, *Memoirs*, 1:279.

16. Peregrine Langton Massingberd, manuscript letter books (Lincolnshire Archives, Lincoln, UK). See also Boswell, *Correspondence of Boswell with Members of the Club*, lxix–lxx.

17. Boswell, *Life of Samuel Johnson*, 3:62.

18. Johnson, *Letters*, Redford, 3:118–19.

19. Boswell, *Boswell in Extremes*, 177, and Boswell, *Life*, 3:186.

20. Piozzi, *Thraliana*, 106.

21. Johnson, *Letters*, Redford, 3:119.

22. Boswell, *Boswell for the Defence*, 172.

23. Boswell, *Boswell in Extremes*, 341, and Boswell, *Life*, 3:348.

24. Boswell, *Boswell in Extremes*, 303. See also Boswell, *Life*, 3:317.

25. Boswell, *Boswell in Extremes*, 292.

26. Hawkins, *Countess and Gertrude*, 1:355.

27. Hayward, *Autobiography*, 1:93.

28. Thomas Campbell, *Dr Campbell's Diary of a Visit to England in 1775*, ed. James L. Clifford (Cambridge: Cambridge University Press, 1947), 53.

29. Ibid., 67.

30. Boswell, *Ominous Years*, 105.

31. Ibid., 256.

32. Joseph Baretti's marginal annotations in his copy of *Letters to and from the Late Samuel Johnson, LL.D.*, 1:370 and 1:216. (British Library shelf mark C.45.e.5-6.) The two octavo volumes are in good condition, Baretti's manuscript notes written in a small neat hand in blue ink.

33. Hayward, *Autobiography*, 1:94.

34. "Stricture the Third," *European Magazine* 14 (August 1788): 91.

35. Baretti, Marginal Annotations, 1:278.

36. Ibid., 1:277.

37. "Stricture the Second," *European Magazine* 13 (June 1788): 394.

38. Baretti, Marginal Annotations, 1:232.

39. Collison-Morley, *Giuseppe Baretti*, 294.

40. Johnson, *Letters*, Redford, 2:248.

41. Boswell, *Ominous Years*, 298.

42. Baretti, Marginal Annotations, 1:206. For the likely cause of Ralph Thrale's death, see Hyde, *The Thrales of Streatham Park*, 115–16 and 122–125.

43. Baretti, Marginal Annotations, 1:307.

44. "Stricture the First," *European Magazine* 13 (May 1788): 315.

45. Baretti, Marginal Annotations, 1:319.

46. Ibid., 1:338.

47. Piozzi, *Thraliana*, 419.

48. Ibid., 626.

49. Burney, *Early Journals*, 1:216.

50. Ibid., 1:246–47, and Burney, *The Early Diary of Frances Burney*, ed. Annie Raine Ellis, 2 vols. (Freeport: Books For Libraries Press, 1971), 1:206–7.

51. Burney, *Diary & Letters*, 4:32.

52. Piozzi, *Thraliana*, 475.

53. Ibid., 43.

54. Ibid., 137.

55. Joyce Hemlow, *The History of Fanny Burney* (Oxford: Clarendon Press, 1958), 109.

56. Burney, *Early Journals*, 3:35.

57. Frances Burney, *Memoirs*, 2:87.

58. Burney, *Diary & Letters*, 1:85.

59. Frances Burney, *Memoirs*, 2:87–88.

60. Burney, *Early Journals*, 3:94.

61. Ibid., 3:165.

62. Piozzi, *Thraliana*, 368.

Chapter Nine

A Variety of Private Cases

Charles Burney received the degree of Doctor of Music from Oxford University in June 1769. While an important event in Burney's career and in the fortunes of his growing family, it was not a solemn or heavy occasion, for the Burneys were not solemn, heavy people. It was an occasion for lightheartedness and laughter. Fanny, seventeen at the time, commemorated the event by sending her father a comical poem in which she said that he must now be much fatter, taller, and graver than formerly,

> For I never can think of a Doctor, not big
> As a Falstaf, [*sic*] or without a full bottom'd wig.

She titled her poem "To Doctor Last" because her father was "of Doctor's the Last & the Best," but the title was also a pun on Doctor Last, a popular character in Samuel Foote's comedy *The Devil upon Two Sticks*.

On the Sunday evening that Dr. Burney returned from Oxford, he stood talking in the parlor with Fanny, her sister Hetty, and her cousin Charles, when the latter happened to mention a new play in town called *Doctor Last in His Chariot*. Dr. Burney glanced at Fanny, and Fanny looked away, embarrassed. "O you sawcy Girl!" he said in mock sternness. "What do you think," he said to the others; "do you know this abominable girl calls *me* Dr. Last?" Charles and Hetty laughed. Dr. Burney then took Fanny's poem from his pocket and handed it to her, asking her to read it.

Feeling embarrassed and ashamed, she wanted to seize the paper and tear it up, but Dr. Burney pulled it back and prepared to read it himself. Fanny begged him not to, but in vain, "so I ran out of the Room—but to own the truth, my curiosity prevail'd so far, that I could not forbear running down stairs again with more speed than up, & into the next Room to hear [his] comments."

She listened as Dr. Burney read the poem in a loud voice. Then everyone laughed, and her father declared, "'tis very *good stuff*!"

Fanny had heard enough—"I ran once more up stairs, & lighter than a Feather felt my Heart!"[1]

Always painfully shy and self-conscious, she hated being singled out for special notice or, as she once put it, being "exposed to a *deliberate* examination."[2] She loved praise, but she feared more than anything being made to appear ridiculous. Consequently, she ran from situations in which she felt threatened, or if she could not run, she tried to shrink into insignificance, hoping to be overlooked.

Young Fanny had been the least promising child in a family of talented people. Her father was an outgoing, amiable, industrious man whom everyone liked and whom his children adored. He was musician, composer, musicologist, teacher, and travel writer. He played the organ, harpsichord, violin, and viola; had been apprenticed to the composer Thomas Arne; and spoke French and Italian fluently. Fanny's older sister Hetty had been a child prodigy, an accomplished harpsichordist by the age of ten, and younger sister Susan was a passable singer and keyboard artist herself. Both had inherited not only their father's love of music, but also his charm and sociability. But Fanny as a young child showed little promise for much of anything. Most people found her a quiet youngster, small for her age and decidedly backward. At age eight she scarcely knew her letters, and her father thought her unable to read. Her brother Charles sometimes teased her by pretending to teach her to read from a book turned upside down. She confessed years later to having been a "little dunce" and thought the humiliation of being a slow learner as a child planted the conviction in her mind that whatever she might write later on, "if seen, would but expose [me] to ridicule."[3]

Only among her young companions was she lively and fun-loving and showed that she possessed humor and ingenuity. A former playmate wrote to her years later, "*You* were so merry, so gay, so droll, & had such imagination in making plays, always something new, something of your own contrivance."[4] She gained inspiration from the comedies her father took her to see, particularly when Garrick acted. After these performances she would imitate the players and invent speeches for their characters. "But in company," her father recalled,

> or before strangers, she was silent, backward, and timid, even to sheepishness: and, from her shyness, had such profound gravity and composure of features, that those of my friends who came often to my house, and entered into the dif-

ferent humours of the children, never called Fanny by any other name, from the time she had reached her eleventh year, than The Old Lady.[5]

Yet she made up ground fast, for despite the lack of a formal education, by her eleventh year she had begun, she said, "scribbling, almost incessantly, little works of invention; but always in private."[6] She also began keeping a diary but considered her passion to write a fruitless occupation, so she burned the diary along with all her imaginative works in a ceremonial bonfire on her fifteenth birthday.[7] But too shy to express her personality any other way, at least in public, she discovered writing to be a necessary outlet, so she once again took up scribbling romances in private and keeping a journal.

Dr. Burney, due to his profession and his genial personality, enjoyed a large acquaintance drawn from England and abroad. He often hosted concerts in his home and frequently attended dinners, dances, and other festivities elsewhere. His children routinely accompanied their father, and while Hetty and Susan enjoyed mixing in these social gatherings, Fanny preferred sitting quietly in corners out of the way. It was at these social events that she closely studied the great, the brilliant, the elegant, the refined, the arrogant, the foolish, the coarse, and the vulgar—the whole range of characters, in fact, that society produced, and that eventually filled her novels. Although she liked to listen in on the conversations around her and to observe the people, she always endeavored to remain inconspicuous. When she went into company, she tried, she said, "to catch at the first chair in my way, and take possession of it, merely to sink from notice."[8] Often she felt like "a poor sheepish wretch . . . among strangers *whom* I *fear*."[9] Sometimes, when frightened, the only alternative was flight: "How often have I relinquished all the pleasure of an Evening merely from a watchful eye or curious glance!"[10] She once described her expression when under someone's deliberate gaze as that of "a poltroon, either smelling something unsavory, or expecting to be Bastinadoed."[11] Her expressive face contributed to her fear of being watched, for it seldom seemed under her control. Whatever thought or emotion passed through her mind also played across her features. "Poor Fanny's face tells what she thinks, whether she will or no,"[12] said her father, and she admitted that "Nobody, I believe, has so *very* little command of Countenance as myself!"[13]

Compounding the problem was her sensitivity to the world around her. Her absorbing interest in people and how they interacted was more emotional than intellectual. "I am very earnest & warm in whatever interests me—not of a philosophick—or phlegmatick turn," she said.[14] In this, as in many other things, she took after her father, who was not a meditative man—not a thinker. He possessed a wholly artistic temperament, his mind engrossed with music, musical instruments, and general impressions rather than abstract ideas. Yet more than any other member of the family, "I have an uncommonly soft Heart," said Fanny.[15] Her stepmother once remarked, "Here's a Girl will *never* be happy! *Never* while she Lives! for she possesses perhaps as feeling a Heart as ever Girl had!"[16] One of her father's friends dubbed her Feeling Fanny.[17] This emotional sensitivity later became a dominant feature of her novels and helped inaugurate the feminine school of sentimental fiction.

Like her father, she was short and slightly built, and she always looked younger than her age. At nearly thirty she still looked like a girl. At sixty she appeared to be in her forties. She had a lively, engaging face, greenish gray eyes, and brown complexion. Once a gentleman, anxious to meet the creator of the fair and beautiful Evelina, asked Mrs. Thrale if Miss Burney was not very pretty. "Very pretty?—no," said Mrs. Thrale.

"I was in hopes she was like her own Evelina."

"No, no such thing," replied Mrs. Thrale, "unless it is in timidity,—but niether [*sic*] in beauty, nor in ignorance of Life."[18]

When Mrs. Montagu, in a letter to Mrs. Thrale, sent her regards to "the truly lovely Miss Burney," Fanny commented, "I fancy she meant love-able."[19] Dreadfully near-sighted, Fanny had a tendency to stoop as if straining to see what lay before her. She could not make out faces clearly from across a room, and this added to her discomfort around strangers, especially after she became the celebrated author of *Evelina*, for she could not be certain that people were not gawking at her as a curiosity.

Also like her father, she possessed a strong sense of the comic and a love of the ridiculous in others. Her early diaries are filled with word sketches of the ludicrous idiosyncrasies of those she observed in society, types that found their way into her fiction. She wrote in a letter that "the world, and especially the Great World, is so filled with absurdity of various sorts, now bursting forth in impertinence, now in pomposity, now giggling in silliness, and now yawning in dulness, that there is no occasion for invention to draw what is striking in every possible species of the ridiculous."[20] All the Burneys loved to laugh. Dr. Burney spoke of himself as "always a *gigler*,"[21] and years later, Fanny wrote an epitaph for her father in which she cited "the Genial Hilarity of his Airy Spirits."[22] Her journals during the periods of her late adolescence and early adulthood testify to her own "tittering & ridiculous fits" of laugh-ing.[23] For example: an amateur singer performs his part "so ludicrously, as to make me Laugh immoderately."[24] A foolish middle-aged couple make "the young Ladies titter unmercifully . . . &, for my part, I Laughed most heart-ily."[25] An absurd young man-of-fashion "made me Laugh to so immoderate a degree that I was quite ashamed."[26] And a silly Miss W. has Fanny in agony "almost killing myself by restraining my Laughter," until finally the young lady departs, allowing Fanny to laugh "without controul or disguise."[27] She goes to a village church with her stepsister and husband, the Rishtons, and finds the singing "the most extraordinary I ever heard":

> no Comedy could have afforded more Diversion: Mrs Rishton & I Laughed ourselves sick—though we very much endeavoured to be grave—Mr Rishton was quite offended, & told his Wife that the Eyes of the whole Congregation were on her—but nothing could restrain us, till the Dean began his prayer.[28]

The ludicrous conduct she observed in others, and the amusement she got from it, only increased her dread of appearing ridiculous in public herself. She feared there might be people who watched her with as keen an eye for the ridiculous as she watched them, so when in company, except with the most intimate friends, she fell silent and became so guarded in her demeanor that people often thought her proud, conceited, and artificial.

Mrs. Thrale hardly knew what to think of Fanny Burney's timidity even as she felt perfectly at ease with her father. "The Doctor is a Man quite after my own Heart," she said. If he had one fault, it was obsequiousness. She thought his following closely after Johnson or Baretti made him softer than the other two, but, after all, it was probably only a *"Vice de Profession*—so God a Mercy Burney! I do love the Man; he is so much to my natural Taste."[29] His gifted daughter, however, was another matter.

On Miss Burney being introduced into the Streatham group immediately following the success of her novel *Evelina*, Mrs. Thrale thought her terribly affected. She failed to see that her reserve hid a painful self-consciousness. She wrote that Dr. Burney's "Daughter is a graceful looking Girl,"

> but 'tis the Grace of an Actress not a Woman of Fashion—how should it? her Conversation would be more pleasing if She thought less of herself; but her early Reputation embarrasses her Talk, & clouds her Mind with scruples about Elegancies which either come uncalled for or will not come at all: I love her more for her Father's sake than for her own, though her Merit cannot as a Writer be controverted.[30]

Although Mrs. Thrale proved a kind and generous hostess, buying Fanny stylish clothing, taking her on trips to Bath and to Brighton, and fitting up a room at Streatham for her exclusive use whenever she chose to visit, friendship between the two women, separated in age by eleven years, developed slowly. Miss Burney's diffidence, in contrast to Mrs. Thrale's exuberance, presented a formidable barrier. So too did Fanny's uneasy sense of the disparity in their social status and fortunes. Although sincerely pleased to have Miss Burney at Streatham,

> yet She makes me miserable too in many Respects [said Mrs. Thrale]—so restlessly & apparently anxious lest I should give myself Airs of Patronage, or load her with the Shackles of Dependance—I live with her always in a Degree of Pain that precludes Friendship—dare not ask her to buy me a Ribbon, dare not desire her to touch the [servants'] Bell, lest She should think herself injured.[31]

Fanny actually seemed most comfortable around older men who fit the general pattern set by her father—men who were intelligent, accomplished, fun-loving, and, of course, exceedingly fond of her. Garrick, for instance, had been a favorite in the Burney household since Fanny was a small girl. His comical nonsense delighted her. He lacked consistency of character and had too volatile a temperament to become an intimate friend, but she felt at ease with him and enjoyed his company nevertheless. Yet "with all my partiality for Mr. Garrick," she wrote, "I cannot help noticing, that he has by no means the Virtue of *Steadiness* in his attachment, &, indeed, is almost perpetually giving offence to some of his friends." He even managed to quarrel with Dr. Burney over some theatrical business and snubbed the Burneys for a time. "Dr. Johnson told my Father, that he attributes almost all the ill errors of Mr. Garrick's Life, to the *fire* & hastiness of his Temper, which is continually misleading him."[32]

She found Sir Joshua Reynolds, whom she met through her father in about 1773, much more companionable. He possessed an easy manner that made everyone comfortable in his presence. On one occasion, as on many others, he "kept with me, to my great satisfaction, the principal part of the evening. He is so pleasant, unaffected, and agreeable, that there is no one, among those who are of celebrity, I can converse with half so easily and comfortably."[33] She particularly valued his sensitivity to her shyness. He avoided, for instance, flattering remarks about her literary work or pointed inquiries about herself, all of which he knew would embarrass her, and he sometimes gently steered the conversation of others into different channels when he saw that its personal nature made her uncomfortable.

Johnson could also be surprisingly understanding in this regard. He petted and pampered and affectionately teased her, but he never scolded her about what she said or how she dressed and behaved as he sometimes did Mrs. Thrale, and Fanny seemed to bring out the jovial side of his disposition. She noted that "Dr. Johnson has more *fun*, & comical humour, & Laughable & [*tear in MS*] nonsense about him than almost any body I ever saw: I mean, though, when with those he likes; for otherwise, he can be as severe & as bitter as Report relates of him."[34] In one of his sportive moods at Streatham, while mimicking Miss Biddy Branghton, a character in *Evelina*, Johnson, "with a refinement of delicacy of which I have the deepest sense, never once cast his eyes my way." He endeavored to spare her the embarrassment that direct notice might cause her. "He clearly wished to draw the little snail from her cell, and, when once she was out, not to frighten her back. He seems to understand my *queeralities*—as some one has called my not liking to be set up for a sign-post—with more leniency than any body else."[35]

Another older man she adored was her father's longtime friend Samuel Crisp—or "Daddy Crisp" as Fanny sometimes called him—a large man, about Johnson's size, twenty years older than her father. Intelligent and learned, he was gruff–humored, a lover of music, an amateur tenor of merit, the first to bring a pianoforte into England, and a failed playwright. A former man of the world, he now lived a secluded life in an old, dilapidated, nearly inaccessible manor house at Chessington, near Kingston-on-Thames, not far outside London. Crisp loved all the Burney girls about equally at first, but the small, bashful second daughter's pointed observations on people and manners delighted him. He noticed, furthermore, a steadiness of character that set her apart from the frivolous young girls often encountered in society. In 1776 he wrote her that "there are not above two or three people in the world that I love so well as *Fanny Burney*."[36] Soon after, she was his "Fannikin, the dearest thing to me on earth."[37] Fanny sent him "journal letters" filled with observations on the festivities she attended and the people she saw. Crisp encouraged her to write him often, for "I most sincerely, nay ardently, interest myself in whatever concerns a Fannikin."[38] Her letters were always "full of excellent portraits, as like, and as strongly painted as Sir J. Reynolds's."[39] When she coyly hinted that she might not, in future, write him such long letters because she did not wish to bore him, he wrote back, "You Young Devil You, You know in your Conscience I devour greedily your Journalizing letters."[40]

In return for her letters, Fanny asked Crisp to criticize her writing and her character unsparingly. Crisp did so in his frank, brusquely humorous, slightly profane style. He also took her father to task occasionally in the same manner, often chastising him for his irregular hours, for Dr. Burney frequently got only three or four hours sleep a night, so occupied was he with writing, performing, giving music lessons, and socializing. "Perhaps he is like a season'd old Drinker," wrote Crisp to Fanny, "whose inside is so lin'd with a Coat of Tartar, that his Brandy only goes in at one End, & out at the other, like a Worm in a still, without affecting the Vessel it passes thro'—certain it is, that he Uses his thin Carcass most abominably."[41]

Crisp performed a valuable service as Fanny's mentor. He helped raise her confidence as a person and as a writer, providing her with supportive but honest criticism. He likewise benefited, much the same way Johnson did, for nothing proved more gratifying in quite the same way as having the affection of this precocious young woman. "I observe we old Fellows," said Crisp, "are inclinable to be very fond of You."[42]

Even Mrs. Thrale succumbed eventually to the solid qualities that lay beneath Fanny's shy exterior. "Fanny Burney has secured my Heart," she wrote in her diary. "I now love her with a fond & firm Affection, besides my Esteem of her Parts, & my Regard for her Father. her lofty Spirit dear Creature! has quite subdued mine; and I adore her for the Pride which once revolted me."[43] Fanny did not deny being proud. That is, she recoiled at being made to feel subservient, another way of being made to feel ridiculous. People of Mrs. Thrale's social standing put her in mind of her own humble status. Her father earned his livelihood as a music teacher and musician—not prestigious callings at the time. *The London Tradesman*, an advice book published in 1747 to help guide youths in seeking suitable professions, spoke disparagingly of musicians: "Music is reckoned among the Liberal Arts; . . . but in this Country especially, those who practice it for Bread are in but small Repute."[44] Lord Chesterfield also reflected the prevailing attitude when he cautioned his son against associating with people "such as fiddlers, pipers, and *id genus omne* [all that sort]; most unedifying and unbecoming company for a man of fashion."[45] Dr. Burney's acceptance at Streatham and elsewhere had more to do with his amiable personality than his social position.

Fanny Burney had now put herself forward as a novelist, also not an illustrious profession at the time, especially for a woman. "I would a thousand Times rather forfeit my character as a *Writer*, than risk ridicule or censure as a *Female*," she said. An authoress was always thought to be "flippant, assuming & loquacious," and "the dread of these kind of censures have been my principal motives for wishing *snugship*."[46] So long as she could sit quietly in corners and watch and listen, her bashfulness went largely unnoticed. But the success of *Evelina* brought her out of the corners and into the middle of the room, making her the center of attention whether she liked it or not.

In writing her first novel, she drew encouragement from Daddy Crisp's praises of her journalizing letters, so replete were they with wit, humor, fascinating character studies, and social insights. She therefore decided in her mid-twenties to try her strength on a wider and more critical audience. She doubted that anything she wrote would ever cause much stir, but she hoped it would all the same. *Evelina* appeared anonymously in January 1778. She had worked on it surreptitiously at odd moments, particularly late at night, able to write little more than half a page a day. Only her sisters and her brother

Charles knew about the work until months after publication. Not even her father knew about it until two months after it appeared in the bookstalls, and then he was afraid to let Fanny know that he had learned her secret. "Why, Susan," he said to his older daughter, "I have got Fan's book."

"Lord sir! have you?"

"Yes—but I suppose you must not tell her—Poor Fan's *such* a prude."[47] Later Dr. Burney confessed that he opened the first volume with fear and trembling, afraid Fanny had disgraced the family. He did not think his shy daughter could write a novel worth reading.[48] But after looking into it he saw its merit and was thoroughly delighted.

The novel's amazing popularity astonished Fanny and placed her in the greatest confusion of her young life, for it both gratified and terrified her. She was visiting Samuel Crisp at Chessington when she wrote to her sister Susan that the complimentary newspaper reviews had agitated her so much that she could hardly catch her breath. She had been walking around the garden trying to calm her nerves:

> Good God! My dear Susy!—what a wonderful affair has this been!—& how ex-traordinary is this *torrent* of success, which sweeps down all before it!—I often think it *too much*, nay, almost *wish* it happenned [*sic*] to some other person, who had more native ambition, whose hopes were more sanguine, & who could less have borne to be Buried in the oblivion which *I* even sought.—But tho' it might have been better bestowed, it could by no one be more gratefully received.[49]

Before the writer's identity became known, Mrs. Thrale thought the author a man. She found the book a little "flimzy" when compared to *The Female Quixote, Tom Jones,* and *Joseph Andrews,* yet she liked it well enough to loan to Johnson. He praised it, saying there were parts in it good enough to honor Richardson.[50] When Fanny learned of Johnson's remarks, she became ecstatic: "*Dr. Johnson's* approbation!—Good God, it almost *Crazed* me with agreeable surprise!—it gave me such a flight of spirits, that I Danced a Jigg [around a mulberry tree in the garden] to Mr. Crisp, without any preparation, *music*, or explanation, to his no small amazement, & diversion."[51]

Interest mounted to discover who the writer could be. Mrs. Thrale eventually learned it from Dr. Burney. She then told Dr. Johnson and a few others, which distressed Fanny, who pleaded with Mrs. Thrale not to tell anyone else, but the secret was already out, and it spread quickly. Literary London was soon abuzz. To think that Dr. Burney's bashful young daughter Frances should have written such a remarkable work as *Evelina*. Miss Burney must be a phenomenon. Her book displayed so much knowledge of the world for such a young and seemingly unsophisticated individual. (Fanny was rumored to be but seventeen and looked it, though she was actually twenty-six.) After seeing her name in periodicals for the first time, she declared that she was unable to eat, sleep, or drink for more than a week. Writing to her sister Susan, she said that she had always feared discovery, sought concealment, and now hoped to escape personal abuse. "Let them Criticise, cut, slash, without mercy my *Book,*—& let them *neglect me,*—but may God avert my becoming a public Theme of Ridicule."[52]

That she both courted recognition and sought concealment was the chief dilemma of her life. She always found herself caught between a desire for notice and a fear of being thought ridiculous. Thomas Twining, an old and respected family friend, noted her ambivalence when he remarked to her, "Plutarch says, I think, that fame is an object to all mankind; but that some pursue it like rowers in a boat, with their backs towards it. Is this your way?—Nay, nay, it is not the worst way."[53]

Ideally, she would like to have eavesdropped on her own celebrity as she had eavesdropped on her father years before when he read and praised her comic poem. She would have preferred running into an adjoining room to listen through the wall to the comments of people on the other side. But instead she now had to suffer the excruciating torment of complete strangers stopping to stare at her in public places. Some brazenly accosted her in private gatherings to heap on her the most embarrassing and fulsome tributes. At a tea one evening, not long after being publicly exposed as the author of *Evelina*, a group of chattering women approached her: "What! is that the lady that has favoured us with that excellent novel?" said one. "Very extraordinary, indeed!" said another. "Dear heart, who'd have thought it?" exclaimed a third. "I never saw the like in my life!" cried a fourth. Then they began praising details of her book until, said Fanny, "I had almost thrown myself out of the window, in my eagerness to get out of the way of this gross and noisy applause."[54] She confessed that she really loved "these agreeable flummeries,"[55] yet praise was "always embarrassing to me except taken *en passant.*"[56] Yet notwithstanding her mortification, she carefully preserved in her diary all tributes that reached her ears.

To help shield herself from the embarrassment that scrutiny caused her, she more and more retreated behind a barrier of strict propriety. The tittering, fun-loving girl yielded in public to the grave and decorous young woman. She had for some time been adopting and refining society's rules of feminine conduct, for she found these rules a useful protection against potentially threatening people and situations. Not only Mrs. Thrale complained of her excessive attention to propriety, but Mr. Crisp also occasionally twitted her about it. Following the success of her novel, Crisp urged her to write a comedy for the stage. She obviously had the comic touch. Yet comedy, he said, required certain unrestrained freedoms that ladies might not wish to be known the authors of, "especially if they were Prudes, (And You know You are one)."[57]

Fanny agreed about the risks involved in dramatic composition and conceded that she was not willing to purchase fame "at the expense of all my own ideas of propriety. You who *know* me for a *Prude* will not be surprised, & I hope not offended at this avowal."[58] Always uppermost in her mind was the ridicule she might incur as a female. Fear, she acknowledged, kept her out of a lot of embarrassing predicaments. She told Mr. Crisp, "I run no risks that I see—I run—but it is always away from all danger that I perceive."[59] Yet despite her outward timidity, she possessed a determined spirit. Her standards and principles, once fashioned, became firm—even rigid. She formed strong opinions, especially about people, whose characters she quickly sized up and judged. "Mr Mackintosh is a very stupid young man," she jotted in her diary, "who is unhappily possessed of a very great fortune, which could hardly be worse bestowed."[60] A Miss Dalrymple "is about 28 or 9, rather handsome, lisps affectedly, simpers designedly, & lookes conceitedly. She is famed for never speaking ill to any ones Face, or well behind their Backs: an amiable Character."[61] Fanny confided these judgments to few, however. Through her efforts at concealment, the world at large saw only a demure young woman with few opinions and apparently little knowledge.

She firmly believed that a woman must live on two levels if she was to avoid undue attention. Conduct legitimately open to public inquiry must be carried on irreproachably according to society's strictures. Private affairs, on the other hand, must be conducted discretely, secretly, even surreptitiously. Take a simple matter like reading. Fanny did not like for people to see her poring over a book because they might think her a bluestocking, and "I am always ready enough to enter into any caution to save that pedantic charge."[62] Dr. Johnson, concerned that he never saw her with a book in her hand, once asked her very gravely if she loved reading. She explained to him that she was always afraid of being caught reading "lest I should pass for being *studious*, or *affected*, & therefore, instead of making a *Display* of Books, I always try to *hide* them,—as is the case at this very Time," and she immediately pulled out from under her gloves, behind where she sat, a copy of his own *Life of Waller*, which she had been reading when Johnson entered the room.[63]

As female intellectuals were ever a target of sarcasm, Fanny did not advocate learning in women. She thought it simply not worth being pointed out as singular: "I think it has no recommendation of sufficient value to compensate its evil excitement of envy and satire."[64] On this point Fanny and Mrs. Thrale disagreed. While Fanny shrank from being thought a learned and singular female, Mrs. Thrale eagerly cultivated the role.

Hester Thrale's transformation from submissive wife and daughter to wit and *salonière* had been remarkable. Yet she attracted attention more by her ebullience and eccentricities than by her features, for she was not physically imposing nor remarkably good–looking. Like Floretta, she was attractive rather than beautiful. As she admitted, "I had always too many strong points in my face for beauty."[65] In keeping with her husband's wishes, she had begun dressing more fashionably, even extravagantly, in the smart, colorful fashions of the Continent. She usually wore makeup, still considered vulgar by many in England, and often topped off her ensemble with a stylish wig surmounted by some kind of striking headdress. A later editor of her letters termed her a frenetic hummingbird—an appropriate image considering her small size, her nervous energy, and her showy attire.[66] She described herself as standing only four foot eleven with a narrow waist and rather longish neck that was remarkably white, "so much so as to create Suspicions of its being painted—This however is particular only because the Woman is a brown one." She had chestnut colored hair and large light grey eyes. Her pale eyes, she thought, washed out the expression in her face, for although large, they were "neither sweet, nor bright, nor any thing else but common ordinary Eyes." Her complexion, however, was "perfectly clear—the Red very bright, & the White eminently good & clean."[67]

She heightened the red in her cheeks with rouge, using greater amounts as she got older. Her flamboyant dress and rouged cheeks often led strangers to think her foreign—"*no doubt on't*" she suspected people of saying when they first saw her; "do not you see how She is painted?"[68] Queen Charlotte, many years later, once caught a glimpse of her in Windsor Chapel and asked her attendants, including the embarrassed Fanny Burney, "Who was that *painted Foreigner*?"[69] When in her eighties, she explained to a friend that she continued to wear rouge, not to appear younger, but to hide a dull yellow that years of using the cosmetic when young had introduced into her complexion.[70] Cosmetics at the time commonly contained lead.

Fanny Burney did not approve of the rouge nor the flamboyant dress: "It is truly vexatious she will descend to singularity so unbecoming. For the paint was nothing to the rest of the glare, though high enough for the Opera Stage!"[71] Mrs. Thrale occasionally drew a sharp word or cautionary lecture from Johnson, who felt obligated to check her growing eccentricities. He once admonished her not to wear bandeaus, a style of headband then in fashion. He said that Henry Thrale's sister, Lady Lade, could get away with such a thing, for she was large enough to carry it off, "but *you*," he said, "are too *little* for any thing ridiculous; that which seems *nothing* upon a Patagonian, will become very *conspicuous* upon a Lilliputian; & of *you* there is so little in *all*, that one single absurdity would swallow up *half* of you."[72]

She stated that her poise came from keeping genteel company, studying paintings, learning to dance, and copying foreign fashions, not English patterns of dress. The general character of her mind was "wholly Italian, or rather Welsh perhaps," for her temperament was "warm even to Irascibility; Affectionate and tender," and she claimed to spare neither money nor pains to help a friend. She was "by Nature a rancorous and revengeful Enemy, but having conquered that Quality thro' God's Grace."[73] She had inherited her father's temper but managed to restrain it.

Fanny placed Mrs. Thrale's social talents on a level with the most distinguished women in society. They shone to advantage even when compared to those of the extraordinary Elizabeth Montagu, queen of the bluestockings. Mrs. Montagu, said Fanny, reasoned well and harangued well, but she possessed no wit. "Mrs. Thrale has almost too much; for when she is in spirits, it bursts forth in a torrent almost overwhelming."[74] The longer Fanny observed Mrs. Thrale, in fact, the more she wished Mrs. Thrale would restrain her exuberance. She regarded her as the most unguarded of human beings, "& though with my whole soul I most affectionately & most truly Love her as she *is*, I cannot help Daily wishing she would a *little* more guide herself like other folks."[75] Mrs. Thrale was far too impetuous, for she never restrained her tongue nor her feelings about anything: "she laughs, cries, scolds, sports, reasons, makes fun,—does everything she has an inclination to do, without any study of prudence, or thought of blame."[76]

Fanny probably realized that had she tried, as she stated early on, to record all that Mrs. Thrale said as all Dr. Johnson said, the result would have been disappointing, for Mrs. Thrale's talk required her vivacious personality to give it life. Her constant flow of words sparkled with brilliance that gained more from its manner than from its substance. Her wit found expression not so much in the sharp and incisive comment, but in her amusing banter. She particularly loved plays on words and clever associations. Johnson drove to the heart of the matter with an arresting phrase or apt metaphor while Mrs. Thrale playfully danced about her subject, illuminating it with associations, fancy, and feeling.

Most people quickly succumbed to her vivacious spirits. "Rattling," as she called her clever and effusive manner of talk, became her medium, and "flashing" is what she took most delight in exhibiting. She once half-seriously joked with Fanny about the two of them printing a weekly paper filled with good-natured nonsense for their gentlemen friends in London attending Parliament. Fanny took up the joke and suggested they call their paper *The Flasher*. Mrs. Thrale explained in her diary that "we have a Hack Phrase here at Streatham of calling ev'ry thing *Flash* which we want other folks to call *Wit*."[77]

Johnson loved Mrs. Thrale's talk, which he characterized as "a stream of Sentiment—enlivened by Gaiety."[78] Once, in the month of October, he debated whether or not to join the Thrales at Brighton. He complained that the sea was so cold and Brighton society so dull that time of year, "Yet I do love to hear the sea roar and my Mistress talk. For when she talks ye Gods, how she will talk."[79] The gaiety, however, as Fanny Burney noted early on, was extravagant, even to some extent contrived. Her excessive spirits actually helped conceal a rising degree of anxiety and discontent. "I have an odd Power of working myself up into artificial Spirits," she confessed. It was a talent she had developed in childhood to placate her parents and make things easier at home, but she gave a specific instance from 1778 when another potential business disaster terribly frightened her and further incapacitated Henry Thrale. She was within a month or so of lying in when she and her husband invited Johnson and Boswell to dine at Streatham. She described her husband as looking "Woe-begone," but she carried on with Johnson as though nothing troubled her: "we talked, we rattled, we flashed, we made extempore Verses, we did so much that at last Mr Boswell said why Mrs Thrale (says he) you are in most riotous Spirits to-day—So I am reply'd I gaily, & actually ran out of the Room to cry—his observation went so to my Heart."[80]

Over time the gap increasingly widened between her outward gaiety and the frustration it concealed. She still had not entirely slipped the yoke about her neck. She remained bound to Henry Thrale and his interests by a sense of duty, yet she received no affection or understanding in return. Johnson had also started to become a burden, for he increasingly demanded more of her attention and felt compelled to check her growing enthusiasms and eccentricities, often speaking to her in the rudest terms. At the dinner of a friend, for instance, "I once inadvertently commended the Pease . . . taste these Pease Mr Johnson do, are not they charming?—Yes Madam replied he—For a Pig."[81] If she still entertained any serious intentions of being an author, Johnson's domineering presence dissuaded her. She yearned for greater independence, for genuine love and affection, and for creative self-expression. The perceptive Miss Burney may have noted the affectation in her gaiety, yet she did not detect the underlying reason for it. Nor did anyone else. Mrs. Thrale, with her ebullient personality and lively talk, beguiled nearly all who met her, and they were charmed. Most of them were, at any rate.

Only now and then did she encounter the odd individual who remained completely unimpressed by her flash and her riotous spirits. She once remarked that she loved to spoil people and hated those she could not spoil.[82] She did not like Dr. William Heberden, for instance, the eminent physician who attended Johnson in his final hours in 1784. Heberden was far too cold and dry for her, "and seems to have so little notion of *Who I am* as I say sometimes in Joke, that I can hardly bear him: I am not used to People that do not worship me, & of course grow very fastidious in my desire of Flattery."[83] Neither did Sir Joshua Reynolds's placid disposition appeal to her. Joseph Baretti was another she came to dislike mostly because of his indifference to her charms. She much preferred people like Father Cowley, Prior of the English Benedictine Convent in Paris, whom the Thrales and Johnson met on their trip to France with Baretti in 1775. Father Cowley seemed to her "learned & polite, and likes me, I believe, which is always the first good Quality in my Eyes."[84]

She eventually made as if Johnson's rebukes and ill-mannered comments had no effect on her. She carried on in her own way, spoke her own mind, and did not allow his petulance to disturb her. "My Mind is an active whirling Mind," she said, "which few Things can stop to disturb, & if disturbed, it soon recovers its Strength & its Activity."[85] One day at Streatham the company were shocked to hear the way Johnson spoke to her. They were nearly as surprised to see how calmly she bore it. Afterward one of the women expressed amazement that Johnson should use such harsh language to her, and Mrs. Thrale answered merely, "*Oh! Dear good man!*"[86] Outwardly and defiantly she would not allow Johnson to disturb her mind or spirits. Inwardly, though, she must have smarted on such occasions. She was, after all, as she herself admitted, naturally rancorous and vengeful. It seems questionable then just how inadvertent her praise of the peas, or anything else that set Johnson off, really was. She knew how he disliked exaggeration and displays of sentiment, and she also knew how he would react when she indulged in them. Yet she seemed to have an urge to bait Johnson at times, feeling safe perhaps in the confidence of his genuine regard for her and his growing dependence on her attachment to him. Her refusal to accede completely to his authority shows an element of rebellion that gained a more prominent place in her character with time. It was not only to irritate Johnson, however, that she grew more eccentric and defiant in her dress, speech, and behavior. Her extravagant actions, her seemingly careless talk, her flashy dress, the way she swept into a room—all were calculated to announce "It's I!—No less a person than Mrs. Thrale!" Yet unlike David Garrick, who called attention to himself for reasons of vanity, her unconventional dress and behavior seemed to be a way of staking out territory, declaring a measure of independence from those who would dictate how she must conduct her life.

Boswell accused Oliver Goldsmith of being very much what the French call *un étourdi*, one who acts without thought.[87] Mrs. Thrale left herself open to the same charge. Her actions and speech certainly were not as ridiculous as Goldsmith's, but both Johnson and Fanny Burney, the two people who knew her best, accused her of lack of prudence and restraint. But just as her excessive gaiety was partly contrived, so was the appearance of being *un étourdi*. "I have a great deal more Prudence than People suspect me for," she maintained;

> they think I act by Chance, while I am doing nothing in the World unintention-
> ally: and have never I dare say in these last 15 Years uttered a Word to Husband,
> or Child; or Servant or Friend without being very careful & attentive what it
> should be. Often have I spoken what I have repented after, but that was want of
> *Judgment*—not of *Meaning*; what I said, I meant to say at the Time; & thought
> it best to say—I do not err from Haste, or a Spirit of Rattling as People think
> I do: when I err, tis because I make a false Conclusion, not because I make no
> Conclusion at all. When I rattle, I rattle *on purpose*.[88]

Johnson had assured Fanny Burney that nothing angered the Thrales, and Fanny herself determined that Mrs. Thrale never got angry. In the case of Henry Thrale, this was certainly the case. But Hester Thrale never entirely freed herself from what she saw as the necessity, acquired in childhood, to please everyone, but then to hate those not captivated by her charms—to feel she must yield to the authority of others, and then to harbor resentment for the oppressive position they placed her in. She always spoke of her mother in later years with the highest regard for her character and general excellence, yet her tone often betrayed an abiding resentment and barely suppressed hostility. This layering of respect, admiration, subservience, and suppressed anger became a familiar pattern in her relations with those closest to her. Her relationship with Henry Thrale exemplifies the point.

In her diary, she presents a thumbnail sketch of her husband's character. She says, first of all, that he is nice looking, with steady eyes of the deepest blue, his features thoughtful and intelligent. His manner is civil and courteous, though not demonstrative. She concedes that he loves money and is diligent to acquire it, but that he is also generous and willing to spend fashionably. She maintains that his passions are either not strong or he keeps them under control so that they seldom disturb his tranquility. To illustrate his steady composure, she mentions the time they were awakened in the night by a report that Thrale's sister's house was on fire. Thrale did not bother to get up but told the servant who had awakened him to provide what assistance he could, then he rolled over and slept until his usual hour. Another time, after he had built some great vats, each holding more than 63,000 gallons, he returned home for dinner and conversed a great while on a number of trivial matters, "but I forgot says he to tell you how one of my great Casks is burst & all the Beer run out." She further states that her husband is extremely

Henry Thrale, after Sir Joshua Reynolds, 1777.
Source: Trustees of the British Museum.

easy to live with, "while the easiness of his Temper and slowness to take Offense add greatly to his Value as a domestic Man." He is reserved and uncommunicative to the point that his servants don't like him, and even his children show him little affection, for "he is obliging to *nobody*; & *confers* a Favour less pleasingly than many a Man *refuses* to confer one." Nonetheless, "Johnson has a very great Degree of Kindness & Esteem for him, & says if he would talk more, his *Manner* would be very completely that of a perfect Gentleman."

Thrale was evidently tranquil and detached not only by nature, but also upon principle as a man of wealth and social standing. His emotional and sensitive wife could not help feel some exasperation when he would sometimes boast that his friends' misfortunes had little power of disturbing his tranquility. Certainly his wife's troubles never much disturbed him. He seldom showed any tenderness or concern for her, and he lacked skill, she said, to dissemble feelings he did not possess. Even so, he appreciated her intellectual abilities: "with Regard to his Wife," she said, "tho' little tender of her Person, he is very partial to her Understanding."[89]

Thrale's dress and demeanor bespoke his wealth and good breeding. On first meeting him at Streatham, Fanny Burney described him as being extremely civil to her. "He is a very Tall, well looking man, & very well bred; but shy & reserved: however, he was attentively obliging to me all the Day."[90] She also found him to be generous. When once accompanying Fanny and his wife on a shopping excursion in town, "he absolutely insisted upon presenting me with a complete suit of gauze lino, and that in a manner that showed me a refusal would greatly disoblige him. And then he very gravely desired me to have whatever I pleased at any time, and to have it added to his account."[91] Few people wished to disoblige Henry Thrale. His quiet but firm address invariably commanded respect and obedience. Johnson told Boswell, "I know no man, (said he,) who is more master of his wife and family than Thrale. If he but holds up a finger, he is obeyed." Even Johnson heeded the upraised finger. It was Thrale, after all, who got the slovenly Johnson to dress better and who restrained much of his unsocial behavior when no one else dared attempt it. "There, there, now we have had enough for one lecture, Dr. Johnson," Thrale once told him; "we will not be upon education any more till after dinner, if you please."[92]

Perhaps in further keeping up the image of the fine English gentleman, Thrale continued his philandering long after marrying Hester. Everyone knew about these adventures, for his escapades occasionally got into the papers. Johnson remained discreetly quiet on the subject, and Mrs. Thrale accepted things as best she could. She felt there was nothing she could do to change the situation, and creating a scene would only make matters worse. Thwarting a husband was a dangerous business for a wife to undertake. She may have recalled her mother's difficulties in dealing with Mr. Salusbury. She certainly remembered her father's warnings about what kind of husband Thrale would make. His infidelities became just another affront she had to pocket, a grievance she had to bury and try not let disturb her active, whirling mind. She attempted to adopt the principle that specific injuries are not hurtful if accepted with the right attitude. They may even prove beneficial: "whoever can resolve to *swallow* injuries, may assure himself of finding their general utility; and I venture (as the advertizers of medicine express themselves) to recommend the practice from *long tried experience* in a variety of *private cases*."[93]

Yet the suppressed injuries festered over time, the resentment surfacing only now and then in a private note in her diary, in the casual remark to a friend, or in the marginalia of a book. Years later, in her copy of Boswell's *Life*, where Johnson agrees that a man's infidelities are not as serious as a woman's, for a husband imposes no bastards on his wife, Mrs. Thrale wrote in the margin, "*Sometimes* he does: Johnson knew a Man who did; & the Lady took very tender Care of them."[94]

Hester Thrale endured the humiliation of knowing that her husband occasionally brought bastards into the world, and she keenly felt the embarrassment of once literally getting down on her knees to help treat the venereal disease he had contracted from another woman. She believed that Jeremiah Crutchley, a cheeky, rather disagreeable young man who frequented Streatham, was Thrale's illegitimate son, and for this reason she grew uneasy when Crutchley took a fancy to her daughter Queeney.[95] In one of her diaries she records that on September 3, 1776, Thrale informed her that he had an ailment, "& shewed me a Testicle swelled to an immense Size: I had no Notion but of a *Cancer*—Poor *Fool*!" When she pressed Thrale to get the best medical attention, he merely smiled and said it was nothing dangerous. But after more urging, he agreed to send for a man named Osborne, whom she described as something of a quack and who followed the practices of "a famous Practitioner in the *Venereal* Way":

> I now began to understand where I was, and to perceive that my poor Father's Prophecy was verified who said If you marry that Scoundrel he will catch the Pox, & for your Amusement set you to make his Pultices. This is now literally made out; & I am preparing Pultices as he said, and Fomenting [applying moist heat to relieve pain] this elegant Ailment every Night & Morning for an Hour together on my Knees, & receiving for my Reward such Impatient Expressions as disagreeable Confinement happens to dictate. however tis well tis no worse— he has I am pretty sure not given it me.[96]

Thrale at first protested that his ailment was not an infection but the result of an injury he received nearly a year before, during the trip to France, when he had leaped from a runaway carriage. Mrs. Thrale, however, did not easily accept his explanation. His having spent fifty guineas about seven years earlier to cure a similar complaint and his not having mentioned such an injury until now made her hesitant to believe him. She found his lack of kindness and confidence in the present situation particularly galling considering her exemplary behavior on the previous occasion. This involved setting him down at the doctor's door "and keeping his Secret inviolable even from my Mother, as that he needed not have neglected any Ailment he might contract for fear of my Suspicions or Resentment." Even if she felt resentment, Thrale need not have feared she would show it. "What need of so many Lyes about it!—I'm sure I care not, so he recovers to hold us all together."[97] She may have had the temerity to bait Johnson occasionally and to endure his rebukes, but she was particularly cautious not to provoke Thrale about his mistresses or anything else, "conscious that a Misunderstanding there could never answer; as I have no Friend or Relation in the World to protect me from the rough Treatment of a *Husband* shou'd he chuse to exert his *Prerogatives*."[98]

While Thrale was at the peak of his building mania, an acquaintance tried convincing him to spend £20,000 on a new structure. Thrale grew so enamored of the plan that he hung the architect's drawing on the wall of his bedchamber. When Mrs. Thrale told Johnson, he advised her to take some action to prevent this foolish scheme. "So little did Dr. Johnson even *then* comprehend the strict awe I stood in," of Thrale, "that I well recollect his saying to me, 'Madam! You should tear that foolish paper down: why 'tis like leaving a wench's loveletter in the apartments of a man whom you would wish to cure of his amorous passion.'" But Mrs. Thrale knew better than to make such a move. "God knows I durst as well encounter death as disturb Mr. Thrale's loveletters or his building plans."[99] She found some consolation and even took pride in never having crossed or fretted her husband: "never had I a desire beyond his Will—or a Will [of my own]—except about *my Trees*."[100]

Her trees were an exception. They stood on land she had inherited in Wales, land that represented memories of her early childhood, esteem for her mother, and pride in her ancient Welsh ancestry. At a time when Thrale needed money, he proposed cutting down some of the trees and selling the timber. Mrs. Thrale protested with many "Intreaties, Tears, and Sullens," and she also enlisted Johnson to help dissuade Thrale from his plan. But after some delay, Thrale went ahead and cut down the trees, sold them for £4,000, "and bid me not set my old Bulldog on *him*; for He w^d bear teizing only from a *Lady*."[101] Her old bulldog, of course, was Johnson.

In her seventeen-and-a-half-year marriage to Thrale, probably the greatest blow to her pride, the situation that required the greatest suppression of anger and resentment, was Thrale's infatuation with the lovely Sophia Streatfeild. Miss Streatfeild had also once been a student of Dr. Collier. She was young, beautiful, learned, and chaste, but she was also a brazen flirt. She turned heads and captured hearts wherever she went. Even the proper Dr. Charles Burney fell under her spell for a time and acted foolishly in her presence.[102] Thrale had continued to sink under the crush of financial worries and increasing depression, especially after the death of his nine-year-old son Harry. Baretti, who then still lived with the Thrales, hurried to Southwark on news of the tragic death and later described the scene: "Mr. Thrale, both his hands in his waistcoat pocket[s], sat on an arm-chair in a corner of the room with his body so stiffly erect, and with such a ghastly smile in his face, as was quite horrid to behold."[103]

It was a blow from which he never fully recovered. Two years after the boy's death, Johnson wrote to Mrs. Thrale, "Is my Master come to himself? Does he talk and walk and look about him, as if there were yet something in the world for which it is worth while to live? or does he yet sit and say nothing?"[104] Thrale, in fact, lost all interest in his business and seemed to care only for traveling and hosting dinner parties. In 1779, at fifty, he suffered a stroke that left him more despondent than ever, although he soon regained his speech and motor skills. Having always been moderate in his habits, he now developed a compulsion to gorge himself and to fawn over the fair and charming Miss Streatfeild. "*I* do not observe with any *Pleasure* I fear, that *my* Husband prefers Miss Streatfield [*sic*] to *me*," wrote Mrs. Thrale in her diary, "tho' I must acknowledge her both Younger, handsomer, & a better Scholar."[105]

The company at Streatham sometimes played a game, inspired by Oliver Goldsmith, in which they tried to determine what food, flowers, or animals certain people most resembled. In his poem "Retaliation," Goldsmith had written that everyone resembles some type of food. He wrote that Reynolds, for instance, was lamb. Garrick was a salad, "for in him we see / Oil, vinegar, sugar, and saltness agree." Playing the game at Streatham one evening, the group determined that Johnson was a haunch of venison, Henry Thrale roast beef, Sophy Streatfeild a white fricassee, Charles Burney a dish of fine green tea, and Fanny Burney a woodcock due to the bird's extreme shyness and ability to conceal itself. Mrs. Thrale later jotted in her diary that Sophy Streatfeild would soon make her, the lady of the house, a *brown* fricassee because "my Husband is in Love with her." Playing the game on another occasion, only this time associating particular persons with animals, the group set Johnson down for the elephant, Baretti for the bear, Fanny Burney for the doe or antelope, and Sophy Streatfeild for the dove. Johnson declared that Mrs. Thrale most resembled the rattlesnake, for she had its attractions, its venom, "and all the World knows you have its *Rattle*." Mrs. Thrale wrote in her diary afterward that her husband was most unfortunate to be enamored of a pigeon and married to a serpent. The company set down Thrale for a beaver due to his rage for building.[106]

Whatever the occasion, the gatherings at Streatham these days always included Sophy Streatfeild, and Mrs. Thrale took careful notice of her husband's increasing obsession with the alluring temptress. One afternoon the Thrales hosted a large gathering for tea, cards, and supper: "Miss Streatfield was one, & as Mr Thrale sate by her—he pressed her Hand to his Heart (as She told me herself,) & said Sophy we shall not enjoy this long, & tonight I will not be cheated of my *Only Comfort.*—Poor Soul! how shockingly tender!"[107] Such an open display of affection for Miss Streatfeild, when he never showed much fondness for his wife, finally caused Mrs. Thrale to erupt in an angry outburst, all the more violent for being so long suppressed. She realized that Thrale's behavior was symptomatic of his deteriorating physical and mental condition, but being once again close to term and consequently irritable and depressed herself, she could no longer restrain her emotions. On this occasion the Thrales gave a large dinner party. Among the guests were Johnson, Edmund Burke, and Miss Streatfeild. With Mrs. Thrale occupying the seat at the head of the table, Johnson on one side of her and Burke on the other, she had barely taken a spoonful of soup when Thrale asked her to change places with Sophy. Miss Streatfeild, he said, had a sore throat and might be injured by sitting so close to the open door. Mrs. Thrale grew so upset at the proposal "that I burst into tears, said something petulant—that perhaps ere long, the lady might be at the head of Mr. T.'s table, without displacing the mistress of the house," after which she jumped up and hurried from the room.

An hour or two later Johnson and Burke came up to the drawing room where she had retired. She asked Johnson if he had noticed what passed at the table, what offense she had suffered, and if, given her pregnant condition, she was much to blame for speaking as she did. Johnson said, "Why, possibly not; your feelings were outraged."

"Yes, greatly so," she replied, "and I cannot help remarking with what blandness and composure you *witnessed* the outrage. Had this transaction been told of others, your anger would have known no bounds; but, towards a man who gives good dinners &c., you were meekness itself!" She noted that Johnson turned color and Burke stood by looking foolish, neither saying a word. Yet it hardly seems surprising that the two most eloquent men in England should have kept silent. They were probably embarrassed and surely not eager to involve themselves in a domestic squabble between a man and his wife, especially in the couple's home. But Mrs. Thrale had a point in accusing Johnson of looking the other way on a moral issue when it proved in his best interests to do so. He never expressed disapproval of Thrale's moral laxity, probably because it would have jeopardized the comfortable lodgings, good company, and fine dinners he enjoyed at Streatham. At least Mrs. Thrale thought so. She agreed that "Johnson was, on the whole, a rigid moralist; but he could be ductile, I may say, servile," when it suited him.[108]

The treatment she received from the two most prominent men in her life was now a constant source of irritation to her. Her husband's philandering and self-indulgence, Johnson's captiousness and demands for attention, both men's lack of sentiment and affection, and their total disregard for her own needs and desires—all threatened to produce in Hester Thrale more anger and resentment than she could possibly contain.

NOTES

1. Burney, *Early Journals*, 1:76–78 and 81.
2. Ibid., 1:82.
3. Frances Burney, *Memoirs*, 2:124.
4. Hemlow, *The History of Fanny Burney*, 14.
5. Frances Burney, *Memoirs*, 2:168.
6. Ibid., 2:123.
7. Ibid., 2:125.
8. Burney, *Diary & Letters*, 2:207–8.
9. Burney, *Early Journals*, 3:108.
10. Hemlow, *The History of Fanny Burney*, 189.
11. Burney, *Early Journals*, 2:243.
12. Frances Burney, *Memoirs*, 3:401.
13. Burney, *Early Journals*, 3:440.
14. Ibid., 1:27.
15. Ibid., 1:26.
16. Ibid., 1:6.
17. Ibid.
18. Ibid., 3:335.
19. Burney, *Diary & Letters*, 1:373.
20. Ibid., 1:312.
21. Charles Burney, *Letters of Dr Charles Burney, 1751–1784*, ed. Alvaro Bibeiro (Oxford: Clarendon Press, 1991), 1:136.
22. Margaret Anne Doody, *Frances Burney: The Life in the Works* (New Brunswick, NJ: Rutgers University Press, 1988), 370.
23. Burney, *Early Journals*, 3:256.
24. Ibid., 2:262.
25. Ibid., 2:276.
26. Ibid., 1:54–55.
27. Ibid., 2:278.
28. Ibid., 1:303.
29. Piozzi, *Thraliana*, 368 and 458.

30. Ibid., 368.

31. Ibid., 400.

32. Burney, *Early Journals*, 1:322.

33. Burney, *Diary & Letters*, 2:149.

34. Burney, *Early Journals*, 3:255–56.

35. Frances Burney, *Memoirs*, 2:167.

36. Burney, *Early Diary*, 2:143.

37. Ibid., 1:lii.

38. Ibid., 2:160.

39. Ibid., 2:160.

40. Burney, *Early Journals*, 2:108.

41. Ibid., 1:321.

42. Ibid., 1:320.

43. Piozzi, *Thraliana*, 470.

44. *The London Tradesman. Being a Compendious View of All the Trades, Professions, Arts, Both Liberal and Mechanic, Now Practised in the Cities of London and Westminster* (1747; reprint, Newton Abbot, Devon: David & Charles Reprints, 1969), 89.

45. Lord Chesterfield, *Letters to His Son*, June 6, 1751 (London: J. M. Dent & Sons, 1935), 238.

46. Burney, *Early Journals*, 3:212 and 3:135.

47. Burney, *Early Diary*, 2:222.

48. Hemlow, *The History of Fanny Burney*, 99.

49. Burney, *Early Journals*, 3:38–39.

50. Piozzi, *Thraliana*, 329, and Burney, *Early Journals*, 3:60.

51. Burney, *Early Journals*, 3:61.

52. Ibid., 3:211, 194, 163.

53. Burney, *Diary & Letters*, 2:376.

54. Ibid., 1:366.

55. Frances Burney, *Memoirs*, 2:297.

56. Burney, *Diary & Letters*, 4:44.

57. Burney, *Early Journals*, 3:187.

58. Ibid., 3:212.

59. Burney, *Diary & Letters*, 3:392.

60. Burney, *Early Journals*, 1:115.

61. Ibid., 1:124.

62. Burney, *Diary & Letters*, 4:65.

63. Burney, *Early Journals*, 3:171–72.

64. Burney, *Diary & Letters*, 4:222.

65. Edward Mangin, *Piozziana; or, Recollections of the Late Mrs. Piozzi, with Remarks. By a Friend* (London, 1833), 10.

66. Hester Lynch Thrale Piozzi, *The Piozzi Letters: Correspondence of Hester Lynch Piozzi, 1784–1821 (formerly Mrs. Thrale)*, ed. Edward A. Bloom and Lillian D. Bloom, 6 vols. (Newark: University of Delaware Press, 1989–2002), 1:22.

67. Piozzi, *Thraliana*, 321–22 and 271.

68. Ibid., 321.

69. Hemlow, *The History of Fanny Burney*, 185.

70. Mangin, *Piozziana*, 212–13.

71. Hemlow, *The History of Fanny Burney*, 185. To illustrate Mrs. Thrale's love of showy attire and the attention it brought her, she once had a dress made to wear to court based on an article brought back from Tahiti by Captain James Burney, Fanny Burney's brother. "The Owyhee is to be trimmed with grebeskins and gold to the tune of £65—the trimming only," Mrs. Thrale wrote to Fanny (Burney, *Diary & Letters*, 1:460). The day after the court ceremony, the *Morning Herald* printed the following notice: "Mrs. Thrale appeared in a striped sattin Otaheite pattern, trimmed with crape, gold lace, and foil, and ornamented with a profusion of stones, of a new composition, very little inferior in point of lustre to the most brilliant jewels;—the *toute ensemble* of this dress was magnificent as well as singular!" (Clifford, *Hester Lynch Piozzi*, 1968], 194).

72. Burney, *Early Journals*, 3:153.

73. Piozzi, *Thraliana*, 321.

74. Burney, *Diary & Letters*, 1:352. In a letter to Mrs. Thrale Johnson said that he had spoken that morning with Sir Philip Jennings Clark on business related to Streatham: "We then talked about our Mistress, and [Mrs. Montagu], and I said You had most wit, and most literature" (Johnson, *Letters*, Redford, 3:253). In comparing herself to Mrs. Montagu, Mrs. Thrale said, "Mrs. Montagu's Bouquet is all out of the Hot-house—mine out of the Woods & Fields & many a Weed there is in it" (Clifford, *Hester Lynch Piozzi*, 153).

75. Burney, *Early Journals*, 3:440.

76. Burney, *Diary & Letters*, 1:406.

77. Piozzi, *Thraliana*, 375.

78. Ibid., 149.

79. Johnson, *Letters*, Redford, 3:81. Johnson here alludes to a line in Nathaniel Lee's play *The Rival*: "Then he will talk, good gods, how he will talk!"

80. Piozzi, *Thraliana*, 415.

81. Ibid., 167.

82. Hayward, *Autobiography*, 1:349.

83. Piozzi, *Thraliana*, 416.

84. Piozzi, *French Journals*, 99.

85. Piozzi, *Thraliana*, 339.

86. Frances Reynolds, "Recollections of Dr. Johnson," in Hill, *Johnsonian Miscellanies*, 2:273.

87. Boswell, *Life*, 1:413.

88. Piozzi, *Thraliana*, 726.

89. Ibid., 52–53.

90. Burney, *Early Journals*, 3:71.

91. Burney, *Diary & Letters*, 1:332.

92. Boswell, *Life*, 1:494; Piozzi, *Anecdotes*, 155. Boswell speculates at one point in the *Life* that a certain improvement in Johnson's dress was suggested by Mrs. Thrale. She has written in the margin of her copy, "no truly—it was Mr. Thrale &

not his Wife who attempted such Corrections. He would no more have suffer'd *me* to have chosen his Coat than the very Youngest of my Children" (Boswell, *Life With Comments*, 3:31).

93. Broadley, *Doctor Johnson and Mrs. Thrale*, 115.

94. Boswell, *Life With Comments*, 3:95.

95. See Piozzi, *Thraliana*, 497 and 515.

96. Hyde, *Thrales of Streatham Park*, 165–66.

97. Ibid., 167 and 174.

98. Piozzi, *Thraliana*, 43.

99. Hayward, *Autobiography*, 2:40–41.

100. Piozzi, *Thraliana*, 469.

101. Ibid., 222 and n2.

102. Sophia Streatfield (1754–1835) was born at Chiddingstone, Kent. Fanny Burney records Mrs. Thrale saying "that she had a power of captivation that was irresistible; that her beauty, joined to her softness, her caressing manners, her Tearful Eyes, & alluring looks, would insinuate her into the Heart of *any* man she thought worth attacking" (Burney, *Early Journals*, 3:303). She had the ability to shed tears at will. Johnson was also charmed by her, saying in 1778, "she is a sweet Creature, & I love her much,—but my little Burney writes a better letter" (Burney, *Early Journals*, 3:137). But Johnson later remarked that except for her mastery of Greek, she was ignorant as a butterfly (Burney, *Early Journals*, 3:303).

103. "Stricture the First," *European Magazine* 13 (May 1788): 314.

104. Johnson, *Letters*, 3:128.

105. Piozzi, *Thraliana*, 423. Boswell first met Sophia Streatfeild at a dinner party in March 1781 and afterward wrote in his journal that "I really fell in love with Miss Sophy Streatfield [*sic*], a beautiful young lady of family and some fortune, exceedingly accomplished and even a Greek scholar." She told Boswell that she highly respected Dr. Johnson but was afraid of him (Boswell, *Laird of Auchinleck*, 302–3).

106. Piozzi, *Thraliana*, 347–48 and n1, 70, 414.

107. Ibid., 432.

108. Hayward, *Autobiography*, 1:122–3. Johnson wrote in *Idler* #13 that "few men of prudence are much inclined to interpose in disputes between man and wife" (Johnson, *Works*, 2:42).

Chapter Ten

Like Embroidery upon Gauze

Hester Thrale quickly formed strong opinions about people. She tended to like or dislike them intensely and did not hesitate to express her feelings to those she trusted. Johnson once scolded her in the presence of Boswell for praising some people too extravagantly and condemning others too violently. "And yet," he added, giving her a sidelong glance and smile while speaking to Boswell, "she is the first woman in the world, could she but restrain that wicked tongue of hers;—she would be the only woman, could she but command that little whirligig."[1]

She liked persons of spirit and took no pleasure at all in "the sneakers & Fawners" and their "Obsequious Civility." People of strong minds, discernment, and sarcastic wit attracted her especially. "What an odd Partiality I have for a rough Character!" she admitted, "and even for the hard parts of a soft one!" She found herself at times, for example, "distractedly fond" of David Garrick. His spirited conversation, sharp wit, and playful mimicry of others delighted her. She also appreciated his mastery of the well-turned phrase. She once told him that no other town but Lichfield ever produced two such men as he and Johnson, and Garrick responded, "Oh I am only the Gizzard Madam, trussed under the Turkey's Wing."[2] She did not know him as intimately as did Johnson and Boswell, though she had met him years before meeting the other two. At age six, when her parents moved from Wales to London in 1747, she had sat on his lap, and he had fed her dainties.[3] Arthur Murphy brought them together again when he introduced Garrick into the Thrale household in 1760, five years prior to Johnson being introduced.[4]

Garrick and the Thrales liked one another well enough but never became intimate. Although Garrick's portrait by Reynolds hung in the library as one of the "Streatham worthies," there is no indication the Thrales took an active interest in his professional career. Hester Thrale does not mention a specific instance of seeing him on stage. And while the Southwark brewer and his wife were rich, they were not of sufficient social position, perhaps, to claim much of Garrick's time. Besides, Henry Thrale was not the sort to kindle warm feelings in the outgoing and vivacious actor. Still, Hester Thrale took careful note of Garrick's personality and ranked his general abilities on a scale of zero to twenty along with the same characteristics of other friends. His highest mark was a nineteen for both "wit" and "humour." In these two areas no one ranked higher in her estimation. His lowest mark was zero for "Good humour ne[ce]ssary to Conversation." Johnson, Baretti, Beauclerk, and Langton also received zeroes in this category. Boswell and Dr. Burney scored highest with nineteen. For religion Garrick got ten, morality fifteen, scholarship three, general knowledge sixteen, person and voice eighteen, and manner seventeen.[5]

Although she sometimes found herself distractedly fond of Garrick, she was the only one among the Johnson circle who did not admire Sir Joshua Reynolds. He was simply too bland for her. "He is . . . not much a Man to my natural Taste," she stated. "He seems to have no Affections, and that won't do with me." Reynolds, in fact, appeared more reserved in her presence than around most people, indicating that he may have been intimidated by her assertiveness or that he disapproved of her eccentricities. While she appreciated his artistic talents and valued his series of portraits that hung in her library, she had no appreciation for the personal characteristics everyone else admired: "I always told Johnson that they overrated that Man's mental Qualities; he replied Everybody loves Reynolds except *you*. The Truth is I felt that he hated *me*; & suspected that he encouraged Mr Thrale's Attachment to Sophia Streatfield—the charming S.S. as we called her."[6] She did not rank him very high on her scale of personal attributes. For scholarship, wit, and humor, she gave him the lowest mark, a zero. For "Manner" he received a ten, "Good humor" a ten, and "Person & voice" a twelve. His highest mark was fourteen for general knowledge.

Her criticism that he lacked affection Reynolds himself acknowledged, and his devoted assistant, James Northcote, granted that "If Sir Joshua had come into the room where I was at work for him and had seen me hanging by the neck, it would not have troubled him."[7] Perhaps somewhere along the way, in his conscious attempt not to be disturbed by anything, Reynolds had lost the faculty of close personal attachment. When Goldsmith died in 1774, Reynolds, stunned at the loss of his closest friend, surprised many by not touching his brushes for an entire day. But then he raised critical eyebrows when he picked them up again the following morning and went back to work with his usual zeal. Boswell also felt Reynolds's stoic indifference. During one his severe bouts of melancholy, he confided to his journal, "It was not pleasing to find that Sir Joshua had all this time known that I was in sad spirits, and never once called or sent to inquire about me. We must take our friends as they are."[8]

It was nevertheless impossible for Reynolds to preserve his equanimity entirely. Rents in the fabric of his placid disposition occasionally appeared. Being a man of consequence, he was sometimes pestered by hangers-on, people who felt it their privilege to call on him during the working part of the day and to lounge about his house. "Those idle people," he once said in exasperation, "those idle people do not consider that my time is worth five guineas an hour." Young painters, anxious to gain the master's commendation, would sometimes bring him their work to look at. "What's this in your hand? A portrait?" said Reynolds impatiently to one young student. "You should not show such things. What's that upon her head—a dish-clout?"[9]

But the one who disturbed Reynolds's equanimity the most was his younger, unmarried sister, Frances. She lived with Reynolds as a sort of housekeeper, running the day-to-day operations of the household. In return for her services, Reynolds provided her with a small allowance. Generally pleasing and intelligent, she possessed traits that nettled her complacent brother. Mrs. Thrale said that she had "an odd dry Manner, something between Malice and Simplicity, which was entertaining enough,"[10] but certainly not entertaining to her brother. She would ask questions and make comments that appeared innocent on the surface but that Mrs. Thrale believed concealed a strain of calculated mischievousness.

Perhaps even more annoying to Sir Joshua was that Frances could never settle on any fixed purpose or course of action. She seemed to live in a constant state of indecision. Fanny Burney, who came to like her, despite her "excessive oddness & absurdity," later described her as

> a woman of worth and understanding, but of a singular character; who, unfortunately for herself, made, throughout life, the great mistake of nourishing that singularity which was her bane. . . . It was that of living in an habitual perplexity of mind, and irresolution of conduct, which to herself was restlessly tormenting, and to all around her was teazingly wearisome.[11]

Johnson, who had great affection for her, showed his impatience with her indecisiveness when he once said to her, "Ponder no more, Renny,—whatever you do do it, but ponder no more!"[12]

Besides looking after the household, Frances Reynolds also painted portraits, which Northcote said were precise imitations of all her brother's faults. The pictures embarrassed Reynolds, and he attempted to keep them out of sight as much as possible, saying that they made others laugh and him cry.[13] For the most part, he tried to ignore Frances and her irritating traits, but when driven to the edge of his patience, he occasionally spoke harshly to her and treated her like one of the domestic servants. In his will, he left her the generous sum of £2,500, yet Frances claimed she had seen nothing in her brother but "a *gloomy tyrant*."[14] Not that he showed any greater affection for his older married sisters, Elizabeth Johnson and Mary Palmer. He treated them with much the same indifference that he treated Frances. His behavior seems all the more strange considering his obligations to them, because they had helped finance his trip to Italy when he was a young man so that he could study the Renaissance masters. But his sisters were in a unique position to interrupt the orderly pattern of his life, and he was careful to seal off every approach where he might be vulnerable. Naturally his sisters resented it.

In 1775, when Elizabeth Reynolds Johnson experienced financial problems because of a bad marriage, her sister Mary tried to persuade their brother to settle £50 a year on Elizabeth in fulfillment of a promissory note he had agreed to sometime earlier. But Reynolds demurred, saying, "If she suffers it is her own fault."[15] Elizabeth's son, Samuel, wrote his mother from London:

> There is no comfort for you from this quarter. Your suppos'd Brother and you could never have had the same parents or be known to one another in your infancy. He desires He may be look'd on as if He did not exist, for He will do nothing for you. He did not know hardly how to get off, My Aunt says, about the £50.[16]

Frances suggested that Elizabeth sue to get the money promised her. "I would go to law with a Brother for the sake of my children," she said, "and the law will undoubtedly give it to her."[17]

Elizabeth finally wrote to her unsympathetic brother, "Thy soul is a shocking spectacle of poverty. When thy outside is, as thy inside now is, as I told thee ten year since I will not shut the door against thee. But it may be, thy soul is past all recovery. If so, I shall never see thee more."[18]

Frances Reynolds grew so annoyed with her brother that she decided to address her grievances to him a letter, but she could not determine how best to go about it, so she solicited Johnson's advice. He offered to write the letter for her, but when she read what he had composed, she rejected it, for she saw that it sounded too much like Johnson and not enough like her. It would no more have deceived her brother, she said, than if Johnson had attired himself in her cap and dressing gown and presented himself to Sir Joshua as his sister.[19]

Aside from his disgruntled relations, however, Reynolds impressed nearly everyone else as a happy, well-balanced, unperturbable individual. Johnson claimed that he was the most invulnerable man he knew, "the man with whom if you should quarrel, you would find the most difficulty how to abuse," and he told Fanny Burney that Sir Joshua possessed the greatest share of inoffen-siveness of any friend he had.[20] His only weaknesses in Johnson's view were a willingness to subordinate his mind to others and his occasional excessive drinking. Northcote believed that Reynolds's normally mild disposition ac-counted for the charm and repose that characterize his paintings. His portraits typically convey an ease and amiability not attributable to the sitters alone. They communicate a tranquility largely derived from the artist himself.

Reynolds distinguished himself as a portrait painter in three key areas: the way he varied the posture of his sitters, the manner in which he conveyed the character of each subject, and his adept use of color. Prior to Reynolds, English portrait painters worked from a few fixed poses to which all they had to do was add a likeness of the face. Reynolds said of these painters, "They have got a set of postures which they apply to all persons indiscriminately: the consequence of which is that all their pictures look like so many sign-post paintings."[21] He, of course, learned the practice while apprenticed to the por-trait painter Thomas Hudson. Reynolds reportedly often told the story of how he and a young partner contrived to make some quick money by turning out small portraits at a guinea apiece of naval officers stationed at Portsmouth. Reynolds did the heads while the friend furnished the draperies.

> All the variety there was in these portraits I endeavoured to give to the airs of the heads [said Reynolds]; as my friend, who had the chief management of the bodies, had a favourite attitude which he gave to all the figures, whether they were in front, oblique or profile. This was one hand in the bosom and the other upon the sword or in the breeches pocket, with the hat under the arm.

Their portrait factory ran smoothly until Reynolds one day decided that a particularly fine head would look better and more military wearing "a fierce cocked hat," so he painted it in. The officer must have been surprised when he received his portrait and saw himself with a hat under his arm and one on his head.[22]

Considering the vast number of people that Reynolds painted throughout his career and how little he knew some of them personally, it is no wonder that he still resorted occasionally to standard poses and that we sometimes find the same posture duplicated in different portraits. The freshness and vari-ety of his ideas, nevertheless, are remarkable. The spontaneity and animation of his work surpasses anything that came before in England, witness the static portraits by Hudson and Hogarth. Dr. James Beattie, who sat for his picture in 1773, discussed with Reynolds this aspect of his work:

> It is, he tells me [said Beattie], the study of Nature in all its varieties, that enables him to give that variety of graceful and expressive attitudes to his pictures, in which in my opinion no painter antient or modern has ever equalled him. Other painters too often imitate one another; he always imitates nature.[23]

Thomas Gainsborough, Reynolds's chief rival, paid him the highest tribute when he exclaimed, "Damn him, how various he is!"[24]

Reynolds successfully adapted even standard poses in his attempt to convey the characters of his subjects, portraying character being one of his chief aims. Mere likeness was not enough. Reynolds said that in about half a year's time he could teach any boy that chance threw in his way to paint a likeness, "but to give a just expression and true character to the portrait . . . proved the great master."[25] Dr. Beattie was immediately struck by this aspect of Sir Joshua's paintings. Beattie wrote in his diary, "His portraits are distinguished from all others by this, that they exhibit an exact imitation not only of the features, but also of the character of the person represented."[26] Edmond Malone made essentially the same point in his introduction to Reynolds's written works:

> Instead of confining himself to mere likeness, in which however he was eminently happy, he dived, as it were, into the minds, and habits, and manners, of those who sat to him; and accordingly the majority of his portraits are so appropriated and characteristick, that the many illustrious persons whom he has delineated, will be almost as well known to posterity, as if they had seen and conversed with them.[27]

Northcote offered only one caveat, that in trying to give character where it did not exist, he sometimes sacrificed likeness.

Reynolds worked rapidly, using exceptionally long brushes with nineteen-inch handles. Lady Burlington remembered him always in motion: "His plan was to walk away several feet, then take a long look at me and the picture as we stood side by side, then rush up to the portrait and dash at it in a kind of fury. I sometimes thought he would make a mistake and paint on me instead of the picture."[28]

He often finished a portrait in two or three days. He explained to a prospective client, "It requires in general three sittings about an hour and half each time but if the sitter chooses it the face could be begun and finished in one day . . . when the face is finished the rest is done without troubling the sitter."[29] The first sitting usually began with Reynolds laying a ground of white on a light colored canvas. Then, while this was still wet, and using only flake white, lake (a purplish red), and black, he produced a flat, monochrome like-ness with the face done in considerable detail and the rest of the figure more or less sketched in. During subsequent sittings, he worked up flesh colors and fine points of expression, leaving the mundane work of draperies and back-ground to assistants. Finally he touched up and finished off the completed work.[30]

Joseph Baretti, after Sir Joshua Reynolds, 1773.
Source: Trustees of the British Museum.

When James Beattie sat for his portrait, he chose one long sitting and afterward jotted in his diary, "I sate to him five hours, in which time he finished my head, and sketched out the rest of my figure:—the likeness is most striking and the execution masterly." More complicated pictures, of course, took longer, but still the rapidity of his work was remarkable. He told Beattie that he finished the painting of Garrick between Comedy and Tragedy in a week, and Beattie learned that the portrait of Joseph Baretti, which hung in the Thrale library, took Reynolds but eight hours to paint.[31]

It was at the stage of working up color that Reynolds focused his greatest attention. He told his pupil Northcote that no person then living knew anything about coloring, but that all artists had an obligation to rediscover this lost art.[32] Not since the Italian Renaissance had anyone been a master of coloring. With Reynolds it became a passion, one might even say an obsession. During the 1750s and 1760s in particular, he experimented with various combinations of pigments, oils, waxes, varnishes, and other materials. These experiments produced many works of brilliant color, subtle shading, and remarkably clear tones, but the experiments also produced some disastrous results. He became impatient to advance this branch of his art while his speed and facility in drawing made him additionally careless in the use of materials. As glowing as his colors were when first set down, they often proved chemically unstable and soon lost their brilliance and began to fade. The lakes, madders, and carmine in particular were subject to speedy decay. Some people understandably got upset to see their portraits deteriorate within only a few years of purchase. One indignant sitter wrote the following epigram:

> Painting of old was surely well designed
> To keep the features of the dead in mind,
> But this great rascal has reversed the plan,
> And made his pictures die before the man.[33]

In the worst cases, the colors entirely flew, leaving a shadowy, chiaroscuro effect. John Thomas Smith, former pupil and later biographer of the sculptor Joseph Nollekens, told of an Irish nobleman whom Reynolds painted in early 1761:

His lordship shortly after went abroad, and remained there between twenty and thirty years, during which time he ran into excesses, became bilious, and returned to Ireland with a shattered constitution. He found that the portrait and the original had faded together, and corresponded, perhaps, as well as when first painted.[34]

Reynolds himself did not seem much disturbed by the impermanence of his colors. Once a painting left his studio, he dismissed it from his mind.

His assembly-line approach to turning out portraits, along with his continuing search for that elusive brilliance of the Renaissance painters, was more important to him than the ultimate fate of a single experiment. A recent art critic has charged that Reynolds's adherence to practices that he knew were detrimental to the life of his pictures amounted to perversity.[35] When someone addressed a poetic epistle to him in 1777, praising his work but referring to the "fleetiness" of his colors, Reynolds good-naturedly remarked that it must be conceded, then, that he "came off with flying colours."[36] But speaking more seriously, he remarked,

> I had not an opportunity of being early initiated in the principles of colouring: no man, indeed, could teach me. If I have never been settled with respect to colouring, let it at the same time be remembered that my unsteadiness in this respect proceeded from an inordinate desire to possess every kind of excellence that I saw in the works of others; without considering that there is in colouring, as in style, excellences which are incompatible with each other: however, this pursuit, or, indeed, any similar pursuit, prevents the artist from being tired of his art. . . . My fickleness in the mode of colouring arose from an eager desire to attain the highest excellence. This is the only merit I assume to myself from my conduct in that respect.[37]

He often ground his pigment directly into wax and stirred it all into a buttery paste. One sitter watched him dab such a mixture onto a canvas. Then he "laid the Picture on its back, shook it about till it settled like a batter pudding, and then painted away."[38] This sort of practice produced a rich, creamy texture and color, but over time the pigment rose to the surface and formed blisters or cracks. Reynolds also used considerable bitumen, a substance similar to tar. Bitumen, like wax, produces a rich, creamy, vibrant texture, but it never completely dries. The result in Reynolds's portraits was often cracking and even peeling of the paint from the canvas. Northcote explained to his brother that Sir Joshua preferred using varnishes to oils, for "the oils give the colours a dirty yellowness in time, but this method of his has an inconvenience full as bad, which is that his pictures crack; sometimes before he has got them out of his hands."[39] Reynolds also tended to apply numerous layers of paint to his portraits, a practice that may have contributed substantially to the cracking. Once when an amateur painter objected that a waxy material Reynolds recommended to him would crack, Reynolds replied, "All good pictures crack."[40]

Reynolds painted twelve portraits for the Streatham library. The centerpiece, a full- length picture of Mrs. Thrale and Queeney, hung over the fireplace. "The rest of the pictures were all three-quarters," wrote Fanny Burney. "Mr. Thrale was over the door leading to his study. The general collection [arranged in pairs, one above the other] then began by Lord Sandys and Lord Westcote, two early noble friends of Mr. Thrale. Then followed

Dr. Johnson.   Mr. Burke.   Dr. Goldsmith.
Mr. Murphy.   Mr. Garrick.   Mr. Baretti.
Sir Robert Chambers, and Sir Joshua Reynolds himself."

A portrait by Reynolds of Dr. Burney was added in 1781. Fanny noted that Sir Joshua took great delight in his Streatham gallery. All the portraits, despite some cracking, have survived in otherwise good condition.[41]

Worthy Bennet Langton never achieved the distinction of becoming a Streatham worthy. Due mainly to family obligations, he seldom attended the gatherings at Streatham Park during its peak years in the 1770s, and, besides, it was during this period that he became more withdrawn and taciturn than usual. While still single, he had been outgoing and talkative, many thought beyond his natural inclinations, but after taking on the responsibilities of a growing family and after experiencing a decline in his limited finances, he grew silent and uncommunicative. "Do you ever hear from Mr. Langton?" wrote Johnson to Boswell in 1776. "I visit him sometimes, but he does not talk. I do not like his scheme of life; but, as I am not permitted to understand it, I cannot set any thing right that is wrong. His children are sweet babies."[42]

Boswell, during a visit to London in the spring of 1778, told Johnson that Langton remembered well what passed in conversation the night before. "So he may," replied Johnson. "For he said nothing." Boswell then remarked that Mrs. Cholmondeley, sister of the actress Peg Woffington, had observed that Langton had first been a talker from affectation and then became silent for the same reason.[43] But whether Langton's silence actually sprang from affectation or was symptomatic of some inner distress that he kept to himself, we can only conjecture, yet Boswell provides a possible insight in one of his journal entries. Feeling dejected in being separated from his family in Edinburgh, Boswell turned to Langton for sympathy as he sometimes did in such circumstances. "Talking seriously with Langton on the deceitfulness of all our hopes of enjoyment on earth," he wrote, "while I at this moment languished for the comfort of being at home with my wife and children, the worthy man, from whom one would not expect it, suggested how domestic happiness was deceitful and how often we feel disgusted and weary when with our family."[44]

Boswell always enjoyed and usually profited from these tête-à-tête conversations. Langton was a man with whom he could exchange minds and compare sentiments. There were no contests for superiority or conflicts of vanity.

The two men conversed as equals and, in fact, had several things in common: both were young married fathers; each was, or was soon to be, head of an ancient landed family; and both venerated Dr. Johnson. Their conversations touched on many topics but usually focused on Johnson, general observations about life, and considerations of religious questions that Boswell had not resolved in his own mind. In their talks on Johnson, Boswell often gathered useful anecdotes from Langton's wealth of Johnsoniana. When they spoke of religion, Langton's thoughtful opinions helped pacify Boswell's vacillating mind.

Another of Langton's appealing features was his gift for making Boswell feel good about himself. Upon Boswell once mentioning that he had spent all Good Friday with Johnson, Langton replied, "Having your company is not fasting."[45] Another time, following a quick and unexpected visit from Langton, Boswell wrote in his journal, "I was glad to relish him, and he always raises me in my own opinion."[46] In addition, after one of their many late night dialogues, Boswell wrote, "The influence of this excellent friend upon me is truly salutary to my mind."[47] But as much as Boswell prized his worthy friend, he had to take him in small doses, for Langton's mild disposition and dormant existence did not accord with his own lively spirits. "It was rather dull compared with what society I can have in London," Boswell said after one visit. "It was dining on plain boiled and roast, with some sauce too. But I am used to variety and high relish."[48] Calling on Langton another evening, Boswell found him so lethargic and the evening so dull that he could not stand it and made his exit as soon as he decently could.[49] Two weeks later, however, he found himself obliged to dine at Langton's again. "I had no great mind to it, but I valued him for his learning and worth, and thought I should get some anecdotes of Johnson from him. . . . It was rather dull at Langton's with him and his lady and a Mrs. Tadwell, and no elegance of living. He seemed to be quite dull and recluse and gloomy from too strict notions of religious duty."[50]

In trying to animate his friend and help extricate him from the idle state into which he had sunk, Boswell urged him to become an author as many of their friends had done. "Your learning and talents in composition should do more than entertain yourself and a smal [sic] circle of correspondents." Recalling Langton's sensitivity to criticism, Boswell tried to reassure him: "There is indeed the risk of censure but that you have no reason to fear. I shall not be satisfied till I have you in my Library in due form. You once I think mentioned to me that you had thoughts of Biography. Mr. Johnson told me that he was for your writing the History of Lincolnshire. That would be an excellent Work for you."[51] But in spite of this urging, Langton remained as torpid as ever.

"Let us go and dine with Langton and sit upon him," Boswell said to Johnson one day, "hold a court of oyer and terminer (A criminal court, at which we can try him for all his offences)."

"We can do nothing for him but send him away," replied Johnson.

"Well, let us do so. We can banish [him]. I'd rather send him to the *Justitia* [a prison ship at Woolich]."[52]

Inertia had become such a part of Langton's personality that friends eventually gave up trying to inspire him to meaningful action. Peregrine Langton remembered his father as an extremely indolent, cautious man, describing him as

> mild, hesitating, considerate; reflecting deeply before he would venture upon the most trifling undertaking—always weighing & consulting the opinions of others before he would act—putting off to a more convenient season whatever he could defer doing—expecting that every shower of rain was to be a deluge—every breath of wind a hurricane—any publick expression of the people was to turn to a revolution, any opposition to the ministry what would overthrow the state.[53]

Langton's most successful efforts had no direct link to his children, to his youthful ambitions, or to his London friends. Attempting to be a writer or a painter required more self-discipline than he could muster, and managing his Lincolnshire estate and his financial affairs seemed beyond his capabilities. But his annual duties as an officer in the Royal North Lincolnshire Militia directed his energies into purposeful activity. Military life provided him with the structure, routine, and discipline that he could not supply himself. Having been commissioned a captain in March 1770, he served periodically in one capacity or another for the next twenty-five years, discharging his military duties intelligently and dependably.

Langton's ability to raise Boswell in his own estimation was not always necessary, for sometimes Boswell needed taking down a peg. One evening at the Thrale house in Southwark, as he began telling Mrs. Thrale how he had given up wine drinking and now drank only water, an exasperated Johnson exclaimed, "Who cares whether you drink water or not? As the French critic quoted in *The Spectator* says of Montaigne's mentioning that he liked white wine better than red, 'Who the devil cares?'"[54] On another occasion, and in a more patient tone, Johnson cautioned his friend against boasting, telling him that he vaunted so much that it provoked ridicule.[55] The worst part was that Boswell spoke as unguardedly about others as about himself, prompting a friend to confide to him that the caustic manner in which he often portrayed people made others think him malevolent. Boswell admitted to indulging himself too freely "in a sort of abusive licentiousness of characterizing" but claimed to be just the reverse of malevolent.[56] Langton once presented him with a book titled *The Government of the Tongue*, asking him to read it, but saying nothing further. Boswell recognized the gesture as "a delicate admonition."[57]

Even Boswell's wife gave him a lecture one morning on the coarse and abusive way he now spoke. She said that it was so distasteful that he was losing friends. She pointed out that he received only a tenth of the social invitations he used to get before they were married. Although he found her criticism just, he claimed to have fallen into the habit unconsciously. The rough manners and language of his fellow Scots barristers had been a bad influence on him, "and I have carried it to excess, as I do everything. I resolved to amend."[58] But fourteen years later, his friend William Temple was still censuring him for the same behavior, writing in his diary that Boswell "has a strange way of saying every thing he knows of people that he thinks will undervalue them.—What he says of one to others seldom turns out to ones praise or credit."[59] Talking about himself and others was one of his many defects he hoped to amend, but he was finding it difficult to root out.

"Another shocking fault which I have," he noted in his journal, "is my sacrificing almost anything to a laugh, even myself. . . . This is indeed a fault in the highest degree to be lamented and to be guarded against."[60] He realized that he cheapened himself by such conduct, but laughing, making jokes, and talking nonsense helped to ward off depression. Unable to mend the fault of being too jocular, he often tried to justify it, saying that he loved nonsense and that it often did him good. "I deluge my mind with it at times, as Egypt is overflowed by the Nile, and I think I produce better crops. To be perpetually talking sense runs out the mind, as perpetually ploughing and taking crops runs out land. The mind must be manured, and nonsense is very good for the purpose."[61]

Manuring his mind with nonsense presents a curious image and is perhaps a more appropriate metaphor for his behavior than he intended. His wife complained to him that his conversation with her was seldom rational but only childish nonsense. "The reason of it may be partly indolence, to avoid thought; partly because my wife, though she has excellent sense and a cheerful temper, has not sentiments congenial with mine. She has no superstition, no enthusiasm, no vanity."[62] Temple urged him to be more prudent in his conduct and said he should force himself to be more grave and reserved, "otherwise I would just be Jamie Boswell, without any respect."[63] Boswell agreed with all these admonitions. He realized that while he enjoyed the pleasure of laughing, the pleasure of being a respected gentleman was more to be desired.[64] Yet as much as he tried to become more grave and regular in his habits, and as often as he attempted to control his low jocularity and buffoonery, he found it impossible. Despite his constant resolutions to study proper conduct, he could never persist with any steadiness.

Irresolution, in fact, was the frailty that plagued him most. He could adopt strong positions on certain questions of national or family pride such as monarchy (he was for it), male succession (for it), and the war in America (against it), but he had difficulty deciding more immediate and personal issues. Often when confronted with a decision, his mind fluctuated radically, seizing upon ideas one after another as quickly as they tumbled through his head. "I have a weakness of mind which is scarcely credible," he confessed. "My mind is like an air-pump which receives and ejects ideas with wonderfull [*sic*] facility."[65] He usually embraced the attitudes and beliefs of the person he conversed with at the moment. After attempting for some time to acquire a more grave and proper character, he had to admit that he still had "a great degree of imbecility of mind; I am easily persuaded by what other people say, and cannot have a firm enough judgment."[66]

All these things resulted mainly from lack of self-esteem and lack of a clearly defined sense of identity. In once drawing up a summary of his life and character, he conceded that he was weaker than could be imagined and that his brilliant qualities were "like embroidery upon gauze"—attractive on the surface with nothing substantial underneath.[67] On one occasion he upbraided himself for having been of seven or eight differing opinions on one subject during the day. Writing to himself a week later he said, "You *are* imbecile. You are made by company."[68] One example of his indecisiveness occurred in Edinburgh when he became anxious over the trivial matter of whether to ride horseback or take a post chaise to the family estate at Auchinleck, a distance of almost eighty miles. He fretted for nearly two days before his wife and a friend finally decided for him and in favor of the chaise.[69]

He continued writing in his journal over the years, a ritual that became the unifying activity of his life and the foundation of those works for which he is yet celebrated. Preserving the daily minutes of his life became almost an obsession. He would stay at his desk throughout the night bringing his journal up to date, making it as full and complete as possible. It was important for him to get down as much as he could, for once preserved on paper, his life and character became fixed, no longer subject to fluctuations of mind or spirit. He cautioned himself that he should live no more than what he could record, "as one should not have more corn growing than what one can get in. There is a waste of good if it be not preserved."[70] The journal functioned, in part, as a mooring, an object to which he might secure himself in order to steady his mind. He attached himself to great men for much the same reason. These were men of impressive achievements, strong wills, and resolution.

"It is certain that I am not a great man," he once remarked, "but I have an enthusiastic love of great men, and I derive a kind of glory from it."[71] More important than glory, he derived stability and confidence. Being intimate with great men gave him a sense of worth by association. Due to his insecurity, he felt more comfortable when under someone else's authority. With no inner compass of his own, no reliable means of self-navigation, he had to depend on the guidance of others. "Will you, Sir, assume direction of me?" he asked Rousseau during one of their interviews at Môtiers.[72] Rousseau begged off, saying he had enough to do to take care of himself.

At other times he tried to place himself under the authority of various friends. Unable to restrain himself from consorting with London prostitutes, for instance, and afraid of becoming infected as a result, he jotted in a memorandum: "Tell Temple your risk, and make him lay restrictions upon you never to have any connection without permission from him."[73] Three days later he wrote again, "At two call Temple, confess errors, and not only resolve but promise. So as to be under his power."[74] When making plans to wed Margaret Montgomerie, his sensible and even-tempered cousin, he wrote in his journal, "That valuable woman will make me the man I wish to be."[75]

His attachment to Dr. Johnson demonstrated the same urgent need for dependence. "Will you really take charge of me?" he asked Johnson soon after they met, the same question he put to Rousseau six months later.[76] Like most people, Boswell venerated Johnson for his character, intellect, and achievements. But more importantly, he worshipped him as a man of strength, courage, and resolution. Under shelter of Johnson's decisive personality, Boswell eagerly sought refuge, and in the great man's strength he found solace. Johnson never seemed to waver. He did not hesitate or back down from decisions. He seemed born, in fact, to resolve difficult issues that harassed inferior minds with uncertainty and indecision. Considering Johnson the final arbiter, the preeminent judge in all matters doubtful or controversial, Boswell often deluged him with questions in order to hear his views on everything from free will and necessity to why a pear has its peculiar form.

He often felt astonished at the force and assurance with which Johnson seized upon every question that arose in conversation, no matter how trivial, and quickly settled it. A man, for instance, once praised a bulldog he owned as being well shaped. "He is not well shaped," exclaimed Johnson, "for there is not the quick transition from the thickness of the forepart to the *tenuity*— the thin part—behind, which a bulldog ought to have."

Boswell afterward remarked to himself, "My father and most men whom I know would no more think of discussing a question about a bulldog than of attacking a bull."[77]

Delighting in the security that Johnson's decisive character gave him, Boswell experienced a serenity of mind in his presence that he found nowhere else. Describing in his journal the sensations he felt during an evening with Johnson, he wrote,

> I complained [to Johnson] of a wretched changefulness—that I could not preserve for any long continuance the same views of anything. It was most comfortable to me to experience in Dr. Johnson's company a relief from this uneasiness. His steady, vigorous mind held firm before me those objects which my own feeble and tremulous imagination presented, for most part, in such a wavering state that my reason could not judge well of them.[78]

The sense of steadiness and security he experienced in Johnson's presence also helped shield him from Johnson's occasional angry explosions. Johnson one day grew impatient with him for asking too many frivolous questions, and finally when Boswell asked if he would not permit a man burdened with cares (Boswell himself) to drink in order to cheer himself up, Johnson replied, "Yes; if he sat next you."

The rebuke, however, did not faze Boswell. He dismissed it as being typical of Johnson. "Langton, who is a timorous man, said, 'I saw that you would bring something upon yourself.' I never was disturbed."[79] On the contrary, he rejoiced in having such a powerful friend to guide him, to curb his extravagancies, to praise him at times, and to scold him at others. "I thought I could die easily in company with him," he exulted. "I was like a weak-sighted passenger at sea who acquiesces in the assurance of a steady, strong-eyed pilot that he sees land."[80] But as much as Johnson helped to steady his mind, and as meticulously as Boswell recorded his own activities and feelings in his journal, he continued to be an enigma to himself. He found it amazing how different he could be at different times and how he was composed of many opposite qualities. "Sometimes I think myself good for nothing, and sometimes the finest fellow in the world."[81] After having scrutinized his character for many years, pointing out his own conceit, melancholy, disordered imagination, fluctuating mind, and other weaknesses, he had to acknowledge that he possessed some good qualities as well. He admitted to having no profound learning, strong judgment, nor constant gaiety, but credited himself with possessing an original sense of humor, turn of expression, and exceptional knowledge of human nature. These attributes, he thought, placed him ahead of many in society with more solid endowments. He claimed, in addition, to having a pleasing manner that put everyone at ease and that provided him with much happiness in return. "Were it not for my black Hypochondria, I might be a practical Epicurean."[82]

Most people were not aware that Boswell was manic depressive, that his character rested on a foundation of gloom and uncertainty, and that he was by nature timid. They saw instead a boisterous, outgoing individual whose good humor and affability made him universally welcome. Johnson once told him, "You make yourself agreeable wherever you go. Whoever has seen you once wishes to see you again."

"That is a very pleasing circumstance, Sir."

"Yes, Sir, very pleasing indeed."[83]

Unlike some of his other traits, Boswell's good humor was not contrived. It welled up naturally and was an attribute he increasingly relied on to advance himself in life as another might use learning, wealth, or rank. Edmund Burke claimed that he possessed so much good humor that it was scarce a virtue,

James Boswell, after George Langton.
Source: Trustees of the British Museum.

and David Garrick once wrote to him in Edinburgh, saying, "pray Let us See You Soon, & bring your Spirits, good humour & unaffected Mirth along with You."[84] His charm, in fact, could be nearly irresistible.

Standing about five foot six inches high and weighing 166 pounds in 1775, he carried himself in a stately manner—chin in, chest out—a deportment that communicated pride, dignity, a trace of arrogance, and a shade of self-deprecating humor. An Edinburgh acquaintance remarked, "It was impossible to look in his face without being moved by the comicality which always reigned upon it."[85] His characteristic demeanor was captured in a drawing by George Langton, Bennet Langton's eldest son.

One of those to feel his immediate charm was Fanny Burney's younger sister Charlotte. She first met him at a dinner party in 1781, and although Dr. Johnson sat across from her, the one who captured her attention was "Mr. Boswell, the famous Mr. Boswell, who is a sweet creature. I admire and like him beyond measure. He is a fine, lively, sensible, unaffected, honest, manly, good-humoured character." Johnson, feeling a bit morose, did not shine that evening, and though other clever people graced the table, the one who captivated her was Boswell. "He idolizes Dr. Johnson, and struts about, and puts himself into such ridiculous postures that he is as good as a comedy."

The most memorable of his *bon mots* that evening came at dinner during a discussion of women in India burning themselves on their husband's funeral pyres. Boswell called out from one end of the table, "Miss Burney, and what do *you* think of this burning scheme?"

"Oh," another of the guests cut in, "she had much rather *live*, I dare say!"

"Ay," replied Boswell, "then, Miss Burney, you would not like to be a *flaming beauty* in India, I fancy."[86]

Not so easily charmed by Boswell's good humor was older sister Fanny. Due to her increasing reserve and sense of decorum, she did not feel comfortable around the sprightly Scotsman. She thought his behavior too free and even impertinent. She did not like his speaking openly of his private affairs and the affairs of others, and she greatly disapproved of his taking down what people said in casual discourse. "I feel sorry," she remarked, "to be named or remembered by that Biographical, anecdotal memorandummer."[87] She recalled him once paying a morning visit to Streatham. As the guests assembled for breakfast, Boswell prepared to take the seat next to Johnson, but one of the other guests motioned for him to move further down, saying that the seat was for Miss Burney. Boswell looked amazed, considering the chair next to Johnson as his by prior rights. "But," wrote Fanny later, "after looking round for a minute or two, with an important air of demanding the meaning of this innovation, and receiving no satisfaction, he reluctantly, almost resentfully, got another chair; and placed it at the back of the shoulder of Dr. Johnson."

Feeling greatly embarrassed, Fanny quietly took her place next to Johnson, who did not notice where Boswell had gone. He assumed that he had taken a seat at the other end of the room. But a few minutes later, when Johnson made some good-natured remark about "Bozzy" and discovered by Boswell's reaction "that Bozzy had planted himself, as closely as he could, behind and between the elbows of the new usurper and his own, the Doctor turned angrily round upon him, and, clapping his hand rather loudly upon his knee, said, in a tone of displeasure, 'What do you do there, Sir?—Go to the table, Sir!'"

Boswell instantly complied, taking a seat at the far end of the table, but then remembering something he wished to show, he jumped up and started after it. Johnson called out to him, "What are you thinking of, Sir? Why do you get up before the cloth is removed?—Come back to your place, Sir!" Boswell again obeyed as Johnson muttered half to himself, "Running about in the middle of meals!—One would take you for a Brangton [*sic*]!" The Branghtons were an uncouth family in Fanny's *Evelina*.

"A Brangton, Sir?" asked Boswell. "What is a Brangton, Sir?"

"Where have you lived, Sir," said Johnson, suddenly laughing, "and what company have you kept, not to know that?"[88]

NOTES

1. Boswell, *Life*, 4:81–82.
2. Piozzi, *Thraliana*, 470, 484, and 125.
3. Hayward, *Autobiography*, 2:13.
4. Boswell, *Life*, 1:493n2.
5. Piozzi, *Thraliana*, 330.
6. Ibid., 382 and 728–29.
7. Leslie and Taylor, *Life and Times of Sir Joshua Reynolds*, 2:601.
8. James Boswell, *Boswell: The Great Biographer*, ed. Marlies K. Danziger and Frank Brady (New York: McGraw-Hill, 1989), 128.
9. Allan Cunningham, *The Life and Writings of Sir Joshua Reynolds, First President of the Royal Academy* (New York, 1860), 28 and 66.
10. Piozzi, *Thraliana*, 268.
11. Burney, *Early Journals*, 5:233; Frances Burney, *Memoirs*, 1:331–32.
12. Frances Burney, *The Journals and Letters of Fanny Burney (Madame d'Arblay)*, ed. Joyce Hemlow et al., 12 vols. (Oxford: Clarendon Press, 1972–1984), 4:256.
13. Hazlitt, *Conversations of James Northcote*, 138.
14. Wendorf, *Sir Joshua Reynolds*, 74; Joseph Farington, *The Diary of Joseph Farington*, ed. Kenneth Garlick et al., 16 vols. (New Haven: Yale University Press, 1978–1984), 4:1137–38.
15. Radcliffe, *Sir Joshua's Nephew*, 123.

16. Ibid.

17. Ibid., 122.

18. Hill, *Johnsonian Miscellanies*, 2:455–56n1.

19. Northcote, *Life*, 1:203.

20. Boswell, *Tour to the Hebrides*, 73; Frances Burney, *Memoirs*, 1:343.

21. Leslie and Taylor, *Life and Times of Sir Joshua Reynolds*, 1:100.

22. Whitley, *Artists and Their Friends*, 1:104.

23. James Beattie, *James Beattie's London Diary 1773*, ed. Ralph S. Walker (Aberdeen: Aberdeen University Press, 1946), 49.

24. Hudson, *Sir Joshua Reynolds*, 75.

25. Northcote, *Life*, 49.

26. Beattie, *London Diary*, 83.

27. Reynolds, *Works*, xxiv–xxv.

28. W. P. Frith, *My Autobiography and Reminiscences* (1888), 3:124.

29. Reynolds, *Letters*, 69.

30. For a detailed discussion of Reynolds's technique, see M. Kirby Talley Jr., "'All Good Pictures Crack': Sir Joshua Reynolds's Practice and Studio," in *Reynolds*, ed. Nicholas Penny (New York: Abrams, 1986), 55–70.

31. Beattie, *London Diary*, 83 and 82.

32. Northcote, *Memoirs*, 182.

33. Penny, *Reynolds*, 55.

34. Leslie and Taylor, *Life and Times of Sir Joshua Reynolds*, 1:111n2.

35. Penny, *Reynolds*, 55.

36. Northcote, *Memoirs*, 201.

37. Leslie and Taylor, *Life and Times of Sir Joshua Reynolds*, 1:116–17.

38. B. R. Haydon, *The Diary of Benjamin Robert Haydon*, ed. Willard Bissell Pope, 5 vols. (Cambridge, MA: Harvard University Press, 1960–1963), 5:585.

39. Whitley, *Artists and Their Friends*, 2:282.

40. Leslie and Taylor, *Life and Times of Sir Joshua Reynolds*, 1:113. See also "Reynolds, Paint and Painting: A Technical Analysis," in which Alexander Gent, Conservator for the Reynolds Research Project, writes, "Extensive layering, sometimes of incompatible materials, seems more often to have been the significant factor in the cracking and drying defects in his paintings, rather than simply the behaviour of the individual pigments and binders alone" (Lucy Davis and Mark Hallett, eds., *Joshua Reynolds: Experiments in Paint* [London: The Wallace Collection, 2015], 49).

41. Frances Burney, *Memoirs*, 2:80–81. Edwin Sandys, Second Baron Sandys (1726–1797), was a Member of Parliament and served for three months in 1757 as a Lord Commissioner of the Admiralty. "Lord Sandys," wrote Mrs. Thrale in her diary, "is a quiet man with a low-toned Voice, but when I want a Fact, or good Information as to Ecclesiastical History—I go to Lord Sandys for it." She later described him as "a vast, large, tall, fat Man, & his Breath excessively offensive" (Piozzi, *Thraliana*, 471n1 and 533). The present location of the Lord Sandys portrait is untraced.

William Henry Lyttelton, First Baron Westcote (1724–1808), was a colonial administrator who served as Governor of South Carolina, in America, in 1755, and as Governor of Jamaica in 1760. He was raised to the Irish peerage as Baron Westcote in

1776 and to the British peerage in 1794 as Baron Lyttelton of Frankley. Young Henry Thrale, after leaving Oxford without taking a degree, had traveled extensively on the Continent with Lyttelton. Henry's father, Ralph Thrale, is reported to have paid the expenses of both (Clifford, *Hester Lynch Piozzi*, 35).

Tall and thin, Lyttelton did not much impress Johnson. Mrs. Thrale wrote in her diary, "Of Mr Lyttelton—now Lord Westcote he [Johnson] observed—that he had more Chaff than Grain in him; as every thing *indeed* says he which grows up to so prodigious a Length—has." In the verses Mrs. Thrale penned as commentaries on the Reynolds library portraits, she said of Lord Westcote, in part,

> With power well-natur'd, with Science well bred,
> He had studied, had travell'd, had reason'd, had read;
> Yet the Mind as the body was wanting in Strength,
> For in Lyttelton every thing ran into Length.
> *(Piozzi, Thraliana, 200 and 471)*

Lord Westcote was the younger brother of George Lyttelton, of whose poetical works Johnson wrote a critical evaluation in his *Lives of the Poets*, an evaluation that greatly offended Elizabeth Montagu and others. The present location of the Lord Westcote portrait is untraced.

The full-length portrait of Queeney and Mrs. Thrale, which hung over the fireplace as the centerpiece of the library's picture collection, is now at Beaverbrook Art Gallery, Fredericton, New Brunswick, Canada. Henry Thrale's portrait is in the Houghton Library, Harvard University. The Streatham library's "blinking Sam" portrait of Johnson is now at the Huntington Library, Art Collections, and Botanical Gardens, San Marino, California. The National Portrait Gallery, London, houses the Reynolds portraits of Edmund Burke and Charles Burney. Goldsmith's portrait hangs in the National Portrait Gallery of Ireland, Dublin. The portraits of Arthur Murphy, Joseph Baretti, and Sir Robert Chambers are in private collections. Reynold's self-portrait, showing him holding a hand up to his left ear to hear better, is in the Tate Gallery, London. And the Streatham portrait of David Garrick is part of the Hyde Collection, Glens Falls, New York. See images of the Streatham portraits at www.thrale.com/library_and_streatham_worthies.

42. Johnson, *Letters*, Redford, 2:360.
43. Boswell, *Boswell in Extremes*, 261.
44. Boswell, *English Experiment*, 81.
45. Boswell, *Boswell in Extremes*, 302.
46. Boswell, *Great Biographer*, 133.
47. Boswell, *Laird of Auchinleck*, 82.
48. Boswell, *Ominous Years*, 97.
49. Ibid., 307.
50. Ibid., 339.
51. Boswell, *Correspondence with Members of the Club*, 50.
52. Boswell, *Boswell in Extremes*, 250 and n7.
53. Manuscript letter books.
54. Boswell, *Ominous Years*, 324.

55. Boswell, *Life*, 4:193.

56. Boswell, *Boswell in Extremes*, 21.

57. Boswell, *Life*, 3:531; Tinker, *Young Boswell*, 15–16.

58. Boswell, *Boswell in Extremes*, 69–70.

59. Temple, *Diaries*, 81.

60. Boswell, *London Journal*, 192.

61. Boswell, *Ominous Years*, 89.

62. Ibid., 72.

63. Boswell, *London Journal*, 269.

64. Boswell, *Boswell in Holland*, 389.

65. Boswell. *Journal of German and Swiss Travels*, 223.

66. Boswell, *London Journal*, 151.

67. Boswell, *Boswell In Search of a Wife*, 40.

68. Boswell, *Boswell in Holland*, 196–97 and 206.

69. Boswell, *Laird of Auchinleck*, 32.

70. Boswell, *Ominous Years*, 265.

71. Boswell, *Grand Tour: Germany*, 44.

72. Ibid., 231.

73. Boswell, *London Journal*, 262n7.

74. Ibid., 265n2.

75. Boswell, *Boswell In Search of a Wife*, 249.

76. Boswell, *London Journal*, 285.

77. Boswell, *Boswell in Extremes*, 179–80.

78. Ibid., 181.

79. Boswell, *Boswell for the Defence*, 122.

80. Boswell, *Boswell in Extremes*, 210.

81. Boswell, *Boswell in Holland*, 223.

82. Boswell, *Journal of German and Swiss Travels*, 327.

83. Boswell, *Boswell in Extremes*, 250.

84. Boswell, *Tour to the Hebrides*, 53; Garrick, *Letters*, 994.

85. Boswell, *Boswelliana*, 191–92.

86. Boswell, *Laird of Auchinleck*, 310–11.

87. Frances Burney, *The Court Journals and Letters of Frances Burney*, ed. Peter Sabor et al., 5 vols. (Oxford: Clarendon Press, 2011–2017), 2:97.

88. Frances Burney, *Memoirs*, 2:193–96.

Chapter Eleven

The Flight of Time

Topham Beauclerk venerated Johnson, tolerated Boswell, and took little interest in the Thrales of Streatham Park. His indifference to the charms of Hester Thrale may help to account for her strong dislike of him. Johnson, on the other hand, loved Beauclerk for his good qualities and hoped to rectify the bad, while Boswell envied his wealth and parts and was willing to value him solely for his attachment to Johnson. But Mrs. Thrale had no use for him at all. "Oh Lord!" she said years after his death, "how I did hate that horrid Beauclerc!"[1]

She recognized his talents and acknowledged his strict adherence to truth (unlike Baretti and Boswell in her view), but she did not care for the man's haughty manner and the influence he exercised on fashionable society. She placed him at the top of the list of languid *ton* people—those persons of quality who affected a bored attitude toward life after having seen and done it all. She said that Beauclerk "helped to bring up the Mode of speaking in a Monotonous Tone, and putting on a Face of Vacant Insipidity as The Ton-Talkers have been doing these last 20 Years." The only difference, she conceded, was that he actually had much to say while they had nothing.[2] The monotonous tone and vacant look that irritated her, however, fascinated Johnson. While it seemed to him that he expended much effort in conversation, Beauclerk delivered what was often excellent without appearing to exert himself at all. In once extolling the ease with which Beauclerk spoke, Johnson said that "no man ever was so free when he was going to say a good thing, from a *look* that expressed that it was coming; or, when he had said it, from a look that expressed that it *had* come." Johnson admitted to having a greater disposition to envy Beauclerk's conversational talents than any other person he knew.[3]

Boswell remarked to Johnson one day, "Beauclerk has a keenness of mind which is very uncommon."

211

"Yes, sir; and everything comes from him so easily. It appears to me that I labour when I say a good thing."

"You are loud, sir," said Boswell, "but it is not an effort of mind."[4]

In addition to his ease of expression was Beauclerk's understated sarcasm punctuated by occasional flashes of mischievous wit. One time years earlier, Oliver Goldsmith, in his role of medical doctor, wrote out a prescription for a sick friend, but the apothecary who was to fill the order objected to either the type of medicine Goldsmith prescribed or to the dosage, and an argument ensued. Finally the apothecary and Goldsmith asked the patient to decide between them, and she chose the apothecary as the one best qualified to judge her needs. Goldsmith left the house in a rage, later declaring at Sir Joshua's that he would stop prescribing for his friends. "Do so, my dear Doctor," replied Beauclerk; "whenever you undertake to kill, let it be only your enemies."[5]

Not even the great man himself escaped Beauclerk's pointed gibes. When Johnson received his pension in 1762, Beauclerk told him, "I hope you'll now purge and live cleanly like a gentleman."[6] Most of the time Johnson relished such banter, and he allowed Beauclerk more leeway in this regard than anyone else among his circle of friends. When the two visited Cambridge together in 1765, Johnson spoke slightingly to those around him of Catharine Macaulay, historian and political writer. "Come, come, Doctor," Beauclerk interposed, "take care what you say, and don't be too saucy about Mrs. Macaulay; for, if you do, I shall find means of setting her upon you as soon as we return, and she will comb your wig for you pretty handsomely." Johnson asked how he meant to achieve this remarkable feat. "Oh! I'll soon tell you that, Doctor. You can't deny that it's now a full fortnight since Mrs. M. made you a present of her history; and to my certain knowledge it still remains in your study without one of the leaves being cut open; which is such a contempt of the lady's genius and abilities, that, should I acquaint her with it, as perhaps I shall, I wouldn't be in your place, Doctor, for a good deal, I assure you." Johnson laughed, admitting to the charge but denying that all Beauclerk's oratorical powers could persuade Mrs. Macaulay that he would leave a work of hers lying about without looking into it.[7]

Johnson could usually laugh at Beauclerk's sallies, though sometimes they became too malicious and cut too deeply. He would then feel compelled to check them. He said to Beauclerk on one such occasion, "You never open your mouth but with intention to give pain; and you have often given me pain, not from the power of what you said, but from seeing your intention."[8]

In deference to his great friend's sensibilities, Beauclerk restrained his more outrageous comments in Johnson's presence, yet he refused to be intimidated. He would not allow Johnson to shout him down or be rude to him as often happened to others. Beauclerk told Boswell that he wondered some violent man by this time had not struck Johnson, considering the severe things he sometimes said to people. He wished to see it, in fact, as a means of teaching him to behave. "To be sure, a man would be a brute who did it. But it would do good."

"O no," Boswell answered, "at his age."

"At his age he should be thinking of better things than to abuse people."[9]

At a meeting of the Club one evening, the members began talking about the current *cause célèbre*, the trial of one James Hackman, twenty-six, charged with the murder of Martha Ray, aged about nineteen. Miss Ray had spurned Hackman's advances, and as she left Covent Garden Theatre one night in the company of a gentleman friend and was stepping into a carriage, Hackman ran up with two loaded pistols, shot her in the forehead, and then shot himself in the temple. Miss Ray fell dead instantly, but the ball he fired at himself failed to penetrate and inflicted only a minor wound.

Arguments presented at Hackman's trial centered on whether Miss Ray's killing had been premeditated or spontaneous. A suicide note found in Hackman's pocket seemed to indicate that he had meant to kill only himself and had killed Miss Ray in a momentary frenzy. Johnson contended that Hackman's carrying two pistols proved that he meant to shoot two people. Beauclerk disagreed. He argued that a person intent on suicide might charge two pistols to ensure success. After all, he maintained, Lord Charles Spencer's cook shot himself with one pistol and lived ten days in great agony, but when Mr. Delmis killed himself, he took care to have two pistols in readiness. "One was found lying charged upon the table by him after he had shot himself with the other."

"Well," Johnson countered. "You see here one pistol was sufficient."

"Because he was dead," said Beauclerk sharply, and angered by Johnson's triumphant manner, he added, "This is what you don't know, and I know."

Several minutes passed, during which time the conversation passed on to other things. Johnson, meanwhile, remained silent, deciding if he should respond to Beauclerk's insolence. Suddenly he exlaimed, "Mr. Beauclerk, how come you to talk so petulantly to me as, 'This is what you don't know and I know'? One thing I know which you don't know: that you are very uncivil."

"Because you began by being uncivil," returned Beauclerk, adding, "which you always are," a remark Johnson may not have caught.

A short time later someone again mentioned Hackman's violent temper, and Johnson said, "It was his business to *command* his temper, as my friend Mr. Beauclerk should have done a little ago."

"I should learn of you," Beauclerk responded.

"You have given *me* opportunities enough of learning, when I have been in your company. No man loves to be treated with contempt."

With a polite bow, Beauclerk said, "You have known me twenty years and however I may have treated others, you may be sure I could never mean to treat *you* with contempt."

"Sir," replied Johnson, "you have said more than was necessary."[10]

Beauclerk once angered Boswell in one of the few ways Boswell *could* be angered, and that was by injuring his pride. Boswell had called at Beauclerk's around midnight, unannounced and uninvited, and found Beauclerk entertaining some persons of rank and distinction. "Who's that?" asked Beauclerk. Someone said that it was Mr. Boswell. "How did you get in at this time of night?" asked Beauclerk as Boswell came around to shake hands. Boswell said that he had called twice during the day and not found him in, so he decided to call at night. The servant had told him that his master was in, so Boswell came up. "I have not been at home at this time o' night this month," replied Beauclerk.

"Then I'm in luck."

As Boswell sat down, Beauclerk asked when he was going to Scotland. The question irritated Boswell, who had just arrived from there. "I won't tell you," he answered. Beauclerk said the reason he asked was that he had some bonds in Scotland that he wanted paid. Edward Gibbon protested that this was in the way of his profession. Boswell felt uncomfortable, seeing clearly he was not wanted there, and when supper came up, he stole off without Beauclerk asking him to remain.[11] Beauclerk had obviously been annoyed at Boswell's intrusion, and Boswell did not like Beauclerk's brusque manner, his addressing him professionally at a social affair, and his treating him like a solicitor rather than a barrister.

At another gathering several nights later hosted by Langton, Beauclerk again mentioned being eager about his bonds in Scotland and said he would have written to Boswell had he not seen him that night. Boswell replied coldly that he would recommend an attorney to him. Near midnight Dr. Johnson prepared to leave, and Boswell offered to accompany him part way home. "Beauclerk came to the door and pressed me to go back," noted Boswell in his journal. "But I was resolute, and would not stay and watch late, especially at *his* desire."[12]

Two weeks later Beauclerk wrote to Langton, "Pray tell Boswell that notwithstanding the Nonsense of his Anger that I really want to see him, and that he need not doubt it that it is of Consequence to myself. To ballance this, pray tell him that he is the only Man in the World that I ever made an Apology to when I was not in the wrong."[13]

Beauclerk expected Langton and Boswell to call on him the following day, yet Boswell could not decide if he should go or not. "But pride or fear of seeming weak made me resolve not to go. So I was set down at home by Langton, who worthily regretted my not going with him."[14]

Aside from his genteel bearing and acid wit, Topham Beauclerk displayed two conspicuously odd traits. Samuel Rogers, a young man at the time but closely associated later with such literary figures as Byron, Wordsworth, and Coleridge, recalled that Beauclerk was exceptionally absentminded. Rogers told of Beauclerk having once arranged a dinner party, and just before his guests arrived, he went upstairs to change his clothes, forgot what he was doing, thought it was bedtime, got undressed, and climbed into bed. A servant, who came into the room to tell him his guests had arrived, found him sound asleep.[15] Another time he invited a group of friends to dinner that included Sir Joshua Reynolds, David Garrick, and the Dean of Derry, Dr. Thomas Barnard. On the appointed evening, Beauclerk got so absorbed in gaming at one of his clubs that he forgot to show up at the party himself. The incident prompted Garrick to write the following lines:

> Our choice British Raphael and rare Dean of Derry,
> With Drury's Tom Fool, to be wise and be merry
> By Beauclerk were ask'd, but the dice came between,
> And quite were forgotten Play'r, Painter and Dean.
>
> Nor indeed did they want him, for sweet Lady Di
> Did more than the loss of ten Beauclerks supply.
> At nine of next morning I saw with these eyes
> His Honour sneak home, neither merry nor wise.[16]

A much more annoying trait than absentmindedness was Beauclerk's neglect of personal hygiene. Dr. Johnson claimed to hate immersion and to dislike clean linen, but Beauclerk went even further. Someone who knew him remarked that he was "what the French call *cynique* in his personal habits beyond what one would have thought possible in anyone but a beggar or a gypsey."[17] Horace Walpole said that Beauclerk was so filthy in his person that he generated vermin and that when he and Lady Di occasionally passed a few days at Strawberry Hill House, Walpole's Gothic-style villa at Twickenham, they slept in separate beds.[18]

Lady Louisa Stuart recalled that one year during a Christmas celebration at Blenheim all the guests found themselves annoyed "by certain visitants— '*in all their quarters*'" and that the "distress became unspeakable. Its origin being clearly traced to M[r] Beauclerk, one of the gentlemen undertook to remonstrate with him, and began delicately hinting how much the ladies were inconvenienced—'What! said Beauclerk, Are they so nice as that comes to? Why I have enough to stock a parish.'" Lady Di surprised the servants by insisting on clean sheets and linen every day, and "after this discovery," said Lady Louisa, "they understood why."[19] This disregard for cleanliness carried over into a general neglect of his health. Never a robust individual to begin with, he undermined what strength he possessed by irregular hours and deleterious habits. His chief indulgence was attending fashionable all-night gaming clubs, where he won and lost large sums as a matter of course. As Garrick indicated in his poem, he seldom got to bed before dawn and did not usually rise before mid-afternoon. Edmond Malone complained that Beauclerk successfully beat others to the purchase of fine books by sending his servant at six or seven in the morning to scout out sales. If they looked promising, Beauclerk came along to snatch up anything rare. This did not inconvenience him, said Malone, for it meant only that he had to stay up half an hour past his usual bedtime.[20]

Subject to recurring illnesses, he often resorted to laudanum to help relieve his discomfort. As early as January 1775, when Beauclerk was only thirty-five, Johnson wrote to Boswell in Edinburgh that Beauclerk was so ill that his life was thought to be in danger and that Lady Di was nursing him with great care.[21] Johnson by this time had come to respect Lady Di and to have cordial social relations with her. When Boswell arrived in London two months later, Johnson informed him that Beauclerk remained ill but was no longer thought to be in danger.[22] But then in June, Langton wrote Boswell, once again in Edinburgh, that Beauclerk had been placed by his physician on a solanum and milk diet for fear that his case had again become serious.[23] Langton noted the depth of Johnson's concern and the strength of his affection when he heard him say, his voice trembling with emotion, "Sir I would walk to the extent of the diameter of the earth to save Beauclerk."[24]

His greatest comfort during these episodes of illness was the company of Langton, his closest friend. Early in their relationship, Beauclerk regretted any long absences and lamented that the two sometimes allowed their correspondence to lag. But then, he said, both were afflicted with idleness. "By what cursed accident does it happen," he wrote, "that we are both of us persecuted by it in so wonderful a manner? Shall we shake it off and become great men? Come to London however, you know the Idiot says, that an Idle man in London must learn something in spight of himself."[25] The "Idiot" was a comical reference to Johnson. Beauclerk often encouraged Langton to visit him, for his friend's gentle disposition and learned conversation soothed his own inflamed nerves. "I have many things which I can talk to you about," he wrote, that all other Company interrupt. Our long and uninterrupted friendship makes this natural. You know at all times I preferred your Company to any other, and that preference is not decreased by a very long and painfull Illness, particularly as I have reason to think that it will not be very long before that Illness puts an End to our connection for Ever.[26]

A short time later he again begged Langton to come and rescue him from his misery:

I have been in constant pain night and day for this whole Week, and I am reducd [*sic*] to a feebleness of Body and mind that you cannot imagine. It is no great wonder considering that even my old Friend Laudanum has failed at giving me ease. . . . I know if you can come, you will take pity upon me, for I can neither read, nor think nor hardly bear my Existence, my pain and lowness of Spirits are so intolerable.[27]

David Garrick, by the early 1770s, was also experiencing health problems. He had suffered from gout since 1768 and had been troubled periodically by painful kidney stones. But he seldom complained or gave much indication that he ailed. "Great Stone, & Sore Throat! yet I am in Spirits—" he wrote to a friend in characteristic fashion.[28] He realized, however, that he could not sustain the demands of acting and managing a theater much longer. He wrote to Boswell in Edinburgh, "I have been confin'd very near two Months with the Gout; Nothing till lately could subdue my Spirits, but I begin to discover that I am growing Old, & tho I have no Apollo at my Elbow, Yet Sickness vellit et admonuit [plucked my ear and warned me], that it is time for me to get into port, & drop my Anchor."[29]

When Boswell came to London in the spring of 1776, he called on Garrick and spent the morning with him drinking port and water and eating a light meal. "He was quite easy and gay as usual," recorded Boswell.[30] Now in the final season of his acting career, he was giving farewell performances of some of his greatest roles, and planned to retire in June. Later that day, as Boswell rode with Johnson in a coach, he observed that once Garrick left the stage, he would have an easier life, but Johnson expressed doubt. "Why, Sir," said Boswell, "he will be Atlas with the burthen off his back." Johnson thought he would be less steady without the load. Still, he agreed that Garrick should not act anymore but live the life of a gentleman. Boswell suggested that he should act once a year "for the benefit of decayed actors, as it has been said he means to do."

"Alas, Sir! he will soon be a decayed actor himself."[31]

Garrick made his final stage appearance on June 10, 1776, as Don Felix in Susannah Centlivre's *The Wonder*. Following the play, he addressed the audience, saying it was customary for retiring actors to deliver a farewell epilogue, and he had considered doing so, but, "The jingle of rhyme and the language of fiction would but ill suit my present feelings. This is to me a very awful moment: it is no less than parting for ever with those, from whom I have received the greatest kindness, and upon the spot, where that kindness your favours were enjoyed." Overcome at this point with emotions, and with tears running down his cheeks, he paused to regain his composure. "Whatever may be the changes of my future life, the deepest impression of your kindness will always remain here—here, in my heart, fixed, and unalterable." After a few more brief remarks, in the words of Arthur Murphy, "he bowed respectfully to all parts of the house, and in a slow pace, and much hesitation, withdrew for ever from their presence."[32] Over the course of his thirty-five-year professional career, he had acted 2,251 times and played about one hundred different characters.[33]

Once in retirement, he retained his buoyant, lighthearted spirits, though his body was quickly giving way to gout, kidney stones, and other ailments. Murphy visited him in November of 1778 and had no idea of his true condition: "His spirits were as lively as ever. [We] walked together several turns in the garden: Mr. Garrick told two or three pleasant stories with such a degree of vivacity, that now . . . Mr. Murphy looks back with astonishment to the gaiety of a man, who was in so desperate a state of health, and, in fact, so near his end."[34]

Early in January 1779 he began experiencing severe pains in the abdomen. During the night of January 20 he frequently apologized to those who attended him, and then at about eight o'clock in the morning, just after taking a dose of medicine, he said softly, "Oh! dear" and quietly died.

On receiving the news in Scotland, Boswell wrote to Johnson, "Garrick's death is a striking event; not that we should be surprised with the death of any man, who has lived sixty-two years; but because there was a *vivacity* in our late celebrated friend, which drove away the thoughts of *death* from any association with *him*."[35]

The magnificence of Garrick's funeral stood in marked contrast to the simple interment of Oliver Goldsmith nearly five years before. On Monday, February 1, 1779, Garrick was buried in the Poets' Corner of Westminster Abbey beneath Shakespeare's monument. The carriages of those attending the services stretched back along Fleet Street and the Strand to Charing Cross. Among the mourners were people of rank and wealth, a host of actors from the theaters of Drury Lane and Covent Garden, along with the foremost names in art, science, and literature. The magnificence of the funeral and the numbers of people in attendance had seldom before been seen. It demonstrated England's love and admiration for a great artist and represented Garrick's vast retinue of acquaintances. Yet among them was not one really close friend, for Garrick had not been capable of true friendship. No one besides his wife, perhaps, ever reached his inmost soul. He had wrapped himself so completely in his art that he remained insulated from those about him. Furthermore, his ever-shifting, ever-pliable character made it difficult to establish a firm base on which to establish a friendship. "He had friends, but no friend," observed Johnson. "Garrick was so diffused, he had no man to whom he wished to unbosom himself." Johnson thought Lord Chesterfield was another man who had no friend, yet there "were more materials to make friendship in Garrick, had he not been so diffused."[36]

Reynolds expressed a similar opinion: "Garrick died without a real friend, though no man had a greater number of what the world calls friends. Garrick had no friends to whom he gave orders that he was always at home, except to his doctors, of which he had two sorts, one sort administering for his body, the other for his diseased mind—in other words, his vanity."[37]

On her thirty-eighth birthday, Mrs. Thrale felt uncommonly low spirited. She had just learned that a lifelong friend was dying of breast cancer. "The Flight of Time is now so shocking to me, I can hardly bear to see the *Winter* going," she wrote; "there are so *few* Winters to be *now* expected!" Garrick had died the week before and that "too has crushed the Spirits of many People among whom I now live—Johnson, Murphy—[Charles] Burney." Not that she herself felt much grief over Garrick's passing. "*I* knew him only just well enough to be proud of knowing him, not well enough to care about his Death, except as at the stopping up a Source of Merriment in the midst of a miserable World."[38] Understandably, Johnson's grief ran far deeper and was more complex than Mrs. Thrale's or almost anyone else's. Not that Johnson felt closer to Garrick than to others. He decidedly had greater affection for Henry Thrale, the young Richard Bathurst, and Sir Joshua Reynolds. But having known Garrick for so long, having come from the same town, and having traveled down to London together in the early days of poverty and obscurity, their association seemed closer to kinship than to friendship. Eight years separated their ages. Exactly when they first met is not known, but in 1727, at age eleven, Garrick got up his first theatrical production. Neighborhood children performed *The Recruiting Officer*, a comedy by Farquhar, and Garrick asked eighteen-year-old Samuel Johnson, already demonstrating his abilities in verse, to supply a prologue, but for some unknown reason Johnson did not do it.[39]

Garrick having once been a student at his failed academy at Edial, Johnson always retained something of the schoolmaster when dealing with his former pupil, chiding or scolding him on apparently little provocation. As an example, when Garrick once whimsically remarked that now he had left the stage, he would sit down and read Shakespeare, Johnson replied, "'Tis time you should, for I much doubt if you ever examined one of his plays from the first scene to the last."[40] Being still treated like a schoolboy was not something Garrick relished. He often felt intimidated by Johnson's presence, not so much by his physical and intellectual dominance, but mainly by the fear that Johnson would find some way to embarrass him in company. Frances Reynolds recalled Garrick expressing concern at a formal gathering "that the attention of the ladies to him would provoke Johnson to say something rude to him."[41] In addition, Garrick sometimes complained, and was visibly hurt, that Johnson did not think so highly of his theatrical accomplishments as others did.

Johnson had also offended Garrick earlier by a *Rambler* essay that purported to be a letter from a correspondent complaining about the extravagance and ostentation of his friend Prospero. Friends could easily see that Prospero represented Garrick. Johnson had written:

> We set out in the world together; and for a long time mutually assisted each other in our exigencies, as either happened to have money or influence beyond his immediate necessities. You know that nothing generally endears men so much as participation of dangers and misfortunes; I therefore always considered Prospero as united with me in the strongest league of kindness, and imagined that our friendship was only to be broken by the hand of death. I felt at his sudden shoot of success an honest and disinterested joy. . . .
>
> While we were conversing upon such subjects as imagination happened to suggest, he frequently digressed into directions to the servant that waited, or made a slight enquiry after the jeweller or silversmith; and once as I was pursuing an argument with some degree of earnestness, he started from his posture of attention, and ordered, that if Lord Lofty called on him that morning, he should be shewn into the best parlour. . . .
>
> Prospero had now an opportunity of calling for his Dresden china, which, says he, I always associate with my chased tea-kettle. The cups were brought; I once resolved not to have looked upon them, but my curiosity prevailed. When I had examined them a little, Prospero desired me to set them down, for they who were accustomed only to common dishes, seldom handled china with much care.[42]

Garrick never mentioned to Johnson the resentment he felt on reading this essay. Outwardly it did not seem to affect their relationship, yet Boswell stated that Garrick never entirely forgave his friend. Thomas Percy said that afterward "there was no great cordiality between Garrick and Johnson."[43] One wonders if the two would ever have become friends to begin with had circumstances not thrown them together in their youth. In reading the correspondence of both, one notices how few times each mentions the other. When they occasionally met, it was usually at the home of someone else. Johnson seldom made up one of the party at Garrick's sumptuous table, and Garrick rarely called at Johnson's dirty apartments. Garrick complained privately that when Johnson did visit his magnificent estate at Hampton on the banks of the Thames, he took little notice of the splendid house and gardens that so impressed everyone else, and he said of Johnson's residence that one could find little comfort at the lodgings of a man who spent his life absorbed in thought and gave no attention to the comfort of visitors.[44]

Johnson had always felt ambivalent about Garrick. He spoke with genuine conviction when he praised the actor for being "a very good man; the cheerfulest man of his age and a decent liver," but he spoke with equal conviction in styling him nearly illiterate: "what does he know? He is not a linguist, he is not a reasoner. A pleasant companion he is; but the mere power of exciting laughter is an unsubstantial talent; and who rises up contented from a table on which whipt syllabub was the principal dish?"[45]

Envy lay at the heart of this ambivalence. Arthur Murphy noted the "corrosions of jealousy" in the relationship,[46] and Boswell thought that Johnson

insensibly fretted a little that *Davy Garrick*, who was his pupil . . . , should be so very general a favourite and should have fourscore thousand pounds, an immense sum, when *he* has so little. He accordingly will allow no great merit in acting. Garrick cannot but be hurt at this, and so unhappily there is not the harmony that one would wish.[47]

Garrick understood the situation. One day when Hannah More asked him why Johnson often spoke to him so roughly and why he spoke of him so unkindly to others, Garrick answered, "Why, it is very natural; is it not to be expected he should be angry, that I, who have so much less merit than he, should have had so much greater success?"[48] Whatever resentment Garrick may have felt, he paid his old master back by sometimes making him the object of his mimicry. One day he entertained the Burneys by see-sawing back and forth, contorting himself with Johnson's odd tics and gestures, assuming the familiar expression and voice, and exclaiming, "Yes, yes, Davy has some convivial pleasantries in him; but 'tis a futile Fellow."[49] In another comical display, Garrick portrayed Johnson sitting at a table, next to his wife's bedside, working on his play *Irene*. As he excitedly answers Tetty's appeals to come to bed, he tries to recite from his play, meanwhile tucking the bed sheets into his breeches.

Johnson, however, for all his critical abuse, would allow no one else to attack Garrick. Woe to the person who tried it, especially if a casual acquaintance. One unlucky word against Garrick and Johnson flew to his defense like a hen to her chick. When Mrs. Thrale accused him of browbeating anyone who spoke against Garrick, Johnson said that it was because others did not know *when* to abuse him and *when* to praise him. He was not going to let anyone speak ill of David that he did not deserve. When Boswell, on another occasion, observed that Johnson attacked Garrick himself but would not suffer others to do it, Johnson merely smiled and said, "Why, Sir, that is true."[50]

When Johnson learned toward the close of 1778 that Garrick was ill, he did not choose to think it serious. He believed that to admit a man was sick was almost to wish it so. Garrick's death, then, came as a surprise, and the sudden extinction of his mirth and conviviality brought a shocking reminder of his own mortality. In his *Life of Edmund Smith*, Johnson paid a final public tribute to Garrick when he wrote,

> At this man's table [Smith's] I enjoyed many cheerful and instructive hours, with companions such as are not often found; with . . . one who has gladdened life . . . David Garrick, whom I hoped to have gratified with this character of our common friend: but what are the hopes of man! I am disappointed by that stroke of death, which has eclipsed the gaiety of nations, and impoverished the publick stock of harmless pleasure.

Several persons, including Boswell, found this tribute inadequate. They thought it little more than empty hyperbole and surprisingly devoid of personal sentiment considering the two men's long intimacy. Boswell even had the temerity to ask Johnson if "harmless pleasure" was not a very tame phrase. Johnson defended it by saying that to furnish pleasure that is pure and harmless is the greatest power a man can possess.[51] George Stevens, a longtime acquaintance of Johnson's, told Boswell that he thought this defense weak. He said that "'eclipsed the gaiety of nations, and impoverished the publick stock of harmless pleasure,' sounds to my ear like the chill though elegant praise of one who lamented the actor, but not the man."[52]

Johnson attended Garrick's funeral, and whatever his settled opinions may have been later, his emotions on this occasion were strong. It could hardly be otherwise, for he had known Garrick as a boy in Lichfield and as a youthful traveling companion when they first came to London together. He had seen him rise to international eminence and become wealthy, had seen him grow old and retire, and finally had seen him die. Johnson had witnessed his entire remarkable passage through life. In looking back over his own life, Johnson could hardly recall a time when David Garrick was not a part of it. Following the services, Richard Cumberland saw Johnson "standing beside his grave, at the foot of Shakespeare's monument, and bathed in tears."[53] Almost six years later Johnson would follow his former pupil and be laid next to him, close to Shakespeare's monument, in the Poets' Corner of Westminster Abbey.

The health of Beauclerk, meanwhile, remained precarious. Shortly before Garrick's death, he wrote to Langton that any long absence between friends was disagreeable, "but much worse to any Body in my Situation, because the Chances of not meeting again are so much increased. However that may be, you may be assured that whenever I die you will lose a very sincere Friend, and one who is perfectly sensible of your Value."[54] No one understood, apparently, the underlying nature of Beauclerk's disorder, but it was certainly aggravated, and perhaps occasioned, by his late hours, irregular habits, and liberal use of opium. As his illness grew worse and his periods of recovery shorter, he became abusive toward his wife and their three children. He would go into tirades that resulted in long disputes and recriminations. Lady Di's friends grew increasingly alarmed and resentful that Beauclerk treated his wife so badly. Her first husband, Lord Bolingbroke, had at last become deranged from years of drink, dissipation, and laudanum, and in 1779 he nearly died from what some thought an intentional drug overdose. Said Horace Walpole in a letter, "It would have been monstrous injustice in opium to kill him, when it will not dispatch Beauclerc."[55] Walpole, who now detested Beauclerk for his ill-treatment of his wife, wrote to another friend, "Lady D.'s case is melancholy indeed. It is patched up for the present; but there is *an affection upon the brain* in both husbands that I believe incurable. It is pity that one is not in as much danger as the other."[56]

Lady Di and Beauclerk's relationship reached its nadir in 1779. They no longer visited Muswell Hill, their estate near Hampstead. They had since moved to a house in Great Russell Street, a short distance from the British Museum and not far from Tottenham Court Road. Here Beauclerk set up his vast book collection, thousands of volumes, in a newly built library wing that Walpole said "reaches halfway to Highgate. Everybody goes to see it; it has put the Museum's nose quite out of joint."[57]

The couple visited Brighton during the summer to help mend what still remained of Beauclerk's health. The change did him good, and he soon felt well enough to resume his customary habits of gaming and keeping late hours. Lady Pembroke, Lady Diana's sister, thought Lady Di by this time had reached the end of her endurance. "I have been almost distracted these ten days," she wrote a friend, "with miseries of my poor Sister's." But Beauclerk's disposition, along with his health, so much improved at Brighton that

Lady Di "consented to bear a little longer." Reflecting on her sister's two difficult marriages, Lady Pembroke could not help but observe, "Husbands are dreadfull & powerfull Animals." Fortunately for Lady Di, she soon came down with chickenpox and was therefore able to enjoy additional peace and seclusion for a time. "Mr B keeps such odd hours," said Lady Pembroke, "that she does not see him above a minute in the day, & she lyes in the next house, & there have been no disputes at all since they came here." But by year's end, as Beauclerk's health again deteriorated, his disposition once more soured, Lady Pembroke reported that her sister "is quite broken in her looks, & leads the life of a Dog with him. He lives to be a torment to himself & all about him."[58]

By spring of the new year, 1780, Beauclerk's health declined to such an alarming extent that he truly seemed to have reached his end. He begged his wife to forgive his mistreatment of her, made out his will leaving care of his children to Lady Di, and in case she did not survive, to Bennet Langton, and on March 11, at his house in Great Russell Street, at the age of forty, he died.

Reactions to his passing varied. Lady Pembroke wrote to a friend, "Mr. Beauclerk dyed last Friday night after ten days illness which was more than sufficient to put an end to the sufferings of his wretched constitution, it is certainly much happier for himself, & he did not act in a manner to be regretted by others. . . . My Sister was shocked at first, but the way they lived in together makes it quite unnatural that it shou'd be a lasting sorrow."[59]

"Poor dear Beauclerk—" wrote Johnson in a different vein, informing Boswell of Beauclerk's passing. "His wit and his folly, his acuteness and maliciousness, his merriment and reasoning, are now over. Such another will not often be found among mankind. He directed himself to be buried by the side of his mother, an instance of tenderness which I hardly expected."[60]

Boswell felt depressed on hearing the news, "for the death of one so fashionable and spirited and knowing and witty as he was damped my spirits."[61] He wrote to Langton that Beauclerk's loss "never can be repaired, though his acidity sometimes made me smart."[62]

The library Beauclerk left behind comprised one of the largest and finest private collections in England. It sold at public auction in the spring of 1781, fetching £5,011. The auction lasted fifty days. The sale catalog described the library as being an excellent choice of books "To the Number of upwards of Thirty Thousand Volumes, In most Languages, and upon almost every Branch of Science and Polite Literature." There were dictionaries and grammars in various languages; volumes on philosophy, logic, ethics, metaphysics; books covering medicine, surgery, anatomy; books on architecture, sculpture, numismatics, music, mythology, and typography. There were thousands of books on history. Eight days alone were devoted to auctioning off nearly fifteen hundred volumes containing works by classical authors. Five days went to the sale of plays in Latin, Italian, Spanish, French, and English. It took another eight days to dispose of over eleven hundred books on geography, voyages, and travels.[63]

John Wilkes and Dr. Johnson, staunch political opposites who went out of their way to be exceedingly polite to one another the two times they met, discussed at their second meeting Beauclerk's extensive library. Wilkes said that he was surprised to find such a large number of sermons in it. "Why, Sir," replied Johnson, "you are to consider that sermons make a considerable branch of English literature, so that a library must be very imperfect if it has not a numerous collection of sermons; and in all collections, Sir, the desire of augmenting grows stronger in proportion to the advance in acquisition, as motion is accelerated by the continuance of the impetus. Besides, Sir," added Johnson with a smile, "a man may collect sermons with intention of making himself better by them. I hope Mr. Beauclerk intended that some time or other that should be the case with him."[64]

One of the items Langton received upon settlement of Beauclerk's estate was a copy by Reynolds of his portrait of Johnson, the original commissioned by Henry Thrale for the Streatham library. Beauclerk had placed on the frame an inscription from Horace: "*Ingenium ingens/Inculto latet hoc sub corpre*" (Underneath this rude, uncouth disguise, / A genius of extensive knowledge lies). When Langton told Johnson that he had removed the inscription, Johnson said, "It was kind in you to take it off," and after a short pause he added, "and not unkind in him to put it on."[65]

Lady Di soon moved to a house at Richmond, a short distance from the country home of Sir Joshua Reynolds. One afternoon during a dinner party at which Johnson and Boswell were not present, Reynolds pointed out to his guests her attractive white dwelling nearby. Edmund Burke expressed pleasure in seeing her so well situated: "I never, myself, so much enjoyed the sight of happiness in another, as in that woman when I first saw her after the death of her husband. It was really enlivening to behold her placed in that sweet house, released from all her cares, a thousand pounds a year at her own disposal, and—her husband dead! Oh! it was pleasant, it was delightful to see her enjoyment of her situation!" Edward Gibbon mentioned that without considering the circumstances, her behavior might seem strange. "Very true," replied Burke, "if the circumstances are not considered, Lady Di may seem highly reprehensible."

Burke then turned to Fanny Burney, who recorded the incident, and explained to her the character of Beauclerk, whom she did not know well, drawing it "in strong and marked expressions, describing the misery he gave his wife, his singular ill-treatment of her, and the necessary relief the death of such a man must give."[66]

Unfortunately for Lady Di, the balance of her life did not remain free from sorrow. She never remarried, but spent most of her time drawing and painting, as well as attending social functions. The worst of her trials came in 1789 when her daughter, Mary Beauclerk, and her eldest son, George, by Lord Bolingbroke, fell in love and eloped. Only then did Lady Diana learn that the incestuous couple already had two illegitimate offspring and were expecting a third. The shock and humiliation devastated her. "I have certainly seen the most unfortunate of all mothers upon earth," wrote Walpole, who hastened to her to offer consolation. "The blow was very nearly killing her. She is but lately come to Twickenham [where she then had a house], and looks as deplorably as you may imagine."[67] Financial problems also plagued her later years. Never having learned to manage money, she eventually dissipated her fortune, dying in reduced circumstances in 1808 at age seventy-three. She left behind a quantity of artistic work that, while not great, is at least of high quality. As one critic has stated, Lady Diana Beauclerk excelled in the modest walks of art, chiefly as a designer.[68]

Topham Beauclerk for his part would hardly be remembered today but for the extensive library he amassed and for his association with Samuel Johnson. He possessed all the qualities necessary to become a prominent and useful individual like other members of the Johnson circle, yet he chose to squander his life in excess. As Bennet Langton wrote to Boswell in 1780, confirming news of their friend's passing, "The melancholy information you have received concerning Mr. Beauclerk's death is true. Had his talents been directed to any sufficient degree as they ought, I have always been strongly of opinion that they were calculated to make an illustrious figure."[69]

NOTES

1. Hayward, *Autobiography*, 2:112.
2. Boswell, *Life With Comments*, 3:111.
3. Boswell, *Life*, 3:424–25.
4. Boswell, *Tour to the Hebrides*, 53.
5. Prior, *Goldsmith*, 2:105.
6. Boswell, *Life*, 1:250. Beauclerk alludes to Falstaff's comment, "I'll purge, and leave sack, and live cleanly, as a nobleman should do" (*Henry IV, Part I*, 5.4.155–56).
7. John Nichols, *Illustrations of the Literary History of the Eighteenth Century*, 8 vols. (London, 1831), 6:158.
8. Boswell, *Life*, 1:249.
9. Boswell, *Laird of Auchinleck*, 83.
10. Ibid., 90–91. Hackman was found guilty of murder and hanged.
11. Boswell, *Boswell in Extremes*, 259–60.

12. Ibid., 278.

13. Boswell, *Correspondence with Members of the Club*, 82.

14. Boswell, *Boswell in Extremes*, 325.

15. Samuel Rogers, *Recollections of the Table-Talk of Samuel Rogers* (New York, 1856), 40.

16. *An Exhibition of Sketches & Watercolours by Lady Diana Beauclerk Held at Gerald M. Norman Gallery, 8, Duke Street, St. James's S.W.1.* (London, 1971), 9.

17. Lady Louisa Stuart, *Notes by Lady Louisa Stuart on George Selwyn and His Contemporaries by John Heneage Jesse*, ed. W. S. Lewis (New York: Oxford University Press, 1929), 22–23.

18. Farington, *Diary*, 1:221.

19. Stuart, *Notes*, 23.

20. Erskine, *Lady Diana Beauclerk*, 170–71.

21. Johnson, *Letters*, Redford, 2:170.

22. Boswell, *Ominous Years*, 87.

23. Boswell, *Correspondence with Members of the Club*, 55–56.

24. Boswell, *Correspondence Relating to the* Life, 280.

25. Boswell, *Correspondence with Members of the Club*, 4.

26. Ibid., 51.

27. Ibid., 66–67.

28. Garrick, *Letters of Garrick*, 855.

29. Ibid., 733.

30. Boswell, *Ominous Years*, 275.

31. Boswell, *Life*, 2:438–39.

32. Murphy, *Life of David Garrick*, 2:135–37.

33. Joseph Knight, *David Garrick* (London, 1894), 335.

34. Murphy, *Life of David Garrick*, 2:335–36.

35. Boswell, *Life*, 3:371.

36. Ibid., 3:386–87.

37. Reynolds, *Portraits*, 98.

38. Piozzi, *Thraliana*, 363–64.

39. Davies, *Life of Garrick*, 1:4–6.

40. Boswell, *Life*, 5:244n2.

41. Hill, *Johnsonian Miscellanies*, 2:258.

42. Johnson, *Works*, 5:278–80.

43. Boswell, *Life*, 1:216; Hill, *Johnsonian Miscellanies*, 2:211.

44. Boswell, *Correspondence Relating to the* Life, 118.

45. Boswell, *Laird of Auchinleck*, 98; Boswell, *Correspondence Relating to the* Life, 118.

46. Hill, *Johnsonian Miscellanies*, 1:456.

47. Boswell, *Boswell for the Defence*, 119.

48. Roberts, *Memoirs*, 1:238.

49. Burney, *Early Diary*, 2:282.

50. Burney, *Early Journals*, 3:76; Boswell, *Life*, 1:393n1.

51. Boswell, *Life*, 3:388.

52. Boswell, *Correspondence Relating to the* Life, 118.

53. Cumberland, *Memoirs*, 2:210.

54. Boswell, *Correspondence with Members of the Club*, 84.

55. Walpole, *Correspondence*, 33:107.

56. Ibid., 30:269.

57. Ibid., 33:136.

58. Henry Pembroke, *Pembroke Papers (1734–1780), Letters and Diaries of Henry, Tenth Earl of Pembroke and His Circle* (London: Jonathan Cape, 1942), 208, 301, 351.

59. Ibid., 429.

60. Johnson, *Letters*, Redford, 3:231.

61. Boswell, *Laird of Auchinleck*, 199.

62. Boswell, *Correspondence with Members of the Club*, 114.

63. *Bibliotheca Beauclerkiana: A Catalogue of the Large and Valuable Library of the Late Honourable Topham Beauclerk, F.R.S. Deceased; Comprehending an Excellent Choice of Books, To the Number of Upwards of Thirty Thousand Volumes, In Most Languages, and Upon Almost Every Branch of Science and Polite Literature* (London, 1781).

64. Boswell, *Laird of Auchinleck*, 350.

65. Boswell, *Life*, 4:180–81.

66. Burney, *Diary & Letters*, 2:91–92.

67. Walpole, *Correspondence*, 34:56.

68. Erskine, *Lady Diana Beauclerk*, 95.

69. Boswell, *Life*, 3:424.

Chapter Twelve

A Wicked, False,
Ungrateful Little Vixen

In the spring of 1778, before Henry Thrale's stroke at the age of fifty, Parliament was dissolved. This was always hateful news to Mrs. Thrale, for it meant weeks away from home and countless hours canvassing votes for her husband toward the next general election. Thrale had first been elected to Parliament in 1765 representing Southwark Borough, a position his father once held. With his wife and sometimes Johnson helping him canvass, he was returned to Parliament in 1768 and 1774. But now he hardly seemed mentally or physically capable of undertaking the grueling campaign that lay ahead. He lacked the energy even to manage the brewery properly. It survived only through the efforts of his wife and the superintendent, John Perkins. "Mr. Thrale is I find brooding in Silence over Schemes of Ruin," said Mrs. Thrale. "My Master's Depression at any ill Fortune or ill Management of his own—for no other Mishap has he had—will if he takes no Care be as fatal as his Elevation when Matters go grand; and he will not listen to Advice."[1]

Following his stroke in 1779, he continued to grow worse. He now suffered from diarrhea, could barely keep awake during the day, and when awake, seemed bent on killing himself by overeating. A friend encountered him at Bath gorging on stewed lampreys and said to him, "for Gods Sake Thrale why wilt thou eat so violently?—thou'lt die Apoplectick at last—& tis surely worse than any thing to see you swallowing these *black* Devils so."[2] One of his doctors told him that any apothecary's apprentice in London could see he was injuring his health by overeating, and he further pleaded with him, "For God's Sake dear Sir do not *stun* your Senses so; neither Sir Richard Jebb [Thrale's primary physician] nor I can restore them you when they are lost."[3] Baretti said that Dr. Jebb called one evening before dinner, and seeing some cucumbers on the table, asked Thrale not to eat them, but Thrale only laughed and ate a huge plateful as if to spite him.[4] Mrs. Thrale became terrified that he would eat himself into another stroke, and Johnson told him bluntly that after all his physicians' warnings, such eating was little better than suicide. But nothing did any good. One day he had eight generous helpings of food washed down with such a great quantity of strong beer that even the servants grew frightened. That evening Sir William Weller Pepys, a longtime family friend, stopped in and told Mrs. Thrale that things could not go on like this— there must either be legal restraints or certain death, but Mrs. Thrale rejected the idea of forced measures.[5]

As the general election approached, Thrale insisted on campaigning despite his narcolepsy, diarrhea, and depression. Early in September 1780 he began his canvass of St. Savior's Parish, "but so feebly," noted Mrs. Thrale, "that his friends said I must go with him to all the others, which I did." A week later he attended an election meeting at St. George's Church where all the candidates for Southwark presented themselves to the constituents. Mrs. Thrale accompanied her husband and "had the Mortification to see him seized with such Illness as made him look a perfect Corpse in the full View of an immense Congregation assembled to see the Gentlemen who wished to represent them."[6] With his inability to represent the borough so apparent, Thrale lost the election by a wide margin. He thereupon turned his attention to new building schemes and plans for travel. In the spring, he talked of going to Italy. This proposal reduced his wife to near despair: "how shall we drag him thither? a Man who cannot keep awake four Hours at a Stroke, who can scarce retain the Fæces &c. Well! this will indeed be a Tryal of one's Patience." But she had not long to fret. Her next diary entry reads, "No Danger of all these Distresses it seems. Mʳ Thrale died on the 4th of April 1781."[7] Another stroke had carried him off at age fifty-three.

In later life Hester never repented marrying Henry Thrale. Despite her ardent temperament, she understood life's realities. She had taken the measure of men and knew the average. Thrale was better than most, though his frigid disposition often annoyed her. She had passed seventeen and a half years with Thrale and never wished she had remained single nor ever preferred another man to him.[8] Thrale had been essentially easygoing, companionable, and reservedly kind. Unfortunately, he had also been phlegmatic and undemonstrative, the opposite of his wife. Her occasional, though increasing, frustration was not only with Henry Thrale the individual, but with Henry Thrale as representative of the stoic English gentleman, the embodiment of studied detachment and composure. She was a romantic in an age of reason, a woman of fervid emotions living among people who took pride in suppressing their feelings and who often derided the sentiments of others. From Thrale she got no love or sympathy. She had no shoulder to cry on when she needed it, nor would Thrale accept sympathy or consolation from her. Such things meant nothing to him but almost everything to his wife. As she once remarked, "How differently does one feel when one is wanted & when one is not."[9]

When it came to a lack of empathy for the needs of others, Johnson could be just as aggravating as Thrale—perhaps more so. When Thrale, shortly before his death, talked of going to Italy, Mrs. Thrale said that Johnson would be the only one to enjoy himself. Because he valued nothing but his own mind, he would be invigorated by the addition of new ideas, and "if Mr Thrale dies on the Road, Johnson will console himself by learning *how it is* to travel with a Corpse—& after all, such Reasoning is the true Philosophy—one's heart is a mere Incumbrance—Would I could leave mine behind."[10] She conceded that Johnson had more tenderness for poverty than any man she ever knew but less for other misfortunes. As an example, she pointed out that he felt little pity for anyone who lost a friend or relation, for these were merely "the Distresses of Sentiment—which a Man who is *indeed* to be pitied—has no leisure to feel." He claimed that poverty was such a common sight in London that anyone who lives in the city "has no Compassion to spare for the Wounds given only to Vanity or Softness."[11] Once when she grew particularly anxious about the health of her children, she found no one with whom she could share her concerns. One child had something wrong with her eyes, another had a black eye, and another was cutting teeth. She felt a mother's distress, "but I have nobody to tell how it vexes me," she said. "Mr. Thrale will not be conversed with by *me* on any subject, as a friend, or comforter, or adviser. Every day more and more do I feel the loss of my Mother." Mrs. Salusbury would at least have listened to her concerns and shown sympathy, but not the present company. "One cannot disburthen one's mind to people who are watchful to cavil, or acute to contradict before the sentence is finished."[12]

As for Johnson in particular, "he always said he hated a *Feeler*."[13] He rejected the notion, for instance, of innate feelings of parent for offspring. He thought such display of sentiments mere affectation. He told Mrs. Thrale that her husband felt sorry for his son Harry's death just as a man might feel when his newly built house tumbles down, "but *no more*." Johnson "denied parental Feelings entirely; & said the Cow low'd after the Calf, only because it eased her of the Pain in the Udder: was She constantly kept dry-milked said he, you would hear her low no more."[14] Little wonder Mrs. Thrale declared in disgust, "My present Companions have too much philosophy for me."[15]

During the trip to France in 1775, the Thrale party experienced a near fatal accident, the one in which Henry Thrale, a year later, claimed to have injured himself when, in fact, he had contracted a venereal infection. Johnson and

Mrs. Thrale rode in one post chaise and Baretti, Henry Thrale, and Queeney in another. During a steep descent, Thrale's postilion fell off his horse, the traces broke, a horse got run over, and the carriage raced headlong toward a precipice. Thrale leaped from the carriage in a desperate attempt to do something just before a quick-thinking servant managed to stop the horses and avert disaster. Mrs. Thrale became frantic until she learned that everyone had escaped injury. But then she got angry to find Johnson sitting composedly in his coach, completely unperturbed by what had just occurred. "Dr Johnson's perfect unconcern for the Lives of three People, who would all have felt for his, shocked and amaz'd me," she jotted in her diary, "but that, as Baretti says, is true Philosophy." Later she forgave Johnson, who protested that it was not unconcern for the three passengers that prompted his sullenness, but anger with her for getting so hysterical that she could give no ready or rational account of what had happened. Besides, "nothing came of it (he said), except that Mr. Thrale leaped out of the carriage into a chalk-pit, and then came up again, looking *as white!*"[16]

Immediately following Henry Thrale's death, a number of men who had recently been family friends now became Mrs. Thrale's suitors. The charming, wealthy, and still attractive widow of forty stirred the ambitions of many admirers. But Mrs. Thrale was not tempted. She said that love and friendship were two distinct things, and there were many men she would go through fire to serve "whom nothing less than Fire would force me to go to Bed to." Thrale's death presented her with prospects of freedom and independence that she found at once exhilarating and frightening. She had spent her life serving the wishes of others, and now she had the opportunity to gratify her own. She felt, for instance, that should she choose another mate, she was obligated to please no one but herself. An attractive woman of ancient family and respectable character, with uncommon talents and an income of three thousand pounds a year, had a right to think herself any man's equal, "& has nothing to seek but return of Affection from whatever Partner She pitches on."[17] And the man she pitched on was not among the wealthy or well-heeled gentlemen of English society. She chose instead Queeney's Italian singing master, Gabriel Mario Piozzi.

Piozzi was a minor composer, fine tenor, and keyboard virtuoso who had come to England—along with other Italian composers, singers, dancers, and musicians—in order to take advantage of the current enthusiasm in London for Italian music and performers. Susan Burney, who, like her father, had a keen interest in music, Italian opera in particular, acknowledged that Piozzi

Gabriel Piozzi by George Dance, 1793.
Source: National Portrait Gallery, London.

sang divinely.[18] Charles Burney thought highly enough of his voice that he introduced him to the Thrales as a suitable singing master for Queeney. Fanny Burney, who described him as "a first-rate singer, whose voice was deliciously sweet, and whose expression was perfect,"[19] claimed that Mrs. Thrale did not know a flat from a sharp and cared nothing for music. Yet a diary entry nearly a year before her husband's death shows how captivating she found this particular Italian singer. She wrote that he had become an exceptional favorite with her,

> he is so intelligent a Creature, so discerning, one can't help wishing for his good Opinion: his Singing surpasses every body's for Taste, Tenderness, and true Elegance; his Hand on the Forte Piano too is so soft, so sweet, so delicate, every Tone goes to one's heart I think; and fills the Mind with Emotions one would not be without, though inconvenient enough sometimes—I made him sing yesterday, & tho' he says his Voice is gone, I cannot some how or other get it out of my Ears,—odd enough![20]

Tenderness, soft, sweet, and *delicate* are terms she never associated with her usual companions, but Piozzi touched her in ways that Thrale and Johnson could not. He differed from them by responding to life emotionally, not just intellectually or philosophically. Sentiment for him was not something to deride but to express in song. In addition to being handsome, polite, and deferential, he possessed a warmth of spirit that fully accorded with her own. He was a "feeler," just as she was.

It has generally been assumed that the pair did not consummate their relationship until after Henry Thrale's death, but Joseph Baretti later gave a different account. According to him, Mrs. Thrale by this time had grown so disgusted with her husband's lascivious conduct over the years, especially his recent displays of affection for Sophy Streatfeild, that she proceeded to serve him in kind. Baretti stated:

> Mr. Thrale made lewd by an apoplectick fit, was guilty even in the presence of Johnson of some indecent attachment with the pretty Miss Sh_____, which Johnson resented; but was appeased by the Bitch, who cuckolded her husband presently by the help of Piozzi. Johnson, who told me the first part of this story, turned it to the great praise of Mrs. Thrale, that could put up with such flights from her husband, as labouring under a disease: but I knew her better, and was far from giving her credit for her pretended magnanimity, as the simple Johnson did.

From this time forward, Baretti contended, "Piozzi never turned his attention but to her money, and she to his battering-ram."[21]

To live on equal terms with a man she had chosen for herself now seemed within Hester Thrale's reach. "Oh how my Soul loves his Soul!" she wrote of Piozzi more than a year and a half after her husband's death, "& how happy am I since the hour in which I confessed my Affection for him. . . . All will go well at last; and I shall once in my Life, (I *think* I shall)—be happy in my own Way." As soon as she and Piozzi agreed to marry, she disclosed her plans to Queeney and to Fanny Burney. Her eldest daughter was now eighteen, cold and reserved like her father, but unlike Thrale, capable of malice—at least her mother brought out the worst in her personality. Mrs. Thrale called her daughter into her room and confessed the great passion she felt for Piozzi, how impossible it was for her to live without him, and how determined she was to marry him. She then called in Fanny Burney and told her the same thing. Both, as Mrs. Thrale expected, strongly opposed the match and tried to dissuade her from it. She then carefully wrote out a note explaining her position, which

> I shew'd in a Transport of Passion to Queeney & to Burney—sweet Fanny Burney cried herself half blind over it: said there was no resisting such pathetic Eloquence . . . but that while She possessed her Reason, nothing should seduce her to approve what Reason itself would condemn: that Children, Religion, Situation, Country & Character . . . were too much to Sacrifice to any **One** Man.[22]

Fanny later recalled that during this time Mrs. Thrale wavered in her determination to marry Piozzi, "and oh! what scenes followed! Sometimes I prevailed entirely:—then she repented her compliance—then she repented her engagement, then her senses seemed to fail her;—then she raved—then she was seized with a sort of stupor—then she used to fall suddenly asleep, and talk aloud . . . frightful period! I had no peace nor rest."[23]

During one of these heart-rending sessions, Mrs. Thrale threw herself on her bed, groaning in agony,

> which My fair Daughter beheld with frigid Indifference . . . but said coldly that if I *would* abandon my Children, I *must*: that their Father had not deserved such Treatment from me; that I should be punished by Piozzi's neglect, for that She knew he hated me, . . . that for her Part She must look herself out a Place like the other Servants, for my Face would She never see more.[24]

Hester now found herself in the greatest quandary of her life. It was the culmination of her life-long dilemma. The question she must decide was whether to yield once more to the wishes of others or follow her own desires. She grew increasingly determined to have Piozzi the more others opposed him. Her Welsh temper and spirit of independence bridled at the onslaught of disapproval, not only from Queeney and Fanny Burney, but also from other friends as they learned of her plans. How could she so degrade herself, the argument went, by marrying a Roman Catholic, a singing master, and a foreigner? An opportunist who sought only her social position and fortune? A scoundrel who would soon abandon her to shame and poverty? Such a foolish woman. This is what happens when passion triumphs over reason.

Mrs. Thrale wrote in her diary that according to Queeney and Fanny Burney,

> I am not to think about myself, I married the first Time to please my Mother, I must marry the second Time to please my Daughter—I have always sacrificed my own Choice to that of others, so I must sacrifice it again:—but why? Oh because I am a Woman of superior Understanding, & must not for the World degrade my self from my Situation in Life. but if I *have* superior Understanding, let me at least make use of it for once; & rise to the Rank of a human Being conscious of its own power to discern Good from Ill—the person who has uniformly acted by the Will of others, has hardly that Dignity to boast.[25]

Despite Queeney and Fanny Burney's fierce opposition, the alienation of most of her friends, and the condemnation of society at large, Hester finally married Gabriel Piozzi in a Roman Catholic ceremony in London on July 23, 1784, and an Anglican service at Bath two days later. She put off disclosing anything to Dr. Johnson until preparations were too far advanced for him to interfere. She wrote to him in June apologizing for having concealed the matter: "Indeed, my dear Sir, it was concealed only to spare us both needless pain; I could not have borne to reject that Counsel it would have killed me to take; and I only tell it you now, because all is *irrevocably settled*, & out of your power to prevent."[26]

Johnson was stunned by the news. He felt angry and hurt. "If I interpret your letter right," he responded, "You are ignominiously married, if it is yet undone, let us once talk together. If You have abandoned your children and your religion, God forgive your wickedness; if you have forfeited your Fame [reputation], and your country, may your folly do no further mischief."[27]

She found Johnson's letter so unfriendly that she wrote back saying that she could no longer bear to continue their correspondence. She added that she had not abandoned anyone—they were abandoning her. She particularly resented Johnson's implied censure of Piozzi, stating that the birth, sentiments, and profession of her second husband were no meaner than those of her first. Nor was she renouncing her country and religion, and for him to claim that she was forfeiting her reputation was the greatest insult she had ever received. "Farewell Dear Sir," she concluded,

> and accept my best wishes: You have always commanded my Esteem, and long enjoy'd the Fruits of a Friendship never infringed by one harsh Expression on

my Part, during twenty Years of familiar Talk. never did I oppose your Will, or controal your Wish: nor can your unmerited Severity itself lessen my Regard— but till you have changed your Opinion of M[r]. Piozzi—let us converse no more. God bless you![28]

Johnson wrote another, more conciliatory letter, but Mrs. Thrale, now Mrs. Piozzi, did not reply. For her it was over. Brighter days lay ahead, and she wished to put behind her the oppressive world of Henry Thrale's cold indifference, Johnson's stern rebukes, and Fanny Burney's prudish decorum.

Hester Thrale's break with Johnson occurred ostensibly due to her marriage to Piozzi, but the relationship truly ended, for all practical purposes, with Henry Thrale's death. Not long after that event, with the help of Johnson, she disposed of the brewery, which had become, she said, a millstone around her neck. But Johnson had become a millstone as well. She still admired him, but his growing irascibility strained friendship, not only with her, but also with others, and the demands he placed on her totally subordinated her life to his. Streatham from the beginning had been his private hospital and Mrs. Thrale his special nurse. Whenever he became ill, it was she who took care of him, and after Thrale's death, he expected the arrangement to continue. But now that he was older and more irritable than ever, his demands became greater. Mrs. Thrale thought he might live another ten years, and she could not bear the idea of supporting such a burden for so long. Henry Thrale had been able to manage him, "But as I never had any ascendancy at all over Mr. Johnson, except just in the things that concerned his health, it grew extremely perplexing and difficult to live in the house with him when the master of it was no more; the worse indeed, because his dislikes grew capricious."[29]

Johnson could always be rough with people. Reynolds once observed that his pet macaw and Johnson were much alike, very good humored at times, but suddenly, for no apparent reason that anyone could see, would grow irritated and peck at you.[30] But Johnson was now in such terrible humor most of the time, as Fanny Burney noted when she accompanied Johnson and Mrs. Thrale to Bath in 1782, that he "has really frightened all the people, till they almost ran from him."[31] She was sorry to witness "how unmercifully he attacks & riots the people." He so terrified everyone that they stopped inviting him to social events. What a pity, she thought, that he could not restrain himself "upon every occasion from such bitter or cruel Speeches as eternally come from him!"[32] Hardly anyone now escaped his attacks. "To me only I think he is now kind, for Mrs. Thrale fares worse than any body."[33]

Once her husband was gone, Mrs. Thrale felt she could no longer tolerate such abuse and domination, so she determined to avoid him as much as possible. Prior to her marriage to Piozzi, she spent most of her time at Bath or at Brighton, keeping away from Streatham so as not to attract Johnson there. "Poor Johnson did not ever *mean* to use me ill," she said, "he only grew upon Indulgence, till Patience could endure no further."[34]

Baretti later indicated that the break was not due primarily to Johnson's ill temper. He insisted that as Mrs. Thrale began to see possibilities with Piozzi, she started picking quarrels with Johnson in an attempt to shake him off: "The charming Piozzi came crossways, and battered down Johnson with his battering-ram." Baretti further maintained that Mrs. Thrale had first been attracted to Johnson by "vanity and strong desire of literary fame: but when the love of a battering-ram succeeded, her friendship cooled, and ended soon."[35]

Johnson naturally felt abandoned at a time when he had most need of Mrs. Thrale's care and attention. It seemed to him that without Henry Thrale's stabilizing influence, and his own counsel, she had grown ever more willful. She was far too impulsive a woman, he said, to navigate life on her own. He told Boswell that she had done everything wrong "since Thrale's bridle was off her neck."[36] He failed to appreciate the fact that it was the bridle on her neck, both Thrale's and his own, that she longed to escape. He saw only that the woman he had long thought "the first of humankind" had abandoned him, and it filled him with bitterness and pain.[37]

Fanny Burney visited him in Bolt Court before word of the impending remarriage became public. It was nearly a year since Mrs. Thrale had begun avoiding him. Fanny suspected that he knew more about the situation than he let on, though their conversation that day began agreeably enough. She carefully skirted the subject of Mrs. Thrale, but soon Johnson grew quiet and "a sudden change from kind tranquillity to strong austerity took place in his altered countenance." A silence "almost awful succeeded." He began "seesawing violently in his chair, as usual when he was big with any powerful emotion," and he stared into the fire. The frightened Fanny observed "the laborious heaving of the ponderous chest, and the roll of the large, penetrating, wrathful eye." Several minutes passed in which she scarcely breathed, "while the respiration of the Doctor, on the contrary, was of asthmatic force and loudness." Then suddenly he turned to Fanny, and "with an air of mingled wrath and woe, he hoarsely ejaculated: 'Piozzi!'"[38]

Mrs. Thrale regretted the split with Fanny Burney perhaps more than her break with Dr. Johnson. She had constantly addressed Fanny in terms of

"My dearest and most delicate-minded Friend," and "my ever dearest, my ever-kindest Friend."[39] Eleven years her junior, Fanny was something of a surrogate daughter, more tender, sympathetic, and affectionate than her actual daughters. For a time the two women were almost inseparable, preferring each other's company to anyone else's. Following Henry Thrale's death, Fanny asked Mrs. Thrale to still love and think of her as the sincerest, fondest, and most grateful of her friends.[40] The problem for Mrs. Thrale was Fanny's nearly pathological concern for society's opinion. "The fear of doing wrong," Fanny once said, "has been always the leading principle of my internal guidance."[41] She objected to Mrs. Thrale's marrying Gabriel Piozzi not only because he was a Catholic, a foreigner, and a singing master. She also objected to Mrs. Thrale taking the lead in the courtship: "*Ladies* chusing openly for themselves, never appeared to me a *right* thing,—nor does it prove *prosperous.*"[42] It simply was not an acceptable way for a woman to act. She asked rhetorically, "What Woman, again, shall chuse for herself?—No, no, we seem, at last, destined to be elected, not to elect,—the two Disciples of Dr. Collier [Sophia Streatfeild and Hester Thrale], two Women, in their different ways, of the rarest attractions, have suffered nothing but disgrace from making the experiment."[43] For several years Sophy Streatfeild had talked openly about her love for a parson of Lambeth, only to end up in 1779 having the parson jilt her.[44]

Once word got around that Hester Thrale had married her daughter's Italian singing master, friends, acquaintances, and people of quality at large rejected her as being not in her right mind. Elizabeth Carter, one of society's leading bluestockings, expressed sorrow but not surprise, for Mrs. Thrale "always seemed to be a genius of that eccentric kind, which is mighty apt to be accompanied by 'a plentiful lack' of common sense."[45] Elizabeth Montagu wrote even more pointedly:

> I am myself convinced that the poor Woman is mad and indeed have long suspected her mind was disordered. She was the best Mother, the best Wife, the best friend, the most amiable member of Society.... I would give much to make every one think of her as mad, the best and wisest are liable to lunacy. If she is not considered in that light she must throw a disgrace of her sex.[46]

Mrs. Thrale understood the fear and awe that such attitudes excited in Fanny's breast. She realized that her young friend "loves me *kindly*, but the World *reverentially*."[47] During the difficult period leading up to the marriage, Fanny, in a delicate balancing act, continued to express sympathy for Mrs. Thrale's feelings but at the same time to voice opposition to her alliance with Piozzi. Mrs. Thrale began to think Fanny duplicitous and perhaps in league with Queeney in trying to prevent the marriage. "I am sometimes ready to think Fanny Burney treacherous," she said, "but tis a sinful Thought & must not be indulged."[48] But the suspicion eventually grew in her mind to a certainty. She became convinced that Fanny only pretended to be sympathetic in order to retain her confidence while she and Queeney conspired behind her back. She wrote to Fanny on August 6, 1784, "I not only thought you unkind, but I think so still: True Tenderness does not express herself ambiguously."[49]

Following her marriage, and after leaving England on her honeymoon, Hester Piozzi refused to have anything more to do with Fanny Burney and her delicate sense of propriety. She wrote to Queeney, "Had it not been for Miss Burney's Interposition with you, I might it seems have been happy long ago: but I forgive her from my Soul: let us however not encourage Mischiefmakers now we are parted, for there are enough who will take up the employment."[50] Putting all such enmities and disputes behind her, she rolled through France on her way to Italy with Piozzi, exclaiming that she was happier at the present moment than she had been in the past twenty-two years.[51] She looked forward to new friends and new opportunities for personal growth. "I shall let loose . . . in this Journey the Fondness for Painting which I was forced to suppress while Dr. Johnson lived with me, and ridiculed my Taste of an Art his own Imperfect Sight hindered him from enjoying."[52] She did not expect her remaining days to be without difficulties, but she at least intended to live them in her own way. In her letter to Johnson announcing her intention to marry Piozzi, she had claimed to be "perhaps the most independent Woman in the World." She now felt certain that she really was.[53]

Shortly after Mrs. Thrale's break with Johnson, another longtime relationship ran into trouble. Joseph Baretti, Johnson's oldest London friend after David Garrick, always acknowledged Johnson's superiority over every other man he had ever known. The great man's preeminence in the field of letters aroused in him no jealousy or sense of rivalry as it had in Goldsmith, and he used to say that if he possessed Johnson's genius, and if Johnson's had *his* "Spirit of Application & Drudgery; we might have driven our Coaches and Six long ago."[54] From their earliest acquaintance, Baretti acknowledged his obligations to Johnson in directing his intellectual growth, and he later proclaimed Johnson "the best friend I ever had." To their many conversations and disputes, said Baretti, "I am indebted for the best part of that little knowledge I have; and if there is any kind of rectitude and solidity in my ideas, I will ever remember with gratitude as well as with pride, that I owe more of it to him and to his books, than to any other man I ever knew, or any other books I ever studied."[55]

Johnson regretted that in the heat of dispute he sometimes exerted his powers too harshly against a man who was poor, a foreigner, and his friend. Yet despite occasionally being tossed and gored, Baretti reverenced Johnson's compassion and generosity, not only to himself in the early years of his English residence, but to others as well. He occasionally told the story of going with Johnson to dinner one evening. On their way to the tavern, a foreigner, with a bogus tale of distress, wheedled from Johnson all the money he had in his pocket. Subsequently, after dinner, Johnson found that he could not pay his portion of the reckoning, but luckily Baretti had enough to cover the amount. In telling the story, Baretti claimed it impossible not to respect a man who could give away all he had without considering his own needs.

The first serious breach in their friendship came during the trip to Paris in 1775. Baretti grew angry that Johnson and Mrs. Thrale laughed at French accommodations and cookery. How supercilious it seemed to him for the English to be laughing at French cookery. But the two also ridiculed French manners and sentiments. When Johnson later told others of Baretti's resentment, a woman suggested that it might be because France lay on the road to Italy and French manners perhaps resembled those of Italy. "No," said Johnson. "He was the showman, and we did not like his show; that was all the reason."[56]

But this was not all the reason from Baretti's perspective. Apart from finding the French stupid, Johnson seemed unwilling to enjoy the things he saw or to take much interest in the people he met. This could not but offend one who made every effort to please in his capacity as guide. Johnson was simply not fit to travel, Baretti claimed, for every place he visited was the same as every other place. "He mused as much on the road to Paris as he did in his garret in London, as much at a French Opera as in his room at Streatham."[57] In writing home to Italy in January 1776 telling of his trip, Baretti attempted to describe Johnson to his brother Amedeo:

> Johnson is a dreadful old man, a giant both in mind and body, always absent-minded, fierce, touchy, dirty, with a number of unpleasant habits. His body is continually in motion while he is seated and he ruminates ceaselessly with his mouth like an ox; but as he is rightly considered to possess more knowledge than any other man in the kingdom, he is feared and respected by every one, perhaps more than he is loved. Though he is a great critic in French, and knows almost as much Italian as I do, he cannot speak either language, but he talks Latin with all Cicero's fury.[58]

Following the French trip, Frances Reynolds noticed a change in Baretti's manner. She attributed the change to a false sense of his own importance and stated that the cordial friendship between him and Johnson did not continue following the excursion.[59] The decisive break, however, did not come until some months before Johnson's death. Baretti, as he did with everyone, often teased Johnson, usually about his idleness. Johnson bore this well, for it contained no real malice and was simply a display of Baretti's saturnine humor and playfulness. Johnson, in fact, usually reciprocated by needling Baretti, and on this occasion

> he recollected that Omiah [a native of Raiatea, an island near Tahiti in the South Pacific] had once conquered me at Chess; a subject, on which, whenever chance brought it about, he never failed to rally me most unmercifully, and make himself mighty merry with.
>
> This time, more than he had ever done before, he pushed his banter on at such a rate that at last he chafed me, and made me so angry, that, not being able to put a stop to it, I snatched up my hat and stick, and quitted him in a most choleric mood.[60]

Blind Anna Williams, however, who overheard the dispute, told a slightly different story. According to her, Baretti countered Johnson's accusation by claiming to have beaten Omai twice at chess at Sir Joshua's house, an assertion Johnson knew to be false, and he said so. "Do you think," exclaimed Baretti, "that I should be conquered at Chess by a savage?"

"I know you were," replied Johnson.

Upon Baretti insisting he had not, "Johnson rose from his seat in a most violent rage, [saying] 'I'll hear no more,'" at which Baretti fled the house in alarm.[61] The two men never met again.

Johnson said that from his twentieth year his health had seldom afforded him a single day of ease. In addition to impaired vision and defective hearing, he had long suffered from depression, hypochondria, and a variety of painful physical disorders. But as he approached his seventieth year, bodily ailments crowded upon him so fast that he seldom got much rest at night.

He now suffered from asthma that made breathing so difficult he often could not lie down but had to sit up nights in a chair. In 1782, not long after he published his last major work, *Lives of the English Poets*, he complained to Boswell that for most of the year he had been battered by one disorder after another. The asthma had been complicated by the onset of gout, making it impossible for him to leave his lodgings for weeks at a time. His letters during this period were often little more than registers of diseases and chronicles of the means he took to combat them.

At times, however, his chief complaints almost entirely disappeared, leaving him hopeful that he had conquered them. But they would soon return with increased vigor, depriving him of sleep at night and leaving him dull and drowsy all day. Then early in the morning of June 17, 1783, he suffered a mild paralytic stroke that temporarily deprived him of speech and made it difficult for him to write legibly. He recovered fully within a month, though he continued to have difficulty breathing. "The asthma, however, is not the worst," he wrote to Boswell. "A dropsy gains ground upon me; my legs and thighs are very much swollen with water, which I should be content if I could keep there, but I am afraid that it will soon be higher. My nights are very sleepless and very tedious. And yet I am extremely afraid of dying." He reiterated his fears of approaching death to another friend, saying, "I am afraid to think on that which I know, I cannot avoid. It is vain to look round and round, for that help which cannot be had. Yet we hope and hope, and fancy that he who has lived to day may live tomorrow."[62] At a meeting of the Club in June 1783, the last that Johnson attended, his friends noted how ill he looked. All addressed him with special concern, and they discussed with him the possibility of his retiring to Italy during the upcoming winter. Johnson approved of the idea, so without his further knowledge, they began devising a plan.

The main obstacle was money, for Johnson's annual pension of £300 would not cover expenses. With Reynolds's encouragement, Boswell wrote to Lord Chancellor Edward Thurlow suggesting that if the king were made aware of the situation, his Majesty might increase the pension, allowing Johnson to make the trip. Lord Thurlow replied favorably in a letter, saying that it would reflect badly on all of them if such a man as Johnson should die for lack of money to care for his health. When shown Lord Thurlow's letter, Reynolds suggested that it was time to lay everything out for Johnson, who might get upset if the plan was too long concealed from him. So Boswell hurried to Bolt Court, explained to Johnson what had been done, and read to him Lord Thurlow's letter. Johnson listened attentively and then said that this was taking extraordinary pains about a man. Boswell told him that his friends would do everything they could for him. "He paused," noted Boswell in his journal, "grew more and more agitated, till tears started into his eyes, and he exclaimed with much emotion, 'GOD bless you all.' I was so affected that I also shed tears. After a little while he renewed his grateful benediction, 'GOD bless you all for JESUS CHRIST's sake.' We remained for some time unable to speak." Johnson then got up and left the room until he could compose himself.

The following day Boswell and Johnson dined with Reynolds so the three could discuss the upcoming trip in greater detail. Boswell and Reynolds were so optimistic that the king would at least double his pension, and perhaps do more, that Johnson got caught up in their enthusiasm and declared that doubling his pension would give him the consciousness of being able to live the rest of his life in splendor. The other two began imagining the happiness he should enjoy in Italy, but Johnson replied, "Nay, I must not expect that. Were I going to Italy to see fine pictures, like Sir Joshua, or to run after women, like Boswell, I might to be sure have pleasure in Italy. But when a man goes to Italy merely to feel how he breathes the air, he can enjoy very little."

At the close of the evening, Boswell accompanied Johnson in Reynolds's coach to the entrance of Bolt Court. Johnson asked if Boswell would not go in with him. Boswell declined, as he wrote in his journal, fearing he would get too emotional. They bid an affectionate adieu to each other in the carriage before Johnson stepped out. "When he had got down upon the foot-pavement, he called out, 'Fare you well!' and without looking back sprung away with a kind of pathetic briskness (if I may use that expression), which seemed to indicate a struggle to conceal uneasiness, and was to me a foreboding of our long, long separation." Boswell left for Scotland two days later without seeing Johnson again.[63]

As things turned out, the king chose not to act in the matter, though Johnson's health deteriorated so rapidly that he probably could not have made the trip anyway. When Bennet Langton learned how dangerously ill Johnson had become, he set aside his own affairs in Lincolnshire and came to London. There he rendered what assistance he could. Hannah More saw him in company at Elizabeth Montagu's. "I am sure you will honour him," she wrote to one of her sisters, "when I tell you he is come on purpose to stay with Dr. Johnson, and that during his illness. He has taken a little lodging in Fleet-street, in order to be near, to devote himself to him. He has as much goodness as learning, and that is saying a bold thing of one of the first Greek scholars we have."[64]

As Johnson grew worse into the month of December, Langton spent long hours watching. He was one of the few now allowed by doctors into the sickroom. Dr. Burney tried for a week to see Johnson but could gain no admittance. Finally he saw him briefly on December 11, at which time Johnson seemed better and appeared more composed. Burney reported to his daughter Fanny that Johnson wished to see her, so she hurried to Bolt Court the following day and waited a considerable time in the parlor before Langton came down. He seemed greatly moved. Fanny noted that he could not look at her, and she avoided looking at him. A Mrs. Davis who was present, the former companion or assistant to Anna Williams, asked how the doctor was doing, and Langton replied, "Going on to Death very fast!" She asked if he had taken any nourishment. "Nothing at all!—we carried him some Bread & milk,—he refused it, & said, *The less the better.*" Another quarter of an hour passed in awkward silence before Fanny realized that Langton wished to say more. He finally remarked, "This poor man, I understand, ma'am, desired yesterday to see you?"

"My understanding that, sir, brought me to Day."

"Poor man! it is pity he did not know himself better,— & that you should have had this trouble." Fanny exclaimed that it was no trouble. She would willingly come a hundred times for the chance to see him. "He hopes, now," said Langton, "you will excuse him,— he is very sorry not to see you,—but he desired me to come & speak to you myself, & tell *You* he hopes you will excuse him, for he feels himself too weak for such an interview."[65]

Johnson died quietly the following day at the age of seventy-five. One week later his body was interred in the Poets' Corner next to that of David Garrick, Bennet Langton serving as one of the pall-bearers. Boswell was in Edinburgh when he received a letter on December 17 from Richard Brocklesby, Johnson's physician, announcing that Johnson had died on the thirteenth. Boswell had long dreaded the event but felt stunned all the same. He did not shed tears nor get emotional. "My feeling was just one large expanse of stupor."[66] Some days later he felt troubled to learn that he had not been mentioned in Johnson's will, yet he consoled himself with the thought that he possessed several books given to him by Johnson as gifts, and other tokens as well. Besides, other longtime friends, such as Edmund Hector and Charles Burney, had not been mentioned in the will either. He also felt uneasy knowing that he would now be expected to produce a memoir of his friend. He feared that habits of idleness, coupled with his constitutional melancholy, would prevent him from putting forth the tremendous effort necessary. "I wished I could write now as when I wrote my *Account of Corsica*," he said, meaning with energy and inspiration. Yet despite his misgivings, he immediately set to work arranging and revising the journal he had kept during his trip with Johnson through the Scottish Highlands and Hebrides in 1773. This would be a preparation, a testing of the water, for what he already thought of as his magnum opus. The journal would be a prelude to a larger work, Johnson's life.[67]

The Journal of a Tour to the Hebrides, with Samuel Johnson, LL.D. appeared in late 1785 to generally favorable notices. *The London Review* thought the book provided much information and entertainment, the reviewer's primary caveat being the author's lack of delicacy in publishing private conversations. Otherwise, the writer thought Mr. Boswell told his anecdotes in a sprightly and agreeable manner.[68] *The Critical Review* found the work a mixture of many things as it passed successively from "the most illiberal sarcasms, and the most trifling vanity, to judicious remarks, and the most interesting conversations." Although the *Critical Review* criticized Boswell's egotism, it thought the spirited style "enlivened the didactic gravity of the literary Colossus," and it recommended the work to readers "as a pleasant, lively, and sometimes useful companion."[69] Other journals reflected similar views, and the book became an unqualified success. The first edition of 1,500 copies sold out quickly and was followed by two more editions in the subsequent year.

Mrs. Piozzi was in Italy with her husband at the time of Johnson's death. She had recently written to a friend in England urging him not to neglect Dr. Johnson, for he would find no other person so wise or so good. She kept Johnson's picture in her room, she said, and some of his words on her chimney.[70] She finally learned of his passing while in Milan around January 2 and wrote but one sentence in her diary—"Oh poor Dr Johnson!!!" It took three weeks before she could write anything more: "I have recovered myself sufficiently to think what will be the Consequence to me of Johnson's Death, but must wait the Event as all Thoughts on the future in this World are vain."[71] Certain things, though, quickly became clear. She learned that six people were preparing to write Johnson's life, and her husband strongly encouraged her to enter the competition. After all, she possessed a unique perspective on much of Johnson's life, habits, and conversation. One immediate consequence of Johnson's death, then, was that she once more considered becoming a published author, an ambition that Henry Thrale's indifference and a fear of Johnson's undue influence had long suppressed. She felt at a disadvantage, however, in being so far from home, for she lacked the necessary sources to help confirm incidents and fix dates. But relying mainly on her recollections, she set to work, and her *Anecdotes of the Late Samuel Johnson LL.D.* appeared in March 1786, six months after Boswell's *Tour to the Hebrides.*

The *Anecdotes*, as the title implied, turned out to be a patchwork of often unrelated impressions that produced no unified portrait of its subject, a fact that some readers and reviewers seized on immediately. Horace Walpole pronounced the book "wretched—a high-varnished preface to a heap of rubbish in a very vulgar style, and too void of method even for such a farrago." He found the work full of contradictions. "Her panegyric is loud in praise of her hero—and almost every fact she relates disgraces him. She allows and proves he was arrogant, yet affirms he was not proud—as if arrogance were not the flower of pride."[72]

Dr. Burney anonymously attacked the volume in the *Monthly Review*. He censured it for "exposing his [Johnson's] failings and his weaknesses, to the curious, yet fastidious eye of the Public." He further complained, as others did, that the book merely attempted to justify Mrs. Piozzi's abandonment of Johnson in his last years.[73]

Despite these and similar criticisms, the work sold well and the general public seemed to like it. Several of her few remaining friends in England praised the work. One wrote to her expressing delight

> in the way every body goes on admiring you and your pretty book—and says how nicely You have cooked your Ragout of Elephant—that you have given all the Flavor of the Substance—without the Rankness and Heaviness of the Beast—and done with such pure clean Hands too—whereas Boswell has *pawed* his Scotch Collops about so—that they stink of himself to such a degree that they turn every body's stomack.[74]

Boswell found the *Anecdotes* entertaining and granted that Mrs. Piozzi had preserved a good deal of useful Johnsoniana, "but she has proved herself to be a wicked, false, ungrateful little vixen" in the way she portrayed Johnson as a burden. He particularly did not like the "Postscript" to her book, in which she objected to "a passage from Mr. Boswell's Tour to the Hebrides, in which it is said, that *I could not get through Mrs. Montagu's Essay on Shakespeare*," a claim she strongly denied. What upset Boswell is that he had earlier given her his manuscript journal to read, and she had made no comment at the time on Johnson's remark. Furthermore, it was Johnson who made the accusation, not himself. He had merely recorded what Johnson said. Mrs. Piozzi, maliciously it seemed to him, made it appear that Boswell made the false assertion. She had attacked his veracity, something for which he prided himself. "She is a little artful impudent malignant Devil," he said, and he vowed to pay her back in his projected "Life of Johnson."[75]

NOTES

1. Hyde, *Thrales of Streatham Park*, 204 and 202–3.

2. Piozzi, *Thraliana*, 442.

3. Samuel Johnson, *The Letters of Samuel Johnson with Mrs. Thrale's Genuine Letters to Him*, ed. R. W. Chapman, 3 vols. (Oxford: Clarendon Press, 1952), 2:352.

4. Baretti, Marginal Annotations, 2:110.

5. Piozzi, *Thraliana*, 441, 488–89.

6. Ibid., 453–54.

7. Ibid., 487.

8. Ibid., 1032.

9. Hyde, *Thrales of Streatham Park*, 201.

10. Piozzi, *Thraliana*, 487.

11. Ibid., 184.

12. Broadley, *Doctor Johnson and Mrs. Thrale*, 193–94.

13. Piozzi, *Thraliana*, 541.

14. Ibid., 740.

15. Broadley, *Doctor Johnson and Mrs. Thrale*, 194.

16. Piozzi, *French Journals*, 88–90.

17. Piozzi, *Thraliana*, 531.

18. Susanna Burney, *The Journals and Letters of Susan Burney: Music and Society in Late Eighteenth-Century England*, ed. Philip Olleson (Farnham, Surrey; Burlington, VT: Ashgate, 2012), 71 and 85.

19. Frances Burney, *Memoirs*, 2:105.

20. Piozzi, *Thraliana*, 452.

21. Baretti, Marginal Annotations, 1:98 and 100.

22. Piozzi, *Thraliana*, 553, 549, 550.

23. R. Brimley Johnson, *Fanny Burney and the Burneys* (Freeport, NY: Books for Libraries Press, 1971), 105.

24. Piozzi, *Thraliana*, 558–59.

25. Ibid., 544–45.

26. Johnson, *Letters*, Chapman, 3:172–73.

27. Johnson, *Letters*, Redford, 4:338.

28. Johnson, *Letters*, Chapman, 3:175.

29. Piozzi, *Anecdotes*, 106–7.

30. Boswell, *Ominous Years*, 335.

31. Burney, *Diary & Letters*, 2:122.

32. Burney, *Letters of Dr Burney*, 1:349–50n10.

33. Burney, *Diary & Letters*, 2:122.

34. Piozzi, *Thraliana*, 617.

35. Baretti, Marginal Annotations, 1:190 and 2:7.

36. Boswell, *Applause of the Jury*, 213.

37. Johnson, *Letters*, Redford, 4:338.

38. Frances Burney, *Memoirs*, 2:360–61.

39. Piozzi, *Piozzi Letters*, 1:59–60 and 1:73.

40. Burney, *Diary & Letters*, 1:471.

41. Ibid., 6:363.

42. Burney, *Early Journals*, 3:374.

43. Marquis of Lansdowne, *The Queeney Letters: Being Letters Addressed to Hester Maria Thrale by Doctor Johnson, Fanny Burney, and Mrs. Thrale-Piozzi* (New York: Farrar & Rinehart, 1934), 94.

44. Abraham Hayward writes: "The parson was the Rev. Dr. [William] Vyse, Rector of Lambeth. He had made an imprudent marriage early in life, and was separated from his wife, of whom he hoped to get rid either by divorce or by her death, as she was reported to be in bad health. Under these circumstances, he had entered into a conditional engagement with the fair S. S.; but eventually threw her over, either in despair at his wife's longevity or from caprice" (Hayward, *Autobiography*, 1:118–19). See also Burney, *Early Journals*, 3:304n87 and 374. Sophia Streatfeild never married.

45. Piozzi, *Piozzi Letters*, 1:102n2.

46. Ibid., 1:99–100.

47. Piozzi, *Thraliana*, 593.

48. Ibid., 581.

49. Piozzi, *Piozzi Letters*, 1:107.

50. Ibid., 1:109.

51. Tyson and Guppy, *French Journals*, 203.

52. Piozzi, *Piozzi Letters*, 1:385.

53. Johnson, *Letters*, Chapman, 3:173.

54. Piozzi, *Thraliana*, 164.

55. "Stricture the Third," *European Magazine* 14 (August 1788): 91 and 89.

56. Hill, *Johnsonian Miscellanies*, 2:290.

57. Baretti, Marginal Annotations, 1:315.

58. Collison-Morley, *Giuseppe Baretti*, 84–85.

59. Hill, *Johnsonian Miscellanies*, 2:292–93.

60. "Mr. Baretti's Relation of his Rupture with Dr. Johnson," *European Magazine* 12 (August 1787): 111–12. Omai had been brought to England in one of Captain James Cook's ships in July 1774. Next to a passage in her copy of Boswell's *Life* describing Omai, Mrs. Piozzi wrote, "When Omai played at Chess and Backgammon with Baretti, every body admired at the Savage's good Breeding, & at the European's Impatient Spirit" (Boswell, *Life With Comments*, 2:265).

61. Hill, *Johnsonian Miscellanies*, 2:292–93.

62. Johnson, *Letters*, Redford, 4:285 and 4:312.

63. Boswell, *Applause of the Jury*, 253–55.

64. Roberts, *Memoirs*, 1:178.

65. Frances Burney, *The Additional Journals and Letters of Frances Burney*, vol. 1, 1784–1786, ed. Stewart Cooke (Oxford: Oxford University Press, 2015), 152.

66. Boswell, *Applause of the Jury*, 271.

67. Ibid., 272–73n3.

68. *London Review, and Literary Journal* 8 (December 1785): 450.

69. *Critical Review, or Annals of Literature* 60 (November 1785): 337–45.

70. Piozzi, *Piozzi Letters*, 1:120.

71. Piozzi, *Thraliana*, 624–25.

72. Walpole, *Correspondence*, 25:636.

73. *Monthly Review* 74 (May 1786): 374.

74. Piozzi, *Piozzi Letters*, 1:196n1.

75. Boswell, *Correspondence Relating to the* Life, 117 and 114; Piozzi, *Anecdotes*, 161.

Chapter Thirteen

Torn Friendships

The years immediately following Johnson's death brought significant changes in the life of Fanny Burney. In her second novel, *Cecilia*, published in 1782, she had written of her heroine, "A strong sense of DUTY, a fervent desire to ACT RIGHT, were the ruling characteristics of her mind."[1] These also continued to be the ruling characteristics of the author's mind. For a woman to act right from Fanny's perspective, and by the prevailing standards of the day, she must act in accordance with society's prescribed rules of conduct rather than follow her own desires and ambitions. A man might take pride in his highly valued sense of independence, but a woman ran too many hazards. Fanny's rift with Mrs. Thrale centered primarily on the issue of whether a woman's first duty was to social convention or to her own happiness. Mrs. Thrale, after much torment and inner struggle, chose her own happiness even as Fanny cautioned her that women were not born for themselves.[2]

One of Fanny's main obligations as she saw it was to act right as a daughter. She worshipped her father. "How strongly, how forcibly do I feel to whom I owe All the happiness I enjoy!—" she wrote in her diary, "it is to my Father! to this dearest, most amiable, this best beloved—most worthy of men!"[3] Her obligation was to obey his wishes, even when they ran counter to her own welfare. Although Dr. Burney was among the most lenient of men and left Fanny pretty much to her own devices, she felt it impossible to resist not only his stated wishes, but also any advice he might offer in passing.[4] This conflict between sense of duty and self-interest is best illustrated by the five unhappy years Fanny spent at court.

She had befriended Mary Delany, a favorite of George III and Queen Charlotte. The elderly Mrs. Delany, ill and impoverished, had, in former times, known George Frederick Handel and Alexander Pope and been a friend and correspondent of Jonathan Swift. An artist and amateur botanist, she excelled at decoupage—pictures made from cutout paper of various textures and tints. These "Paper Mosaiks," as she called them, were botanically correct, meticulously detailed, and beautifully colored representations of plants and flowers. Fanny described Mrs. Delany as "an aged lady of rare accomplishments, and high bred manners, of olden times."[5] In 1785 the queen granted her a yearly pension of £300 and provided her with a small house near Windsor Castle. There the royal couple often visited her, and there they met Fanny. Queen Charlotte took a particular interest in the shy young woman—in her reserve, discretion, and steady character—so much so that she considered offering Miss Burney the position of Keeper of the Robes that was soon to fall vacant on the retirement of an old servant who held the post. Fanny sensed the queen's intentions and dreaded the event. She found the king and queen good and kind people. That presented no difficulties. And the position was prestigious and much coveted. But Fanny realized that the sacrifices she would have to make would deprive her of any possible means of happiness. She would have to give up her home, her freedom, and her friends for a life of servitude.

After a period of suspense, in which she hoped the offer would not be made, the royal invitation arrived: "The *Blow* was struck on Monday,—& hard it struck, & almost felled me."[6] The position, said the queen in her offer, was to be permanent. The duties involved assisting the queen at her toilette, for which Miss Burney would receive meals, a room, her own maid and footman, and £200 a year. Fanny wanted to decline the offer outright but thought it would be disrespectful to the queen and discourteous to Mrs. Delany, who had championed the plan. But principally she saw that her father expected her to accept. Two conflicting desires now came together: "a strong sense of duty,—with a disinterested Love of Independence."[7] She realized that her independence rested entirely on her father's generosity. She was now thirty-four and unmarried, and she seemed likely to remain single. Being the only child from his first marriage still at home, she was a drain on her father's meager income.

When Dr. Burney learned of the queen's offer, he felt greatly relieved. He had once observed that a man without a family was an isolated beast, "but a woman without a mate is still more insignificant & helpless."[8] How fortunate to be able to place his spinster daughter under the protection of the king and queen. Now if something happened to him, she would be provided for. Of further consideration was the possibility that Fanny's appointment might lead to royal favors for other members of the family—the post of Master of the King's Band for himself; promotions for son James, a captain in the Royal Navy; and preferment for son Charles, studying for the clergy.

Under these pressures, Fanny felt powerless to refuse the queen's offer. She could think of nothing to save herself from a life of servitude:

> I cannot even to my Father utter my reluctance,—I see him so much delighted at the prospect of an establishment he looks upon as so honourable—but for the Queen's own word *permanent*—but for her declared desire to *attach me entirely*—I should share in his pleasure,—but what can make *me* amends for all I shall forfeit?[9]

She kept her forebodings to herself and accepted the post. Once she arrived at court and began to learn her duties, she understood how justified her fears had been—she would be separated from her friends and family and be committed to a life of unremitting attendance, dress, and confinement.[10] She did not know if she possessed sufficient strength for the task. She often had to be up before dawn, stand in place for hours at a time, not get to bed until after midnight, and then start the routine again early next morning. When not attending the queen, she waited in her room to be called. Her immediate superior, Mrs. Juliana Schwellenberg, a fat, ill-natured German, made the situation even more unpleasant with her "Tyranny, Dissension, & even insult."[11] But the worst part remained the separation from family and friends. Her only recourse, she said, was "to wean myself from myself—to lessen all my affections—to curb all my wishes—to deaden all my sensations."[12] The confinement, long hours, isolation, and general monotony of court life proved to be so exhausting and mind-numbing that her health began to suffer.

Then everything took a sudden turn, and she went from exhaustion and tedium to anxiety and fear. The king became ill in the summer of 1788 and by the fall began to act strangely. "I had a sort of conference with His Majesty, or rather I was the object to whom he spoke," Fanny wrote in her journal in October. The king's manner appeared to her highly unusual and completely out of character—"a rapidity, a hoarseness of voice, a volubility, an earnestness—a vehemence, rather—it startled me inexpressibly." Although his words were gracious, his manner alarmed her. "Heaven—Heaven preserve him!" she wrote.[13] His behavior grew stranger into the winter months, marked by a nervous agitation rising at times to delirium. One day in a fit of anger, he threw his adult son, the Prince of Wales, against a wall. Fanny refused to record in her journal some of the things she witnessed or was told in confidence, but stories of the king's unusual behavior circulated outside of court. Reportedly in one of his fits, he ran naked into the queen's chamber, flung his wife on the bed, and ordered the female attendants to witness how well he did. Another story is that he attempted to rape his eldest daughter, the Princess Royal.[14] Due to such erratic, unpredictable, and sometimes violent behavior, the king finally had to be restrained and kept apart from the rest of the royal household. He was occasionally confined in a straightjacket or tied down to his bed, and only his doctors and a few select male attendants were allowed access to him. Everyone at court, especially the queen, her daughters, and Fanny, were greatly frightened by the entire experience.

By February, however, the king began to improve just as suddenly and mysteriously as he had taken ill, and by month's end he seemed almost fully recovered. Yet the harrowing events of the previous three months left everyone feeling anxious and apprehensive lest the malady recur, which it did many years later, leaving the king permanently insane. But for now at least, life at court returned to its usual routine. Fanny endured the long hours and monotony as best she could for a total of five years before the strain got to be almost unbearable. Friends who were able to visit her on occasion recognized her misery long before her father did. Perhaps for selfish reasons he chose to ignore it. At any rate, during a visit with Fanny—the first intimate conversation between father and daughter in four years—Dr. Burney expressed concern for her welfare and confessed that others had voiced discontent at her seclusion. This encouraged her to speak to her father more candidly and in greater detail than she had planned:

> I spoke my high and constant veneration for my Royal Mistress, her merits, her virtues, her condescension, and her even peculiar kindness towards me. But I owned the species of life distasteful to me: I was lost to all private comfort, dead to all domestic endearment; I was worn with want of rest, and fatigued with laborious watchfulness and attendance. My time was devoted to official duties; and all that in life was dearest to me—my friends, my chosen society, my best affections—lived now in my mind only by recollection, and rested upon that with nothing but bitter regret.

As she poured out her unhappiness, her father listened silently with head bowed, but when he looked up, she saw his eyes filled with tears. "I have long been uneasy," he said, "though I have not spoken; . . . but . . . if you wish to resign—my house, my purse, my arms, shall be open to receive you back!"[15] And with her father's consent, she composed a formal letter of resignation, which the queen reluctantly, though graciously, accepted, and Fanny Burney left the confines of court on July 7, 1791.

Fanny's experience at court illustrated a dilemma faced by many women in England at the time. Caught between personal ambitions and the rules of society, a woman could either rebel and be ostracized as was Mrs. Thrale when she married Gabriel Piozzi, or she could passively submit as Fanny

Frances Burney by Edward Francesco Burney, 1785.
Source: National Portrait Gallery, London.

Burney did when she went to court. Although submission proved difficult, open rebellion was simply not an option for Fanny. A woman's role was one of sacrifice and compliance. She once remarked proudly regarding another difficult situation she faced, "I could not more passively have let it take its course."[16] For her, remaining passive was the right way for a woman to act. Yet her compliance with social convention did not result from weakness of character. She was strongly principled rather than weak willed. It took her as much inner strength to submit as it did for Mrs. Thrale to rebel. Fanny clearly understood the restraints a woman lived under. She understood and articulated them more clearly than any woman of her day. Her diaries, letters, and novels demonstrate a strong underlying urge to mutiny, but she well knew that "no innovations ought to be risked,"[17] so she channeled her rebellious urges into social satire rather than open confrontation. "*Safety & quiet,—*" she said, "those are the Ports I ever try to make for myself."[18]

Her acquiescence to all her father's wishes, particularly his wish that she enter court, a move totally abhorrent to her nature and desires, was more a testament to the strength of her principles of filial duty than an indication of weakness. But either way, revolt or submit, women invariably paid a price. She told her sister Susan, "I am sometimes dreadfully afraid for myself, from the *very* different behaviour which Nature calls for on one side, & the World on the other."[19] And it was this theme—a young woman carefully steering the path between personal desires and social obligations—that distinguished her novels. Her last, *The Wanderer*, bore the subtitle *or, Female Difficulties*, which could have been the subtitle for all her fictional works. She was not a feminist in the sense of crusading for women's rights. She always castigated women like Mrs. Thrale who deviated from society's accepted norms. But as she clearly understood the difficult position of women in society, that is what she dramatized in her fiction.

Fanny Burney *was* a feminist, on the other hand, and an important one in the purest sense of the term, in that she insightfully dramatized the female experience. Her novels were written from a woman's point of view, about a woman's concerns, and with a distinctly female voice. She focused on the interplay of the drawing room, the theater, and the salon. She found drama in the trivialities of daily life. She established the conventions governing the domestic novel of sensibility, a form later perfected by women novelists of the following century. Yet she was not simply a woman's writer. A large part of her audience—perhaps the largest part—was composed of male readers, for she wrote perceptively of the human condition, albeit from a woman's perspective. Much of her success resulted from how she depicted the manners of the day—portraying aristocratic caprices and middle class vulgarities. She excelled in creating striking characters through the witty exchange of realistic dialogue. Dr. Johnson had once said to her, shaking his head in amusement, "O, you little *Character-monger*, you!"[20] Edmund Burke told her, after reading *Cecilia*, "Nothing . . . struck me more in reading your book than the admirable skill with which your ingenious characters make themselves known by their own words."[21]

Her first novel, *Evelina, or a Young Lady's Entrance into the World*— "world" meaning society, especially genteel society—is her most amusing and informal work of fiction with its relatively loose structure and colloquial style. Her expectations of anonymity allowed her freedoms of expression and fancy she would not hazard later. As a result, *Evelina* possesses more humor, simplicity, and charm than her later novels. Dr. Johnson said of it, "*Evelina* seems a work that should result from long experience, and deep and intimate knowledge of the world; yet it has been written without either. Miss Burney is a real wonder. What she is, she is intuitively."[22]

The surprising success of the work, along with the notoriety it brought her, forced her to be more guarded when writing her second novel. As a consequence, *Cecilia, or Memoirs of an Heiress*, published four years before she entered service at court, gave her more trouble than her first novel. "I go on but indifferently,—" she said of her progress at the time, "I don't write as I did, the certainty of being known, the high success of Evelina . . .—these thoughts worry & depress me."[23]

What *Cecilia* lacked in humor and simplicity, it gained in polish, structure, and elegance. It felt more like the work of a professional writer than that of an "accidental author" as she once described herself.[24] Sir Joshua Reynolds kept the multivolume novel in his painting room and became so absorbed in the characters that he neglected his own work. He told actor and educator Thomas Sheridan, "She has, certainly, something of a knack at Characters;— *where* she got it, I don't know,—& *how* she got it, I can't imagine,—but she certainly *has* it."[25] He later jokingly threatened to send Fanny a bill for damages, for he claimed that *Cecilia* had cost him £100 in lost commissions. Dr. Burney reported to Fanny in a letter, "Sr J. says he never yet read a book in wch the Characters are so supported, & discriminated."[26]

Mrs. Thrale had found *Cecilia* a marvelous depiction of manners and fashions of the time, but she also thought it would eventually become passé. "*Cecilia* is the Picture of Life such as the Author sees it," she wrote in her diary, "while therefore this Mode of Life lasts, her Book will be of value, as the Representation is astonishingly perfect: but as nothing in the Book is derived from Study, so it can have no Principle of duration."[27]

In 1790, nearly six years after Johnson's death, while Fanny still resided at court and was attending the queen at Windsor Castle, Boswell got word to her that he wished to call on her. She declined a formal meeting, knowing that a visit from a man so well known for compiling anecdotes would not be appreciated. Besides, except for family members, she was not allowed private meetings with men. "But yet I really wished to see him again, for old acquaintance' sake, and unavoidable amusement from his oddity and good humour," so she agreed to meet him briefly and publicly one day following church service. At the appointed time, she found him awaiting her as she exited the cathedral, and the two greeted each other "with mutual glee: his comic-serious face and manner have lost nothing of their wonted singularity," nor had his manner of thought and speech. He began by expressing alarm at her court confinement, and he urged her to resign immediately. He comically threatened to employ violent measures to bring it about and said that he would get together a group of friends to lay siege to Dr. Burney and convince him that his daughter must resign. He was prepared to make the harangue himself and claimed to have a speech already prepared. "Whether I laughed the most, or stared the most, I am a loss to say; but I hurried away from the cathedral, not to have such treasonable declarations overheard, for we were surrounded by a multitude."

Attempting to change the subject, she asked about Edmund Burke's anticipated book, *Reflections on the Revolution in France.* He replied that it would be out the following week and exclaimed that it was the first book in the world, "except my own, and that's coming out also very soon; but I want your help." He said that Dr. Johnson had long enough been portrayed upon stilts. "I want to show him in a new light. Grave Sam, and great Sam, and solemn Sam, and learned Sam—all these he has appeared over and over." Boswell wanted to do something different. "I want to show him as gay Sam, agreeable Sam, pleasant Sam: so you must help me with some of his beautiful billets to yourself." She tried putting him off as best she could with excuses about how difficult it was in her present situation to access the letters, but Boswell remained persistent, suggesting numerous ways to retrieve them. He then took a proof sheet of his book from his pocket and began reading from a letter Johnson had written to him, doing so with an excellent imitation of Johnson's manner of speaking. As they were now just outside the Queen's Lodge with a crowd gathering, Mrs. Schwellenberg looking down from a window, and the king and queen approaching from the distance, Fanny had to make a quick apology for ending the conversation, and then hurried off to her apartment.

She later remarked in her diary, "I cannot consent to print private letters, even of a man so justly celebrated, when addressed to myself: no, I shall hold sacred those revered and but too scarce testimonies of the high honour his kindness conferred upon me."[28] The meeting with Boswell highlighted for her the dangers in associating with such a notorious collector and public retailer of personal letters and private conversations. She nevertheless had always admired the sprightliness of his early Corsica book and thought his devotion to Johnson laudable, "for his heart," she said, "almost even to idolatry, was in his reverence of Dr. Johnson." She noted, however, that in his devotional zeal, he had cultivated a "kind of farcical similitude" to the man he so admired. Years later, in recalling her general impressions of Boswell, she wrote,

> He had an odd mock solemnity of tone and manner, that he had acquired imperceptibly from constantly thinking of and imitating Dr. Johnson. . . . There was, also, something slouching in the gait and dress of Mr. Boswell, that wore an air, ridiculously enough, of purporting to personify the same model. His clothes were always too large for him; his hair, or wig, was constantly in a state of negligence; and he never for a moment sat still or upright upon a chair.[29]

In contrast to Fanny's guarded though generally favorable opinion of Boswell, Hester Piozzi had never much cared for him. "I thought him a clever & a comical Fellow," she said, and that was all.[30] She had tolerated him mainly because Johnson liked him. Although she acknowledged his charm, he was not the sort to win her affections. Nevertheless, in the table she drew up in her diary, rating certain qualities of various acquaintances, the number twenty being perfect, she gave Boswell a nineteen for "Good humour necessary to Conversation," Charles Burney being the only other friend of Johnson's to rank as high. In the same category, Johnson, Garrick, Baretti, Beauclerk, and Langton all got zero. Reynolds got a ten, and Henry Thrale rated a five.

Joseph Baretti, unlike most others, had little appreciation for Boswell's good humor and certainly no love for the man himself. Ever since Boswell expressed the view that he deserved to be hanged for killing Evan Morgan in the Haymarket in 1769, Baretti seldom encountered him without giving him a look of contempt. In his copy of Mrs. Piozzi's *Letters to and from the Late Samuel Johnson*, Baretti jotted in the margins several disparaging remarks about Boswell. In one of the letters to the former Mrs. Thrale, Johnson mentioned that Boswell had departed for Scotland. "He has been gay and good-humoured in his usual way," wrote Johnson, to which Baretti appended the note, "That is, in his noisy and silly way."[31] Next to a letter in which Johnson said, "Boswell is with us in good-humour; and plays his part with his usual vivacity," Baretti wrote, "That is, He makes more noise, than any body in company, talking and laughing loud."[32]

Peregrine Langton, Bennet Langton's second son, often saw Boswell in the company of his father and could testify to the Scotsman's often loud and raucous manner:

> Boswell was exceedingly talkative, very loud; boisterous at all times, but particularly after dinner; and especially in his latter days, for he seemed to have no command over his appetites, & drank much more than was prudent: his conversation degenerated at that time to any thing but what could be admired

& he broke out into singing & talking so loud that it was quite insufferable—
but at other times, when under due restraint, no man ever made himself more
agreeable: his whole soul seemed to come forth when in the midst of those who
could draw forth, and fully appreciate his stores of information and anecdotes.
. . . It was impossible to be grave in his company—The instant he entered all
was mirth and gaiety—The last time I ever saw him, was one evening in Pall
Mall—my father was in London, and had lodgings opposite to Carlton House—
Boswell came in & spent the evening—he was gay & cheerful to an extreme;
sang, and talked, & laughed & was particularly eloquent in praise of that savage
musick that the butchers in the metropolis indulge in, called marrow bones &
cleavers: which that night happened to be going about the street on some great
publick rejoicing. He used to talk a great deal about liberty and I can not tell
what, so that my father, whose political opinions were so diametrically opposite
to such notions, used to say that had he lived much longer he would have come
to be hanged.[33]

Johnson's mere presence had usually kept Boswell somewhat in check,
and as a result, Johnson was able to appreciate his sprightly good humor
without experiencing much of the boisterousness. Johnson once told him, "I
think you are one of the happiest fellows I know. You have as many ingredients of happiness as anybody: good humour, prospect of a good estate, good
wife and good children."[34] Johnson, however, could not help but get irritated
sometimes at Boswell's egotism and incessant quizzing. He told Langton on
their leaving a party at Sir Joshua's one evening that when Boswell started
drinking wine, his conversation consisted all of questions.[35] Johnson once
got so perturbed that he said to him, "Don't you consider, Sir, these are not
the manners of a gentleman? What man of elegant manners teases one with
questions so?"

"Why, Sir," replied Boswell, "you are so good."

"My being so good is no reason why you should be so ill."

"Sir, I stop whenever you give me a hint, whenever you put a lock upon
the well."

"But that is forcing one to do a disagreeable thing. I will not be baited with
what: what is this? what is that? why is a cow's tail long? why is a fox's tail
bushy?"[36] Another time Johnson complained to Mrs. Thrale that "Bozzy"
had asked him so many questions that he was now panting for breath from
answering them. She wondered what sort of questions he asked. "Why one
Question was Pray Sir can you tell why an Apple is round & a Pear pointed?
Would not such Talk make a Man hang himself?"[37] This relentless quizzing
sometimes provoked Johnson to say such brutal things in response that despite Boswell's declaration that the great man's rough rebukes did not trouble
him, he was occasionally very much hurt. Arthur Murphy claimed to have
seen him on occasion leave the room with tears in his eyes after Johnson had

violently chastised him. Following one such incident, Johnson explained to Mrs. Thrale, "The Man *compels* me to treat him so."[38]

Fanny Burney noted that Johnson generally treated Boswell as a school-boy, scolding and pardoning him alternately, persuaded that no matter how severe the reprimand, after a day or two of pouting, he would return and ask to be forgiven. She said that Johnson, although sometimes greatly irritated, was actually touched by Boswell's attachment to him, and for that reason, Johnson normally granted him extraordinary patience.[39] He realized that no friend showed him more reverence and devotion than James Boswell. At a social gathering one evening before Johnson arrived, a group of men sat talking about him. Allan Ramsay, the painter, said that he found Johnson very polite and that he had great respect for him. Boswell confessed that he worshipped him. A third cautioned that he should not *worship* him. He should worship no man. "I cannot help worshipping him," replied Boswell. "He is so much superior to other men."[40] Johnson could not but feel a reciprocal affection for someone so devoted to him. Boswell told him, "Sir, there is none of your friends on whom you could depend more than on me."

"No, Sir, none who would do more for me of what I'd wish to have done. Were you to die, it would be a limb lopped off. And remember, I tell you this that you may not always be wishing for kind words."[41]

Throughout much of his life, Boswell contemplated various schemes to make himself more prosperous and better known. One of his hopes had long been to secure an important position either in law, perhaps as a judge as his father had been, or in politics. Yet he felt handicapped by his lack of education and by a temperament that shirked prolonged application. He possessed a gregarious personality more suited to the pleasures of the dinner table than to the seclusion of the study. He recalled that some years earlier Sir John Pringle had accused him of knowing nothing. "And now the remark is as just as then," he conceded:

> There is an imperfection, a superficialness, in all my notions. I understand nothing clearly, nothing to the bottom. I pick up fragments, but never have in my memory a mass of any size. I wonder really if it be possible for me to acquire any one part of knowledge fully. I am a lawyer. I have no system of law. I write verses. I know nothing of the art of poetry. In short I could go through everything in the same way.[42]

Influential friends, like Edmund Burke, who were personally fond of Boswell and who could have aided him professionally had they chosen, saw that he was temperamentally unsuited to positions of authority. One area in which he had always exceled, however, was in writing. From the age of nineteen, when he began publishing poems and prose pieces in newspapers, he had shown the ability to attract attention with his pen. His ease of expression, casual turn of phrase, and engaging egotism charmed readers. His was not a studied, "literary" style, but one that captured the rhythms and diction of casual speech. His Scottish friend Andrew Erskine once told him, "I am fond of your Style, it is not the solemn march of your friend [Johnson], but the careless and easy walk of a Gentleman."[43]

He fully valued his literary gift, saying that "words come skipping to me like lambs upon Moffat Hill; and I turn my periods smoothly and imperceptibly like a skilful wheelwright turning tops in a turning-loom."[44] Due to his agreeable style, his amiable personality, and his practice of accumulating minute though significant details, his first book, *An Account of Corsica*, became an instant success. This was the book Baretti said had shown the Corsicans to be nothing better than bloody-minded savages, the book that grew out of Boswell's trip to Corsica in 1765 during his Grand Tour of the Continent. Even before reaching the island, Boswell had become a champion of the Corsicans' struggle for independence. He hoped his book would influence Britain to become an ally of the Corsicans in their fight for liberty. He divided the work into two parts. The first summarized the history of the island while the second part consisted of a journal describing his own experiences and observations while among the freedom fighters. He did not separate the journal portion into daily entries as he did in his later books, but rather presented it as a continuous narrative. He focused attention particularly on the heroic character of the Corsican chief, General Pasquale Paoli, and this is what gave the book its special appeal, for Boswell's genius lay in the dramatic presentation of character and personality. He excelled in creating scenes that came alive through the skillful use of detail and conversation. His friend William Temple told him, "You *do* excell in painting *minds*; nay in making them paint themselves."[45]

Johnson said to him that the history part of his Corsica book was like other histories, but the journal portion was unique and delightful: "You express images which operated strongly upon yourself and you have impressed them with great force upon your readers."[46] Although the volume did not succeed in swaying British foreign policy as he had hoped, it nevertheless brought its author substantial notice. The book was quickly translated into five languages, making "Corsica Boswell," at the age of twenty-seven, a more prominent literary figure for a time than Samuel Johnson. With this success, he achieved what he had longed for since leaving Edinburgh in 1762: he had made himself known. Although he was to produce two finer books in the

James Boswell by George Dance, 1793.
Source: National Portrait Gallery, London.

years ahead, none brought him greater notice in his lifetime than his first. He regarded it at the time as a stabilizing influence in his life. He thought that being elevated to the position of prominent author would force him to be more reserved in the future, for, as he told Temple, he now had a character to support. Henceforth, he said, "I will swear like an ancient disciple

of Pythagoras to observe silence. I will be grave & reserved though chearful
& communicative of what is *verum atque decens* [right and seemly]."[47] His
career as barrister in Edinburgh had brought him little stability, nor had his
wife and five children given him a lasting sense of fulfillment. Becoming a
judge seemed certain if only he remained patient and steadily applied himself,
and his wife and children were as fine as a man could desire. But patience,
prolonged application, and satisfaction with family life lay beyond his capabilities. "It is a sad thing to have so *un*domestic a disposition," he lamented.
"It appeared to me that I should not have married, having no turn for the
regularity of domestic life."[48]

What primarily sustained him was the swirl of London life, hopes of practicing law before the English bar, and Dr. Samuel Johnson. But late in 1783,
when Johnson's deteriorating health indicated that he had not many more
years to live, Boswell reflected on what the loss of his great friend would
mean to him. "I thought of his death with dreadful gloom," he wrote. "It appeared to me that if he were gone, I should find life quite vapid and myself
quite at a loss what to do, or how to think."[49] Following Johnson's death, and
with *The Journal of a Tour to the Hebrides* having proved a success, he set to
work on his magnum opus, determined to stick with his former plan of writing the work in scenes built around Johnson's conversation. This followed his
usual practice in writing his daily journal, though it marked an innovation in
the art of biography. He had no doubt about the correctness of his method nor
about the book's ultimate success. "I will venture to promise," he said, "that
my Life of my revered Friend will be the richest piece of Biography that has
ever appeared."[50] He referred to the work in progress as a "Great Biographical
Monument. I tell every body it will be an Egyptian Pyramid in which there
will be a compleat mummy of Johnson that Literary Monarch."[51] He vowed
to present Johnson as he really was, professing to write "not his panegyric,
which must be all praise, but his Life; which, great and good as he was, must
not be supposed to be entirely perfect." The imperfections he chronicled
were mainly physical—Johnson's uncouth bearing, his dirty clothes, his odd
tics and gestures, his diseased body, his gross manner of feeding, and so
forth. While some readers later objected to these details as trivial and even
offensive, Boswell had a purpose for including them. They were as much a
part of his art as the dramatic use of dialogue and the theatrical presentation
of characters interacting with one another upon the stage of life, for the em-
phasis placed on Johnson's physical imperfections threw what Boswell truly
wished to highlight into sharper focus—the great man's intellectual gifts and
majestic character. Boswell intended to show, by depicting Johnson's many
infirmities, the difficulties he had surmounted in achieving the eminent position he ultimately attained.

Johnson's majestic character became the dominant theme of the *Life*. Boswell described him as "a majestick teacher of moral and religious wisdom" noting the "majestick expression" of his prose. In contrasting Johnson's poetry with that of other writers, he remarked that tastes might differ as to the violin, the flute, and the hautboy, "in short, all the lesser instruments: but who can be insensible to the powerful impressions of the majestick organ?"[52] If the *Life* escaped being panegyric, the tone was nevertheless unmistakable: it was one of "admiration and reverence," the three words that conclude Boswell's literary monument to his friend.

When the *The Life of Samuel Johnson, LL.D.* finally appeared on May 16, 1791, Fanny was still at court with less than two months remaining before her departure. The king immediately began reading the work, and every night he would enter the queen's dressing room to talk with Fanny about it, getting her to explain and enlarge upon certain issues and people mentioned in the book. "He told me once, laughing heartily, that, having seen my name in the Index, he was eager to come to what was said of me; but when he found so little, he was surprised and disappointed." Fanny assured him that she herself had "rejoiced at this very circumstance, and with what satisfaction I had reflected upon having very seldom met Mr. Boswell, as I knew there was no other security against all manner of risks in his relations."[53] Aside from this sense of relief, her overall reaction to the work was one of outrage that Boswell had revealed many instances of Johnson's prejudices and petulant outbursts that would otherwise have sunk and been forgotten under the preponderance of his greater virtues. Encountering Boswell one morning at a social breakfast a year after publication of the *Life*, she was still seething:

I felt a strong sensation of that displeasure which his loquacious communications of every weakness and infirmity of the first and greatest good man of these times has awakened in me, at his first sight; and, though his address to me was courteous in the extreme, and he made a point of sitting next me, I felt an indignant disposition to a nearly forbidding reserve and silence.

But as Boswell continued to talk, she slowly began to thaw, and imperceptibly she yielded to his good humor and affability:

Angry, however, as I have long been with him, he soon insensibly conquered, though he did not soften me: there is so little of ill design or ill nature in him, he is so open and forgiving for all that is said in return, that he soon forced me to consider him in a less serious light, and change my resentment against his treachery into something like commiseration of his levity; and before we parted we became good friends. There is no resisting great good-humour, be what will in the opposite scale.[54]

Mauritius Lowe knew firsthand how successfully Boswell could charm people with his ingratiating speech and manners. Lowe was a second-rate painter of historical scenes whom Fanny once characterized as "a certain poor wretch of a villainous painter, . . . who is in some measure under Dr. Johnson's protection."[55] In 1783, for the annual exhibition of the Royal Academy, Lowe had submitted a work depicting the Deluge. The academy rejected the painting, which Reynolds's assistant, James Northcote, described as execrable beyond belief.[56] Lowe immediately ran to Johnson complaining of the ill-treatment he had received and asking for assistance. Knowing little and caring nothing about painting, Johnson nevertheless agreed to write a letter on Lowe's behalf asking the Academy to reconsider its decision. Boswell came in just as Johnson finished writing, and when Lowe rushed off, letter in hand, Boswell quickly followed and stopped the painter in the street. "Nothing could surprise me more," recalled Lowe. "Till that moment he had so entirely overlooked me, that I did not imagine he knew there was such a creature in existence; and he now accosted me with the most overstrained and insinuating compliments possible."

"How do you do, Mr. Lowe?" said Boswell. "I hope you are very well, Mr. Lowe? Pardon my freedom, Mr. Lowe, but I think I saw my dear friend, Dr. Johnson, writing a letter for you."

"Yes, sir."

"I hope you will not think me rude, but if it would not be too great a favor, you would infinitely oblige me, if you would just let me have a sight of it. Every thing from that hand, you know, is so inestimable."

"Sir it is on my own private affairs, but—"

"I would not pry into a person's affairs, Mr. Lowe; by any means. I am sure you would not accuse me of such a thing, only if it were no particular secret."

"Sir, you are welcome to read the letter."

"I thank you, my dear Mr. Lowe, you are very obliging, I take it exceedingly kind." After looking over the contents, Boswell said, "It is nothing, I believe, Mr. Lowe, that you would be ashamed of."

"Certainly not."

"Why then, my dear Sir, if you would do me another favour, you would make the obligation eternal. If you would but step to Peele's coffee-house with me, and just suffer me to take a copy of it, I would do any thing in my power to oblige you."

Overcome, as he said, "by this sudden familiarity and condescension, accompanied with bows and grimaces," Lowe retired with his companion to the coffeehouse, where Boswell soon made a copy, stuck it into his pocket, and then strode away "as erect and proud as he was half an hour before, and I ever afterward was unnoticed." Lowe said that he could not be certain, but he seemed to recall that Boswell actually left him to pay for his own dish of coffee.[57] The letter subsequently appeared in the *Life.*

Hester Piozzi, when she read the work, found it both engaging and upsetting. "I have been now laughing & crying by turns for two Days over Boswell's Book," she said. "That poor man should have a *Bon Bouillion* and be put to Bed,—he is quite light-headed. yet Madmen, Drunkards, & Fools tell Truth they say." What particularly disturbed her were the deprecating things Johnson on occasion apparently said about her. Boswell quoted him as affirming that she was flippant, that her husband had ten times her learning, and that she possessed the learning of a schoolboy in one of the lower forms. Boswell elsewhere quoted Johnson as agreeing with him that she displayed the arrogance of wealth and the conceit of parts.[58] Boswell's accounts troubled her, for "if Johnson was to me the back Friend he has represented—let it cure me of ever making *Friendship* more with any human Being—let it cure me!"[59]

Boswell published these and similar disparaging remarks partly as a way of paying Mrs. Piozzi back for what he thought her ungrateful comments in her *Anecdotes* about Johnson being a burden. It was also for the way she had impugned his veracity in the "Postscript." But he did not stop there. Throughout the *Life* he continued to point out her book's numerous inaccuracies and "how ready she was, unintentionally, to deviate from exact authenticity of narration." Much of her book, he said, while "smart and entertaining," tended "to represent Dr. Johnson as extremely deficient in affection, tenderness, or even common civility." It troubled him, he wrote, "to animadvert on the inaccuracies of Mrs. Piozzi's 'Anecdotes,'" but her account had left such "an unfavourable and unjust impression" of Johnson that "my duty, as a faithful biographer, has obliged me reluctantly to perform this unpleasing task."[60]

General critical reaction to Boswell's *Life* ran along the same lines as what his *Tour* had received. Most reviewers found the biography highly entertaining and informative though slightly shocking in its disclosure of private conversations and its revelation of intimate details. In our own era, more than two hundred years after the book first appeared, certain commentators have accused the author of misrepresenting, falsifying, and fabricating Johnson's character. One distinguished twentieth-century Johnsonian scholar had discovered in Boswell's representation a persistent strain of "serious distortions."[61] Another stated as a commonplace that "Boswell's 'Johnson' is of course, a fiction."[62] But those who knew Johnson personally did not think so. No one at the time accused Boswell of misrepresenting or distorting his subject. He drew censure for having distorted Goldsmith's character in the *Life*, but not Johnson's. Everyone appeared satisfied that he had indeed represented Johnson as he really was. Edmund Hector, Johnson's oldest friend still living, wrote to Boswell correcting a particular anecdote in the *Life* but expressing pleasure with the work overall: "I thank You, most sincerely thank You for the great and long continu'd entertainment your *Life of Dr. Johnson* has afforded me and others of my particular friends."[63]

Likewise, the Reverend Doctor William Maxwell, another of Johnson's early companions, wrote to Boswell, "You have described our Illustrious Friend with so much Spirit, Truth and Justice, that I make no doubt, but your Name will descend to Posterity, as A Commentator worthy of the Great Original." And Boswell's friend Temple assured him that "never was there so true and exact a picture given of any man."[64]

The most common objection from those who had known Johnson intimately was not that Boswell misrepresented the great man, but that in exhibiting his character to the public, he had represented him *too* fully and *too* accurately. Charles Burney's sentiments, like those of his daughter Fanny, were typical. Dr. Burney wrote Boswell that in the *Life* "too many of the weaknesses, prejudices, and infirmities, of this truly great and virtuous Man have been recorded; but, besides the reputation which you will acquire for the fidelity of your narrative in telling all you knew, it will elevate the Character of our Hero." Burney added that if all Johnson's writings were lost or had never appeared, "your book would have conveyed to posterity as advantageous an Idea of his Character, genius, and worth as Xenophon has done of those of Socrates."[65]

Despite recent efforts to diminish Boswell's achievement, *The Life of Samuel Johnson, LL.D.* remains the finest example in English of the biographer's craft, a "Great Biographical Monument" not only to its subject, but to its author as well.

At the time of Johnson's death, Joseph Baretti had nearly reached the end of his own writing career. He was not in good health or spirits and had not been for some time. Ever since leaving the Thrales in 1776, he had been nearly destitute. One reason for his difficulties was improvidence, for he always lived on money he was soon to earn, not on what he had. Another reason was the American war, which, he said, "has proved my utter ruin, because the printers and booksellers will do no more business either with me or with any of the other numberless authors who live by compiling books," the cost for materials being high and the reading public preoccupied with war news. "I am in a worse plight than I ever was in my life before," he lamented in a letter to his brother Amedeo,

> without money in a country where the price of everything rises daily with the endless growth of taxation. . . . Things have reached such a point that I don't

know which way to turn; and the bitter thought that I have made all these efforts for so many years, without succeeding in keeping my head above water, and that all my high hopes have vanished into empty air, besides the finding myself old, quite white-headed, fat and out of health, with sight so bad that the strongest convex glasses cannot help it, has made me change my tone for some time past. I have become more irritable and depressed than ever, and feel almost angry at having lived so long.[66]

He became dependent on the generosity of various friends, first of all on the goodness of John Cator, a retired lumber merchant, friend, and later the trustee of Henry Thrale. Cator lodged Baretti much of the year at his Beckenham estate in Kent, contributed £10 annually for his maintenance, and solicited money from others. Cator spoke with Mrs. Thrale in 1781 "and gave such a deplorable Account of Baretti as shocked me." He asked Mrs. Thrale to donate £10, "but if one is to do *all one can do* for a professed Enemy—how does one deserve to have a Friend? I thought five enough."[67] Largely through Cator's mediation with the government, Baretti was granted an annual pension of £80 beginning in 1782.

Another benefactor was Francis Barwell of Stanstead House, Sussex, where Baretti spent much of his time in the 1780s, buried alive, he said, in the boredom of a country life. He had little in common with neighboring squires, who regarded him primarily as Barwell's dependent. Yet Baretti had no choice but to swallow his pride and submit to his position. He vowed that while under obligations to Barwell,

I shall always behave with the greatest caution in his house; that I shall never venture to take the wall of any of the fine gentlemen who visit him, however vulgar they may be; that I shall always make a point of sitting last at his table; that I shall never enter into a violent dispute with any one, and shall always give way to these gentlemen, be their opinions good or bad. These are the terms prescribed for those who have not enough to lead an independent life—hard terms, if you like, yet what can I do but accept them? I have fought the world for so many years and have had so little success that I am tired of it.[68]

Yet he still had one fight left in him. This was against the former Mrs. Thrale, now Mrs. Piozzi, concerning her *Letters to and from Samuel Johnson*, published in March 1788. Baretti chafed at certain uncomplimentary references to himself, and felt outraged that Mrs. Piozzi had mutilated and fabricated some of Johnson's letters and evidently rewritten some of her own.[69] He determined to set things straight in a series of "Strictures," published in the May, June, and August 1788 issues of *The European Magazine.* He wrote these articles not in the genial style of his *Journey from London to Genoa*, but in the harsh, bitter, sarcastic manner of *The Literary Scourge.* He noted at the start that he might be criticized for not showing more ceremony and respect to the lady, "But by what right can LA PIOZZI, as my fiddling country-men now term her, claim ceremony and respect from any one of the many whom she has offended by her publication, now that, in the great wisdom of her concupiscence, she has degraded herself into the wife of an Italian singing-master?"[70]

In reading "the blackest pages of thy heart," he accused her of dishonesty, called her "a wicked calumniator," and said, "as far as I have surveyed the circle of life, I could not easily have met with a worse misfortune than that of your acquaintance." As noted earlier, he charged her with beating her chil-dren until they were terrified of her, discussed the episode of her giving tin pills to Queeney, insinuated that she carried on an affair with Gabriel Piozzi before their marriage, and many similar things. But by attacking Mrs. Piozzi in such a savage manner, he accomplished the reverse of what he intended, for his "Strictures" stirred up universal scorn against him.

"I have just read for the first time," said Johnson's friend Anna Seward, the poet known as the Swan of Lichfield, "the base, ungentlemanlike, unmanly abuse of Mrs. Piozzi by that Italian assassin, Baretti. The whole literary world should unite in publicly reprobating such venomed and foul-mouthed railing."[71]

Mrs. Piozzi, writing to a friend, exclaimed, "Have you seen how *I* am treated by that unextinguishable Viper Baretti? who like Aaron the Moor in Shakespear's Titus Andronicus, digs up people's dead Friends, and sets them at their doors-----*even when their Sorrows are almost forgot.*"[72]

The articles supported whatever evil rumors people had heard, or whatever bad opinions they had formed, regarding the Italian's temper and brutality. "I neither know nor care for Madam Piozzi," wrote a correspondent in *The Gentleman's Magazine*, "but yet I think Baretti's attack upon her is in many parts false, and in all malicious, and that he has seldom written but with the stiletto in one hand, and the pen in the other."[73]

Fanny Burney wrote in her journal that a friend, "with a good-humoured note, sent me the *Magazine* with Baretti's strictures on Mrs. Thrale. Good heaven, how abusive! It can hardly hurt her—it is so palpably meant to do it. I could not have suspected him, with all his violence, of a bitterness of invec-tive so cruel, so ferocious!"[74]

Yet Baretti now had more pressing matters to contend with than the pub-lic's indignity. His annuity was three quarters in arrears, and payment of £100 for a revised edition of his Italian dictionary had been delayed. These prob-lems so worked upon his imagination that he developed gout in the stomach, but instead of seeking medical help, he drank copious amounts of ice water, believing that would cure him. John Cator again came to his aid by speaking with the publisher Thomas Cadell, who, when he learned of Baretti's condition, agreed to send him £50 immediately. When Cator told Baretti that the money should be paid next morning, "He pressed my hand with the cold sweat of death upon his palm. 'My dear friend,' said he, 'I thank you for your kind offices, but it is now too late.'"[75] He said little after that except to blame himself for declining medical assistance, fearing his actions might set a poor example for young people.

On the morning of May 5, 1789, still in full possession of his faculties, he said that he had often dreaded this day and had imagined it would be a melancholy one. When his barber came at the usual hour to shave him, Baretti asked him to return next day when he "should be better able to undergo the operation." He requested that his brothers be notified of his death, took leave of several friends at about four o'clock in the afternoon, and once they had gone, asked Mr. Cator to shut the door to the room, for he did not wish to be disturbed by the women, who might be frightened to watch him die. At about 7:45 that evening, shortly after taking a glass of wine, he expired without a struggle.

Four days later in London, attended by a handful of friends, he was buried in the new burying ground just off Paddington Street, near Baker Street, in Marylebone. A monument, containing a medallion portrait by Thomas Banks, R.A., was placed in St. Marylebone Old Church with the following inscription:

> Near this place are deposited the Remains
> of Signor GIVSEPPE BARETTI,
> A native of Piedmont in Italy,
> Secretary for Foreign Correspondence,
> to the Royal Academy of Arts, of London;
> Author of several esteem'd Works in his own
> and of the Languages of France and of England.

Few people truly mourned or much cared about Joseph Baretti's passing. Most learned of his death from obituaries in the newspapers. There they read the names of his eminent friends, almost all of them now dead, and noted the long list of his miscellaneous works. Mrs. Piozzi, on seeing the news, wrote in her diary, "Baretti is dead—Poor Baretti! I am sincerely sorry for him." She summarized what the papers said about his death and concluded with a line from Edward Young's tragedy *The Revenge*:

> And art thou dead? So is my Enmity;
> I war not with the Dust.[76]

The "new burying-ground" where Baretti was laid—subsequently called Paddington Cemetery—now shows no signs of its former use or of where

Baretti was placed. The cemetery was officially closed to new burials in 1814. Nearly all the tombstones were removed, and the grounds were converted to a recreation area. Paddington Street Gardens, as the place is now called, though still consecrated ground containing more than eighty thousand graves, remains a peaceful spot of green lawns, shade trees, and park benches. Something that likely would have pleased Baretti is that one end has been set aside as a play area for small children.

Not much had changed, meanwhile, in the life of Sir Joshua Reynolds. He continued to work day after day in his octagonal painting room, contentedly turning out the finest portraits of the age. But as devoted as he was to his art, he loved social conviviality in the evenings almost as much. Once he had finished the day's work, he took up his fork and glass with the same eagerness he had taken up his brushes and paints that morning. His dinner parties, which cost him about £2,000 annually, were the most celebrated in London. They were easy and unpretentious, like Reynolds himself. No one stood upon ceremony, rank, or formality. The food and wine made the rounds amid raucous, light-hearted conversation. Wit and raillery were more prized than disquisitions, and political talk was discouraged. Sir Joshua had never liked formal gatherings. He said, "I love the correspondence of viva voce over a bottle with a great deal of noise and a great deal of nonsense."[77]

Along with his good spirits, he enjoyed a continuous run of good health. He was hardly ever ill. He once told Northcote, "I have been fortunate in an uninterrupted share of good health and success for thirty years of my life: therefore, whatever ills may attend on the remainder of my days, I shall have no right to complain."[78] He continued to be fortunate for many years more, but suddenly in April 1779, at age fifty-six, he suffered a mild paralytic stroke. Another followed in November 1782. He quickly and fully recovered from both and resumed his usual routine.[79] Then on July 13, 1789, while finishing a portrait of Lady Beauchamp, he noticed a dimness in his left eye as if a curtain had fallen over it. His doctors diagnosed the problem as a *gutta serena*, or decay of the optic nerve. Despite the efforts of various oculists, within a few months he completely lost the sight in that eye. Fearing he would lose the sight in the other if he strained it, he resolved to give up painting.

Wearing a pair of spectacles with a thick dark patch in the left opening and no lens in the other, he remained cheerful, found pleasure in reading, playing cards, and enjoying the society of friends. Boswell was then in town, and two or three nights a week they could be found together at a banquet or a dinner, "two inseparable companions of the illustrious Order of the Knife and

Fork," as Boswell termed it.[80] Later in the summer Edmond Malone and John Courtenay joined their revels, and the four became known as "the Gang."[81] Reynolds also spent part of his days cleaning or repairing earlier works, for he could not give up his paints entirely. He still had a number of unfinished canvases on hand, and he completed some of them at a leisurely pace. One that he finished was a portrait of the lovely Mrs. Sheridan seated at a harpsichord. In sending the painting home, he included a note to her husband, the playwright Richard Brinsley:

> It is with great regret I part with the best picture I ever painted, for tho I have every year hoped to paint better & better and may truly say—nil actum reputans dum quid superesset agendum [think nothing done while anything remained to be done]. It has not been always the case however there is now an end of the pursuit, the race is over whether it is won or lost.[82]

He continued his regular functions at the Royal Academy, and despite the fear of losing the vision in his right eye, he read his fifteenth and final discourse at the Academy on December 10, 1790. The following September his blind left eye gave him more trouble when a painful swelling developed just above it. His surgeon, Mr. William Cruikshank, purged and blistered him, and bled him with leeches, but nothing helped the condition. Convinced it was a tumor that would soon spread to his good eye and leave him totally blind, Reynolds grew dejected. The cheerfulness that had marked his character throughout life now deserted him. His appetite waned. His physicians assured him that his good eye was unaffected and that if he would only be optimistic and exert himself, things would improve. When a friend tried to console him, he replied, "I know that all things on earth must have an end, and now I am come to mine."[83]

Boswell, much depressed at the time himself, tried often to visit Reynolds and amuse him as best he could, with no success. "My spirits have been still more sunk," Boswell wrote to his friend Temple in Scotland,

> by seeing Sir Joshua Reynolds almost as low as myself. He has for more than two months past had a pain in his blind eye . . . and he broods over the dismal apprehension of becoming quite blind. He has been kept so low as to diet that he is quite relaxed and desponding. He who used to be looked upon as perhaps the most happy man in the world is now as I tell you.[84]

Fanny Burney, accompanied by her father, called on Reynolds one evening. She had not seen him in a great while and had been hesitant to visit him while he was ill, but she took pleasure in now climbing his staircase once again. He was at cards when the Burneys arrived, but he rose to greet them. The left eye was bandaged and the other shaded. He seemed greatly dejected and said in a weak voice as he shook hands, "I am very glad to see you again, and I wish I could see you better! but I have only one eye now,—and hardly that." Fanny knew not what to say under the circumstances, but Sir Joshua's niece relieved her embarrassment by engaging her in conversation and recommending that her uncle go on with his cards.[85]

Reynolds continued to grow worse for no reason that his physicians could discern, and Boswell reported in mid-February 1792 that he now stayed in bed, took laudanum, did not wish to see any friends, "and dozes in 'tranquil despondency' as Burke expressed it."[86] Finally at half past eight on the evening of February 23, 1792, he died peacefully, aged sixty-nine, in his house in Leicester Square. An autopsy disclosed liver failure as the probable cause of death. The liver, which should have weighed about five pounds, weighed more than eleven, and was somewhat scirrhous, possibly the result of steady alcohol consumption over the years. The optic nerve of the right eye proved normal, while the nerve of the left eye was shrunken and flimsy.[87] The body lay in state on the evening of March 2 in the rooms of the Royal Academy at Somerset House with burial scheduled for the next afternoon.

When Hester Piozzi heard of Reynolds's death, she wrote in her diary,

Poor Sir Joshua! another of our Library Portraits gone; dismal enough—this Man was never much a personal Favourite with me however; so I only feel that kind of general Sullenness rather than Sorrow, which Death & Defalcation naturally produce.[88]

Fanny Burney recorded her own sentiments in her diary:

He was always peculiarly kind to me, and he had worked at my deliverance from a life he conceived too laborious for me [as Keeper of the Queen's Robes], as if I had been his own daughter; yet, from the time of my coming forth, I only twice saw him. I had not recovered strength for visiting before he was past receiving me. I grieve inexpressibly never to have been able to pay him the small tribute of thanks for his most kind exertions in my cause. I little thought the second time I saw him would be my last opportunity, and my intention was to wait some favourable opening.[89]

Boswell mourned Reynolds's death not only as a personal loss, but also as a loss to the nation of a great artist. Yet he was not ignorant of a significant shortcoming in his friend's attitude toward his art: "He had, I thought, too mechanical a notion as to painting; for he held there was no particular natural genius, and that any child not defective in organs might be taught to do a portrait—some better, some worse, no doubt."[90] And here Boswell touched on a key element in Reynolds's character. Much of his approach to both life and art had been mechanical. Everything had its proper time and place and its due proportion. Emotion and inspiration, while not denied, were of less importance to art than steady application and adherence to established rules. This attitude provided stability to his life, but it constituted a weakness in his theories of art. Just as anyone who carefully followed a recipe could produce an acceptable pudding, Reynolds believed that anyone who diligently followed the rules of art, as set forth in his *Discourses*, could produce a satisfactory picture—some better, some worse. Making a painting was far more complex and difficult, of course, than making a pudding, but the principle was the same. Such attitudes were already under assault by younger artists, who felt they did not take into sufficient account the importance of emotion, spontaneity, and inspiration.

Boswell's observation also goes to the heart of the period's neoclassic principles, of which Reynolds was a leading exponent, and reveals its chief weakness, that over time it grew to be too rigid. It led eventually to standardization, sterility, and a repetition of fixed patterns. Both neoclassicism in general and Reynolds in particular undervalued the nonrational aspects of the creative process. These included inspiration, instinct, sentiment, and imagination. Reynolds had, in many ways, been to art what Johnson had been to literature—an anchor, a foundation, a mainstay. He was of the old guard, a representative of values that were quickly passing away as the century drew to a close. The private friends and public dignitaries who gathered at the Royal Academy rooms of Somerset House on the morning of March 3, 1792, were about to lay to rest not only a very great man, as Johnson had called him, and an exceptional artist, but also an age. Soon afterward would come Blake and Turner and Constable—artists with new approaches and fresh ideas about the role of spontaneity and sentiment in art.

At half past twelve the long funeral procession moved off from Somerset House, Boswell marching with members of the Royal Academy in his capacity as Secretary for Foreign Correspondence, a position Reynolds had secured for him the year before and the position Baretti had held before him. Once arrived at St. Paul's Cathedral, Reynolds was eulogized, and then his body was laid under the pavement in the crypt, directly beneath the perforated brass plate of the main floor, under the center of the dome, and near the tomb of the cathedral's architect, Sir Christopher Wren.

Five years prior to Reynold's death, the Piozzis, still in Italy, thought of once again taking up residence in England. Old animosities had cooled, and with Johnson gone, the country seemed less constraining. The couple, therefore, returned in March 1787 after several years' travel on the Continent. Having access to her papers once again, Hester quickly compiled and edited the *Letters to and from the Late Samuel Johnson, LL.D.*, the work Baretti so fiercely attacked in his "Strictures." Much to her surprise, she learned in December 1789 that her old antagonist, although he had died nine months earlier, could still attack her. "I hear Baretti's Enmity towards me outlived his Powers of exerting it," she wrote in her diary, "and that he left a Libel behind him desiring it might be printed to vex me." She had not seen the work, only been told about it. "Can such Malignity inhabit the Heart of any thing but Dæmons?" The 147-page pamphlet, published anonymously shortly after Baretti's death, bore the title *The Sentimental Mother, A Comedy, in Five Acts; The Legacy of an Old Friend, and his Last Moral Lesson to Mrs. Hester Lynch Thrale, now Mrs. Hetser* [*sic*] *Lynch Piozzi.* The play's storyline bears no relation to actual events, and the work possesses little, if any, literary merit, yet the intent to vex is clear throughout. Mrs. Thrale is represented by the central character, Fantasma Tunskull, depicted as vain, selfish, conniving, and hypocritical. A footnote informs the reader that *fantasma* is Italian for "nightmare." Her husband, Timothy Tunskull, a normally phlegmatic individual who likes to eat, sleep, and flirt with chambermaids, denotes Henry Thrale, and Squalici is Gabriel Piozzi. Although calculated to vex, the work ultimately attracted little attention and caused Hester Piozzi no harm. The only public notice it received was brief mention in the March 1790 issue of *The Monthly Review*:

> Indignation glowed on our cheeks, as we perused the pages of *the Sentimental Mother*; and we feel ourselves hurt in being obliged to notice a pamphlet abounding with the most base and illiberal insinuations. The person whom it labours principally to traduce is sufficiently pointed out: but such gross calumny (for such we must esteem it) defeats its own purpose. The envenomed arrow recoils, without effect, from the object at whom it is thrown, while it wounds and blackens, in the estimation of a candid public, the reputation of him who could calmly and deliberately fit it to his bow, and draw the string.[91]

Mrs. Piozzi quickly dismissed the subject from her mind and turned her attention to other concerns. Perhaps the most important was to gather about her a new set of friends. A few of the old ones desired to renew her acquaintance, but she did not encourage them. "Mrs Montagu wants to make up with me again," she wrote; "I dare say She does; but I will not be taken & left, even at the Pleasure of those who are much dearer and nearer to me than Mrs. Montagu." Arthur Murphy she acknowledged as one of the few who had remained loyal to her. Others she still cared about now appeared sheepish and contrite over their past conduct. "Mr Pepys, Mrs Ord &c now sneak about, & look ashamed of themselves. Well they may!"[92] What still nettled her was the unmerited insult she felt these people had given her husband.

Hester Lynch Piozzi by George Dance, 1793.
Source: National Portrait Gallery, London.

She now felt fully vindicated, for despite the grim predictions of Queeney, Fanny Burney, and others, Gabriel Piozzi had proven himself a kind and considerate husband. His personal integrity and solid character had justified her choice of him as a mate, and after several years of marriage, his warmth and emotions still stirred her passions. She later recalled that after their return to Streatham, she had to consult Milton's *Comus* "when no Words of my own would express the Passion of my Soul which Piozzi's Voice excited & called forth. When in the Summer's Gloom at Streatham Park he used to sing to me under the Trees at Evening how sweetly did his Notes—how cruelly did they float upon the Wind."[93]

Her first marriage, as she herself pointed out as Thrale's new bride, had not been founded on passion. Her marriage to Piozzi was. It was not primarily, or at least exclusively, physical passion, but rather a deeply shared emotional response to the experience of life. Samuel Rogers got to know the couple intimately after their return to England, and he often visited Streatham. He vouched for Piozzi's merit. "The world was most unjust in blaming Mrs. Thrale for marrying Piozzi," he said. "He was a very handsome, gentlemanly, and amiable person, and made her a very good husband. In the evening he used to play to us most beautifully on the piano."[94]

Unlike Henry Thrale, Gabriel Piozzi supported his wife's literary ambitions, and in June 1789, with his encouragement, she published *Observations and Reflections Made in the Course of a Journey through France, Italy, and Germany.* The work recounted her impressions of what she saw on her travels with Piozzi following their marriage. Fanny Burney commented on reading the book, "How like herself, how characteristic is every line!—Wild, entertaining, flighty, inconsistent, and clever!"[95] A reviewer in the *Morning Post* wrote more emphatically:

> In private life Mrs. *Piozzi* displays a *superficial glitter* in her conversation, which supported by some anecdotes of her *former* literary connections, enables her to pass with tolerable credit; but if she properly estimated her powers, or regarded her intellectual character, she would never venture into *print*, for she really can give nothing new in the way of remark or description, and her language, rather distorted than strengthened by a tasteless selection from *Johnson*, and larded with an abundance of *Continental cants*, is destitute of force, elegance, and even ordinary correctness.[96]

Notwithstanding such criticism, she ventured again into print in April 1794 with *British Synonymy*, a running discussion of the subtle differences between terms roughly synonymous. Next she set about writing an anecdotal narrative ("not a History," she emphasized) of the "most Striking and Important Events, Characters, Situations, and Their Consequences" of the last eighteen hundred years.[97] It was an ambitious, almost foolhardy undertaking, but she must now have her mind and pen employed at something. "I would not accept help from Doctor Johnson as you well know," she wrote to Queeney, "or I should not have waited for his Death before I commenced Author----in good Time!"[98]

Hester Piozzi wrote much as she talked. She rattled in her books as did in her parlor. Her writing does not develop linearly as writing commonly does, but circuitously, like informal talk, circling in on a subject only to fly off in pursuit of a new idea before the first is finished, but returning to the original subject later. Her style also does not maintain an even tone or texture. It rises at times to eloquence only to descend to mere chatter. The modern ear probably accepts her style more readily than the classically–trained ear of her own day. Although she possessed a limber pen and an agile mind, she lacked the patience and application to be a serious scholar, just as she lacked the imagination to be a creative writer. She once decided that she wanted to write a comedy, "but as I have not a Spark of Originality about me, I must take a French Model—it shall be *L'Homme Singulier*."[99] Another time she lamented that the highest her genius could attain was to translate a sonnet or an epigram, and that the only thing original she could write was a letter.[100] Her letters, though, are what Johnson rightly called tattle, often entertaining tattle, but tattle nevertheless. They contain little solid matter. They do, however, convey her spontaneous and whimsical personality as she flits from one topic to another. Arthur Murphy, a trained lawyer, and acting for a time as her legal advisor, once grew annoyed with her impetuosity and shot back a response to one of her missives: "In short, I have had nothing to disconcert me, Except your Letters veering and shifting from one point to another, Capricious, *flickering*, Inconsistent, and Contradictory."[101]

The form that suited her best was her "Thraliana" as she called it—part diary, part commonplace book, a miscellaneous collection of anecdotes, sayings, conundrums, quotations, reflections, and poetry—a grab bag, in short, of whatever happened to cross her mind. It is the form most characteristic of her temperament, for it required no sustained application, no continuity of subject matter, and no consistency of mood. She could drop into it whatever occupied her attention at the moment.

In 1790 she encountered Fanny Burney at an assembly in the house of a friend. Six years had passed since the two last met. She still regarded Fanny as a "Traitress" and one of her principal enemies. "She appear'd most *fondly* rejoyced—in good Time!" she wrote in her "Thraliana." The quietly charming and, as she thought, duplicitous Miss Burney "pretended that She had *such* a Regard for me &c. I answered with Ease & Coldness, but in exceeding Good humour; and we talked about the King & Queen, his Majesty's Illness & Recovery—and all ended as it should do with perfect Indifference."[102]

Fanny would like to have renewed the friendship, but Mrs. Piozzi thought such efforts futile:

> When Connections are once broken, 'tis a foolish Thing to splice and mend; They never can (at least with *me*) unite again as before. Life is not long enough for *Darning* torne *Friendships*; and they are always a Proof however neatly done, that the Substance is *worne out*. A new Dress can be better *depended* on.[103]

To Fanny, Mrs. Piozzi remained a cipher, a parcel of inconsistencies and contradictions. Fanny had never been able to fully grasp her nature: "I have seen and judged characters all my life instinctively: but hers passes all my calculations and combinations. I truly cannot comprehend its materials."[104]

NOTES

1. Frances Burney, *Cecilia, or Memoirs of an Heiress* (Oxford: Oxford University Press, 1990), 55.

2. Doody, *Frances Burney*, 162.

3. Burney, *Early Journals*, 1:61.

4. Ibid., 2:146.

5. Frances Burney, *Memoirs*, 2:302.

6. Burney, *Court Journals*, 1:39.

7. Burney, *Additional Journals*, 424.

8. Hemlow, *The History of Fanny Burney*, 196.

9. Burney, *Additional Journals*, 426.

10. Hemlow, *The History of Fanny Burney*, 196.

11. Ibid., 208.

12. Burney, *Diary & Letters*, 3:9.

13. Ibid., 4:120.

14. Janice Hadlow, *The Royal Experiment: The Private Life of King George III* (New York: Henry Holt, 2014), 367.

15. Burney, *Diary & Letters*, 4:391–92.

16. Doody, *Frances Burney*, 156.

17. Ibid., 176.

18. Burney, *Additional Journals*, 84.

19. Doody, *Frances Burney*, 157.

20. Burney, *Early Journals*, 3:110.

21. Burney, *Diary & Letters*, 2:140.

22. Ibid., 1:247.

23. Hemlow, *The History of Fanny Burney*, 139.

24. Frances Burney, *Memoirs*, 3:235.

25. Burney, *Early Journals*, 3:235.

26. Burney, *Letters of Dr Burney*, 1:343.

27. Piozzi, *Thraliana*, 536.

28. Burney, *Diary & Letters*, 4:431–33.

29. Frances Burney, *Memoirs*, 2:191.

30. Boswell, *Life With Comments*, 2:183.

31. Baretti, Marginal Annotations, 1:384.

32. Ibid., 1:370.

33. Manuscript letter books.

34. Boswell, *Boswell in Extremes*, 300.

35. Boswell, *Ominous Years*, 138. See also Campbell, *Diary*, 79.

36. Boswell, *Boswell in Extremes*, 264.

37. Boswell, *Life With Comments*, 2:472.

38. Taylor, *Records of My Life*, 1:193; Boswell, *Life With Comments*, 2:36.

39. Frances Burney, *Memoirs*, 2:192.

40. Boswell, *Boswell in Extremes*, 322.

41. Ibid., 297.

42. Boswell, *Ominous Years*, 203.

43. Boswell, *Correspondence Relating to the* Life, 395.

44. Boswell, *London Journal*, 187.

45. Boswell, *Correspondence of Boswell and Temple*, 415.

46. Johnson, *Letters*, 1:329.

47. Boswell, *Correspondence of Boswell and Temple*, 214.

48. Boswell, *Great Biographer*, 257 and 190–91.

49. Boswell, *Applause of the Jury*, 163.

50. Boswell, *Correspondence Relating to the* Life, 117.

51. Ibid., 79.

52. Boswell, *Life*, 1:201, 1:355, 2:335.

53. Burney, *Diary & Letters*, 4:479–80.

54. Ibid., 5:83–84.

55. Ibid., 1:494.

56. Northcote, *Life*, 2:139–43.

57. Thomas Holcroft, *Memoirs of Thomas Holcroft, Written by Himself and Continued by William Hazlitt* (Edinburgh: Oxford University Press, 1926), 254–55.

58. Piozzi, *Thraliana*, 809–10; Boswell, *Life*, 1:494 and 3:316.

59. Piozzi, *Thraliana*, 810 *Interpretations* 11.

60. Boswell, *Life*, 3:226; 4:346–47. For a detailed look at the Boswell/Mrs. Thrale relationship, see Mary Hyde, *The Impossible Friendship: Boswell and Mrs. Thrale* (London: Chatto and Windus, 1973).

61. See Donald Greene's "Reflections on a Literary Anniversary," in *Twentieth Century Interpretations of Boswells "Life of Johnson,"* ed. James L. Clifford (Englewood Cliffs, NJ: Prentice-Hall, 1970), 97–103; and also Greene's "'Tis a Pretty Book, Mr. Boswell, But—" in *Boswell's "Life of Johnson": New Questions, New Answers*, ed. John A. Vance (Athens: University of Georgia Press, 1985), 110–46.

62. Harold Bloom, ed., "Introduction," in *Modern Critical Interpretations: James Boswell's "Life of Samuel Johnson"* (New York: Chelsea House, 1986), 4.

63. Boswell, *Correspondence Relating to the* Life, 339.

64. Ibid., 382; Temple, *Diaries*, 157.

65. Boswell, *Correspondence Relating to the* Life, 330–31. It should also be noted that on reading an advance copy of the *Journal of a Tour to the Hebrides* in 1785, Sir Joshua Reynolds wrote to the Fourth Duke of Rutland that "Boswell has drawn his [Johnson's] character in a very masterly manner. The Bishop of Killaloo who knew Johnson very well, I think will subscribe to the justness and truth of the drawing" (Reynolds, *Letters*, 151).

66. Collison-Morley, *Giuseppe Baretti*, 311–12.

67. Johnson, *Letters*, Chapman, 2:450.

68. Collison-Morley, *Giuseppe Baretti*, 339–40.

69. *European Magazine* 13 (March 1788): 147.

70. "Stricture the First," *European Magazine* 13 (May 1788): 313.

71. Collison-Morley, *Giuseppe Baretti*, 346.

72. Piozzi, *Letters*, 1:257.

73. *Gentleman's Magazine* 54 (May 1789): 469.

74. Burney, *Diary & Letters*, 4:32.

75. "Anecdotes and Character of the Late Mr. Baretti," *Gentleman's Magazine* 65 (May 1789): 570.

76. Piozzi, *Thraliana*, 745–46.

77. Reynolds, *Letters*, 112.

78. Northcote, *Memoirs*, 295.

79. The first stroke is conjectured based on two pieces of evidence. The first is Mrs. Thrale's entry in her *Thraliana* for May 1, 1779: "I was at the Exhibition yesterday & heard nothing but a general Murmur of Lamentation that poor Sir Joshua Reynolds had had a paralytick Stroke.—I hope it is not true: he is a Man very generally beloved: some say he has lost the Use of his Hands and fingers" (1:382). The second piece of evidence is Fanny Burney's entry in her *Diary* just after the stroke in 1782 when she describes Reynolds as a "man who has had two shakes of the palsy" (*Diary & Letters*, 2:163).

80. Frank Brady, *James Boswell: The Later Years, 1769–1795* (New York: McGraw-Hill, 1984), 416.

81. Ibid., 293 and 355.

82. Reynolds, *Letters*, 199.

83. Northcote, *Memoirs*, 295.

84. Boswell, *Letters*, 441.

85. Burney, *Diary & Letters*, 5:41.

86. Boswell, *Correspondence of Boswell with the Club*, 356.

87. Prior, *Malone*, 192.

88. Piozzi, *Thraliana*, 836.

89. Burney, *Diary & Letters*, 5:67.

90. Reynolds, *Portraits*, 24.

91. *The Monthly Review* (March 1790): 335–36.

92. Piozzi, *Thraliana*, 744–45.

93. Tearle, *Mrs. Piozzi's Tall Young Beau*, 109.

94. Samuel Rogers, *Recollections of the Table-Talk of Samuel Rogers* (New York, 1856), 45. Rogers met the Piozzis in Edinburgh in the summer of 1789 and proposed to the seventeen-year-old Cecilia Thrale in 1794, "but he is too ugly to hope Acceptance," said her mother (Piozzi, *Thraliana*, 868–69).

95. Burney, *Diary & Letters*, 4:300.

96. Piozzi, *Letters*, 1:329–30n3.

97. Clifford, *Hester Lynch Piozzi*, 379; Hester Lynch Piozzi, *Retrospection: or A Review of the Most Striking and Important Events, Character, Situations, and Their Consequences, which the Last Eighteen Hundred Years Have Presented to the View of Mankind*, 2 vols. (London, 1801).

98. Piozzi, *Letters*, 2:140. The phrase "in good time" became one of Mrs. Piozzi's favorite expressions. For her it conveyed scorn. Iago uses the phrase in Shakespeare's *Othello*, I.1.32.

99. Piozzi, *Thraliana*, 386–87. *L'Homme Singulier* ["The Strange Man"] is a five-act comedy by Philippe Néricault Destouches (1680–1754).

100. Piozzi, *Thraliana*, 402.

101. Piozzi, *Letters*, 2:436n6.

102. Piozzi, *Thraliana*, 760–61.

103. Piozzi, *Letters*, 5:194.

104. Lansdowne, *The Queeney Letters*, 65.

Chapter Fourteen

A Pattern of Resignation

Diana Langton wrote to her son, Bennet, in May 1792 telling him that she had been reading Boswell's *Life of Johnson.* She thought the author's "strict adherence to the character of a Faithful Biographer had rather preval'd over his Judgement in Some Instances," meaning that Boswell had discussed certain aspects of Johnson's character that he should have kept to himself. But she admired the book nonetheless. She told her son that she had recently discussed the work with a family friend, and the friend pointed out that Bennet's "learning, fine Genius & long Friendship with the Doctor Qualify'd you more eminently for giving the world his Memory than the Present Author."[1]

Her son, to be sure, had known Dr. Johnson longer than Boswell had. He had also been more often in his company. Yet Bennet's personality clearly disqualified him for the task. For one thing, his natural indolence would have kept him from ever finishing the project, let alone undertaking it in the first place. For another, he felt more comfortable in talking than in writing, as he explained in a letter to a friend regarding some Parliamentary matters:

This earnest preference of oral discussion to the attempt at offering my thoughts in writing, may in part proceed from indolence and my scanty degree of exercise in the habit of writing, but I hope it may proceed likewise from a sense of the very imperfect and inadequate degree of Attention and investigation that I have used towards Those important Objects—which makes it necessary for me to prefer treating on them, rather in the lax manner wherein conversation usually proceeds, than in the more correct and finished form that seems requisite in what is committed to writing.[2]

He could also be verbose. Johnson had pointed this out to Sir John Hawkins years earlier. But although his indolence and verbosity kept him from turning author, they did not prevent him from doing one thing extremely well, which was to discharge his duties as an officer in the Lincolnshire Militia. Throughout the latter half of the eighteenth century, fears of a French invasion made it necessary for England to fortify coastal installations, train new recruits, and maintain veteran soldiers in a state of readiness. In addition, the war in America had drawn regular army troops out of the country, so that local militias were called upon to assist at home. "I have little doubt of a Call in no long time to my *Militia* Duty—" Langton had written to Boswell in the fall of 1775, "as it will surely be necessary to have *Them* embodied [the militia organized] when so large a Force is sent away as seems to be proposed, and indeed must, if any Effect is expected, in reducing the Americans to Obedience—I think it is agreed that less than 40,000 Men cannot be expected to answer that End."[3]

The Lincolnshire Militia usually bivouacked on Warley Common in Essex, and here Dr. Johnson had visited Langton and his men in September 1778. Johnson took great interest in the details of military life—its drills, exercises, equipment, and general protocol. Late one night he even made the rounds with the commanding officer to check on sentries at their posts. "I spent five days amongst them," he wrote to Boswell at the time, and he was pleased to observe that Langton "signalized himself as a diligent officer, and has very high respect in the regiment. He presided when I was there at a court-martial." After returning to London, Johnson wrote to Captain Langton enquiring facetiously, "Pray how many sheepstealers did you convict, and how did you punish them?"[4]

Probably in an effort to increase his income, Langton, in the early summer of 1780, took on further responsibilities by becoming a military engineer. Among his duties were helping to repair and improve the fortifications and ship building facilities around Chatham. Dr. James Beattie visited him in June 1781 just before Langton departed London. "He goes to Chatham in a few days with his family, in quality of engineer," Beattie wrote to Sir William Forbes. "You certainly know that Mr. Langton is an officer of militia. He loves the military life, and has been indefatigable in acquiring the knowledge that is necessary to it. He is allowed to be a most excellent engineer. Indeed, he is excellent in every thing."[5]

Forbes, a prominent Edinburgh banker and occasional author, a close friend of Boswell, and one of his executors, knew Langton a total of thirty years. In his *Life and Writings of James Beattie*, Forbes confirmed that Langton put aside his classical studies and devoted his energy to mastering military tactics and making himself into an outstanding officer:

> He acquired the esteem and admiration of his brother-officers, not only by his worth and learning, but by his elegant manners, and an inexhaustible fund of entertaining conversation; while he procured the love of the soldiers, by his

mildness and humanity, which were so great, that he was never, in a single instance, betrayed into passion, nor ever heard to utter an oath.[6]

In 1793, Boswell, as had Johnson fifteen years earlier, visited the encampment on Warley Common. Langton, now a major, welcomed him and provided a tent for his use. Boswell as a young man had entertained romantic notions of a military life and longed to be a soldier himself. He dreamed of the travel, adventures, honor, esteem, women, and handsome uniforms. But during his first night in the field on Warley Common, he could not sleep and he caught a cold, whereupon he quickly broke camp and beat a hasty retreat back to London. "I was sorry to leave you sooner than you kindly wished," he wrote to Major Langton. "But it was really necessary for me to be in town; and, as I candidly owned to you, I had enough of a Camp. In my convalescent state, another disturbed night would have hurt me much." His convalescent state resulted from his having been severely beaten and robbed a month earlier while intoxicated in Titchfield Street, London, and he had not yet fully recovered from the ordeal.[7]

Besides his work as military engineer, Langton derived further income from what was called his navigation, an older term for canal. He had inherited half interest in a commercial venture that operated and maintained the narrow Wey River, with its numerous locks, as a navigable channel from Guildford in Surrey to the Thames. He received a certain portion of the toll charges from boats and barges using the waterway. In addition, Parliament granted permission in 1778 for a canal to be dug from Basingstoke in Hampshire to join the Wey Navigation near Weybridge. Langton earned a certain amount on tolls collected from boats passing from one canal to the other. Moreover, he entertained hopes of greater profits by one day extending the canal so that it ran through Winchester and down to Portsmouth.[8] He also hoped to improve his situation eventually by some token of royal patronage. Boswell mentions that he was a favorite at court, a slight exaggeration, but the king did take pleasure in talking to him, enquiring how the education of his children progressed, and hearing his opinions on literary matters.[9] When the king was considering a tutor for his own younger children, several names were suggested, at which time the Prince of Wales proposed Langton as being the appropriate scholar and gentleman to instruct his brothers. The position, however, was not offered. Peregrine Langton stated that even if it had been proposed, it would not have been accepted, "at least I trust not, if proposed. I say I trust not—as it is impossible to imagine any man less fit for such an undertaking than was my father—he had no plan in teaching—he was remarkably indolent, and supine—stood in such supreme awe of rank of any kind, much less of that of Royalty, that nothing would have been learnt from him of any kind."[10]

Bennet Langton by George Dance, 1798.
Source: Trustees of the British Museum.

Langton, nevertheless, long held out expectations for some type of royal favor, which never came. He wrote to his mother lamenting that after twenty years' acquaintance with the king, he had received no special appointment or promotion:

> But as it now too plainly appears that any such aspiring hope is not to be realized, I must acquiesce in my Destiny: & thankful for the notice with which he has thought proper to honour me & with the due feelings of an attachment to Him as our Great Political Parent, continue to join in the general wish & Prayer that it may be granted to Him "in Health & wealth long to live" & to experience the subjects of Petitions for Him in the Former Devotion to which I am now.[11]

Boswell thought the king's failure to bestow favor on Langton had more to do with political considerations than with indifference. "The king cannot give to Langton because he is not in the political sphere," wrote Boswell. "He cannot take a handful of the gold upon the faro table, and give it to any man, however worthy, who is only looking on or stalking round the room. Let him play, let him part [the cards], and take his chance."[12] Yet despite the king's neglect, Langton's financial circumstances apparently improved, for by the early 1780s he gave up his long-held taciturnity and returned once more to being outgoing and loquacious. According to Boswell, Johnson had once cited him "as a foolish instance of studied behaviour: that he was first grave and silent and then gay and talkative."[13]

One evening Boswell entertained some people, among them Fanny Burney, with excellent imitations and stories of Johnson. "Mr. Langton told some stories himself in imitation of Dr. Johnson," said Miss Burney, "but they became him less than Mr. Boswell, and only reminded me of what Dr. Johnson himself once said to me—'Every man has, some time in his life, an ambition to be a wag.' If Mr. Langton had repeated anything from his truly great friend quietly, it would far better have accorded with his own serious and respectable character."[14]

At the time Boswell started work on what he boasted would be "the richest piece of Biography that has ever appeared,"[15] he constantly drew upon Langton and his great store of Johnsoniana. He spoke with Langton directly whenever the two happened to be in London, and when Langton had to be in Lincolnshire, Boswell proposed meeting him for a day halfway between Oxford and London so they might compare notes. Boswell further bombarded his friend with letters filled with requests and enquiries. Langton generously, if sluggishly, complied with everything Boswell desired, supplying him with much valuable information. Had it not been for Langton, Boswell's great work would not have been as monumental as it turned out to be.

As he approached the end of his task and began sending out portions of manuscript to be printed, Boswell continued to fire off letters to Langton with more questions for him to answer. When Langton did not respond quickly enough, he followed up with letters urging dispatch. "Now my dear Langton," he wrote in one, "let me request to have your answer to my queries directly; for *one* of the articles will be in the press in a day or two. How *can* you be so indolent?"[16] Another time he wrote, "I hope this request will induce you to write without delay, before the *mould* of indolence has had time to gather."[17] Yet despite his indolence, he managed to edit Johnson's Latin poems for an edition of the author's collected works published in 1787, and in the following year he succeeded Johnson as Professor of Ancient Literature to the Royal Academy. A further distinction came on June 16, 1790, when Oxford University awarded him a doctorate degree. In writing to congratulate him, Boswell hesitated whether to address him as *Doctor* Langton, but he nevertheless wished him "joy of the degree of L.L.D. so *worthily* conferred."[18]

Even with Langton's help and the constant prodding of Edmond Malone, writing Johnson's life had proved a tremendous struggle for its author. It would have been a formidable undertaking in the best of situations, only Boswell had to contend with personal difficulties and constant inner turmoil. His wife died after a long illness in June 1789, leaving him a widowed father of five young children, disconsolate and harassed with guilt, especially because he had not been with Margaret when she died. He had been off on a vain effort to curry political favor that he hoped would lead to a seat in Parliament. Thinking back on his periodic drunken sprees and his whoring binges, together with his protracted jaunts to London that amounted almost to abandonment, he felt completely unworthy of the woman who had borne his excesses with patience and forgiveness. With both Johnson and his wife gone, he had lost two of his greatest supports in life, and he felt adrift. With little chance of now rising in his profession in either Scotland or England, and with no hope of obtaining political preferment or election to Parliament, the only thing left to him that seemed worthwhile was completing the biography. Had not his friend Malone kept him to the task by skillfully advising, praising, scolding, and encouraging him by turns, even that might have come to nothing. Boswell wrote to Temple:

I have an *avidity* for death. I *eagerly* wish to be laid by my dear, dear wife. Years of life seem insupportable. . . . Every prospect that I turn my mind's eye upon is dreary. *Why* should I struggle? I certainly am *constitutionally* unfit for any employment. The law life in Scotland amidst vulgar familiarity would now quite destroy me. I am not able to acquire the law of England. To be in Parliament unless as an independent Member would gall my spirit. To live in the country would either harass me by forced exertions or sink me into a gloomy stupor. Let me not *think* at present, far less *resolve*. The *Life of Johnson* still keeps me up. I *must* bring that forth.[19]

He still enjoyed occasional flashes of vitality and moments of social pleasure, but they came less often and were of shorter duration than formerly. His predominant mood was now despondency. Barely fifty years old, he felt that his life was nearly over. He wished his magnum opus were finished, for sometimes he imagined he would die before completing it.[20] When Temple visited London from Scotland in May 1783, a year and a half before Johnson died, he was disturbed to see his friend so erratic in his conduct. He found Boswell "selfish, indelicate, thoughtless, no sensibility or feeling for others who have not his coarse and rustick strength of spirits." Temple regretted making the journey and felt that Boswell detained him to no purpose. "Seems often absurd and almost mad I think. No composure or rational view of things. Years do not improve him."[21] On a subsequent visit seven years later, Temple was even more displeased. "Never thinks of any one but himself," he wrote in his diary. "Indifferent to other peoples feelings or whether they are amused: envious: solicitous to make known what others wish to conceal: no command of his tongue: restless, no composure. Can never be happy uniform, or be depended on." Temple further noted that by his irregular conduct, Boswell had displeased most of his friends.[22]

For one thing, he had acquired the reputation of being a heavy drinker who might commit any indiscretion while intoxicated. Hannah More, like most others, originally found him pleasant and good natured, but one evening she became "heartily disgusted with Mr. Boswell, who came up stairs after dinner, much disordered with wine, and addressed me in a manner that drew from me a sharp rebuke, for which I fancy he will not easily forgive me."[23] Another time, Fanny Burney's younger sister Charlotte, now Mrs. Charlotte Francis, invited him and his daughters, Veronica and Euphemia, to a dinner party. Charlotte had always found Boswell delightful company, but she was warned half-jokingly that he would not leave her house while sober and might stay a week regardless. He was pleasant as usual during dinner, but growing increasingly drunk as the evening progressed, he hauled his daughter Veronica out of her chair so that he might sit next to Charlotte, and, she said, "He began by attempting to make love to me, but I was so grave that happily the love-fit wore off."[24]

These were not the overtures of a romantic young swain, but the desperate groping of a deeply despondent middle-aged man. One dull December afternoon, feeling ever more wretched and isolated in a city where he once cautioned himself against living more than he could record, he walked out of his lodgings to wander down Bond Street and St. James's Street hoping to meet someone along the way who would invite him to dinner. But now he stood dejected and alone in the court of St. James's Palace and listened to the clock strike half past four.[25] How different had it once been. Three decades earlier, at age twenty-two, he had come to London hoping to attain a proper conduct in life, reflecting how sad it would be if he should turn out no better than he was. Thinking now on his situation, he concluded that he had made little progress during the intervening years:

> What sunk me very low was the sensation that I was precisely as when in wretched low spirits thirty years ago, without any addition to my character from my having had the friendship of Dr. Johnson and many eminent men, made the tour of Europe, and Corsica in particular, and written two very successful books. I was as a board on which fine figures had been painted, but which some corrosive application had reduced to its original nakedness.[26]

Following publication of the *Life* in May 1791, he briefly visited Auchinleck, his Scottish estate, but found the time there heavy and depressing. Haunted by memories of his dead wife, he attempted to flee his despondency by visiting neighbors. "But, alas," he said, "I could not escape from myself." Returning to London, he tried plunging once more into the swirl of life, immersing himself in the activities that he once pursued with such zest, but everything—even the theater—had lost its savor. After attending a dinner one evening with Edmond Malone, Bennet Langton, and John Courtenay, he came away remembering little of what was said. "I have lost the faculty of recording conversations," he wrote in his journal. "Or perhaps I have seen and heard so much now that no conversation impresses me much." Under Malone's steady guidance, he revised the *Life* for a second edition, which appeared in 1793, but the labor brought him no pleasure or satisfaction. He found that his interest in literature had vanished. He could think about little but himself.[27]

People noticed the dramatic changes in his looks and behavior. Joseph Farington recorded in his diary meeting Boswell, "who, I think, is much altered for the worse in appearance." Temple found that his friend's temper had further deteriorated since the two last met and that Boswell had become increasingly more fretful. John Courtenay spoke with him at a party and was startled by the transformation in his usual lively spirits: "Poor Boswell is very low and dispirited and almost melancholy mad—feels no spring, no pleasure in existence—and is so perceptibly altered for the worse that it is remarked everywhere."[28]

Boswell wrote to his son James Jr., now sixteen years old, that as dismal as things now seemed to him, he would try to avoid repining. He was not content with mere literary fame nor mere social pleasures and would still hope for some honorable employment, yet he could see little ahead in life but a thick fog. Attempting to express in verse how apathy, resulting from years of disappointment, eventually supplants the lively hopes of youth, he got no further than the first two lines:

> 'Tis o'er, 'tis o'er, the dream is o'er,
> And Life's delusion is no more.[29]

At a meeting of the Club on April 14, 1795, he suddenly fell ill. He experienced nausea, headache, chills, and vomiting. Carried to his lodgings, he lingered for five weeks, dying quietly at two in the morning on May 19 at age fifty-four. Apparently he had succumbed to uremia, a condition brought on by kidney failure and obstruction of the urethra. It was a condition similar to the one that killed Oliver Goldsmith. Boswell's ailment likely resulted from recurring episodes of gonorrhea picked up during decades of whoring. His journal documents nineteen separate venereal infections over a thirty-year span.[30]

News of Boswell's death went unremarked by Fanny Burney and Mrs. Piozzi. He had long ago ceased to be of interest or concern to them personally. Edmond Malone perhaps felt the loss more keenly than anyone. In a letter of May 21 he wrote that he would miss Boswell more and more every day, adding,

He was in the constant habit of calling upon me almost daily, and I used to grumble sometimes at his turbulence, but now miss and regret his noise and his hilarity and his perpetual good humour, which had no bounds. Poor fellow, he has somehow stolen away from us, without any notice, and without my being at all prepared for it.[31]

Stealing away without any notice had not been Boswell's style. He had always wished to make himself conspicuous, so the absence of some final dramatic gesture, some theatrical display, made his passing seem anticlimactic. He had been whisked off the stage before he could finally determine if he was truly good for nothing or was the finest fellow in the world. Ultimately, of course, his many shortcomings—his vanity and self-indulgence in particular—were more to be pitied than despised, for they grew out of an overwhelming and irrational sense of inadequacy, an affliction he recognized but had not the strength to conquer. The most remarkable thing about him is how successfully he turned his frailties into great art. Had he possessed a steadier, more confident personality, he would have been less malleable, less able to adapt himself to changing circumstances. Had he been a man of stronger character, he would have been less receptive to the characters of much greater men than he. And had he been anyone but James Boswell of Auchinleck, the loud and boisterous, but agreeably charming anecdotal memorandummer, we would not now have the finest biography in the English language. His body was transported to his estate in Scotland, where it was interred on June 8, 1795, in the family vault near his wife.

The year that Boswell died, Bennet Langton resigned his commission in the Lincolnshire Militia. He found himself getting too old for the rigors of military life, although aside from chronic bouts of rheumatism and a persistent cough he picked up in the winter of 1801, his health had been reasonably good as he entered his sixties. Then in December of that year, as he dined with his friend and physician Dr. John Mackie in the city of Southampton, he suddenly grew so ill that he had to return to his lodgings. No one, however, felt especially concerned, for as his son Peregrine said, "he always desponded, fancying himself ill in a 100 ways." But the cough grew worse, and Dr. Mackie prescribed an elixir to help relieve it. Mackie supposed that he would take only a few drops occasionally as the cough required—"instead of which he took so large a dose," said Peregrine, "that when the Dr. attended him on the 17 or 18, he was greatly alarmed, and then, when too late, saw the danger he was in."[32] Langton's sons were not present, but his daughter Elizabeth tended her father to the end, which came easily on the eighteenth. "I was with him to the *last* when he ceased to breathe!" she wrote to a family friend. Following his burial on Christmas Day in the chancel of St. Michael's Church, Southampton, Elizabeth summed up her father's character by stating that "his attention was continually directed to the virtue of Humility, the effect of which was to be seen by those who had the most intimate means of observing, in every action of his life; nor was his piety reserved for particular & important occasions, but *uniformly* and *constantly* practised in the commonest occurrences of life."[33]

It was Samuel Johnson, however, who left the final and most lasting tribute, for on a marble tablet, erected to Bennet Langton's memory on the south wall of St. Michael's Church, are inscribed his words, given to the world in Boswell's *Life*, "*Sit anima mea cum Langtono.*"

In later years, Langton's oldest son and heir, George, expressed some bitterness at the decreased estate his father had left him. In 1812, Mrs. Piozzi wrote her daughter Queeney of being greatly amused at meeting George Langton and his own seventeen-year-old son at her house the day before. "Poor Mr. [George] Langton's Account of his good Father, bursting with Greek and with Religion as he said, and leaving him the Estate—diminished 4000£ o'Year!!—and then exclaims the Man—Johnson could say—Sit anima mea cum Langtono! A fine Fellow to take [a] Chance of Heaven with! that has ruined me and my Seven Children."[34]

Despite her growing circle of new acquaintances, Mrs. Piozzi found society less exciting than in the glory days of Streatham. She had shone among the shiners, she said, but the present shiners were pretty dull compared to the Johnsons, Burkes, Goldsmiths, Boswells, Murphys, and others who once illuminated the scene. Trying to please people now seemed to her a hollow endeavor, and maintaining the reputation of being a wit she found hardly worth the effort. Meeting others' expectations of perpetual gaiety had grown tiresome. She exclaimed in exasperation, "Comical Mrs Piozzi! as the People cry out for ever; Sad or merry—always Comical Mrs Piozzi!" She noted a similarity between cultivating friendships and scrounging votes in a political campaign: "Life has been to me nothing but a perpetual *Canvass* carried on in all parts of the World—not to make *Friends* neither—for I have certainly found very few—but to keep off *Enemies.*" How distasteful had been those times of canvassing votes for Henry Thrale, and how disagreeable had cultivating society now become. "You must *canvass* your Husbands, or they will—(should you not please them)—keep a Mistress: You must *canvass* Your Acquaintance by every possible Method, or they will speak very ill of you, & do You infinite Mischief." Existence itself seemed like one long political campaign. "Life, keeping up one's Acquaintance as 'tis called, I consider as setting out upon a regular Canvass:—The fatigue is the same, & the Pleasure the same, *to me.*"[35]

She and her husband finally decided to quit Streatham and settle on her Welsh land of Bach-y-Graig near Denbigh. Henry Thrale and Dr. Johnson had hated the country, but she loved it. The beauty of this area of Wales seemed to her like paradise. She could now spend time among her papers and books or her chickens and turkeys just as she pleased without anyone chastising her for it. The couple chose to build a handsome Italian villa on a hill overlooking the Vale of Clwyd with the dark peaks of Snowdonia in the distance. From here they could see the romantic ruins of Denbigh Castle and a stretch of Irish Sea eight miles to the north that was often dotted with white sails. They bought a telescope for the front of the house in order to view the far-reaching expanse of beauty more closely. She called their new home Brynbella, *bryn* meaning *hill* in Welsh and *bella* meaning *beautiful* in Italian. The name symbolized for her the happy union of two languages, two cultures, and two people.

They settled into their new home in mid-September 1795. On the seventeenth, Mrs. Piozzi commemorated the event in her diary, emphasizing that she was not the appendage of someone else, but rather an independent woman, happy in her own way: "On this Morn^g the Birthday of my eldest Daughter, do I open my Eyes—and My Thraliana, at *My own house*; my new beautiful Residence built for me in *my own* lovely Country, by the Husband of my Hearts Choice." She could not help contrasting Brynbella with the gloomy house in Deadman's Place where she first took up residence after her marriage to Thrale: "What a black Dungeon did I wake in, this Day one and Thirty Years!! and what a Paradise did I unclose my Eyes upon this Morning!"[36] Streatham Park conjured up more pleasant associations, but lovely Brynbella claimed sole possession of her heart. Streatham, she said, "is an Attachment of more Propriety than Passion, strengthened by the associating agreeable Ideas of Time passed among pleasant Friends &c."[37]

As she approached the twentieth anniversary of her marriage to Gabriel Piozzi, she reflected on her present situation: living in an elegantly furnished new house on a beautiful wooded hill in her native Wales—having only a few bills but no major debt—the nearby church at Tremeirchion, where some of her ancestors lay, being repaired and beautified by her husband, "this *formidable* Foreigner, whom my Daughters & my Friends said was to ruin my Fortune, & change my Religion, and use me I know not how ill besides. He certainly has been a faithful & tender Husband to me notwithstanding their Denunciations now for 19 Years."[38] She thought back over the most important men in her life and chose her words carefully to describe the constraints or freedom she had felt with each of them. She recalled "the venerating solicitude which hung heavily over my whole soul whilst connected with Doctor Johnson, . . . the strong connubial duty that tied my every thought to Mr. Thrale's interest," and finally the "attractive passion which made twenty years passed in Piozzi's society seem like a happy dream of twenty hours."[39] Her greatest regret during these otherwise happy years had to do with her grown daughters. The youngest of the four, Cecilia, did not give her mother much trouble, for she had not the capacity for malevolence that the older daughters possessed, "very unlike her Sisters in everything but Person," said her mother. Mrs. Piozzi further described Cecilia as "a good Girl, but not a bright one, She has neither Genius nor Application I think, but a flexible Temper, and empty Head." The other three, led by the headstrong, intractable Queeney, would have nothing to do with Piozzi and little to do with their mother. Henry Thrale had taken little active role in raising the girls except to make sure they lacked nothing money could buy. Their mother had been as flighty and inconsistent in child-rearing as with everything else, the result being that the three oldest had grown up beautiful, well-bred, rich, self-centered, and spoiled. They also grew up having no affection for their father and hating their mother. "Mr Thrale had not much heart," said Mrs. Piozzi, "but his fair Daughters have none at all."[40]

Sophia and Susanna Thrale had hearts as impenetrable as their older sister's, but Queeney was the ringleader, foremost in nearly everything—the most intelligent, most calculating, and most unfeeling. Yet all three, said their mother, were capable of starving a favorite animal or of looking upon a friend's afflictions with unconcern.[41] Mrs. Piozzi recalled that even Fanny Burney had been appalled by the oldest daughter's frigid malignity. During the time she agonized over whether she should marry Gabriel Piozzi—pulled one way by her own desire and another way by Queeney's strong opposition, when she nearly died from the turmoil in her mind—all three daughters "laughed at my distress, and observed to dear Fanny Burney—that it *was monstrous droll*: *She* [Miss Burney] could scarcely suppress her Indignation."[42] Years earlier, when the sickly baby Harriett Thrale was to be moved from London to Streatham for better air, and Mrs. Thrale felt misgivings, fearing the move might kill her, "She will be nearer the Church Yard replies the eldest, coldly."[43] The baby died soon after.

Mrs. Piozzi made no attempt to keep such deplorable behavior by "the three cruel misses," as she called them, a secret. She told friends of her daughters' insolence and cold neglect. She spoke openly of their demands for money or property they thought their due. Friends often wrote to Mrs. Piozzi if they happened to see the girls at Bath or Brighton or other fashionable resorts, and they sympathized, of course, with her situation. "That naughty Queeny!" wrote the Reverend Thomas Sedgwick Whalley to Mrs. Piozzi:

> What an amiable and pretty dear it *once* was! Will it never be so again! Will its crabbedness, and sourness, and disobedience, and petulant obstinacy never pass away! . . . And the *other* perverse Dears! But *they* are only Satellites to the Elder Planet, and moving in the attraction of her Sphere, will follow her wherever she goes, turn at her influence, and sparkle as she commands.[44]

One would think, said the Reverend Leonard Chappelow facetiously, that her three oldest daughters had been born in Flintshire, their hearts were so hard. Another friend called them Goneril and Regan while others referred to them as the "wayward sisters."[45] To help compensate for her failure to raise respectful, obedient daughters—the kind of daughter she had been to her own mother—she decided to adopt the son of Gabriel Piozzi's favorite brother, Giovanne Battiste. During the Piozzis' visit to Italy on their honeymoon, Giovanne had named his newborn son John Salusbury Piozzi in honor of his brother's wife. Later, when the family suffered personal and financial hardship under Napoleon's occupation of the Milanese region, Mrs. Piozzi saw the opportunity to help alleviate their distress and to serve her own interests. She sent for the five-year-old boy to come and live in England, where he arrived in December 1798.

Except for brief visits to Wales during vacation time, the child lived and attended school at Streatham. Mrs. Piozzi intended to raise him as an English gentleman, "& we will see if He will be more grateful, & rational, & comfortable than Miss Thrales have been to the Mother they have at length *driven to Desperation*."[46] She apparently already intended to hurl defiance at her unkind daughters by making the boy her heir. In due course she had him naturalized, had his name legally changed to John Salusbury Piozzi Salusbury (she liked the idea of perpetuating her maiden name), and saw that he was confirmed in the English Church. Meanwhile, with advancing years, Gabriel Piozzi suffered from increasingly severe fits of gout. His wife said he had become a martyr to the disease that left him a periodic invalid. He could no longer play the pianoforte. "Gout such as I never knew fastened on his fingers," she said, "distorting them into every dreadful Shape, and filling them with solid and liquid Chalkstones almost without example."[47] The disease sometimes confined Piozzi for weeks at a time to bed, where he remained completely delirious from pain. He eventually died in agony on March 26, 1809, from gangrene, the result of his chronic gout having broken through the skin. He was buried at Tremeirchion church, which, to please his wife, he had taken great care to restore.

Nine years after Johnson's death and two years after her escape from court, forty-one-year-old Fanny Burney made a bid to find happiness in the manner Mrs. Thrale had done—in her own way and on her own terms. She met and fell in love with General Alexandre d'Arblay, and soon the two wanted to marry. Like many other French émigrés who had served King Louis XVI, General d'Arblay fled France during the revolution and settled in England. Despite being a soldier, he was a charming, gentle, sensitive man who valued close relationships and who loved literature. Still, he was poor, a Catholic, and spoke no English. As a consequence, Dr. Burney advised his daughter not to marry him. But d'Arblay was simply too valuable for her to pass up, and at her age she might not find so good an opportunity again. She may also have harbored a slight resentment for what she considered her personal sacrifice in having spent five long years at court. Feeling less inclined, therefore, to follow her father's wishes in a matter so important to her future, she married d'Arblay against her father's advice, the first and only time she acted contrary to Dr. Burney's stated wishes. She failed to notice, or chose to overlook, certain similarities between her marriage to d'Arblay and Hester Thrale's marriage to Gabriel Piozzi. Dr. Burney was so surprised and annoyed at his daughter's defiance that he declined to attend the wedding. Later, however, he became reconciled once he saw d'Arblay's merit and recognized his daughter's genuine happiness. A year and a half after the couple's wedding, they had a son whom they named Alexander Charles Louis Piochard d'Arblay, although they called him simply Alex.

D'Arblay, having left everything behind in France, was virtually penniless, and Madame d'Arblay (as Fanny Burney was now known to the public) possessed a yearly income of only £100 by way of an annuity generously provided by the queen at Fanny's departure from court. This amount could hardly support a family, so Madame d'Arblay, through the offices of her brother Charles, arranged to stage one of her plays. The play was *Edwy and Elgiva*, a blank verse tragedy she had composed at odd moments during her most depressed and unhappy period at court. It was performed at Drury Lane Theatre on March 21, 1795, but even the leading actors of the day, Sarah Siddons and John Kemble in the leading roles, could not enliven the inert piece. The opening night performance proved to be its last. She then took up her pen to create a work in prose as a way to raise money. The result was *Camillia: or, A Picture of Youth*, published in July 1796. She refused to call the work a novel, for she did not want to give readers the notion that it was simply a love story. It was actually a hybrid of the popular etiquette book and the novel of manners. Her purpose was to dramatize the problems a young woman encounters in society. "I mean this work to be sketches of characters and morals put in action," she said, "—not a romance."[48] The book brought in enough money to allow the d'Arblays to build a small house, which they called Camillia Cottage, on land owned by Fanny's wealthy friends William and Frederica Locke of Norbury Park near Leatherhead, Surrey, some twenty-one miles southwest of London.

Camillia shows a marked deterioration in the author's style. It is more turgid, dense, and obscure than her previous works. Some critics at the time thought she had taken the *Rambler* for a model of fine writing and turned out a poor imitation of Johnson's worst pomposities. She venerated Dr. Johnson so much, both as man and author, that she almost always wrote his name in larger letters than the surrounding text. She read his *Lives of the Poets* with pleasure and benefitted from the teachings of the *Rambler*. "Oh what a writer he is!" she exclaimed, "what instruction, spirit, intelligence, and vigour in almost every paragraph!"[49] But whatever salutary effect Johnson and his writings had on her character, his influence on her style proved detrimental. Johnson's majestic, resonant prose was, in Madame d'Arblay's estimation, the summit of literary excellence. Previous writers, more practiced than she, had already dashed themselves on the rocks of Johnsonian loftiness, balance, and antithesis, but even if Madame d'Arblay had been capable of maneuvering so ponderous a vehicle with Johnson's facility, it was a style more suited to expository writing than to fiction. The cumbersome style of *Camillia* further demonstrated Madame d'Arblay's painful self-consciousness, a misguided attempt to cover her vulnerability with a layer of correctness, elegance, and decorum foreign to her nature. Her latest style seemed as remote from the simplicity of *Evelina* as her new title "Madame" seemed inappropriate to the shy and personally unpretentious Fanny Burney.

In 1802 she and young Alex followed General d'Arblay to France, where he hoped to reclaim his rank, character, and property from Napoleon's government. Shortly after their arrival, war broke out between England and France, forcing the family to settle in Paris. During the long exile that followed, Fanny was completely cut off from her family, friends, culture, and language. Ten years later she managed to return to England, but by that time tastes had changed. England had changed. Fanny herself had changed. She had put on weight and looked better for it. People also noticed that she spoke English with a slightly foreign accent like an educated Frenchwoman who knew the language fluently.

In 1814 she published her fourth and final novel, *The Wanderer*, a book that repeated many themes and character types found in her previous works and did so in a convoluted, pretentious style whose meaning often proved elusive. Young William Hazlitt, in reviewing the book, said that "we perceive no decay of talent, but a perversion of it."[50] John Wilson Croker accused her of being a mannerist—"that is, she has given over painting from the life, and has employed herself in copying from her own copies. . . . The Wanderer has the identical features of Evelina—but Evelina grown old."[51] Thomas Babington Macaulay thought the author had brought back from her long exile in France "a style which we are really at a loss to describe. It is a sort of broken Johnsonese, a barbarous *patois*, bearing the same relation to the language of Rasselas, which the gibberish of the Negroes of Jamaica bears to the English of the House of Lords."[52]

Her prudishness, merely the leitmotif of youth, had become the dominant strain of her advancing years, at least in her public persona. Her convoluted style made her seem ever more distant and remote as an author, yet to her close friends she remained the simple, humorous, thoughtful person she had always been, even after personal tragedies pressed upon her. In 1811, in Paris, she had undergone the removal of her right breast—a radical mastectomy without anesthetic—and she later wrote a harrowing account of the experience. Then her husband died of colon cancer in 1818 and was buried at Bath. To help alleviate her crushing sorrow, she turned to editing the massive collection of personal papers her father left behind at his death in 1814 at age eighty-eight. At various times, Dr. Burney had worked on a narrative of his life, together with reminiscences of the prominent people he had known. Madame d'Arblay envisioned publishing three octavo volumes of these memoirs followed by three volumes of letters. But as she read through her father's papers, her prudishness rose up stronger than ever to guide her editorial hand.

Dr. Burney possessed an engaging, personable style that exactly expressed his personality. He wrote frankly about himself and his friends. He told, in the beginning of his narrative, about his difficulties growing up, especially about his negligent father and uncaring mother. He evidently hoped to show, by contrasting his deprived childhood with his later successes, how far his diligence and hard work had brought him. But Fanny thought these kinds of revelations opened to public view "a species of Family degradation to which the name of Burney now gives no similitude." She set about, therefore, to score out what she thought offensive passages and even burned heaps of Dr. Burney's papers, fearing they might later fall into the hands of less decorous biographers. She found it a herculean effort "to have dissected this multifarious work, & to have removed all that appeared . . . peccant parts, that might have bred fevers, caused infectious ill-will, or have excited morbid criticism or ridicule."[53] Scholars have regretted the loss of so much valuable material ever since.

Instead of simply editing the papers and letting her father speak in his own words, she proceeded to rewrite his memoirs herself. That way she could be sure that it was done properly. The final product, *Memoirs of Dr. Burney, Arranged from His Own Manuscripts, from Family Papers, and from Personal Recollections. By His Daughter, Madame d'Arblay*, published in 1832, turned out to be a disappointment. She had idealized, sanitized, and generalized Dr. Burney to the point where he possessed no personality. Half the work focused on her own activities rather than her father's, and the work was written in the ponderous, inflated style of her later years. John Wilson Croker, in his review of the work, could hardly contain his outrage. "Madame d'Arblay may have exercised a sound discretion in not giving to the public this mass of materials, *in extenso*," he wrote,

> but we do very much doubt whether what she has suppressed could have been more feeble, anile, incoherent, or "*sentant plus l'apoplexie*," than that which she has substituted for it. In fact, almost the only passages in these volumes, which exhibit common sense, good taste, or intelligible language are the few sentences which are given in Dr. Burney's own words and which, though occasionally somewhat inflated, appear simple and natural in the midst of the strange *galimatias* of pompous verbosity in which his daughter has enshrined them.

Croker further pointed out that "it is her *own Memoirs*, and *not* those of her father that she has been writing; and we confess that we have a strong suspicion, that it was *because* her father's auto-biography did not fulfil *this* object, that *it* has been suppressed."[54]

Macaulay, who was generally more well disposed toward Madame d'Arblay and her works than Croker, still could not defend the *Memoirs*, especially its inflated language, which he called "the worst style that has ever been known among men." He noted specific examples:

An offence punishable with imprisonment is, in this language, an offence "which produces incarceration." To be starved to death is, "to sink from inanition into nonentity." Sir Isaac Newton is, "the developer of the skies in their embodied movements;" and Mrs Thrale, when a party of clever people sat silent, is said to have been "provoked by the dulness of a taciturnity that, in the midst of such renowned interlocutors, produced as narcotic a torpor as could have been caused by a dearth the most barren of all human faculties."[55]

What contemporary critics could not see was that behind the pompous public voice lay hidden the shy, self-conscious, uncertain Fanny Burney trying desperately not to appear ridiculous. She came across, however, as affected, prudish, and old-fashioned. Yet she "survived her own wake, and overheard the judgment of posterity," as Macaulay put it,[56] for despite her bloated style and antiquated notions of proper decorum, the public still regarded her as a cherished relic of that great age of order, restraint, reason, and harmony. But the nineteenth century was now a far different time, one given more to rhapsodies, nonconformity, and fantastic emotional displays. Madame d'Arblay had become to others what Mrs. Delany had once been to her—"an aged lady of rare accomplishments, and high bred manners, of olden times."

Thomas Jefferson Hogg met her on one occasion, thought her a curiosity, and planned to take his friend Percy Shelley to see her. But the meeting never came off, and Hogg thought it just as well: "They were not suited for each other; whatever merit Miss Burney had, and no doubt she possessed much, was not to his taste." Besides, he said, she was actually "a bundle of conventionalities; and these, however clever and well arranged, would not have proved attractive to the Divine Poet. Her conversation was not without ability, but it was wholly about herself, and the self not being at all interesting, the conversation could not be so."[57]

Samuel Rogers brought Walter Scott to call at her home in Bolton Street, Piccadilly, in 1826. Scott found her "an elderly lady, with no remains of personal beauty but with a gentle manner and a pleasing expression of countenance. She told me she had wished to see two persons—myself, of course, being one; the other George Canning." She talked to Scott about her early success with *Evelina* and about dancing around the mulberry tree at Chessington after learning of Johnson's praise. "I trust I shall see this lady again," wrote Scott in his journal. "She has simple and apparently amiable manners, with quick feelings."[58]

With Gabriel Piozzi gone, Brynbella was now too much for Mrs. Piozzi to manage alone, so she gave the place to her stepson, John Salusbury, now grown to manhood with a wife and young children of his own. Mrs. Piozzi delighted in the idea of the Welsh lands being again in the hands of a Salusbury, but giving Brynbella to John proved a bad decision. Salusbury had no occupation, lived like a country squire, and depended largely on his stepmother for support. Ironically, but not altogether surprisingly, Salusbury turned out no better than the three cruel misses. He had little respect or affection for Mrs. Piozzi, thought her "a Superannuated old Goose," she said, and constantly dunned her for money. It eventually became apparent to her that Salusbury "will strip me to the skin I see."[59] Feeling particularly dejected in May 1815, she wrote in her diary that she "Sate at home in the Evening & pitied poor Mrs. Piozzi—squeezed and despised between two Rapacious Families."[60]

But even with so many disappointments crowding upon old age, she never lost her gift of talk, her love of fun, or her flare for extravagant dress. A woman who met her in 1803 when she was sixty-two described her as "skipping about like a kid, quite a figure of fun, in a tiger skin shawl, lined with scarlet, and *only* five colours upon her head-dress—on top of a flaxen wig a bandeau of blue velvet, a bit of tiger ribbon, a white beaver hat and plume of black feathers—as gay as a lark."[61] William Macready, the Irish-born actor and theater manager, attended a select gathering at Bath twelve years later and described the scene as she was announced:

> It seemed almost as if a portrait by Sir Joshua had stepped out of its frame, when the little old lady, dressed *point de vice* in black satin, with dark glossy ringlets under her neat black hat, highly rouged, not the end of a ribbon or lace out of its place, with an unfaltering step entered the room. And was this really "the Mrs. Thrale," the sage monitress of "The Three Warnings," the indefatigable tea-maker of the Great Insatiable? She was instantly the centre on which every eye was fixed, engrossing the attention of all. I had the satisfaction of a particular introduction to her, and was surprised and delighted with her vivacity and good-humour.[62]

She realized that the world had passed her by and that others regarded her as little more than an oddity, a token, a nostalgic remembrance of the past: "So I am now grown one of the Curiosities of Bath it seems and *one of the Antiquities.*"[63] She remarked that "'tis a melancholy Thing—as Floretta found it in Dr. Johnson's Tale—to outlive Lovers & Haters, & Friends & Foes; & find ones' self surrounded by those with whom one has no Ideas in common."[64] Despite her own romantic temperament, she had little sympathy for the new romantic age, "this Age where every body seeks to be agitated & shuns to be informed."[65] She especially did not approve of the popular gothic novel, which she said taught nothing. She thought Matthew Lewis's *The Monk* a strange and wicked novel, and she found Mary Shelley's *Franken-stein* shocking: "I have never seen such an audacious, and I might add, such an ingenious, piece of impiety."[66] George Crabbe, however, was her favorite among the new poets:

Crabbes Poems please me better than any of the modern Productions—They leave something behind them. Lord Byron gives you frightful Images, but they fade away in Phantasmagoria. Southey sends you to Bed in the Horrors not knowing why: Walter Scott's Marmion is very fine certainly, and his Lay—very Interesting:—They seized my Imagination forcibly on their first Appearance but I return to Crabbe.[67]

Having entered her seventies, she had to pinch pennies and give up the lavish parties and expensive clothes she had loved so much. Maintaining Streatham, which she no longer even visited, had become a severe drain on her resources, so in order to rid herself of the burden and raise money, she sold at auction the entire contents of the house, including furniture, books, and all but one of the eleven Reynolds portraits that hung in the library. The only portrait she kept was that of Arthur Murphy.[68] The auction brought in nearly £4,000. The empty house she leased at £260 a year for the rest of her life. Forced to move periodically into ever smaller accommodations because of the rapaciousness of her daughters and stepson, she resided for a time in "a nut-shell here at Bath, where I used to live gay and grand in Pulteney Street." Her nutshell was two rooms at 17 New King Street. Later she had to move again and referred to herself as "the *little Bundle of black Rags* . . . at No. 8 Gay Street."[69] Her one consolation was that her daughters and stepson, whom she still truly cared about though they cared little for her, benefitted from the Thrale fortune even if she did not:

My daughters rich & I suppose happy. My Grandchildren well provided & pros-perous. My protégé [Salusbury] married & of Age, and I trust living the life he likes [at Brynbella] with the People he loves. Myself, tho' cast off by *him* and by

Them; not despised by *others*, but respected in my ragged Gown, and inhabiting the Parish of Walcote, Bath.[70]

To save even more money, she retired for a year to the dull obscurities of Penzance but then settled in Clifton, not far from Bath.

Toward the end of April 1821, at age eighty, she became ill and continued to decline for ten days. She realized that her time had finally come. "I die in the trust and the fear of God" were the last words she uttered before growing too weak to talk. A longtime Bath friend, Sir George Smith Gibbes, called on her near the end. Unable to speak, she traced the outline of a coffin in the air with her hands.[71] Hester Piozzi died with little suffering at about nine o'clock in the morning on Wednesday, May 2, 1821, and was buried two weeks later next to her second husband in Tremeirchion Church in the Vale of Clwyd, Wales. At her bedside were the three wayward sisters. Now in their fifties, they had grown somewhat reconciled in recent years to their mother's eccentric ways.

On learning of Mrs. Piozzi's death, Madame d'Arblay wrote in her diary,

I have lost now, just lost, my once most dear, intimate, and admired friend, Mrs. Thrale Piozzi, who preserved her fine faculties, her imagination, her intelligence, her powers of allusion and citation, her extraordinary memory, and her almost unexampled vivacity, to the last of her existence. . . . She was, in truth, a most wonderful character for talents and eccentricity, for wit, genius, generosity, spirit, and powers of entertainment.[72]

Hester Lynch Thrale Piozzi had been the most modern of the Johnson circle. Were she dropped into the present age, she would adapt the quickest and enjoy the change the most. Gabriel Piozzi used to laugh at her facility to adapt to every circumstance she encountered. This ability was partly a deliberate strategy for getting on in the world. She claimed that she was always willing to bend and that was the reason she never broke.[73] Her association with Samuel Johnson had been in some ways the most important relationship of her adult life. It was not necessarily the happiest relationship, but it was the most complex, and it defined more than any other who she was and what she might be. In the early years, Johnson had supported her, nurtured her, and given her confidence. He inspired her initial bid for independence even if later, after her mother's death, he assumed the role of domineering parent himself. Yet it seems unlikely that she would have become one of the most socially prominent women of her day without his encouragement, praise, and admonishment over the years. He helped form and define many of her ideas. She once stated that their friendship was founded on "the truest Principles Religion, Virtue, & Community of Ideas—saucy Soul! Community of Ideas with Doctor Johnson: but why not? he has fastened many of his own Notions so on my Mind before this Time, that I am not sure whether they grew there originally or no: of this I am sure, that they are the best & wisest Notions I possess."[74]

She acknowledged that her own mind and Johnson's were not at all alike: "My first friend [Dr. Collier] formed my mind to resemble *his*. It never *did* resemble that of either of my husbands, and in that of Doctor Johnson's mine was swallowed up and lost."[75] She had always found Johnson's colossal presence inhibiting, but as he grew more irritable and peremptory in his manner, he at last became too much for her to support. In her *Anecdotes* she had summed up her attitude toward him:

> Veneration for his virtue, reverence for his talents, delight in his conversation, and habitual endurance of a yoke my husband first put upon me, and of which he contentedly bore his share for sixteen or seventeen years, made me go on so long with Mr. Johnson; but the perpetual confinement I will own to have been terrifying in the first years of our friendship, and irksome in the last; nor could I pretend to support it without help, when my coadjutor was no more.[76]

Of greatest importance, perhaps, was the self-confidence Johnson had given her in the beginning. He had praised her wit, her beauty, and her intellect. He had shown her so much attention that she could not but help think herself remarkable. But Johnson had done his work too well. If he did not sow the seeds of her rebellion, he had at least nurtured the soil from which the rebellion sprang. Confident of her abilities and convinced of her right to live life in her own way, she broke with those who set limits on her independence and happiness. She pushed ahead, doing silly things and making wrong choices now and then, yet always maintaining her lively talk and her buoyant spirits. As Johnson said in one of his last references to her, "if she was not the wisest woman in the world, she was undoubtedly one of the wittiest."[77]

Madame d'Arblay, the former Fanny Burney, was now the last surviving principal figure of the Johnson circle. It had been a loosely formed collection of remarkable persons, from varied backgrounds, with diverse interests, and exhibiting sometimes discordant personalities. The chief things they had in common were a shared love of social conviviality and engaging talk, and a reverence for Samuel Johnson. Johnson had stood at the center, holding the group together by the attraction of his powerful intellect and commanding personality. His wise counsel, ethical conduct, vigorous thought and writing, and capacity for friendship had, in the main, been a quickening influence on their minds and a vitalizing force in their lives. All freely acknowledged their indebtedness to him.

In her final years Madame d'Arblay became increasingly religious and reclusive. Following her husband's death, she grew more dejected and wished that her own death might come soon. Then in January 1837, Alex, the sheltered, bookish, absentminded son, who had become minister of Ely Chapel, Holborn, died unexpectedly at age forty-three of influenza. After the initial shock and grief, opening for her, she said, the most mournful and hopeless year of her long life, she became what her younger sister Charlotte called "a pattern of Resignation to the Divine Will."[78] Not only had she outlived all the other members of the Johnson circle, but she had also outlived her father, her husband, her son, and her sisters Hetty and Susan. She had outlived, as well, a remarkable period, an era painstakingly chronicled in her diaries and sharply delineated in her novels.

Her novels had done much to influence the currently popular novel of manners, and her stature as a professional writer had helped clear the way for Jane Austen, Charlotte Brontë, and subsequent women authors. Jane Austen's first novel, *Sense and Sensibility*, appeared in 1811. A second followed in 1813, its title apparently taken from the last chapter of Madame d'Arblay's *Cecilia.* Here the character Dr. Lyster declares that Mortimer Delvile's nearly fatal misunderstanding with Cecilia "has been the result of PRIDE and PREJUDICE. . . . Yet this, however, remember; if to PRIDE and PREJUDICE you owe your miseries, so wonderfully is good and evil balanced, that to PRIDE and PREJUDICE you will also owe their termination."

But the present age seemed worlds away from the one in which Fanny Burney had flourished, the one in which she had been a principal favorite of Dr. Johnson, David Garrick, Sir Joshua Reynolds, Daddy Crisp, and Mrs. Thrale. Queen Victoria now occupied the throne. Scott, Coleridge, Shelley, Keats, Byron, and Lamb were already dead. Charles Dickens was at work on *The Old Curiosity Shop* following his success with *Pickwick Papers* and *Oliver Twist*. Railway carriages were about to start transporting passengers between London and Birmingham and other English towns and cities. The postage stamp had just come into use, along with the electric telegraph and photography, and some adventurous people were starting to ride bicycles.

Well into her eighties, her sight grew dim and her hearing weak. In late 1839 she fell dangerously ill and lingered into the new year when she saw her end approaching. "I know I am dying, but I am willing to die," she said in her last words; "I commit my soul to God, in reliance on the mercy & merit of my redeemer."[79] She expired peacefully at half past one in the morning on January 6, 1840, aged eighty-eight, the same age as her father when he died. Her remains were carried to Bath where she was buried in Wolcot Churchyard next to her son and not far from her husband.

NOTES

1. From a letter dated May 9, 1792 in the possession of the Langton family.

2. From a letter to John English Dolben, November 1792, in the possession of the Langton family. Boswell mentions that not having been in Johnson's company during the year 1780, he had to compensate by relying on the communications of his worthy friend Mr. Langton. "Very few articles of this collection were committed to writing by himself," says Boswell, "he not having that habit; which he regrets, and which those who know the numerous opportunities he had of gathering the rich fruits of *Johnsonian* wit and wisdom, must ever regret. I however found, in conversation with him, that a good store of *Johnsoniana* was treasured in his mind" (Boswell, *Life*, 4:1).

3. Bowell, *Correspondence of Boswell with the Club*, 61.

4. Johnson, *Letters*, Redford, 3:142 and 3:132.

5. Forbes, *Life and Writings of James Beattie*, 2:75.

6. Ibid., 2:77.

7. Boswell, *Correspondence of Boswell with the Club*, 387; Boswell, *Great Biographer*, 221–22.

8. For an account of the Wey Navigation, see C. N. Fifer, "Boswell's Langton and the River Wey," in *Notes and Queries*, August 1956, 347–49. Peregrine Langton wrote in one of his letter books, "Nothing ever seemed to rouse my father from the natural indolence of his character as did the subject of the Canals—upon all occasions he seemed animated out of himself whenever that topick was brought forward—The Wey, & Basingstoke, had been greatly improved by his attention to them, and he always hoped to see at least begun if not finished an extended branch that should communicate by Winchester from the Lea to join the latter, which would not only have been to his family, an almost incalculable increase of wealth but would have been of equally splendid service, & advantage to the country by thus having a direct communication from the Metropolis, to Portsmouth."

9. "I resolved to go some day [to Court] with Langton," wrote Boswell, "a well-known favourite, and stand close to him, by which means I could not fail to be talked to by Her Majesty" (Boswell, *English Experiment*, 46).

10. Boswell, *Correspondence of Boswell with the Club*, lxviin52.

11. From an undated letter in the possession of the Langton family.

12. Boswell, *Boswelliana*, 299.

13. Boswell, *Applause of the Jury*, 151.

14. Burney, *Diary & Letters*, 5:84.

15. Boswell, *Correspondence Relating to the* Life, 117.

16. Ibid., 244.

17. Ibid., 259. See p. 241n1 for a chronology of Langton's assistance to Boswell.

18. Boswell, *Correspondence of Boswell with the Club*, 302. The degree was a DCL (Doctor of Civil Law, traditionally an honorary degree) rather than an LL.D. (Doctor of Laws).

19. Boswell, *Great Biographer*, 11–12.

20. Ibid., 79.

21. Temple, *Diaries*, 41.

22. Ibid., 79.

23. Roberts, *Memoirs*, 1:210–11.

24. Boswell, *Great Biographer*, 313.

25. Ibid., 256.

26. Ibid., 86.

27. Ibid., 153, 225, 295 and 245.

28. Joseph Farington, *The Farington Diary*, ed. James Greig, 8 vols. (London, 1923–1928), 1:6; Boswell, *Great Biographer*, 236 and 125.

29. Boswell, *Great Biographer*, 307–8.

30. See William B. Ober, M.D., *Boswell's Clap and Other Essays: Medical Analyses of Literary Men's Afflictions* (Carbondale: Southern Illinois University Press, 1979), 1–42.

31. Boswell, *Great Biographer*, 316–17.

32. Account by Peregrine Langton; Boswell, *Correspondence of Boswell with the Club*, lxv–lxvi.

33. From a letter to Augusta Sophia Feilding, December 31, 1801, in the possession of the Langton family.

34. Piozzi, *Letters*, 5:129.

35. Piozzi, *Thraliana*, 907, 752 and 976.

36. Ibid., 941.

37. Piozzi, *Letters*, 2:302.

38. Piozzi, *Thraliana*, 1039–40.

39. Hayward, *Autobiography*, 2:43–44.

40. Piozzi, *Thraliana*, 721 and 564.

41. Ibid., 570.

42. Ibid., 562.

43. Ibid., 563.

44. Piozzi, *Letters*, 1:278 and n1.

45. Piozzi, *Thraliana*, 919 and 717.

46. Ibid., 984.

47. Tearle, *Mrs. Piozzi's Tall Young Beau*, 52.

48. Burney, *Diary & Letters*, 5:264.

49. Ibid., 1:443.

50. *Edinburgh Review* 24, no. 48 (February 1815): 338.

51. *Quarterly Review* 11 (April 1814): 125.

52. *Edinburgh Review* 76, no. 154 (January 1843): 566.

53. Hemlow, *The History of Fanny Burney*, 449–50.

54. *Quarterly Review* 49 (April and July 1833): 107.

55. *Edinburgh Review* 76, no. 154 (January 1843): 524 and 568.

56. *Edinburgh Review* 76, no. 154 (January 1843): 523.

57. Thomas Jefferson Hogg, *The Life of Percy Bysshe Shelley* (London, 1906), 495.

58. *The Journal of Sir Walter Scott, 1825–32* (Edinburgh: 1910), 308–9.

59. Piozzi, *Letters*, 6:265; Tearle, *Mrs. Piozzi's Tall Young Beau*, 161.

60. Clifford, *Hester Lynch Piozzi*, 440.

61. Hayward, *Autobiography*, 1:346–47.

62. William Macready, *Macready's Reminiscences*, ed. Sir Frederick Pollock (New York, 1875), 79–80.

63. Piozzi, *Letters*, 5:416.

64. Clifford, *Hester Lynch Piozzi*, 414.

65. Piozzi, *Thraliana*, 1028–29.

66. Piozzi, *Letters*, 2:411; Hayward, *Autobiography*, 2:390.

67. Clifford, *Hester Lynch Piozzi*, 439.

68. See Hayward, *Autobiography*, 2:170–71.

69. Piozzi, *Letters*, 5:308 and 6:119.

70. Tearle, *Mrs. Piozzi's Tall Young Beau*, 55.

71. Hayward, *Autobiography*, 1:363.

72. Burney, *Diary & Letters*, 6:399.

73. Piozzi, *Letters*, 1:267 and 2:65.

74. Piozzi, *Thraliana*, 445.

75. Hayward, *Autobiography*, 2:44.

76. Piozzi, *Anecdotes*, 156.

77. Thomas Tyers, "A Biographical Sketch of Dr. Samuel Johnson," in Hill, *Johnsonian Miscellanies*, 2:353.

78. Hemlow, *The History of Fanny Burney*, 483.

79. Ibid., 491.

Appendix

Bennet Langton's Children

Lincolnshire historian Terence R. Leach observes that Bennet Langton's children were hardly normal people, and that made them interesting. The children having been mentioned a number of times in this work, it seems appropriate to give a brief account of each.

George Langton (1772–1819) benefited as a child from his father's instruction, for, according to his friend Henry Digby Beste, he became "a man of almost universal, though perhaps superficial, literary knowledge." He attended Christ Church, Oxford, and served for a time as a militia officer. On March 3, 1794, at Lincoln, he married Elizabeth Mainwaring. They had thirteen children before Elizabeth died at age thirty-four. Tall like his father, he is said by Leach to have been "an excellent landlord, and very diligent in the performances of his duties as a country gentleman," but his "blunt manner, and his addiction to drink, alienated him from his family." He possessed artistic talent, as is shown by his drawing of Boswell, an engraving of which is reproduced earlier in this book. (Beste, *Personal and Literary Memorials*, 66; Leach, *Lincolnshire Country Houses & Their Families*, 37)

Mary Langton (1773–1796) died at age twenty-three at Clifton, Bristol. We know very little about the daughters of Bennet Langton and his wife, Lady Rothes. None of them married, and Leach tells us, "The bad health, indiscipline and sullen behaviour of her daughters caused the Countess of Rothes much anxiety" (Leach, *Lincolnshire Country Houses & Their Families*, 37).

Diana Langton (1774–1809) was born and baptized on September 28 at Langton-by-Spilsby, and was buried there on April 6, 1809.

311

Jane Langton (1776–1854) was Johnson's goddaughter, baptized on August 3 at St. Marylebone Parish Church, London. Johnson referred to her as "Jenny." Like her older sister Mary and her younger sister Elizabeth, she received no formal education, but was schooled at home by her father. Leach writes that Jane "was allowed to spend too much time in the kitchen—becoming addicted to drink." Her brother Algernon helped cure her by arranging to have her live for a time with friends and other relations. She later urged her nephew John Stephen Langton to send his children to a good school, telling him in a letter, "For God's sake, my dear John, do not keep them at home." She died at Richmond. (Johnson, *Letters*, Redford, 4:24 and 314; Leach, *Lincolnshire Country Houses & Their Families*, 36)

Elizabeth Langton was baptized on December 30, 1777. Little else is known about her except that she died on December 10, 1804 at Stonehouse near Plymouth.

Peregrine Langton Massingberd (1780–1856) married Elizabeth Massingberd in 1802 and assumed her surname, by grant, in 1803. The Massingberds were the other prominent, long-established family, along with the Langtons, residing near Spilsby in Lincolnshire. The marriage is said to have been troubled, leaving Peregrine "an unhappy and tormented man . . . of rather narrow Anglican views who continually dwelt on the fault of others" (Leach, *Lincolnshire Country Houses & Their Families*, 35–36). He died on September 23, 1856 at Exeter, Devon.

Algernon Langton (1781–1829) is described by Leach as "the most normal member of Bennet Langton's large brood, being both sensible and conscientious. His father bought him a commission in the army before he was twenty." At six foot six inches, he was the British Army's tallest soldier. He was so tall, said an acquaintance, "that when he was in a crowd in St. Peter's [Rome] the Gendarmes ordered him to get down, thinking he must be standing on something." He served in Portugal from 1808 to 1810 during the Peninsular War as Assistant Quarter Master under Sir Arthur Wellesley (later Duke of Wellington). He obtained temporary leave from the army in 1813, returning to England to help straighten out the affairs of his brother George, who had become mentally deranged, but he again took up his military duties in time to participate in the Waterloo Campaign against Napoleon. Holding the rank of captain, he was wounded at the Battle of Quatre Bras on June 16, 1815. This was two days before the Battle of Waterloo, in which he also took part as an aide-de-camp to Lieutenant General Sir Thomas Picton. He attained the rank of major in 1817. Returning to civilian life, he married Marianne Drewe in 1820 and was ordained a deacon on June 13, 1824. (Leach, *Lincolnshire Country Houses & Their Families*, 36; Henrietta Litchfield, ed., *Emma Darwin: A Century of Family Letters, 1792–1896*, edited by her daughter, Henrietta Litchfield, 2 vols. [New York, 1915], 104; Charles Dalton, *The Waterloo Roll Call* [London, 1904], 15.)

Isabella (Bella) Langton (1782–1808) was noted for her piety and for having a number of health problems. Among her various complaints were "hiccoughs and a cough which resembled the barking of a large dog. Any movement threw her into convulsions and three or four people had to help hold her down" (Leach, *Lincolnshire Country Houses & Their Families*, 36).

Charles Langton (1783–1809) is said by Leach to have been "somewhat unstable." After serving in the navy, he joined the East India Company Army as a lieutenant in 1803. Although Leach states (p. 36) that he died in London, it is clear from his brother Algernon's letters dated July 27 and 30, 1810, still in possession of the Langton family, that he died in India.

Margaret Langton (1788–1821) died at Larkbeare House, Exeter, Devon.

Selected Bibliography

"Anecdotes of Joseph Baretti." *European Magazine* (May–August 1789).

Balderston, Katharine C. *The History and Sources of Percy's Memoir of Goldsmith.* Cambridge: Cambridge University Press, 1926.

Baretti, Joseph. *A Journey from London to Genoa, through England, Portugal, Spain and France.* 4 vols. London, 1770.

———. Marginal Annotations in His Copy of *Letters to and from the Late Samuel Johnson, LL.D.*, edited by Hester Lynch Piozzi. 2 vols. London, 1788. (British Library shelf mark C.45.e.5-6.)

———. "On Signora Piozzi's Publication of Dr. Johnson's Letters. Stricture the First." *European Magazine* 13 (May 1788): 313–17.

———. *The Sentimental Mother, A Comedy, in Five Acts; The Legacy of an Old Friend, and his Last Moral Lesson to Mrs. Hester Lynch Thrale, now Mrs. Hetser [sic] Piozzi.* London, 1789.

———. "Stricture the Second." *European Magazine* (June 1788): 393–99.

———. "Stricture the Third." *European Magazine* 14 (August 1788): 89–99.

Beattie, James. *James Beattie's London Diary 1773.* Edited by Ralph S. Walker. Aberdeen: Aberdeen University Press, 1946.

Benedetti, Jean. *David Garrick and the Birth of Modern Theatre.* London: Methuen, 2001.

Beste, Henry Digby. *Personal and Literary Memorials.* London, 1829.

Bibliotheca Beauclerkiana: A Catalogue of the Large and Valuable Library of the Late Honourable Topham Beauclerk, F.R.S. Deceased; Comprehending an Excellent Choice of Books, to the Number of Upwards of Thirty Thousand Volumes, in Most Languages, and upon Almost Every Branch of Science and Polite Literature. London, 1781.

Bloom, Harold, ed. "Introduction." In *Modern Critical Interpretations: James Boswell's "Life of Samuel Johnson."* New York: Chelsea House, 1986.

Boswell, James. *Boswell for the Defence, 1769–1774.* Edited by William K. Wimsatt Jr. and Frederick A. Pottle. New York: McGraw-Hill, 1959.

315

————. *Boswelliana: The Commonplace Book of James Boswell.* Edited by Charles Rogers. London: Printed for the Grampian Club, 1874.

————. *Boswell in Extremes, 1776–1785.* Edited by Charles McC. Weis and Frederick A. Pottle. New York: McGraw-Hill, 1970.

————. *Boswell in Holland, 1763–1764.* Edited by Frederick A. Pottle. New York: McGraw-Hill, 1952.

————. *Boswell in Search of a Wife, 1766–1769.* Edited by Frank Brady and Frederick A. Pottle. New York: McGraw-Hill, 1956.

————. *Boswell: Laird of Auchinleck, 1778–1782.* Edited by Joseph W. Reed and Frederick A. Pottle. New York: McGraw-Hill, 1977.

————. *Boswell on the Grand Tour: Germany and Switzerland, 1764.* Edited by Frederick A. Pottle. New York: McGraw-Hill, 1953.

————. *Boswell on the Grand Tour: Italy, Corsica, and France, 1765–1766.* Edited by Frank Brady and Frederick A. Pottle. New York: McGraw-Hill, 1955.

————. *Boswell: The Applause of the Jury, 1782–1785.* Edited by Irma S. Lustig and Frederick A. Pottle. New York: McGraw-Hill, 1981.

————. *Boswell: The English Experiment, 1785–1789.* Edited by Irma S. Lustig and Frederick A. Pottle. New York: McGraw-Hill, 1986.

————. *Boswell: The Great Biographer.* Edited by Marlies K. Danziger and Frank Brady. New York: McGraw-Hill, 1989.

————. *Boswell: The Ominous Years, 1774–1776.* Edited by Charles Ryskamp and Frederick A. Pottle. New York: McGraw-Hill, 1963.

————. *Boswell's Journal of a Tour to the Hebrides with Samuel Johnson, LL.D. 1773.* Edited from the original manuscript by Frederick A. Pottle and Charles H. Bennett. New York: McGraw-Hill, 1961.

————. *Boswell's London Journal, 1762–1763.* Edited by Frederick A. Pottle. New York: McGraw-Hill, 1950.

————. *The Correspondence of James Boswell with Certain Members of the Club.* Edited by Charles N. Fifer. New York: McGraw-Hill, 1976.

————. *The Correspondence of James Boswell with David Garrick, Edmund Burke, and Edmond Malone.* Edited by George M. Kahrl et al. London: Heinemann, 1986.

————. *The Correspondence of James Boswell and John Johnston of Grange.* Edited by R. S. Walker. New York: McGraw-Hill, 1966.

————. *The Correspondence of James Boswell and William Johnson Temple 1756–1795*, vol. 1. Edited by Thomas Crawford. Edinburgh: Edinburgh University Press and New Haven: Yale University Press, 1997.

————. *The Correspondence and Other Papers of James Boswell Relating to the Making of the* Life *of Johnson.* Second edition, corrected and enlarged. Edited by Marshall Waingrow. Edinburgh: Edinburgh University Press and New Haven: Yale University Press, 2001.

————. *Facts and Inventions: Selections from the Journalism of James Boswell.* Edited by Paul Tankard. New Haven and London: Yale University Press, 2014.

————. *The General Correspondence of James Boswell, 1766–1769.* Edited by Richard C. Cole et al. 2 vols. Edinburgh: Edinburgh University Press, 1993, 1997.

———. *James Boswell: The Journal of His German and Swiss Travels, 1764.* Edited by Marlies K. Danziger. Edinburgh: Edinburgh University Press and New Haven: Yale University Press, 2008.

———. *Letters of James Boswell.* Edited by Chauncey Brewster Tinker. 2 vols. Oxford: Clarendon Press, 1924.

———. *The Life of Samuel Johnson, LL.D. by James Boswell with Marginal Comments and Markings from Two Copies Annotated by Hester Lynch Thrale Piozzi.* Edited by Edward G. Fletcher. 3 vols. New York: Heritage Press, 1963.

———. *The Life of Samuel Johnson, LL.D. Together with Boswell's Journal of a Tour to the Hebrides.* Edited by G. B. Hill and revised by L. F. Powell. 6 vols. Oxford: Clarendon Press, 1934–1964.

Brady, Frank. *James Boswell: The Later Years, 1769–1795.* New York: McGraw-Hill, 1984.

Broadley, A. M. *Doctor Johnson and Mrs. Thrale.* London, 1910.

Bundock, Michael. *The Fortunes of Francis Barber: The True Story of the Jamaican Slave Who Became Samuel Johnson's Heir.* New Haven and London: Yale University Press, 2015.

Burney, Charles. *Letters of Dr Charles Burney, 1751–1784.* Edited by Alvaro Ribeiro. Oxford: Clarendon Press, 1991.

———. *Memoirs of Dr. Charles Burney, 1726–1769.* Edited by Slava Klima, Garry Bowers, and Kerry S. Grant. Lincoln: University of Nebraska Press, 1988.

Burney, Frances. *The Additional Journals and Letters of Frances Burney*, vol. 1: *1784–1786.* Edited by Stewart Cooke. Oxford: Oxford University Press, 2015.

———. *Cecilia, or Memoirs of an Heiress.* Oxford: Oxford University Press, 1990.

———. *The Court Journals and Letters of Frances Burney.* Edited by Peter Sabor et al. 5 vols. Oxford: Clarendon Press, 2011–2017.

———. *Diary & Letters of Madame d'Arblay (1778–1840).* Edited by her niece Charlotte Barrett. With preface and notes by Austin Dobson. 6 vols. London, 1904–1905.

———. *The Early Diary of Frances Burney.* Edited by Annie Raine Ellis. 2 vols. Freeport, NY: Books for Libraries Press, 1971.

———. *The Early Journals and Letters of Fanny Burney.* Edited by Lars Troide, Stewart J. Cooke, and Betty Rizzo. 5 vols. Montreal: McGill-Queens University Press, 1988–2012.

———. *The Journals and Letters of Fanny Burney (Madame d'Arblay).* Edited by Joyce Hemlow et al. 12 vols. Oxford: Clarendon Press, 1972–1984.

———. *Memoirs of Doctor Burney, Arranged from His Own Manuscripts, from Family Papers, and from Personal Recollections by His Daughter, Madame d'Arblay* [Frances Burney]. 3 vols. London, 1832.

Burney, Susanna. *The Journals and Letters of Susan Burney: Music and Society in Late Eighteenth-Century England.* Edited by Philip Olleson. Farnham, Surrey; Burlington, VT: Ashgate, 2012.

Campbell, Thomas. *Dr Campbell's Diary of a Visit to England in 1775.* Edited by James L. Clifford. Cambridge: Cambridge University Press, 1947.

"The Character of Mr. Garrick." *Gentleman's Magazine* 12 (October 12, 1742): 527.

Chesterfield, Lord. *Letters to His Son.* London: J. M. Dent & Sons, 1935.

Cibber, Theophilus. *Dissertations on Theatrical Subjects, as They Have Several Times Been Delivered to the Public, (With General Approbation).* London, 1756.

——. *Theophilus Cibber, to David Garrick, Esq; with Dissertations on Theatrical Subjects.* London, 1759.

Clifford, James L. *Hester Lynch Piozzi.* Oxford: Clarendon Press, 1968.

Coke, Lady Mary. *The Letters and Journals of Lady Mary Coke.* Edited by J. A. Holmes. 4 vols. Bath: Kingsmead Reprints, 1970.

Collison-Morley, Lacy. *Giuseppe Baretti and His Friends.* London, 1909.

Colman, George, Jr. *Random Records.* 2 vols. London, 1830.

Cooke, William. *Memoirs of Charles Macklin, Comedian, with the Dramatic Characters, Manners, Anecdotes, &c. of the Age in Which He Lived.* London, 1804.

——. *Memoirs of Samuel Foote, Esq. with a Collection of His Genuine Bon-Mots, Anecdotes, Opinions, &c. Mostly Original.* 3 vols. London, 1805.

——. "Table Talk; or, Characters, Anecdotes, &c. of Illustrious and Celebrated British Characters, During the Last Fifty Years." *European Magazine* 24 (August 1793): 91–95; (September 1793): 170–74; (October 1793): 258–64.

Cotton, William. *Sir Joshua Reynolds, and His Works. Gleanings from His Diary, Unpublished Manuscripts, and from Other Sources.* London, 1856.

Cradock, Joseph. *Literary and Miscellaneous Memoirs.* Second edition. 4 vols. London, 1826–1828.

Croker, John Wilson. *Johnsoniana; or, Supplement to Boswell.* Philadelphia, 1842.

Cumberland, Richard. *Memoirs of Richard Cumberland.* 2 vols. London, 1807.

Cunningham, Allan. *The Life and Writings of Sir Joshua Reynolds, First President of the Royal Academy.* New York, 1860.

Dalton, Charles. *The Waterloo Roll Call.* London, 1904.

d'Arblay, Madame. See Burney, Frances.

Davies, Thomas. *Dramatic Micellanies [sic]: Consisting of Critical Observations on Several Plays of Shakespeare.* 3 vols. London, 1784.

——. *The Life of David Garrick.* 2 vols. London, 1780.

Davis, Lucy, and Mark Hallett, eds. *Joshua Reynolds: Experiments in Paint.* London: The Wallace Collection, 2015.

Doody, Margaret Anne. *Frances Burney: The Life in the Works.* New Brunswick, NJ: Rutgers University Press, 1988.

Erskine, Beatrice. *Lady Diana Beauclerk: Her Life and Work.* London, 1903.

An Exhibition of Sketches & Watercolours by Lady Diana Beauclerk Held at Gerald N. Norman Gallery, 8, Duke Street, St. James's S.W.1. London, 1971.

Farington, Joseph. *The Diary of Joseph Farington.* Edited by Kenneth Garlick et al. 16 vols. New Haven: Yale University Press, 1978–1984.

——. *The Farington Diary.* Edited by James Greig. 8 vols. London, 1923–1928.

——. *Memoirs of the Life of Sir Joshua Reynolds; with Some Observations on His Talents and Character.* London, 1819.

Fifer, C. N. "Boswell's Langton and the River Wey." In *Notes and Queries*, August 1956, 347–49.

FitzGerald, Emily. *Correspondence of Emily, Duchess of Leinster.* Edited by Brian Fitzgerald. 3 vols. Dublin: Stationery Office, 1949.

Fitzgerald, Percy. *The Life of David Garrick.* 2 vols. London, 1868.

Forbes, Sir William. *An Account of the Life and Writings of James Beattie, LL.D.* 2 vols. London, 1824.

Forster, John. *The Life and Times of Oliver Goldsmith.* London, 1890.

Frith, W. P. *My Autobiography and Reminiscences.* 1888.

Garrick, David. *The Letters of David Garrick.* Edited by David M. Little and George M. Kahrl. 3 vols. London: Oxford University Press, 1963.

Goldsmith, Oliver. *An Inquiry into the Present State of Polite Learning in Europe* in *The Collected Works of Oliver Goldsmith.* Edited by Arthur Friedman. 5 vols. Oxford: Clarendon Press, 1966.

———. *The Collected Letters of Oliver Goldsmith.* Edited by Katharine C. Balderston. Cambridge: Cambridge University Press, 1928.

———. *The Collected Works of Oliver Goldsmith.* Edited by Arthur Friedman. 5 vols. Oxford: Clarendon Press, 1966.

———. *New Essays of Oliver Goldsmith.* Edited by Ronald S. Crane. Chicago: University of Chicago Press, 1927.

Gray, Thomas. *The Letters of Thomas Gray.* Edited by Duncan C. Tovey. 3 vols. London, 1909.

Greene, Donald. "Reflections on a Literary Anniversary." In *Twentieth Century Interpretations of Boswells "Life of Johnson,"* edited by James L. Clifford, 97–103. Englewood Cliffs, NJ: Prentice-Hall, 1970.

———. "'Tis a Pretty Book, Mr. Boswell, But—." In *Boswell's "Life of Johnson": New Questions, New Answers*, edited by John A. Vance, 110–6. Athens: University of Georgia Press, 1985.

Hadlow, Janice. *The Royal Experiment: The Private Life of King George III.* New York: Henry Holt, 2014.

Hardy, Francis. *Memoirs of the Political and Private Life of James Caulfield, Earl of Charlemont.* 2 vols. London, 1812.

Hawes, William. *An Account of the Late Dr. Goldsmith's Illness, So Far as Relates to the Exhibition of Dr. James's Powders.* London, 1774.

Hawkins, Lætitia-Matilda. *Anecdotes, Biographical Sketches and Memoirs; Collected by Lætitia-Matilda Hawkins.* London, 1822.

———. *The Countess and Gertrude; or, Modes of Discipline.* 4 vols. London, 1811.

———. *Gossip About Dr. Johnson and Others, Being Chapters from the Memoirs of Miss Lætitia-Matilda Hawkins.* London: Eveleigh Nash and Grayson, 1926.

———. *Memoirs, Anecdotes, Facts and Opinions, Collected and Preserved by Lætitia-Matilda Hawkins.* London, 1824.

Hawkins, Sir John. *The Life of Samuel Johnson, LL.D.* London, 1787.

Haydon, Benjamin Robert. *The Diary of Benjamin Robert Haydon.* Edited by Willard Bissell Pope. 5 vols. Cambridge, MA: Harvard University Press, 1960–1963.

Hayward, Abraham, ed. *Autobiography, Letters and Literary Remains of Mrs. Piozzi (Thrale).* Second edition. 2 vols. London, 1861.

Hazlitt, William. *Conversations of James Northcote, R.A.* Edited by Edmund Gosse. London, 1894.

Hedgcock, Frank A. *A Cosmopolitan Actor: David Garrick and His French Friends.* London: Stanley Paul and Co., 1912?

Hemlow, Joyce. *The History of Fanny Burney.* Oxford: Clarendon Press, 1958.

Hiffernan, M. D., Paul. *Dramatic Genius. In Five Books.* London, 1772.

Hill, George Birckbeck. *Dr. Johnson: His Friends and His Critics.* London, 1878.

———, ed. *Johnsonian Miscellanies.* 2 vols. New York, 1897.

Hill, John. *The Actor: or, A Treatise on the Art of Playing.* London, 1755.

Hilles, Frederick Whiley. *The Literary Career of Sir Joshua Reynolds.* Hamden: Archon Books, 1967. Reprint Cambridge: Cambridge University Press, 1936.

Hogg, Thomas Jefferson. *The Life of Percy Bysshe Shelley.* London, 1906.

Holcroft, Thomas. *Memoirs of Thomas Holcroft, Written by Himself and Continued by William Hazlitt.* Edinburgh: Oxford University Press, 1926.

Hudson, Derek. *Sir Joshua Reynolds: A Personal Study.* London: Geoffrey Bles, 1957.

Hyde, Mary. *The Impossible Friendship: Boswell and Mrs. Thrale.* London: Chatto and Windus, 1973.

———. *The Thrales of Streatham Park.* Cambridge, MA: Harvard University Press, 1977.

Jesse, John Heneage. *George Selwyn and His Contemporaries.* 4 vols. London, 1843–1844.

Johnson, R. Brimley. *Fanny Burney and the Burneys.* Freeport, NY: Books for Libraries Press, 1971.

Johnson, Samuel. *The Letters of Samuel Johnson.* Edited by Bruce Redford. 5 vols. Princeton, NJ: Princeton University Press, 1992, 1994.

———. *Letters of Samuel Johnson, LL.D.* Edited by George Birkbeck Hill. 2 vols. New York, 1892.

———. *The Letters of Samuel Johnson with Mrs. Thrale's Genuine Letters to Him.* Edited by R. W. Chapman. 3 vols. Oxford: Clarendon Press, 1952.

———. *Samuel Johnson's Dictionary: Selections from the 1755 Work that Defined the English Language.* Edited by Jack Lynch. Delray Beach, FL: Levenger Press, 2004.

———. *Samuel Johnson's Prologue Spoken at the Opening of the Theatre in Drury-Lane in 1747 with Garrick's Epilogue: A Facsimile of the Hitherto Undiscovered First Edition.* With preface by Austin Dobson and introduction and notes by A. S. W. Rosenbach. New York, 1902.

———. *The Yale Edition of the Works of Samuel Johnson.* Edited by E. L. McAdam Jr. et al. 23 vols. to date. New Haven and London: Yale University Press, 1958–2016.

Johnsoniana; or, Supplement to Boswell: Being Anecdotes and Sayings of Dr. Johnson. Edited by John Wilson Croker. Philadelphia, 1842.

Joseph, Bertram. *The Tragic Actor.* London: Routledge and Kegan Paul, 1959.

Kendall, Alan. *David Garrick: A Biography.* London: Harrap, 1985.

Kirkman, James Thomas. *Memoirs of the Life of Charles Macklin, Esq. Principally Compiled from His Own Papers and Memorandums.* 2 vols. London, 1799.

Knight, Joseph. *David Garrick.* London, 1894.

Lansdowne, Marquis of. *The Queeney Letters: Being Letters Addressed to Hester Maria Thrale by Doctor Johnson, Fanny Burney, and Mrs. Thrale-Piozzi.* New York: Farrar and Rinehart, 1934.

Larsen, Lyle. *Dr. Johnson's Household.* Hamden, CT: Archon Books, 1985.

Leach, Terence R. *Lincolnshire Country Houses & Their Families: Part One.* Lincoln: Laece Books, 1990.

Leslie, Charles Robert, and Tom Taylor. *Life and Times of Sir Joshua Reynolds.* 2 vols. London, 1865.

Lichtenberg, Georg Christoph. *Lichtenberg's Visits to England as Described in His Letters and Diaries.* Translated and annotated by Margaret L. Mare and W. H. Quarrell. New York: Benjamin Blom, 1969.

Litchfield, Henrietta, ed. *Emma Darwin: A Century of Family Letters, 1792–1896.* Edited by her daughter Henrietta Litchfield. New York, 1915.

Lloyd, Robert. *The Actor. A Poetical Epistle to Bonnell Thornton, Esq; by the Rev. Mr. Loyd [sic], One of the Masters of Westminster School.* London, 1760.

The London Tradesman. Being a Compendious View of All the Trades, Professions, Arts, Both Liberal and Mechanic, Now Practised in the Cities of London and Westminster. 1747. Reprint, Newton Abbot, Devon: David & Charles Reprints, 1969.

Mack, Maynard. *Alexander Pope: A Life.* New York: W. W. Norton, 1985.

Macready, William. *Macready's Reminiscences.* Edited by Sir Frederick Pollock. New York, 1875.

Mangin, Edward. *Piozziana: or Recollections of the Late Mrs. Piozzi, with Remarks. By a Friend.* London, 1833.

Manuscripts and Correspondence of James, First Earl of Charlemont: Lord Charlemont's Memoirs of His Political Life, 1755–1784. Correspondence 1745–1783. 2 vols. London, 1891.

Massingberd, Peregrine Langton. Manuscript letter books. Lincolnshire Archives, Lincoln, United Kingdom.

McKenzie, Alan T. "Two Letters from Giuseppe Baretti to Samuel Johnson." *PMLA* 86, no. 2 (March 1971): 218–24.

Montagu, Lady Mary Wortley. *The Complete Letters of Lady Mary Wortley Montagu.* Edited by Robert Halsband. 3 vols. Oxford: Clarendon Press, 1966.

Murphy, Arthur. *The Life of David Garrick, Esq.* 2 vols. London, 1801.

Nichols, John. *Illustrations of the Literary History of the Eighteenth Century.* 8 vols. London, 1831.

Northcote, James. *The Life of Sir Joshua Reynolds.* 2 vols. London, 1818.

———. *Memoirs of Sir Joshua Reynolds.* Philadelphia, 1817.

Ober, William B., M. D. *Boswell's Clap and Other Essays: Medical Analyses of Literary Men's Afflictions.* Carbondale: Southern Illinois University Press, 1979.

Old Comedian. *The Life and Death of David Garrick, Esq. The Celebrated English Roscius. In Which His Powers Both in Tragedy and Comedy Are Considered.* London, 1779.

Oman, Carola. *David Garrick.* Great Britain: Hodder and Stoughton, 1958.

O'Keefe, John. *Recollections of the Life of John O'Keefe.* 2 vols. London, 1826.

[Palmer, Mary]. *A Devonshire Dialogue in Four Parts.* Edited by Mrs. Gwatkin. London, 1839.

Parsons, Mrs. Clement. *Garrick and His Circle.* London: Methuen, 1906.

Pembroke, Henry. *Pembroke Papers (1734–1780), Letters and Diaries of Henry, Tenth Earl of Pembroke and His Circle.* London: Jonathan Cape, 1942.

Penny, Nicholas, ed. *Reynolds.* New York: Abrams, 1986.

Pepys, Samuel. *The Diary of Samuel Pepys.* Edited by Robert Latham and William Matthews. 11 vols. Berkeley: University of California Press, 1970–1983.

Percy, Thomas. *The Life of Dr. Oliver Goldsmith.* Edited by Richard L. Harp. Salzburg: Institut für Englische Sprache und Literatur, 1976.

———. *The Percy Letters: The Correspondence of Thomas Percy & Edmond Malone.* Edited by Arthur Tillotson. Clinton, MA: Louisiana State University Press, 1944.

Piozzi, Hester Lynch Thrale. *Anecdotes of the Late Samuel Johnson, LL.D., during the last Twenty Years of His Life* with William Shaw's *Memoirs of the Life and Writings of the Late Dr. Samuel Johnson.* Edited with an introduction by Arthur Sherbo. London: Oxford University Press, 1974.

———, ed. *Letters to and from the Late Samuel Johnson, LL.D.* London, 1788.

———, *The Piozzi Letters: Correspondence of Hester Lynch Piozzi, 1784–1821 (formerly Mrs. Thrale).* Edited by Edward A. Bloom and Lillian D. Bloom. 6 vols. Newark: University of Delaware Press, 1989–2002.

———. *Retrospection: or A Review of the Most Striking and Important Events, Character, Situations, and Their Consequences, which the Last Eighteen Hundred Years Have Presented to the View of Mankind.* 2 vols. London, 1801.

———. *Thraliana: The Diary of Mrs. Hester Lynch Thrale (Later Mrs. Piozzi), 1776–1809.* Edited by Katharine C. Balderston. 2 vols. Oxford: Clarendon Press, 1951.

Pottle, Frederick A. *James Boswell: The Earlier Years, 1740–1769.* New York: McGraw-Hill, 1966.

Prior, James. *Life of Edmond Malone, Editor of Shakspeare. With Selections from His Manuscript Anecdotes.* London, 1860.

———. *The Life of Oliver Goldsmith.* 2 vols. London, 1837.

Quintana, Ricardo. *Oliver Goldsmith: A Georgian Study.* New York: Macmillan, 1967.

Radcliffe, Susan M. *Sir Joshua's Nephew.* London: Murray, 1930.

Reynolds, Sir Joshua. *The Letters of Sir Joshua Reynolds.* Edited by John Ingamells and John Edgcumbe. New Haven: Yale University Press, 2000.

———. *Portraits by Sir Joshua Reynolds.* Edited by Frederick W. Hilles. New York: McGraw-Hill, 1952.

———. *The Works of Sir Joshua Reynolds, Knight; Late President of the Royal Academy.* 3 vols. Edited by Edmond Malone. London, 1809.

Roberts, William. *Memoirs of the Life and Correspondence of Mrs. Hannah More.* 4 vols. London, 1834.

Rogers, Samuel. *Recollections of the Table-Talk of Samuel Rogers.* New York, 1856.

Scott, Sir Walter. *The Journal of Sir Walter Scott, 1825–32.* Edinburgh, 1910.

Stone, George Winchester, Jr., and George M. Kahrl. *David Garrick: A Critical Biography.* Carbondale and Edwardsville: Southern Illinois University Press, 1979.

Stuart, Lady Louisa. *Notes by Lady Louisa Stuart on George Selwyn and His Contemporaries by John Heneage Jesse.* Edited by W. S. Lewis. New York: Oxford University Press, 1929.

Taylor, John. *Records of My Life.* 2 vols. London, 1832.

Tearle, John. *Mrs. Piozzi's Tall Young Beau: William Augustus Conway.* Rutherford, NJ: Fairleigh Dickinson University Press, 1991.

Temple, William Johns[t]on. *Diaries of William Johnston Temple, 1780–1796.* Edited by Lewis Bettany. Oxford: Clarendon Press, 1929.

The Theatrical Review; or, Annals of the Drama. London, 1763.

Thrale, Hester Lynch. See Piozzi, Hester Lynch Thrale.

Timbs, John. *Anecdote Biography; or, Scenes and Events in the Lives of Distinguished Persons.* London, 1860.

Tinker, Chauncey Brewster. *Young Boswell: Chapters on James Boswell the Biographer Based Largely on New Material.* Boston: Atlantic Monthly Press, 1922.

Tyson, Moses and Henry Guppy, eds. *The French Journals of Mrs. Thrale and Doctor Johnson.* Manchester: Manchester University Press, 1932.

Walpole, Horace. *Horace Walpole's Correspondence.* Edited by W. S. Lewis. 48 vols. New Haven: Yale University Press, 1948–1983.

Ward, James. *Conversations of James Northcote R.A. with James Ward on Art and Artists.* Edited by Ernest Fletcher. London, 1901.

Wardle, Ralph M. *Oliver Goldsmith.* Lawrence: University of Kansas Press, 1957.

Wendorf, Richard. *Sir Joshua Reynolds: The Painter in Society.* Cambridge, MA: Harvard University Press, 1996.

White, Jerry. *A Great and Monstrous Thing: London in the Eighteenth Century.* Cambridge: Harvard University Press, 2013.

Whitley, William T. *Artists and Their Friends in England 1770–1799.* London, 1928.

Wilkinson, Tate. *Memoirs of His Own Life.* 4 vols. York, 1790.

———. *The Wandering Patentee: or, A History of the Yorkshire Theatres.* 4 vols. York, 1795.

Wooll, John. *Biographical Memoirs of the Late Revd. Joseph Warton, D.D.* London, 1806.

Young, Edward. *The Correspondence of Edward Young, 1683–1765.* Edited by Henry Pettit. Oxford: Clarendon Press, 1971.

Index

Page references for illustrations are italicized.

BL	Bennet Langton
CB	Charles Burney
DG	David Garrick
FB	Frances Burney
HLT/HLP	Hester Lynch Thrale (Piozzi)
HT	Henry Thrale
JB	James Boswell
OG	Oliver Goldsmith
SJ	Samuel Johnson
SJR	Sir Joshua Reynolds
TB	Topham Beauclerk

An Account of Corsica (JB), 98, 245, 258, 262–63

An Account of the Life and Writings of James Beattie (Forbes), 286

An Account of the Manners and Customs of Italy (Baretti), 50

Addison, Joseph, 47

The Alchemist (Jonson), 113

Anecdotes of the Late Samuel Johnson, LL.D. (HLP), 246, 306

Arblay, Alexander Charles Louis Piochard d' (son of FB), 299, 307

Arblay, Alexandre d' (husband of FB), 298–99, 300

Armstrong, John, 47

Arne, Thomas, 164

Austen, Jane, 307

Barber, Francis, 66

Baretti, Joseph, 14–18, *15*, 17, 49–50, 83, 183, *195*; Burke and, 97–98, 104; death of, 271–72; DG and, 104, 105, 120; FB and, 157, 168, 206–7, 270; fiery disposition of, 14, 16–17, 21, 49, 98, 157, 268–70; financial dependence of, in later years, 268–69; HLT and, 151, 152–57, 189–90, 219, 234, 238, 270; JB and, 49, 98, 104–5, 113, 118, 120, 122, 217–18; JB disliked by, 152, 259; JB's *Account of Corsica* and, 98, 262; OG and 97; Queeney and, 151; Royal Academy and, 50, 97; SJ and, 18, 20–21, 84–85, 97–98, 104, 105, 106, 240–42; SJR and, 97, 104; stabs Evan Morgan, 97, 99; TB and 36, 39, 103

Barry, James, 127, 156

Barry, Spranger, 13, 110–11

Bartoli, Giuseppe, 16

Bathurst, Richard, 64, 66, 219

Beattie, James, 74, 194, 196, 286
Beauclerk, Charles (grandfather of TB), 34
Beauclerk, Diana, formerly Bolingbroke (née Spencer), 88–90, *89*, 215–16, 223–24, 225, 226
Beauclerk, Mary (daughter of TB and Lady Di), 226
Beauclerk, Sidney (father of TB), 34
Beauclerk, Topham (TB), 34–36, *35*, 41, 88–92, 119, 137, 141; absentmindedness of, 215; Baretti and, 36, 39, 103; BL and, 84, 148, 216–17; Burke and, 225; death of, 224, 226; DG and, 36, 215; FB and, 225; HLT and, 211; JB and, 92, 130, 214–15; Lady Di mistreated by, 223–24; library of, 216, 224–25, 226; and neglect of personal hygiene, 215–16; OG and, 130, 132, 212; recurring illness of, 216–17, 223–24; sarcastic wit of, 36, 92, 132, 211–14, 215, 224; SJ and, 34, 130, 213–14, 216; SJR and, 97
Beste, Henry Digby, 32
Betterton, Thomas, 3
Blake, William, 275
Bolingbroke, Frederick St. John, 2nd Viscount, 88–91
Booth, Barton, 3
Boswell, James (JB), 43–50, *205*, *263*; assesses his own character, 44–48, 261, 264; Baretti and, 49, 98, 104–5, 113, 118, 120, 122, 217–18; Baretti dislikes, 152, 259; BL and, 198–200, 289–90; Burke and, 139; death of, 293–94; DG and, 113, 118, 120, 122, 136, 217–18; FB and, 206–7, 257–59, 265, 270; HLT and, 247, 259, 267; hypochondria of, 45–46, 48, 204–5, 273, 290–93; irresolution of, 202–4, 263–64; lively spirits and charm of, 48, 205–6, 259–60, 265–67; OG and, 77, 78, 131, 136, 138–39; SJR and, 128–29, 274–75;

SJ and, 43–44, 200, 203–5, 243–44, 260–61; speaks unguardedly, 48–49, 200–201; TB and, 92, 214–15; vanity of, 45
Boswell, James, Jr., 292
Boswell, Margaret Montgomerie (wife of JB), 46, 203
Boswell, Veronica (daughter of JB), 291
Bracegirdle, Anne, 5
British Synonymy (HLP), 278
Brocklesby, Richard, 245
Brontë, Charlotte, 307
Buckingham, George Villiers, Duke of, 113
Burke, Edmund, 28, 41, 47, 73, 81, 119, 141, 184; Baretti and, 30, 97–98, 104; OG and, 136; FB and, 256; JB and, 139; TB and, 225; SJR thinks, superior to SJ, 52n10
Burney, Charles (CB), 73, 113, 117, 157–59, *158*, 163, 165–67, 183; DG and, 118, 168; FB and, 254, 298–99, 301–2; HLP and, 234, 246; JB and, 268; SJ and, 244, 273–74; SJR and, 273–74
Burney, Charles (son of CB), 164, 171, 252
Burney, Charlotte (daughter of CB), 157, 159, 206, 291, 307
Burney, Esther "Hetty" (daughter of CB), 163, 164, 307
Burney, Frances (daughter of CB), 166–67, 183, *255*, 289, 293, 298–99, 306–7; Baretti and, 157, 168, 206–7, 270; CB and, 254, 298–99, 301–2; death of, 307; DG and, 113, 114, 117–18, 168; exiled in Paris, 300; HLT and, 159, 176, 305, 235–36, 238–40, 277, 278, 279–80; HT and, 180; JB and, 206–7, 257–59, 265–66, 270; on women's role in society, 170, 239, 254–56; prudishness of, 172–73, 239–40, 251, 300; Samuel Crisp and, 169–70, 307; serves at the court of George III, 251–55, 256; shyness of,

163–65, 166, 170, 172–73, 302; SJ
and 244–45, 299–300, 306; SJR and,
273–74; TB and, 225
Burney, James (son of CB), 252
Burney, Susan (daughter of CB), 164,
171, 173, 307
Byron, Lord, 304, 307

Cadell, Thomas, 79
Camillia (FB), 299
Campbell, Thomas, 152
Canning, George, 303
Carmontelle, Louis Carrogis, 8
Carter, Elizabeth, 239
The Castle of Otranto (Walpole), 3
Cator, John, 269, 270
Cecilia (FB), 251, 257, 307
Centlivre, Susannah, 218
Chambers, Robert, 73
Chambers, Sir William, 83
Chamier, Anthony, 41
Chappelow, Rev. Leonard, 297
Charles II, 34, 132
Charlotte Augusta Matilda, Princess
Royal (daughter of George III), 253
Charlotte Sophia, Queen (wife of
George III), 174, 251–52, 279
Chesterfield, Philip Dormer Stanhope,
Lord, 5, 47, 170, 219
Cibber, Colley, 3, 5, 11
Cibber, Susannah Maria, 4–5, 11, 13,
22n7, 33
Cibber, Theophilus, 11–12
The Citizen of the World (OG), 82
The Clandestine Marriage (DG), 110
Clark, John, 100, 101, 102
Club, The, 41, 85, 130, 132, 243, 293
Coleridge, Samuel Taylor, 307
Collier, Arthur, 58, 62, 182, 239, 306
Colman, George (the elder), 110, 120
Colman, George (the younger), 76, 119
Constable, John, 275
Contarine, Thomas, 37–38, 39, 133
Cooke, William, 8, 135, 142
Courtenay, John, 273, 292

Crabbe, George, 304
Cradock, Joseph, 78, 130, 135
Crisp, Samuel, 169
Croker, John Wilson, 300, 301
Crutchley, Jeremiah, 181
Cumberland, Richard, 4, 117, 221–23

Davies, Thomas, 42, 43–44, 98–99, 111,
115–16, 139
Day, John, 142
Day, Robert, 142
Delany, Mary, 251–52, 302
Delap, Elizabeth, 37
"The Deserted Village" (OG), 129, 131,
138, 140
The Devil upon Two Sticks (Foote), 163
Dickens, Charles, 307
*A Dictionary of the English and Italian
Languages* (Baretti), 19
A Dictionary of the English Language
(SJ), 6, 18–19
Diderot, Denis, 115
Digges, West, 47
Discourses (SJR), 127, 275
A Dissertation on the Italian Poets
(Baretti), 19
Dobson, William, 25
Doctor Last in His Chariot (Isaac
Bickerstaffe and Foote), 163
Draycott, Anna Maria, 88
Dr. James's Fever-Powders, 135–36

Edwy and Elgiva (FB), 299
*An Enquiry into the Present State of
Learning in Europe* (OG), 41
Erskine, Andrew, 262
Evans, Thomas, 132
Evelina (FB), 166, 169, 170–72, 207,
257, 303

The Fair Penitent (Rowe), 3, 4
Farquhar, George, 219
The Female Quixote (Lennox), 18, 171
Fielding, Henry, 8, 58, 97
Fielding, Sarah, 58

Fielding, Sir John, 97
Filby, William, 73
Foote, Samuel, 10, 27, 98, 111, 120–21
Forbes, Sir William, 286
"The Fountains" (SJ), 67–69, 151
Fox, Caroline, Lady Holland, 90
Fox, Charles James, 28, 119
Frankenstein (Shelley), 304
Fuentes, Rosina, 20–21

Gainsborough, Thomas, 8, 26, 194
"Garrick between Comedy and Tragedy" (SJR), 196
Garrick, David (DG), *9*, 76, 91, 105, *112*, 141, 148, 164;
Arthur Murphy and, 115; as Abel Drugger in *The Alchemist*, 112–13, 116; as Aboan in *Oroonoko*, 2; as Bayes in *The Rehearsal*, 3, 112–13; as Chamont in *The Orphan*, 112–13; as Clodio in *Love Makes a Man*, 3; as Don Felix in *The Wonder*, 218; as Hamlet, 109, 111–12, 113; as Henry IV, 111–12 113; as Hotspur in *Henry IV, Part 1*, 111; as Lear, 2, 11, 111–12, 113, 114–16; as Lothario in *The Fair Penitent*, 3, 4; as Macbeth, 111, 113–14; as Mahomet in *Irene*, 13; as Othello, 111; as Richard III, 2, 111–12, 113; as Romeo, 110–12; avarice of, 120, 121; Baretti and, 104, 105, 120; BL and, 30; CB and, 118, 168; eyes of, 8, 110, 117; facial expressions of, 8, 10, 110; FB and, 113, 114, 117–18, 168
generosity of, 121; HLT and, 189–90, 219; illness and death of, 217–19, 222–23; JB and, 113 118, 120, 122, 136, 217–18; OG and, 74, 134, 141–42; provincial dialect of, 9–10; short stature of, 30, 110–11; SJ and, 12–13, 78, 120, 121, 122, 219, 220–21, 222; SJR and, 113, 114, 119; "stage business" of, 11–12, 113; TB

and, 36; vanity of, 120–21, 177, 219; voice of, 8–10, 110
Garrick, Eva Maria Veigel (wife of DG), 7
Garrick, George (brother of DG), 1
Garrick, Peter (brother of DG), 2–3
A General History of Music (C. Burney), 117
Gentleman's Magazine, 6
George III, 50, 251–52, 253–54, 279
George, Prince of Wales, 253, 287
Gibbon, Edward, 119, 214, 225
Goldsmith, Ann (mother of OG), 37, 133
Goldsmith, Maurice (brother of OG), 42
Goldsmith, Oliver (OG), 36–42, *43*, 85–86, *141*, 177, 190, 212, 293; as physician, 40–41, 212; Baretti and, 97; beaten by Thomas Evans, 132–33; BL and, 131; blunders of, 41, 75–76, 81–82; buffoonery of, 38, 74–77, 78, 80–81; Burke and, 136; compares Irish to English, 77–78; compassion of, 82–83; deceitfulness of, 79; DG and, 74, 134–35, 141–42; enviousness of, 78–79; gaming and, 133–34; gaudy attire of, 73–74; HLT and, 77, 140; illness and death of, 133, 135–36; in Edinburgh, 39–40; JB and, 77, 122, 131, 136, 138–39; misrepresented in JB's *Life*, 139; prodigality of, 133; Royal Academy and, 50, 97; SJ and, 41, 75, 81–82, 121–22, 136–38, 145; SJR and, 80, 82–83, 125, 128–29, 130, 138, 140; TB and, 130, 132, 212; ugliness of, 37, 42
Goldsmith, Rev. Charles (father of OG), 37, 39
Goldsmith, Rev. Henry (brother of OG), 37, 39
The Good-Natured Man (OG), 77, 129, 131
Globe Theatre, 67
Gray, Thomas, 3–4, 47
Gwyn, Nell, 34, 91

Hamilton, Duke and Duchess of, 39
Hamlet (Shakespeare), 3
The Harlot's Progress (Hogarth), 111
Hawes, William, 135–36, 142
Hawkins, Lætitia-Matilda, 29, 76, 79, 117, 150–51
Hawkins, Sir John, 29, 41, 91–92, 118, 137
Hazlitt, William, 300
Heberden, William, 176
Hector, Edmund, 245, 267–68
A History of the Earth, and Animated Nature (OG), 131
Hodson, Catherine Goldsmith (sister of OG), 37, 39
Hodson, Daniel, 39
Hogarth, William, 8, 26, 111, 194
Hogg, Thomas Jefferson, 302
Holbein, Hans, 25
Hudson, Thomas, 25, 193, 194

The Idler (SJ), 5, 57
An Introduction to the Italian Language (Baretti), 19
Irene, (SJ), 12–13, 221
The Italian Library (Baretti), 19

Jebb, Richard, 155
Johnson, Elizabeth Reynolds (sister of SJR), 192
Johnson, Elizabeth "Tetty", 6, 13–14, 44, 221
Johnson, Samuel (SJ), 6, 18–19; Baretti and, 18, 20–21, 97–98, 104, 105, 106, 240–42; BL and, 14, 20–21, 84–88, 97–98, 105–6, 244–45, 286, 294; declining health and death of, 242–45; DG and, 12–13, 78, 120, 121, 122, 219, 220–21, 222; FB and, 168–69, 256, 257; has greater affection for HT and SJR than for DG, 219; HLT and 64–69, 176, 231–32, 236–37, 240, 305–6; HT and, 64; idleness of, 19, 20–21, 57–5; JB and, 43–44, 200,

203–4, 243–44, 260–61, 262; lacks empathy for others, 231–32; OG and, 41, 75, 78, 81–82, 136–38, 145; on acting, 12; on friendship, ix-x; Royal Academy and, 50; rudeness of, ix-x, 176, 177, 204, 212–13, 220, 237; SJR and, 25, 125, 128; TB and, 34, 213–14, 216
Johnson, Samuel (nephew of SJR), 192
A Journal of a Tour to the Hebrides (JB), 245–46, 264
Journey from London to Genoa (Baretti), 98, 100, 106

Kauffmann, Angelica, 27, 126
Keats, John, 307
Kelly, Hugh, 77, 142
Kneller, Godfrey, 25

Lacy, James, 7
La Frusta Letteraria (Baretti), 21
Lamb, Charles, 307
Lambert, John, 101–102
Langton, Bennet, 29–34, *31*, 41, 105, 198–200, 287–89, *288*; as artist, 146–47; Baretti and, 105; death of, 294; derives income from canals, 287; DG and, 30; HLT and, 84, 148; indolence of, 147, 148–51, 199–200, 285, 290; JB and, 198–200, 287, 289–90; the Lincolnshire Militia and, 200, 286–87, 294; OG and, 79, 131; prodigality of, 147, 150; referred to as "worthy", 83–84, 87, 198, 199, 290; SJ and, 14, 20–21, 84–88, 97–98, 105–6, 244–45, 286, 294; SJR and, 146–47; tall stature of, 14, 30, 31–32; TB and, 84, 148, 216–17
Langton, Bennet, Sr., 32–33
Langton, Diana (mother of BL), 33, 285
Langton, Elizabeth (daughter of BL), 294
Langton, Elizabeth (sister of BL), 33
Langton, George (son of BL), 206, 294–95

Langton, John, 32
Langton, Peregrine (son of BL), 146,
    148–49, 200, 287, 294
Lely, Peter, 25
Lennox, Charlotte, 18
Lettere familiari (Baretti), 19–20, 21
*Letters to and from the Late Samuel
    Johnson, LL.D.* (HLP), 155–56, 276
Levett, Robert, 66
Lewis, Matthew "Monk", 304
The Life of Nash (OG), 129
The Life of Richard Savage (SJ), 6
The Life of Samuel Johnson, LL.D. (JB),
    264–65, 267–68, 285, 292
"London" (SJ), 6
Love Makes a Man (Cibber), 3
Lowe, Mauritius, 266–67
The Lying Valet (DG), 3

Macaulay, Catharine, 212
Macaulay, Thomas Babington, 300, 302
Macklin, Charles, 11–12
Macready, William, 303
Malone, Edmond, 139, 216, 273, 292,
    293
Marischal (George Keith), Lord, 47
Marr, Harry "Dagger", 8, 116–17
Marriott, James, 60
Maxwell, Rev. Dr. William, 268
Memoirs of Dr. Burney (FB), 301–2
*Miscellaneous Observations on the
    Tragedy Macbeth* (SJ), 57
Miscellanies in Prose and Verse
    (Williams), 67
The Monk (Lewis), 304
Monsey, Messenger, 116–17
Montagu, Elizabeth, 88, 166, 175, 239,
    276
Montagu, Mary Wortley, 34
More, Hannah, 109–10, 114, 221, 291
Morgan, Evan, 97, 99–103
Murphy, Arthur, 59, 64, 67, 73, 189;
    DG and, 12–13, 111, 115, 120–21,
    218, 221; HLT and, 219, 276, 279,
    304

Nash, Beau, 42
Newton, Rev. Thomas, 112–13
Nollekens, Joseph, 142, 196
Northcote, James, 80, 126, 127, 190,
    193–4, 196, 197, 272
Nugent, Christopher, 41

Observations and Reflections (HLP),
    278
O'Keefe, John, 106, 116
The Old Curiosity Shop (Dickens), 307
Oliver Twist (Dickens), 307
Ord, Anna, 276
Oroonoko (Southerne), 2
The Orphan (Otway), 3
Otway, Thomas, 3, 75–76

Palmer, Joseph, 142
Palmer, Mary Reynolds (sister of SJR),
    192
Pamela (Richardson), 3
Paoli, Gen. Pasquale, 46, 98, 262
Patman, Thomas, 99, 100
Pembroke, Lady, 223–24
Pepys, Samuel, 34
Pepys, Sir William Weller, 230, 276
Percy, Thomas, 41, 80, 132, 221
Perkins, John, 69
Pickwick Papers (Dickens), 307
Piozzi, Gabriel Mario, 232–34, *233*,
    277–78, 298, 305
Piozzi, Giovanne Battiste, 297
Piozzi, Hester Lynch, formerly Thrale
    (née Salusbury) (HLT/HLP), *65*,
    277, 303–5;   Arthur Murphy and,
    219, 276, 279, 304; Baretti and, 151,
    152–57, 189–90, 219, 234, 238, 270;
    BL and, 84, 148; CB and, 157–59;
    death of, 305–6; describes herself,
    174–75, 176–77, 178; DG and, 189–
    90, 219; education of, 58–59; FB
    and, 159, 167–68, 170, 180, 238–40,
    257, 278, 279–80, ; Gabriel Piozzi
    and, 234, 236–36, 295–96; gives
    tin pills to Queeney, 155; HT and,

62, 178–80; JB and, 247, 259, 267;
lively talk of, 159, 175–76, 177–78,
183, 189, 279; OG and, 77, 140;
Salusbury, Sir John Salusbury Piozzi
and, 297–98, 303; Sophia Streatfeild
and, 182–85; SJ and, 64–69, 176,
231–32, 236–37, 240, 305–6; SJR
and, 177, 190, 274; TB and, 211
Pitfour, James Ferguson, Lord, 47
Pitt, William, 3
The Plays of William Shakspeare (SJ),
19, 20, 57–58
Pope, Alexander, 5
Porter, Henry, 6
Porter, Molly, 5
Pott, Percivall, 134
"Primo Cicalamento" (Baretti), 16–17
Pritchard, Hannah, 13, 33

Quin, James, 3, 4–5, 111

The Ramber (SJ), 13–14, 20
Ramsay, Allan, 261
Rasselas, Prince of Abyssinia (SJ), 57
The Recruiting Officer (Farquhar), 219
Reflections on the Revolution in France
(Burke), 258
The Rehearsal (Buckingham), 113
Reliques of Ancient English Poetry
(Percy), 41
"Retaliation" (OG), 125–26, 142, 183
Reynolds, Frances (sister of SJR), 42,
191–92, 241
Reynolds, Sir Joshua (SJR), 25–29, *28*,
190–93, 272–74; Baretti and, 97;
BL and, 146–47; death of, 274; DG
and, 113, 114, 119; FB and, 257;
HLT and 177, 190, 274; JB and,
125, 128–29, 274–75; OG and, 76,
80, 82, 83, 125, 128, 129, 130, 138;
painting practices of, 26–27, 127,
193–96; placid disposition of, 25, 27,
28–29, 125–27, 128, 177, 191–93;
the problem of coloring and, 196–97;
the problem of pictures cracking

and, 197, 208n40; Royal Academy
and, 50, 97, 273; SJ and, 25, 125,
128; "Streatham worthies" portraits
by, 140, 151, 189, 197, 225; thinks
Burke superior to SJ, 52n10
Richardson, Jonathan, 25
Richardson, Samuel, 3
Rishton, Maria, 167
Rogers, Samuel, 278, 302
Romney, George, 26
Rothes, Mary, Dowager Countess of
(wife of BL), 145, 147, 150
Rousseau, Jean-Jacques, 45, 49, 203
Rowe, Nicholas, 3
Royal Academy, 50, 97, 106, 127, 266,
273, 275
Rubens, Peter Paul, 25

St. John, George (son of Lady Di and
Lord Bolingbroke), 226
Salusbury, Hester Maria (mother of
HLT), 59–61, 62, 66, 70
Salusbury, John (father of HLT), 58–61
Salusbury, Sir John Salusbury Piozzi
(adopted son of HLP), 297–98
Salusbury, Sir Thomas (uncle of HLT),
58–61
Schwellenberg, Juliana, 253, 258
Scott, Sir Walter, 302, 304, 307
Sense and Sensibility (Austen), 307
The Sentimental Mother (Baretti), 276
Seward, Anna, 270
Seward, William, 157–58
Shelley, Mary Wollstonecraft, 304
Shelley, Percy Bysshe, 302, 307
Sheridan, Richard Brinsley, 119, 273
Sheridan, Thomas, 46
She Stoops to Conquer (OG), 80, 131–
32, 138
Smith, John Thomas, 196
Southerne, Thomas, 2
Southey, Robert, 304
Spence, Joseph, 145–47
Spencer, Lord Charles, 213
Steele, Sir Richard, 47

Stevens, George, 139, 222
Stockdale, Percival, 42
Strean, Rev. Annesley, 37, 39, 59–61
Streatfeild, Sophia, 182–85, 190, 239
"Strictures" (Baretti), 269–70, 276

Temple, William Johnson, 49, 147, 201, 203, 268, 291, 292
Thrale, Cecilia (daughter of HLT), 296
Thrale, Harry (son of HLT), 154–55, 183
Thrale, Henry (HT), 59–61, 62–64, 178, *179*, 229–30;   HLT describes, 178–80, 230–31; infidelities of, 91, 180–82, 185; Sophia Streatfeild and, 182–85

Thrale, Hester Lynch. *See* Piozzi, Hester Lynch Thrale
Thrale, Hester Maria "Queeney" (daughter of HLT), 63, 151, 235–36, 270, 277, 278–79, 296–97
Thrale, Ralph (father of HT), 59
Thrale, Ralph (son of HLT), 154–55
Thrale, Sophia (daughter of HLT), 297
Thrale, Susanna (daughter of HLT), 297
Thraliana, (HLT), 279
"The Three Warnings" (HLT), 67

Thurlow, Lord Chancellor Edward, 243
Topham, Richard, 34
"The Traveller" (OG), 129
Turner, J. M. W., 275
Turton, John, 136
Twining, Thomas, 172

Van Dyck, Anthony, 25, 79
Venice Preserved (Otway), 74–75
The Vicar of Wakefield (OG), 129
Victoria, Queen, 307
Voltaire, 49

Walpole, Horace, 3, 75, 88, 142, 246
The Wanderer (FB), 256, 300
Ward, Elizabeth, 99–100, 102
Warton, Joseph, 137
Whalley, Rev. Thomas Sedgwick, 297
Wilkes, John, 91, 139, 225
Wilkie, John, 137
Wilkinson, Tate, 10, 121
Williams, Anna, 43–44, 66, 67, 242
The Wonder (Centlivre), 218
Woodhouse, James "shoemaker poet," 64
Wren, Sir Christopher, 275
Wyatt, John, 102

Young, Edward, 145–46

About the Author

Lyle Larsen is Professor Emeritus of English at Santa Monica College. A native Californian, he received an MA degree in English from California State University, Dominguez Hills, and a PhD in English from Indiana University of Pennsylvania. His area of concentration was eighteenth-century English biography. He has published five previous books, including *Dr. Johnson's Household, Memoirs of His Own Life by Tate Wilkinson* (FDUP 1998) and *James Boswell: As His Contemporaries Saw Him* (FDUP 2008).

Lightning Source UK Ltd.
Milton Keynes UK
UKOW06n0023071117
312294UK00003B/52/P